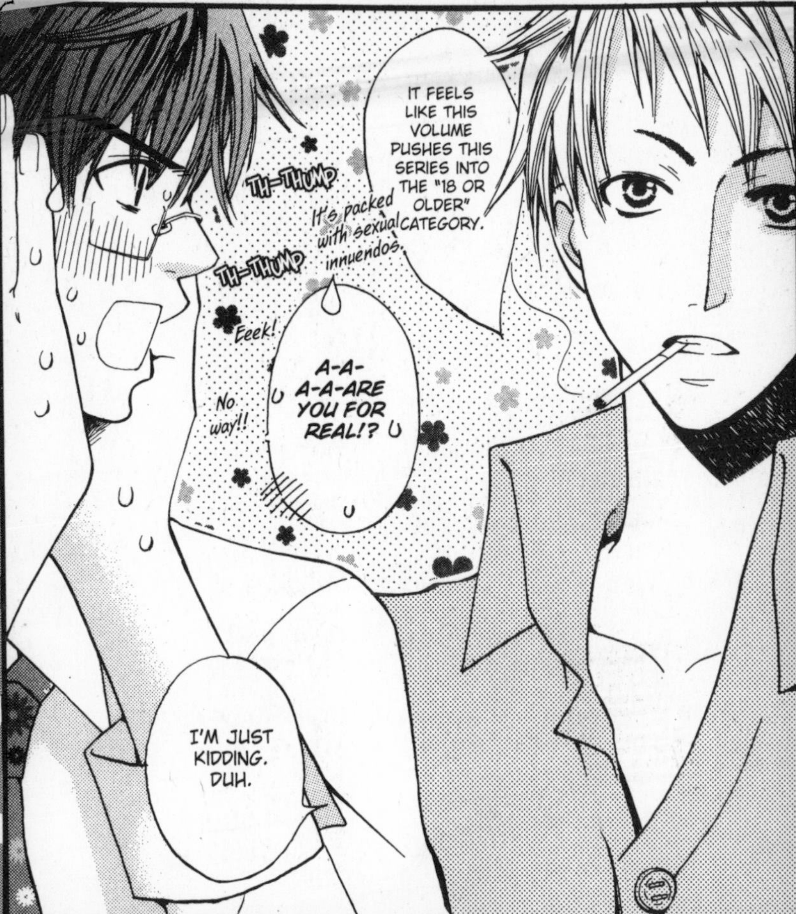
IT FEELS LIKE THIS VOLUME PUSHES THIS SERIES INTO THE "18 OR OLDER" CATEGORY.
It's packed with sexual innuendos.
TH-THUMP
TH-THUMP
A-A-A-A-ARE YOU FOR REAL!?
Eeek!
No way!!
I'M JUST KIDDING. DUH.

TENSHI JA NAI!!

Translation –Christine Schilling
Adaptation -- Jamie S. Rich
Production Assistant – Mallory Reaves
Lettering – Jennifer Skarupa
Production Manager – James Dashiell
Editor – Audry Taylor

A Go! Comi manga

Published by Go! Media Entertainment, LLC

Tenshi Ja Nai!! Volume 5
© TAKAKO SHIGEMATSU 2005
Originally published in Japan in 2005 by Akita Publishing Co., Ltd., Tokyo.
English translation rights arranged with Akita Publishing Co., Ltd.
through TOHAN CORPORATION, Tokyo.

English Text © 2006 Go! Media Entertainment, LLC. All rights reserved.

This book is a work of fiction. Names, places and incidents are either a
product of the author's imagination or are used fictitiously.

No part of this book may be reproduced or transmitted in any form or by any
means physical or digital without permission in writing from the publisher.

Visit us online at www.gocomi.com
e-mail: info@gocomi.com

ISBN 1-933617-12-8

First printed in December 2006

1 2 3 4 5 6 7 8 9

Manufactured in the United States of America

TENSHI JA NAI!!

I'm No Angel!

Volume 5

Story and Art by
Takako Shigematsu

go!comi

Concerning Honorifics

At Go! Comi, we do our best to ensure that our translations read seamlessly in English while respecting the original Japanese language and culture. To this end, the original honorifics (the suffixes found at the end of characters' names) remain intact. in Japan, where politeness and formality are more integrated into every aspect of the language, honorifics give a better understanding of character relationships. They can be used to indicate both respect and affection. Whether a person addresses someone by first name or last name also indicates how close their relationship is.

Here are some of the honorifics you might encounter in reading this book:

-san: This is the most common and neutral of honorifics. The polite way to address someone you're not on close terms with is to use "-san." it's kind of like Mr. or Ms., except you can use "-san" with first names as easily as family names.

-chan: Used for friendly familiarity, mostly applied towards young girls. "-chan" also carries a connotation of cuteness with it, so it is frequently used with nicknames towards both boys and girls (such as "Na-chan" for "Natsu").

-kun: Like "-chan," it's an informal suffix for friends and classmates, only "-kun" is usually associated with boys. it can also be used in a professional environment by someone addressing a subordinate.

-sama: indicates a great deal of respect or admiration.

Sempai: in school, "sempai" is used to refer to an upperclassman or club leader. it can also be used in the workplace by a new employee to address a mentor or staff member with seniority.

Sensei: Teachers, doctors, writers or any master of a trade are referred to as "sensei." When addressing a manga creator, the polite thing to do is attach "-sensei" to the manga-ka's name (as in Shigematsu-sensei).

Onii: This is the more casual term for an older brother. Usually you'll see it with an honorific attached, such as "onii-chan."

Onee: The casual term for older sister, it's used like "onii" with honorifics.

[blank]: Not using an honorific when addressing someone indicates that the speaker has permission to speak intimately with the other person. This relationship is usually reserved for close friends and family.

TENSHI JA NAI!!

CONTENTS

VOL.5

Hikaru Takabayashi

The reluctant star of the series. Hikaru wants nothing more than to be left alone, but ever since she transferred to the prestigious Seika Academy, she's been stuck in the spotlight. Being roommates with a cross-dressing pop idol is bad enough, but now Izumi is blackmailing her into helping with his modeling job. Will Hikaru ever catch a break?

Izumi is one of the hottest new female pop idols in Japan. The only problem is...she's a guy! Only two people knew his secret—Yasukuni, his bodyguard and childhood friend, and Akizuki his manager. When Hikaru finds out, Izumi blackmails her into helping him maintain his secret. Izumi needs the modeling money to pay off his father's medical bills.

Izumi Kido

Yasukuni Inukai

Yasukuni is fiercely loyal to Izumi. A bastard child disowned by his father, Izumi is the only family he has. Now that Hikaru has won his trust, he's taken to looking out for her, as well. Much of his past remains a mystery, such as why he's missing his right eye. He does double duty as the school janitor so he can always be close to Izumi.

SUMIKKO

Momochi

Akizuki

Hikaru's best friend in the world. Yasukuni takes care of her while Hikaru's at school.

Star reporter for the school paper, Momochi is always on the lookout for gossip!

President of the Akizuki Talent Agency and Izumi's manager.

Cast of Characters

Wall of Memories

A New School

When her mom and step-dad move to France, Hikaru transfers to her mother's alma mater, the prestigious Seika Academy, an all-girls finishing school.

Childhood memories

When she was seven years old, Hikaru modeled in a series of ads. Her jealous classmates picked on her relentlessly so now Hikaru's greatest wish is to be left alone.

She's a GUY!?

Hikaru discovers that her roommate, Izumi, is actually a guy!

BLACKMAIL!!!

To keep Hikaru quiet and in order to enlist her help, Izumi and Yasukuni blackmail Hikaru with naked photos.

Izumi's confidant

Hikaru turns out to be a blessing in disguise for Izumi. Having a female conspirator by his side helps him maintain his cover in the trickiest circumstances.

When Fans Attack!

It's not easy being a celebrity on campus. Half the students worship Izumi, the other half resent her. And Hikaru's stuck in the middle!

A Shocking Past

After being betrayed and left for broke, Izumi's father attempted to commit suicide but ended up in a coma. Now Izumi has to work as a model to pay off his dad's medical bills.

TENSHI JA NAI!!
I'm No Angel

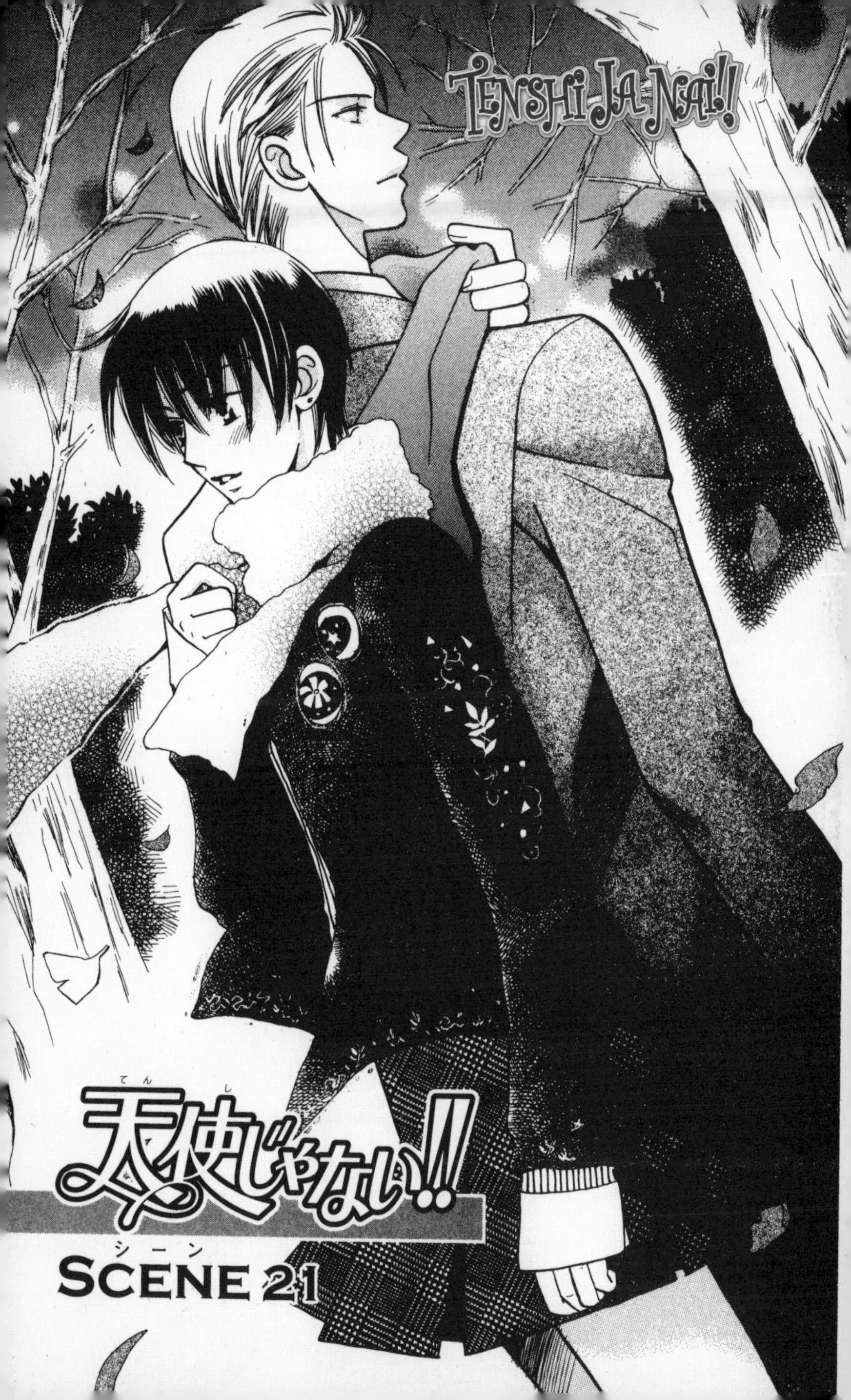
TENSHI JA NAI!!
天使じゃない!!
SCENE 21

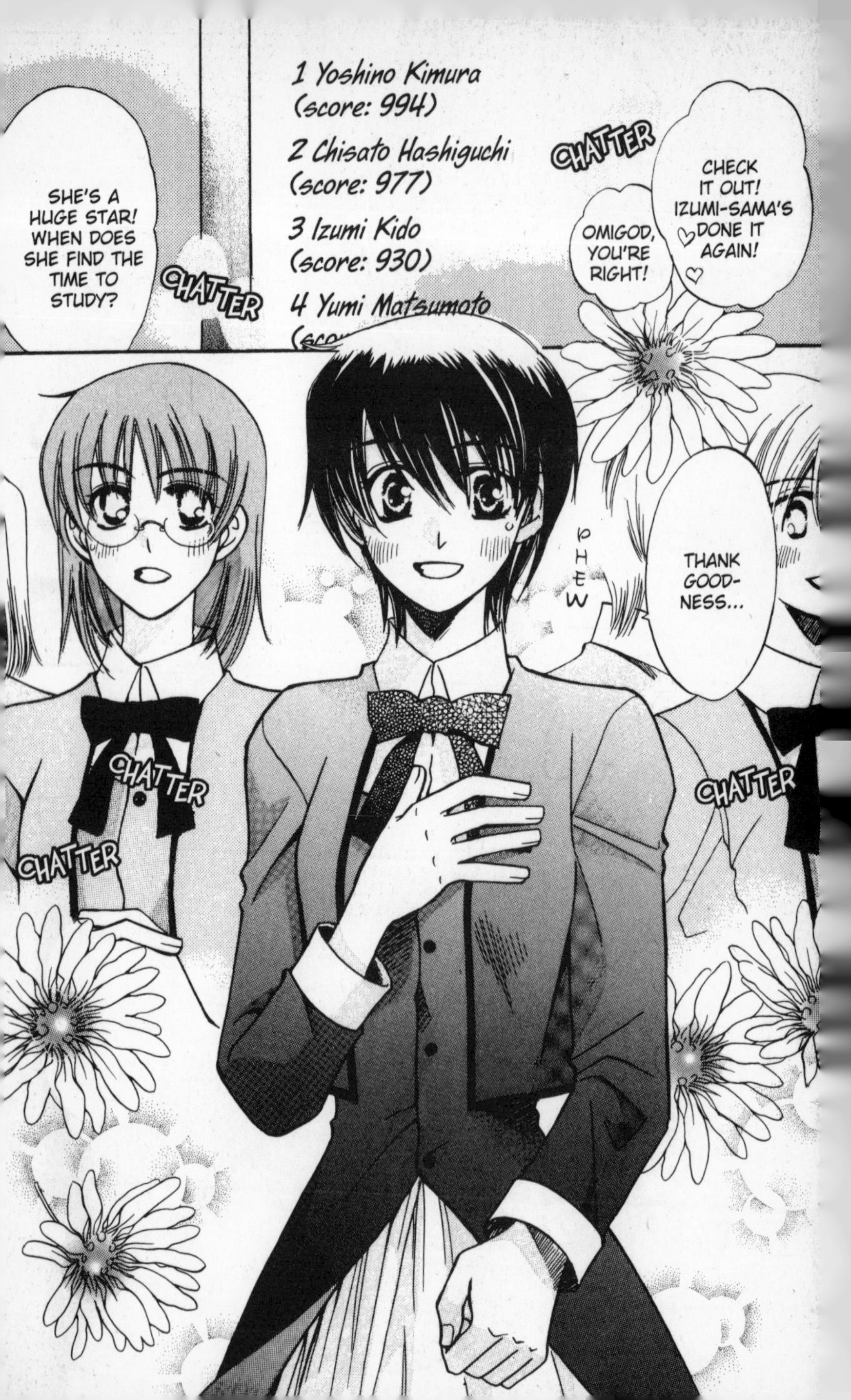
CHECK IT OUT! IZUMI-SAMA'S DONE IT AGAIN!
OMIGOD, YOU'RE RIGHT!
CHATTER
1 Yoshino Kimura (score: 994)
2 Chisato Hashiguchi (score: 977)
3 Izumi Kido (score: 930)
4 Yumi Matsumoto
CHATTER
SHE'S A HUGE STAR! WHEN DOES SHE FIND THE TIME TO STUDY?
THANK GOOD-NESS...
PHEW
CHATTER
CHATTER
CHATTER

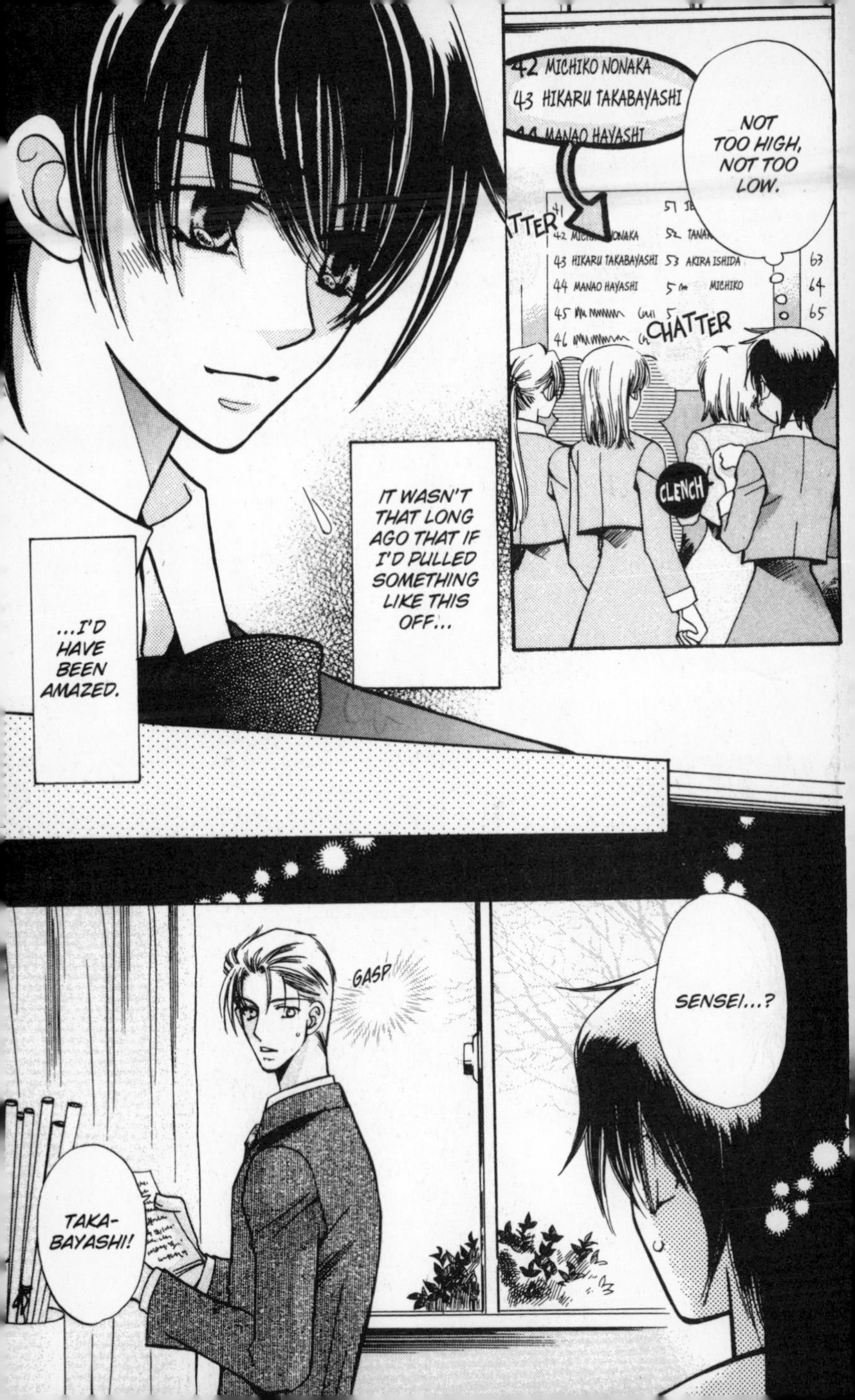

42 MICHIKO NONAKA
43 HIKARU TAKABAYASHI
44 MANAO HAYASHI
NOT TOO HIGH, NOT TOO LOW.
TTER
43 HIKARU TAKABAYASHI
53 AKIRA ISHIDA
63
44 MANAO HAYASHI
MICHIKO
64
45
65
46
CHATTER
CLENCH
IT WASN'T THAT LONG AGO THAT IF I'D PULLED SOMETHING LIKE THIS OFF...
...I'D HAVE BEEN AMAZED.
SENSEI...?
GASP
TAKA-BAYASHI!

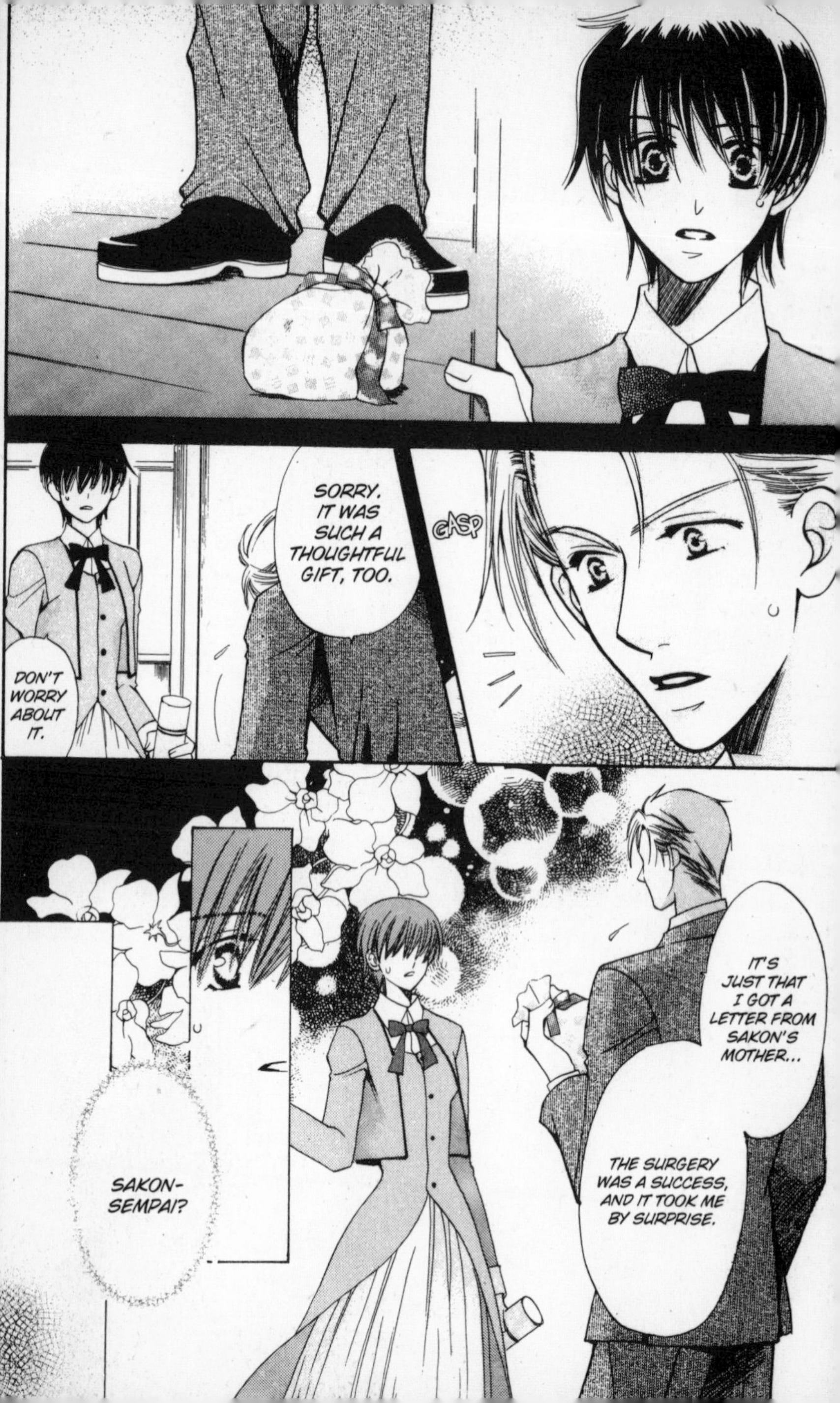
GASP
SORRY. IT WAS SUCH A THOUGHTFUL GIFT, TOO.
DON'T WORRY ABOUT IT.
IT'S JUST THAT I GOT A LETTER FROM SAKON'S MOTHER...
THE SURGERY WAS A SUCCESS, AND IT TOOK ME BY SURPRISE.
SAKON-SEMPAI?

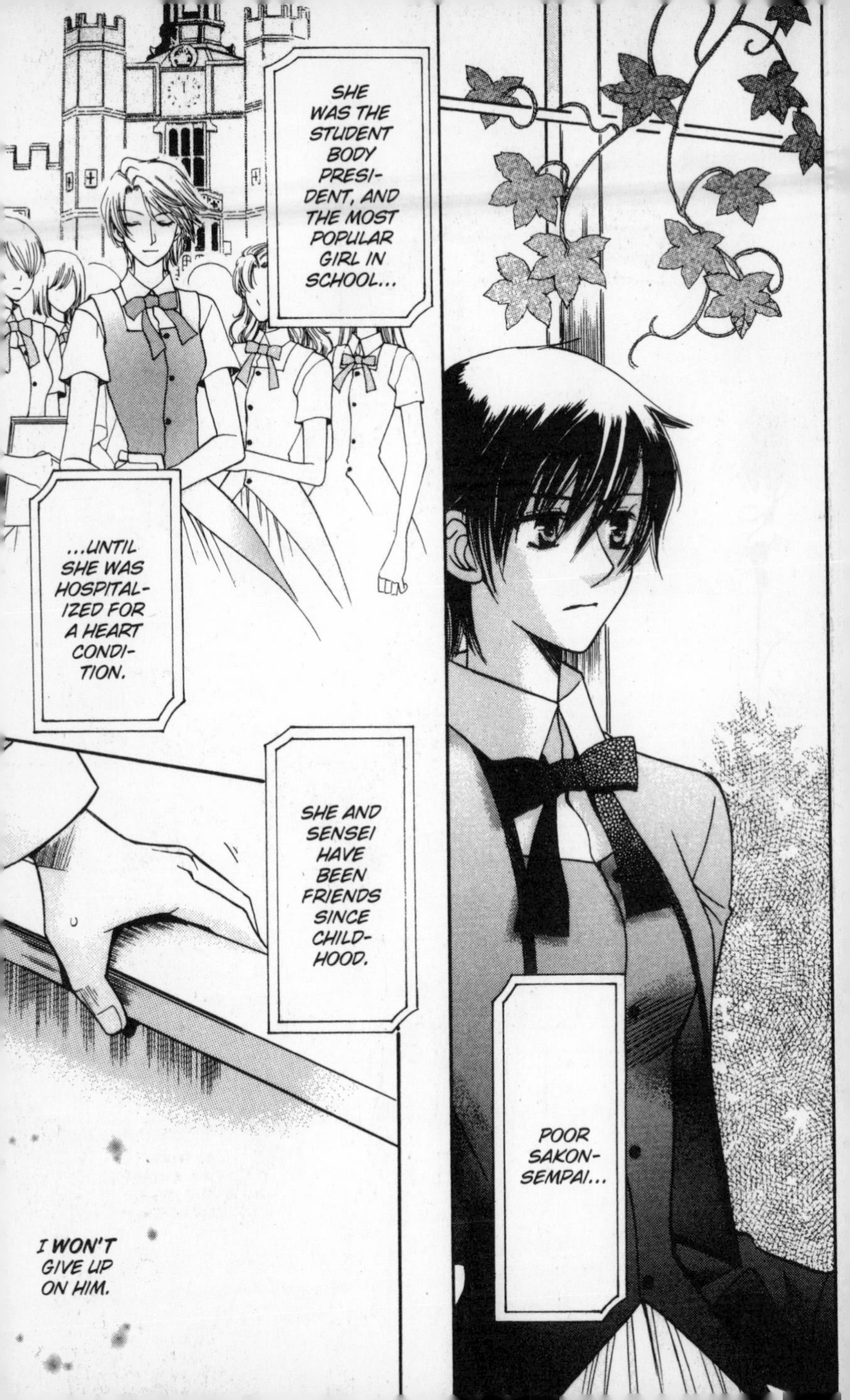
POOR SAKON-SEMPAI...
SHE WAS THE STUDENT BODY PRESIDENT, AND THE MOST POPULAR GIRL IN SCHOOL...
...UNTIL SHE WAS HOSPITALIZED FOR A HEART CONDITION.
SHE AND SENSEI HAVE BEEN FRIENDS SINCE CHILDHOOD.
I WON'T GIVE UP ON HIM.

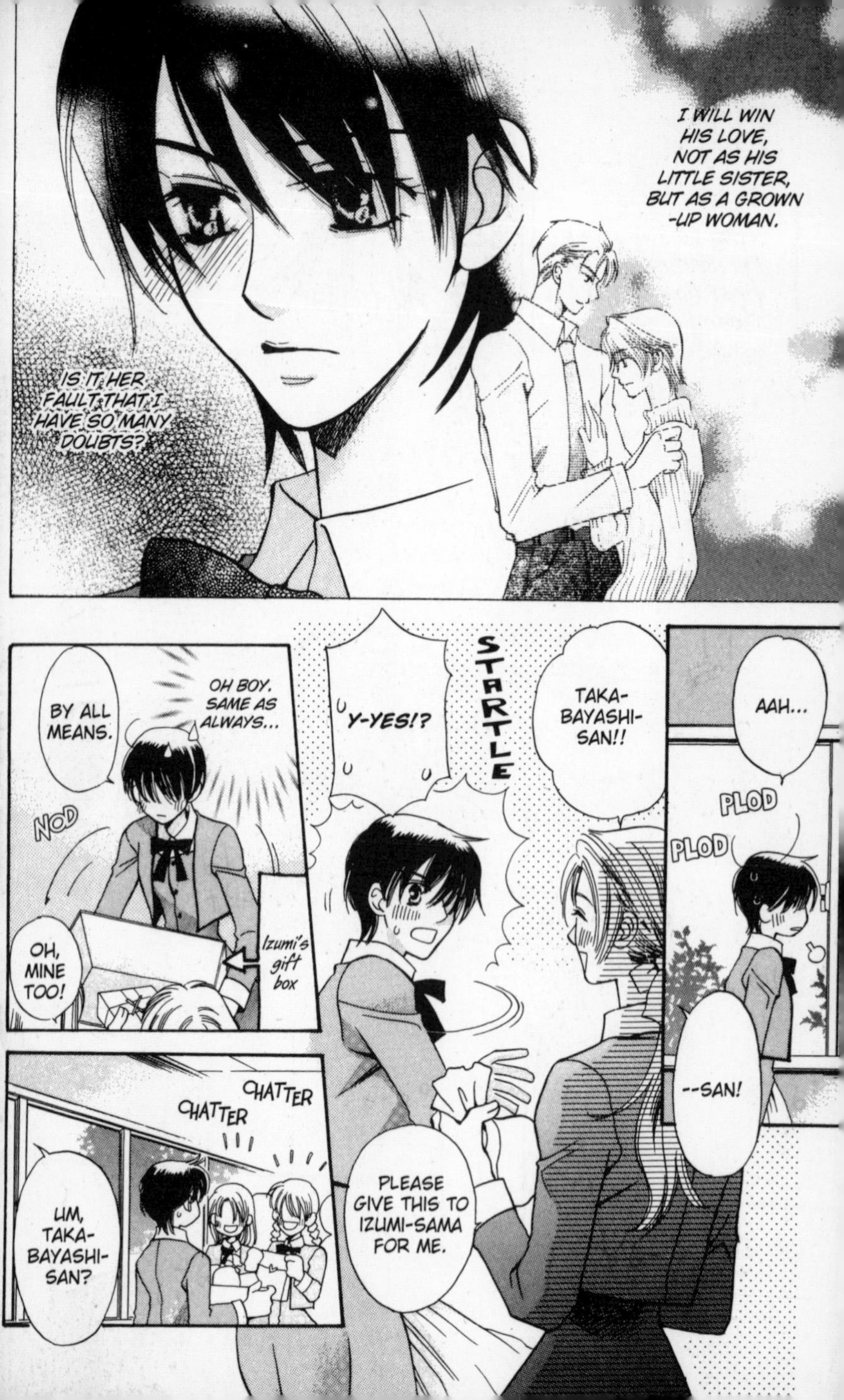
I WILL WIN HIS LOVE, NOT AS HIS LITTLE SISTER, BUT AS A GROWN-UP WOMAN.
IS IT HER FAULT THAT I HAVE SO MANY DOUBTS?
AAH...
PLOD
PLOD
TAKA-BAYASHI-SAN!!
STARTLE
Y-YES!?
--SAN!
PLEASE GIVE THIS TO IZUMI-SAMA FOR ME.
OH BOY. SAME AS ALWAYS...
BY ALL MEANS.
NOD
Izumi's gift box
OH, MINE TOO!
CHATTER
CHATTER
UM, TAKA-BAYASHI-SAN?

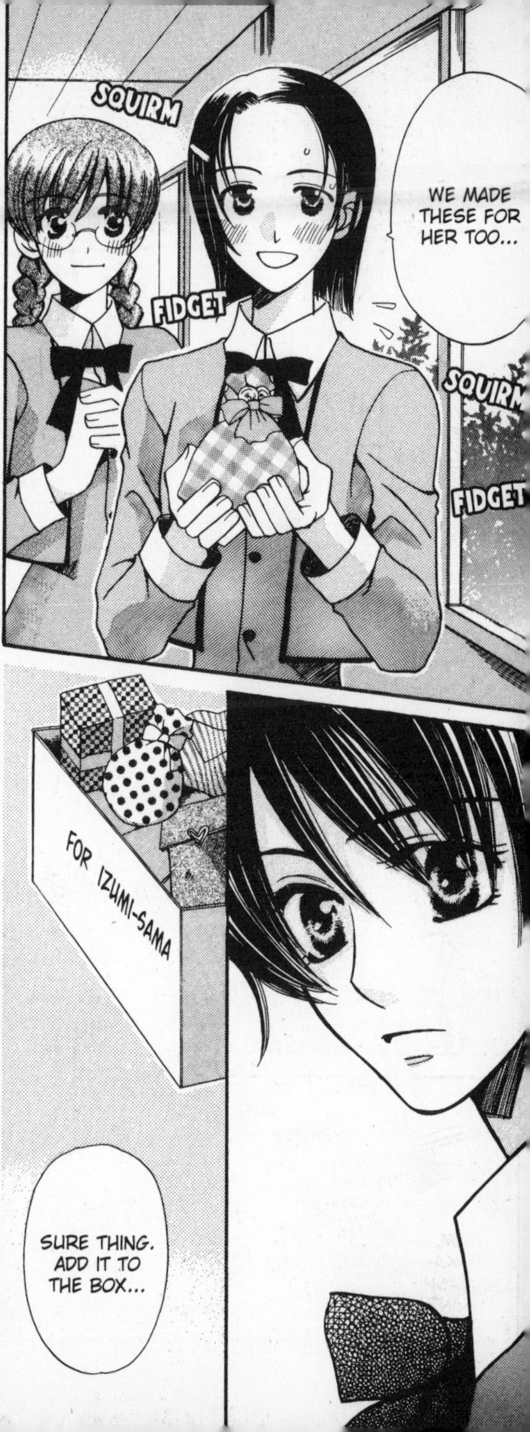
WE MADE THESE FOR HER TOO...
SQUIRM
FIDGET
SQUIRM
FIDGET
FOR IZUMI-SAMA
SURE THING. ADD IT TO THE BOX...

Greetings

Hello, both to those I'm meeting for the first time and to those I'm seeing again!

It happened without me realizing it, but Tenshi Ja Nai!! has reached the 5th volume! I owe it all to each and every one of my faithful readers.

From here on in, I'm going to work even harder as a sign of my gratitude!

So hurry up and finish reading volume 5!

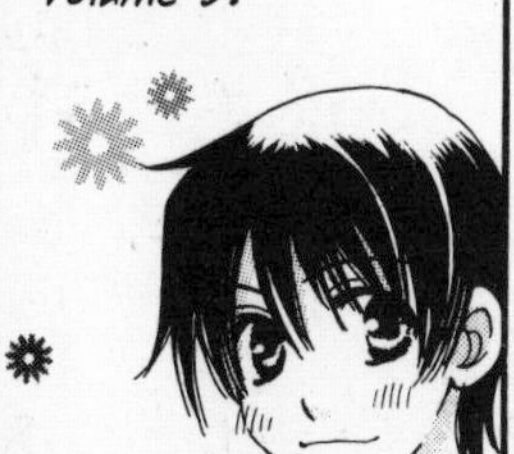

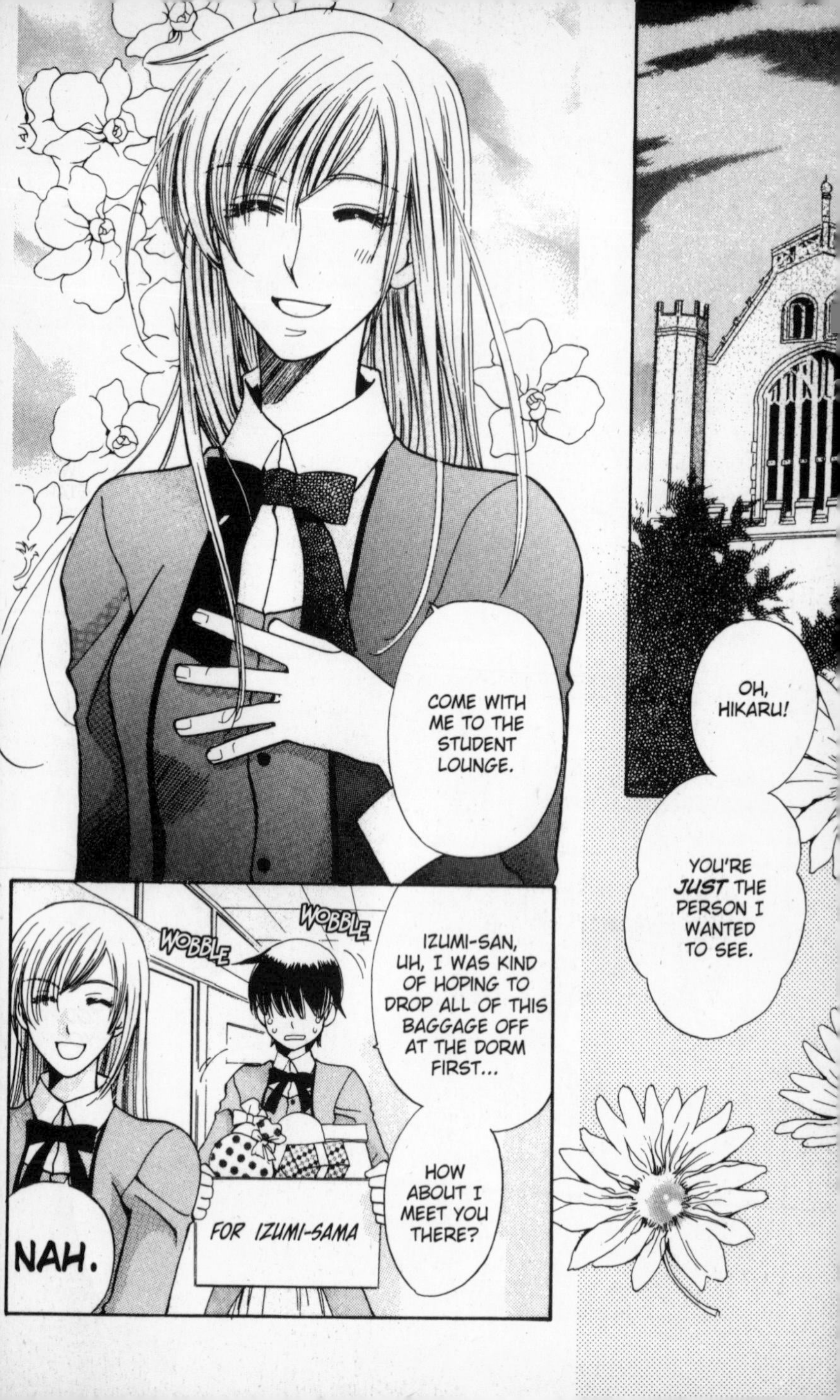
OH, HIKARU!
YOU'RE JUST THE PERSON I WANTED TO SEE.
COME WITH ME TO THE STUDENT LOUNGE.
WOBBLE
WOBBLE
IZUMI-SAN, UH, I WAS KIND OF HOPING TO DROP ALL OF THIS BAGGAGE OFF AT THE DORM FIRST...
HOW ABOUT I MEET YOU THERE?
FOR IZUMI-SAMA
NAH.

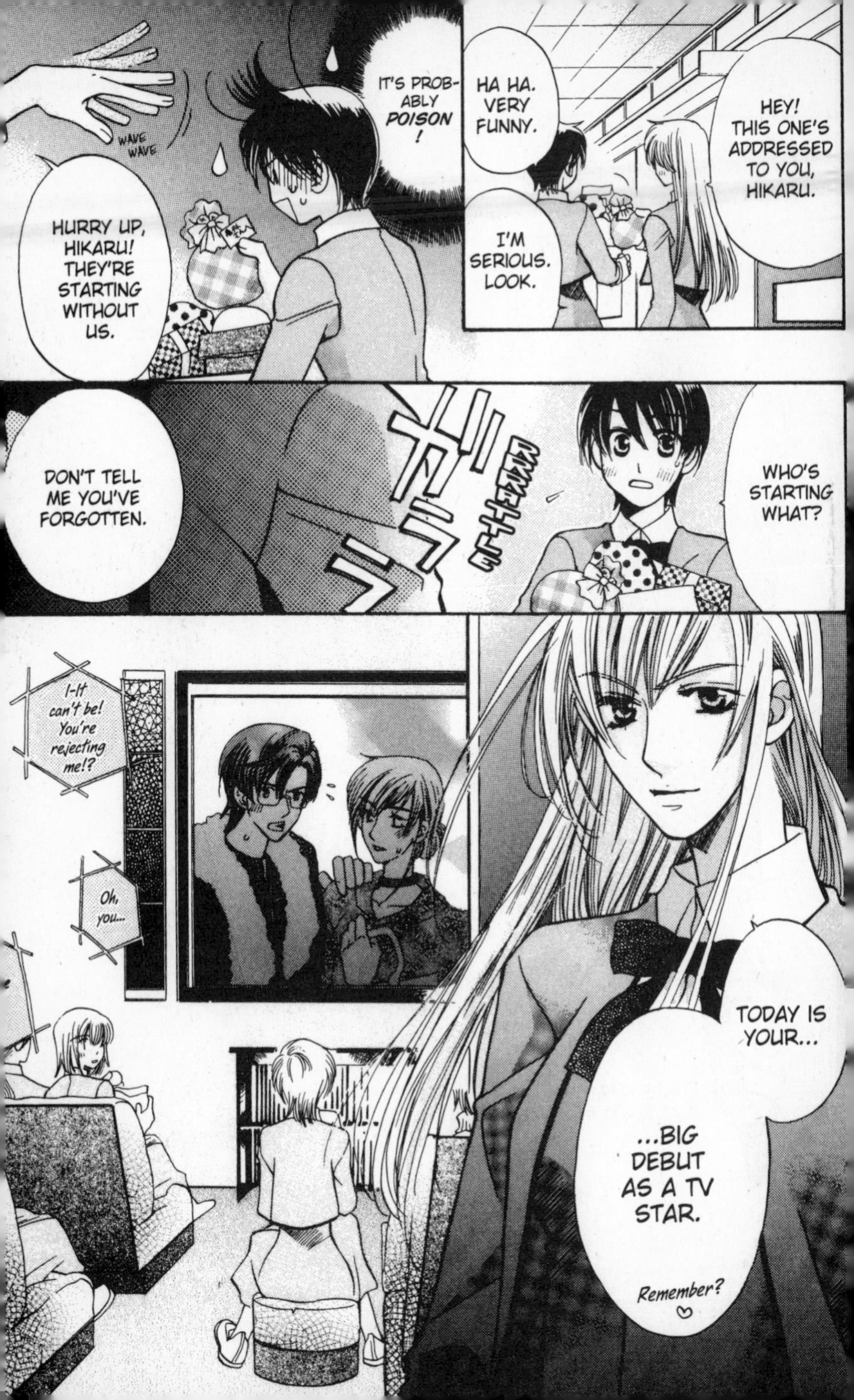
HEY! THIS ONE'S ADDRESSED TO YOU, HIKARU.
HA HA. VERY FUNNY.
I'M SERIOUS. LOOK.
IT'S PROB-ABLY POISON!
WAVE WAVE
HURRY UP, HIKARU! THEY'RE STARTING WITHOUT US.
WHO'S STARTING WHAT?
DON'T TELL ME YOU'VE FORGOTTEN.
TODAY IS YOUR...
...BIG DEBUT AS A TV STAR.
Remember?
I-It can't be! You're rejecting me!?
Oh, you...

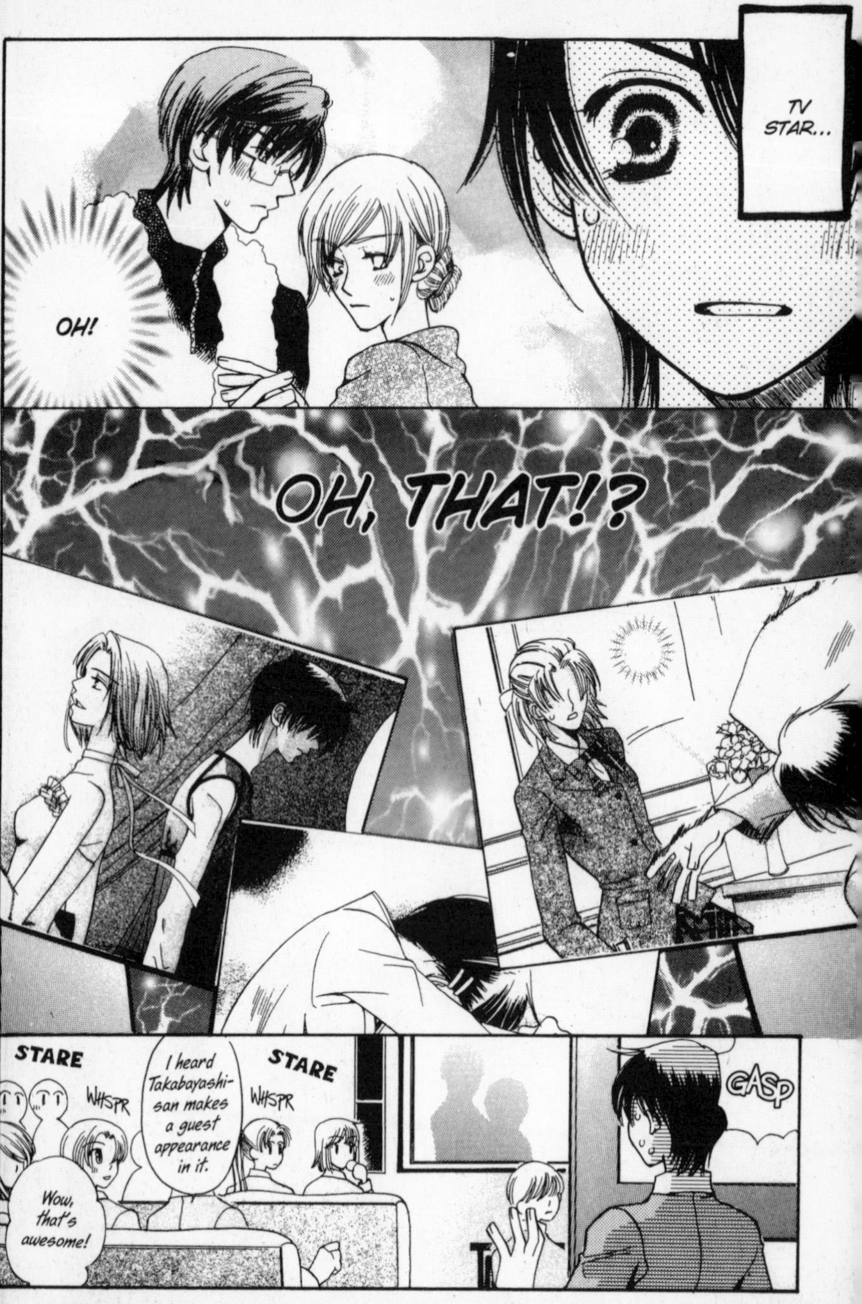
TV STAR...
OH!
OH, THAT!?
GASP
STARE
WHSPR
I heard Takabayashi-san makes a guest appearance in it.
WHSPR
STARE
Wow, that's awesome!

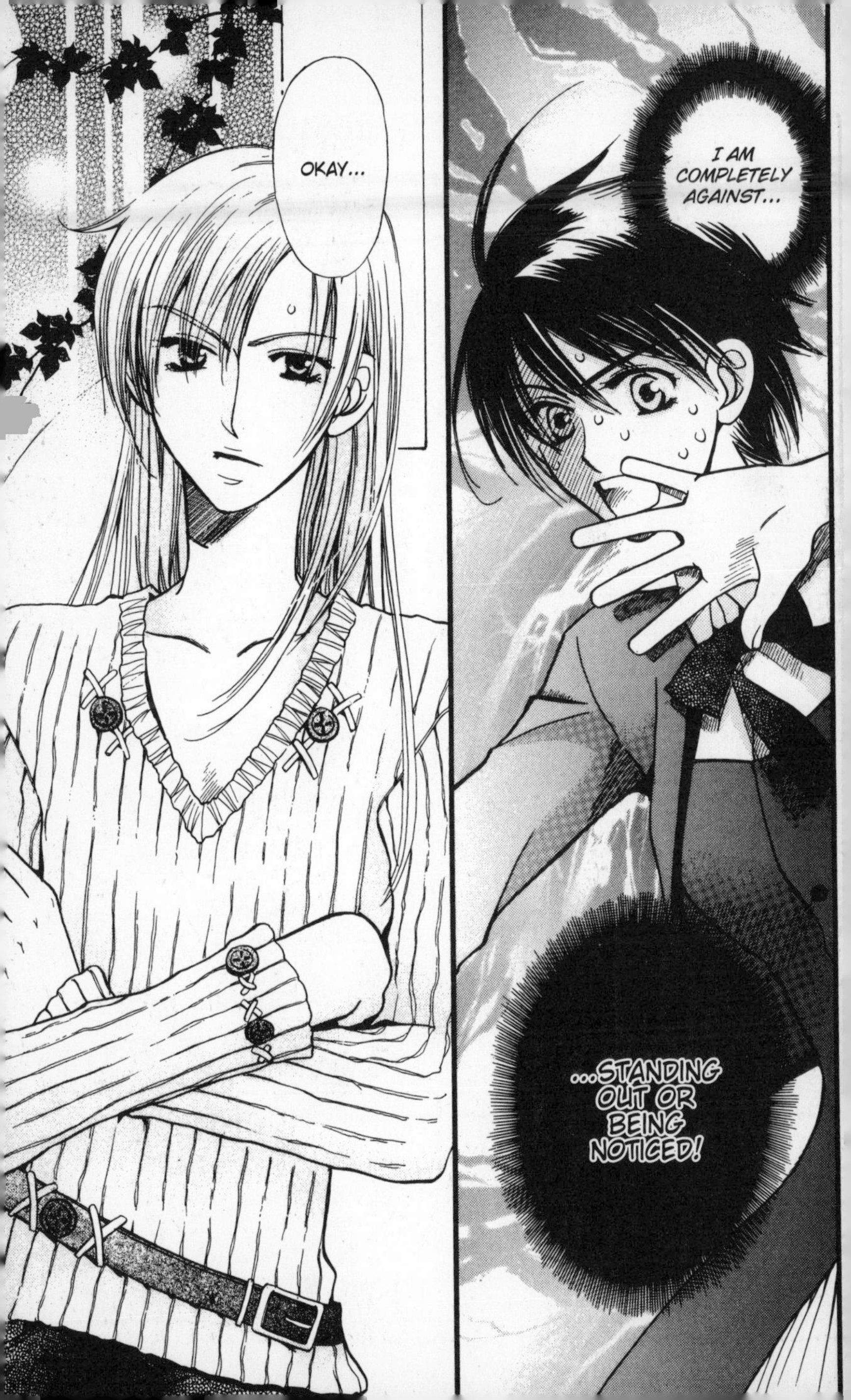
I AM COMPLETELY AGAINST...
...STANDING OUT OR BEING NOTICED!
OKAY...

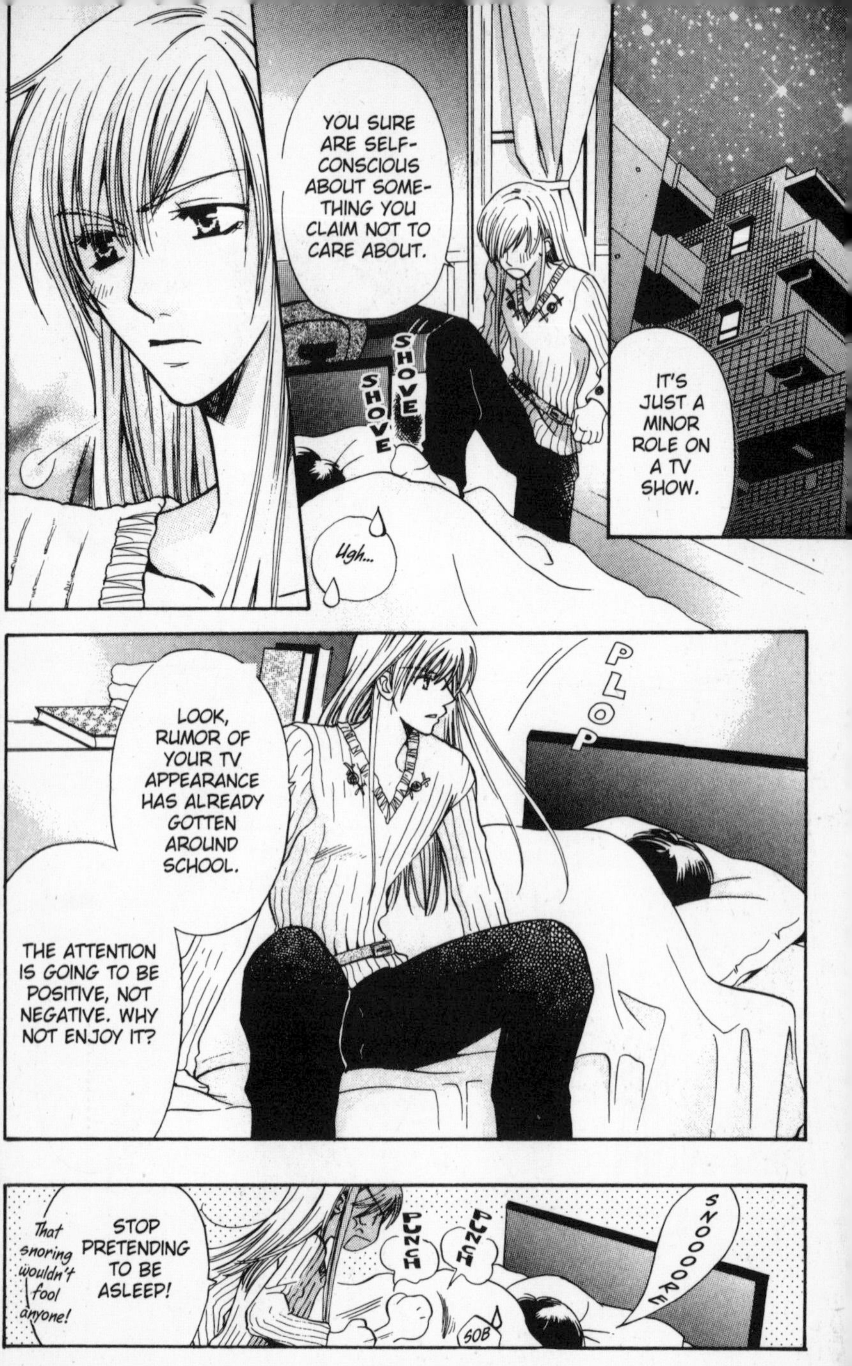
IT'S JUST A MINOR ROLE ON A TV SHOW.
YOU SURE ARE SELF-CONSCIOUS ABOUT SOMETHING YOU CLAIM NOT TO CARE ABOUT.
SHOVE
SHOVE
Ugh...
PLOP
LOOK, RUMOR OF YOUR TV APPEARANCE HAS ALREADY GOTTEN AROUND SCHOOL.
THE ATTENTION IS GOING TO BE POSITIVE, NOT NEGATIVE. WHY NOT ENJOY IT?
SNOOOORE
PUNCH
PUNCH
SOB
STOP PRETENDING TO BE ASLEEP!
That snoring wouldn't fool anyone!

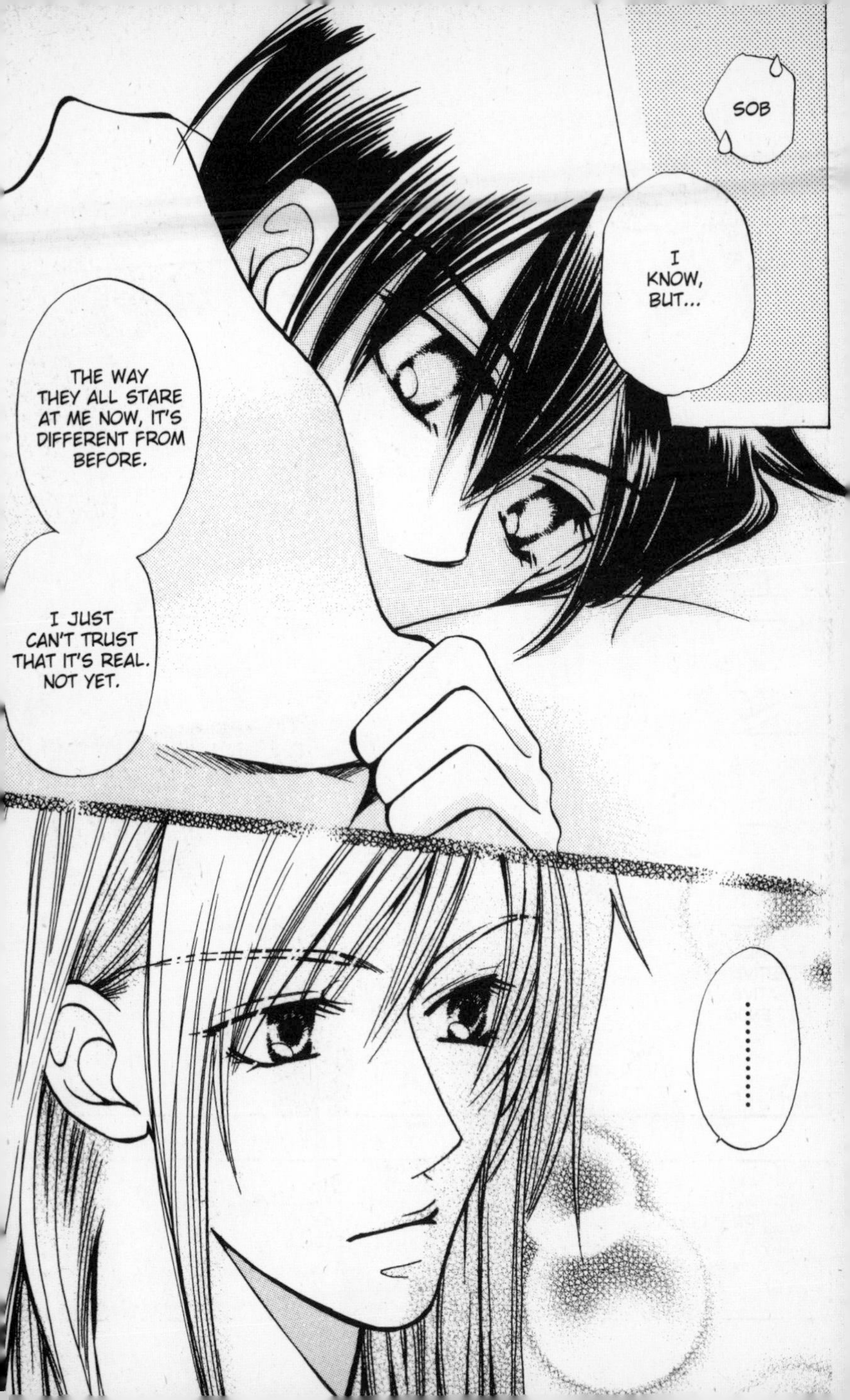
SOB
I KNOW, BUT...
THE WAY THEY ALL STARE AT ME NOW, IT'S DIFFERENT FROM BEFORE.
I JUST CAN'T TRUST THAT IT'S REAL. NOT YET.
....

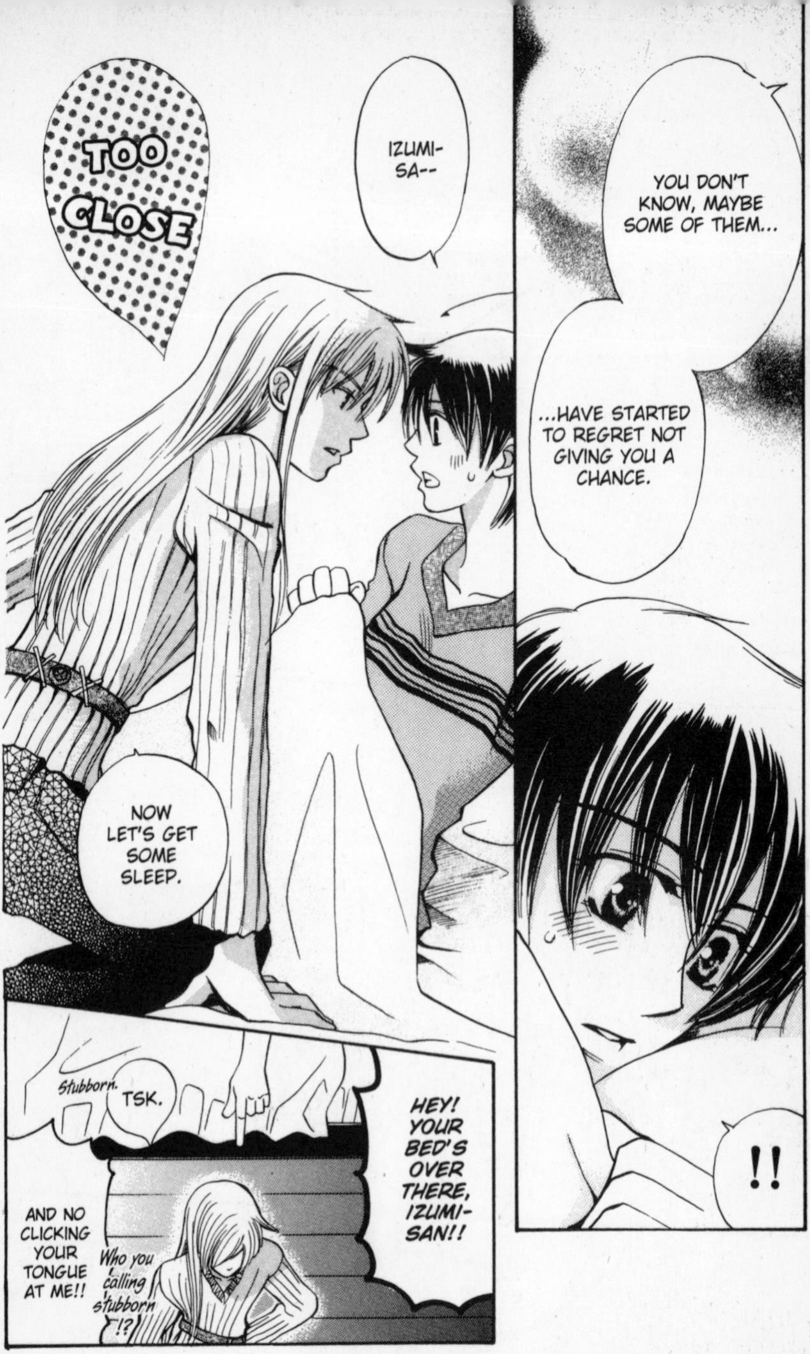
YOU DON'T KNOW, MAYBE SOME OF THEM...
...HAVE STARTED TO REGRET NOT GIVING YOU A CHANCE.
!!
IZUMI-SA--
TOO CLOSE
NOW LET'S GET SOME SLEEP.
HEY! YOUR BED'S OVER THERE, IZUMI-SAN!!
TSK.
Stubborn.
AND NO CLICKING YOUR TONGUE AT ME!!
Who you calling stubborn!?

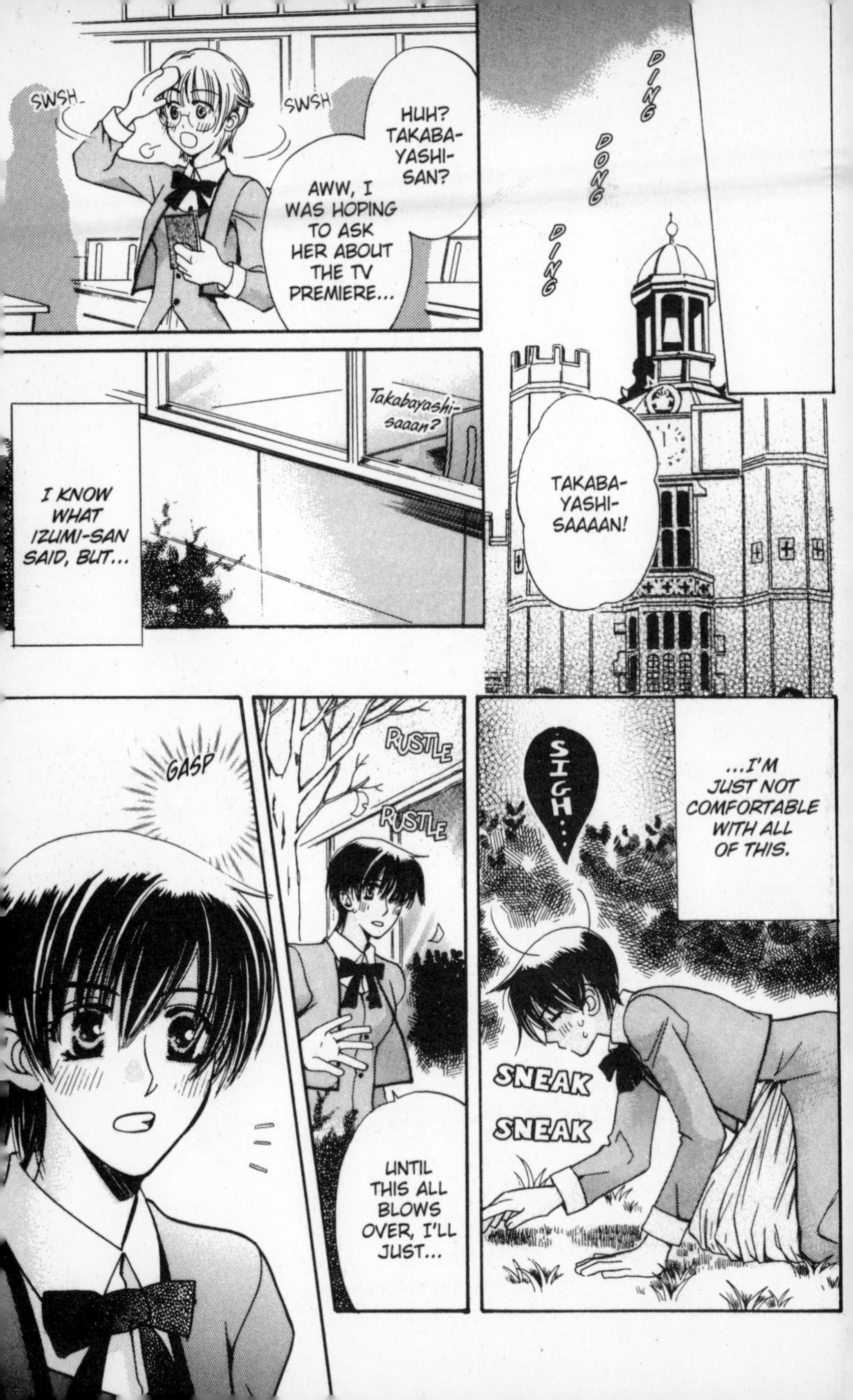
DING
DONG
DING
TAKABA-YASHI-SAAAAN!
SWSH
SWSH
HUH? TAKABA-YASHI-SAN?
AWW, I WAS HOPING TO ASK HER ABOUT THE TV PREMIERE...
Takabayashi-saaan?
I KNOW WHAT IZUMI-SAN SAID, BUT...
...I'M JUST NOT COMFORTABLE WITH ALL OF THIS.
SIGH...
SNEAK
SNEAK
RUSTLE
RUSTLE
UNTIL THIS ALL BLOWS OVER, I'LL JUST...
GASP

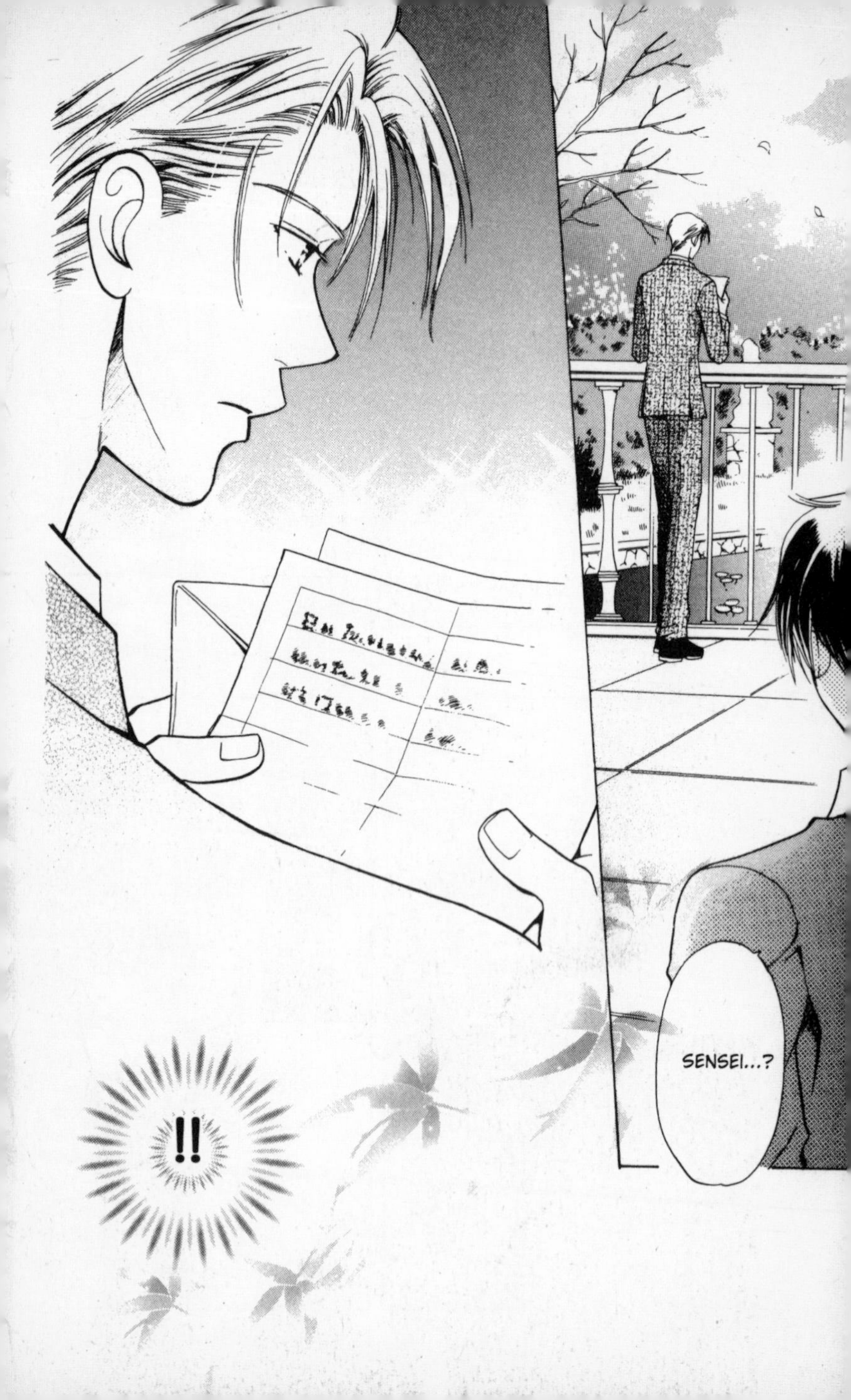
SENSEI...?
!!

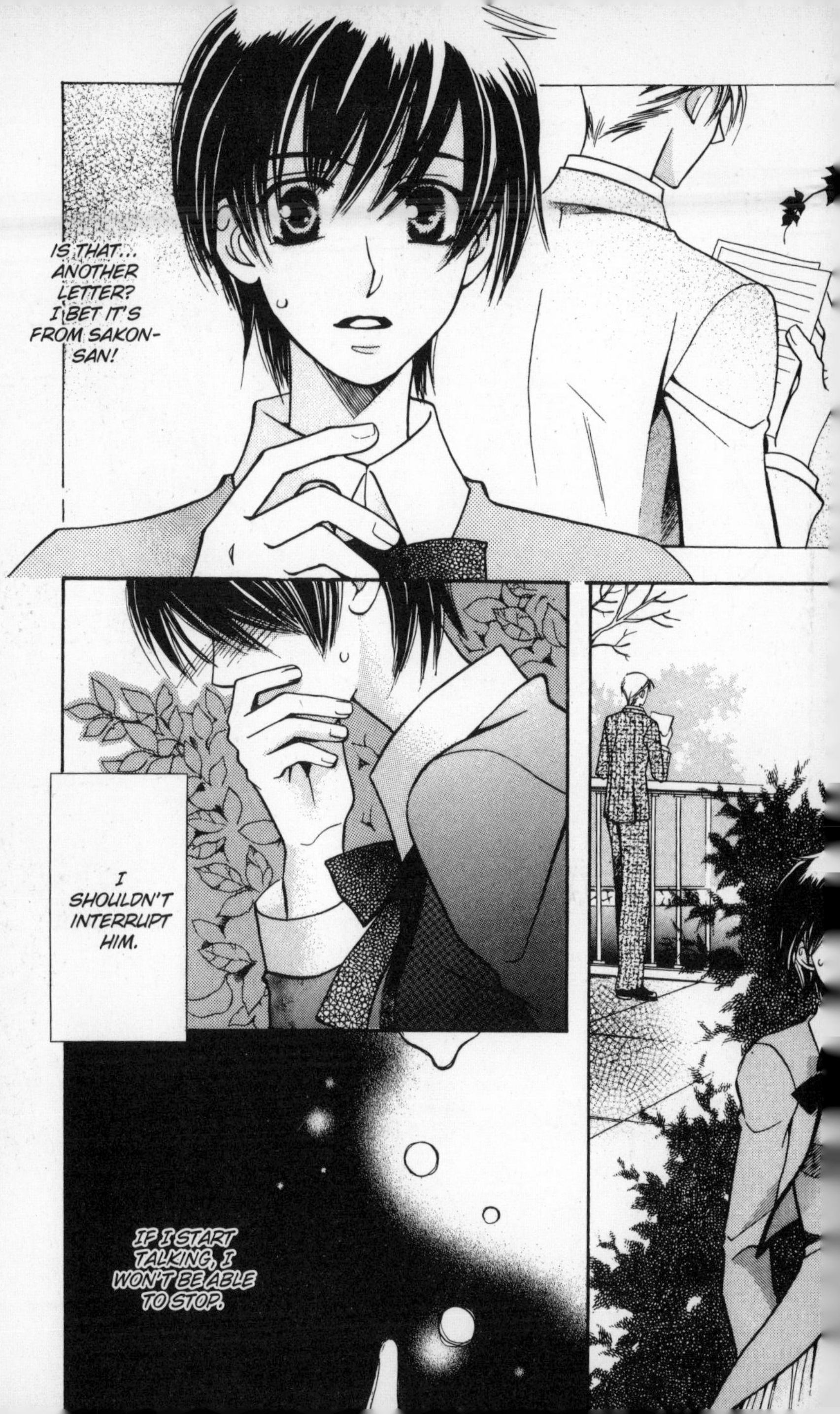
IS THAT... ANOTHER LETTER? I BET IT'S FROM SAKON-SAN!
I SHOULDN'T INTERRUPT HIM.
IF I START TALKING, I WON'T BE ABLE TO STOP.

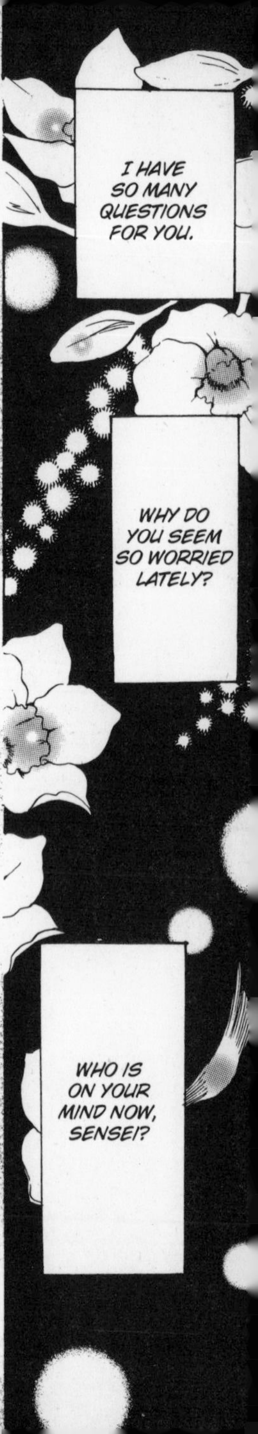
I HAVE SO MANY QUESTIONS FOR YOU.
WHY DO YOU SEEM SO WORRIED LATELY?
WHO IS ON YOUR MIND NOW, SENSEI?

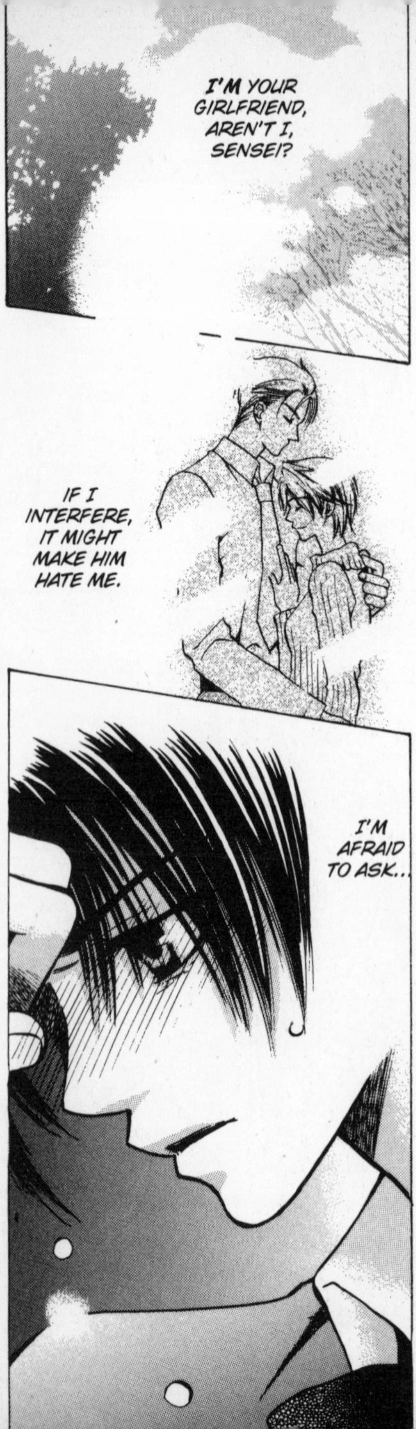
I'M YOUR GIRLFRIEND, AREN'T I, SENSEI?
IF I INTERFERE, IT MIGHT MAKE HIM HATE ME.
I'M AFRAID TO ASK...

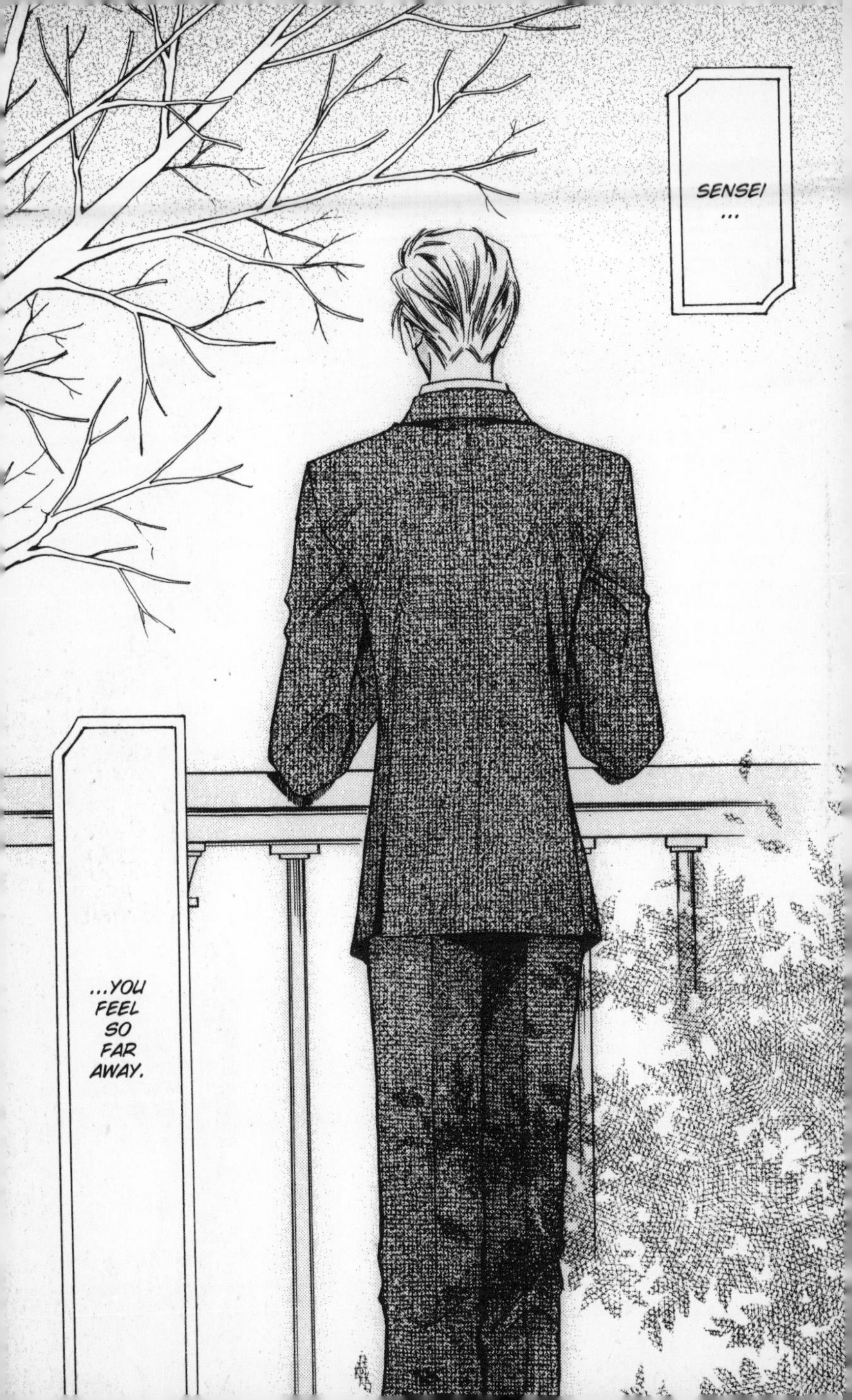
SENSEI ...
...YOU FEEL SO FAR AWAY.

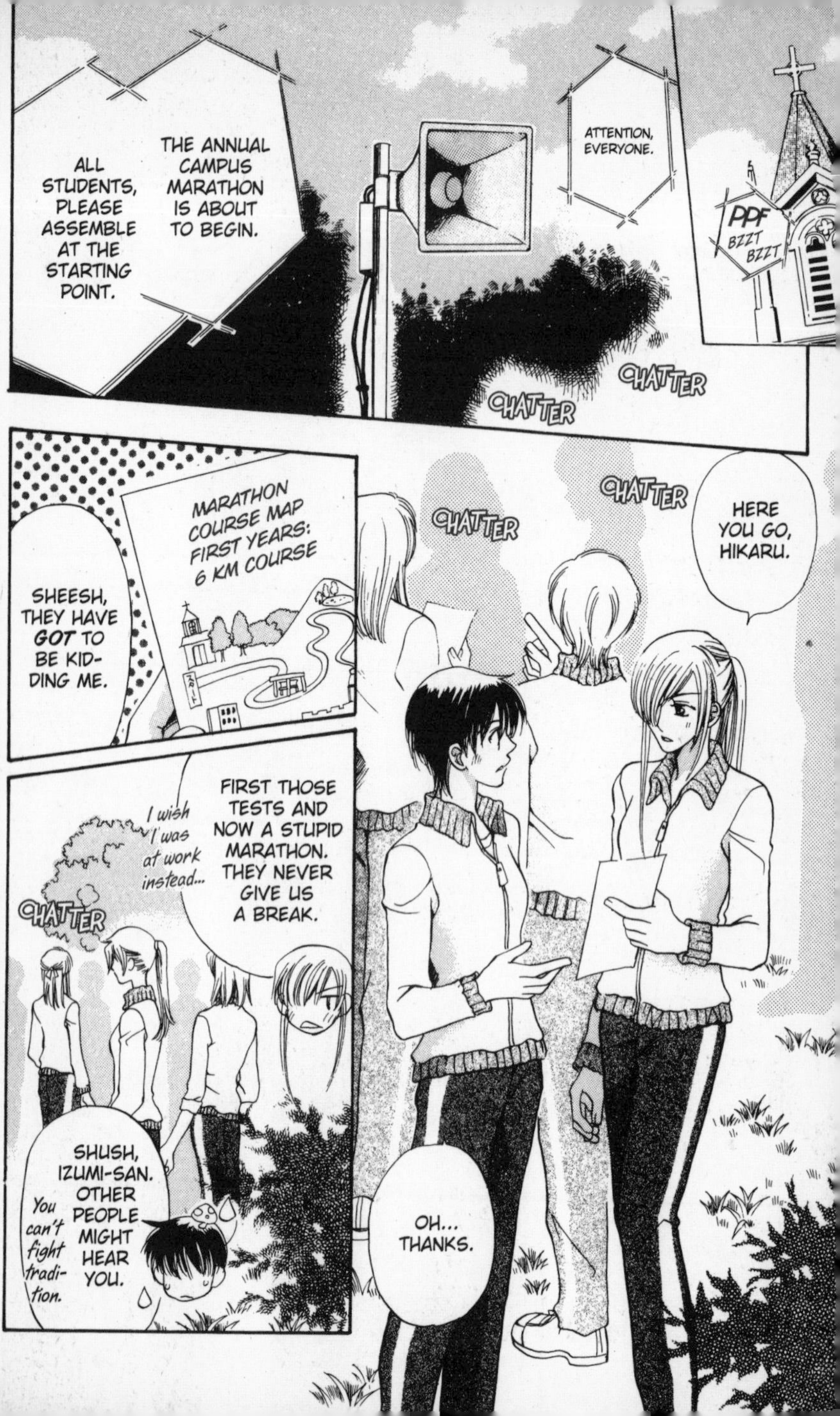

PPF
BZZT BZZT
ATTENTION, EVERYONE.
THE ANNUAL CAMPUS MARATHON IS ABOUT TO BEGIN.
ALL STUDENTS, PLEASE ASSEMBLE AT THE STARTING POINT.
CHATTER
CHATTER
HERE YOU GO, HIKARU.
CHATTER
CHATTER
OH... THANKS.
MARATHON COURSE MAP
FIRST YEARS: 6 KM COURSE
SHEESH, THEY HAVE GOT TO BE KID-DING ME.
FIRST THOSE TESTS AND NOW A STUPID MARATHON. THEY NEVER GIVE US A BREAK.
I wish I was at work instead...
CHATTER
SHUSH, IZUMI-SAN. OTHER PEOPLE MIGHT HEAR YOU.
You can't fight tradi-tion.

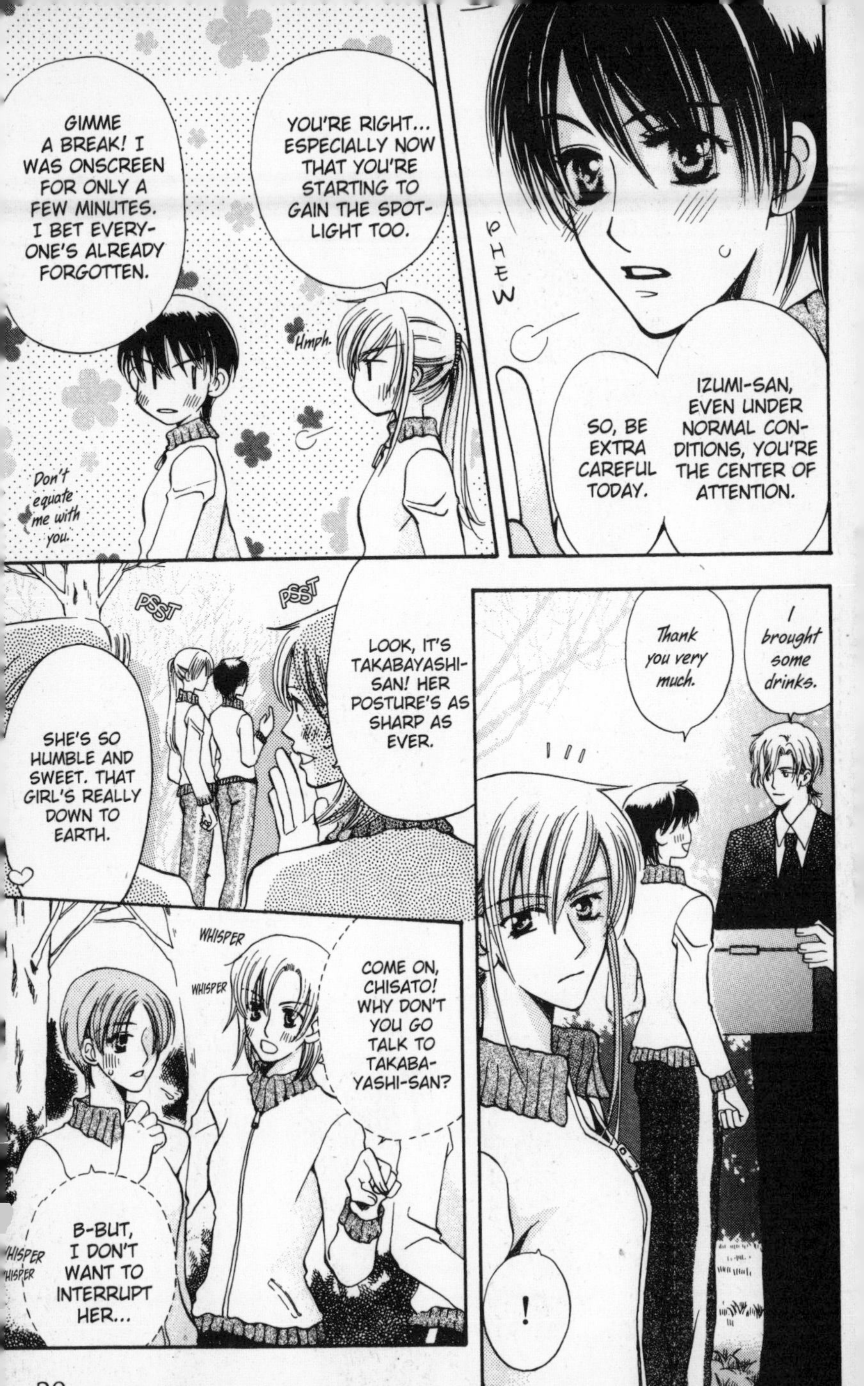
PHEW
IZUMI-SAN, EVEN UNDER NORMAL CONDITIONS, YOU'RE THE CENTER OF ATTENTION.
SO, BE EXTRA CAREFUL TODAY.
YOU'RE RIGHT... ESPECIALLY NOW THAT YOU'RE STARTING TO GAIN THE SPOTLIGHT TOO.
GIMME A BREAK! I WAS ONSCREEN FOR ONLY A FEW MINUTES. I BET EVERYONE'S ALREADY FORGOTTEN.
Hmph.
Don't equate me with you..
PSST
PSST
LOOK, IT'S TAKABAYASHI-SAN! HER POSTURE'S AS SHARP AS EVER.
SHE'S SO HUMBLE AND SWEET. THAT GIRL'S REALLY DOWN TO EARTH.
WHISPER
WHISPER
COME ON, CHISATO! WHY DON'T YOU GO TALK TO TAKABAYASHI-SAN?
B-BUT, I DON'T WANT TO INTERRUPT HER...
WHISPER
WHISPER
I brought some drinks.
Thank you very much.
!

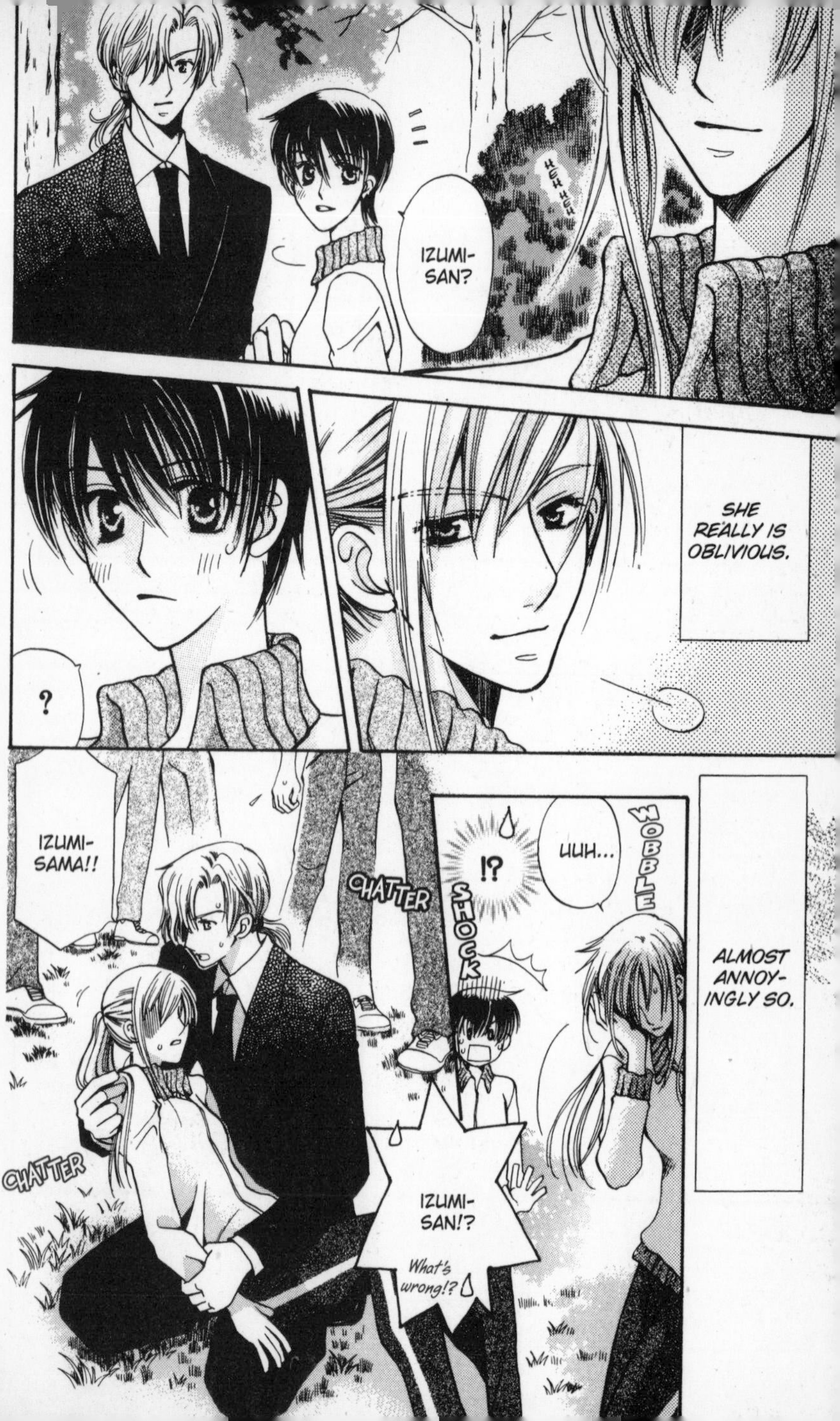
HEH HEH
IZUMI-SAN?
SHE REALLY IS OBLIVIOUS.
?
ALMOST ANNOY-INGLY SO.
WOBBLE
UUH...
SHOCK
!?
CHATTER
IZUMI-SAMA!!
IZUMI-SAN!?
What's wrong!?
CHATTER

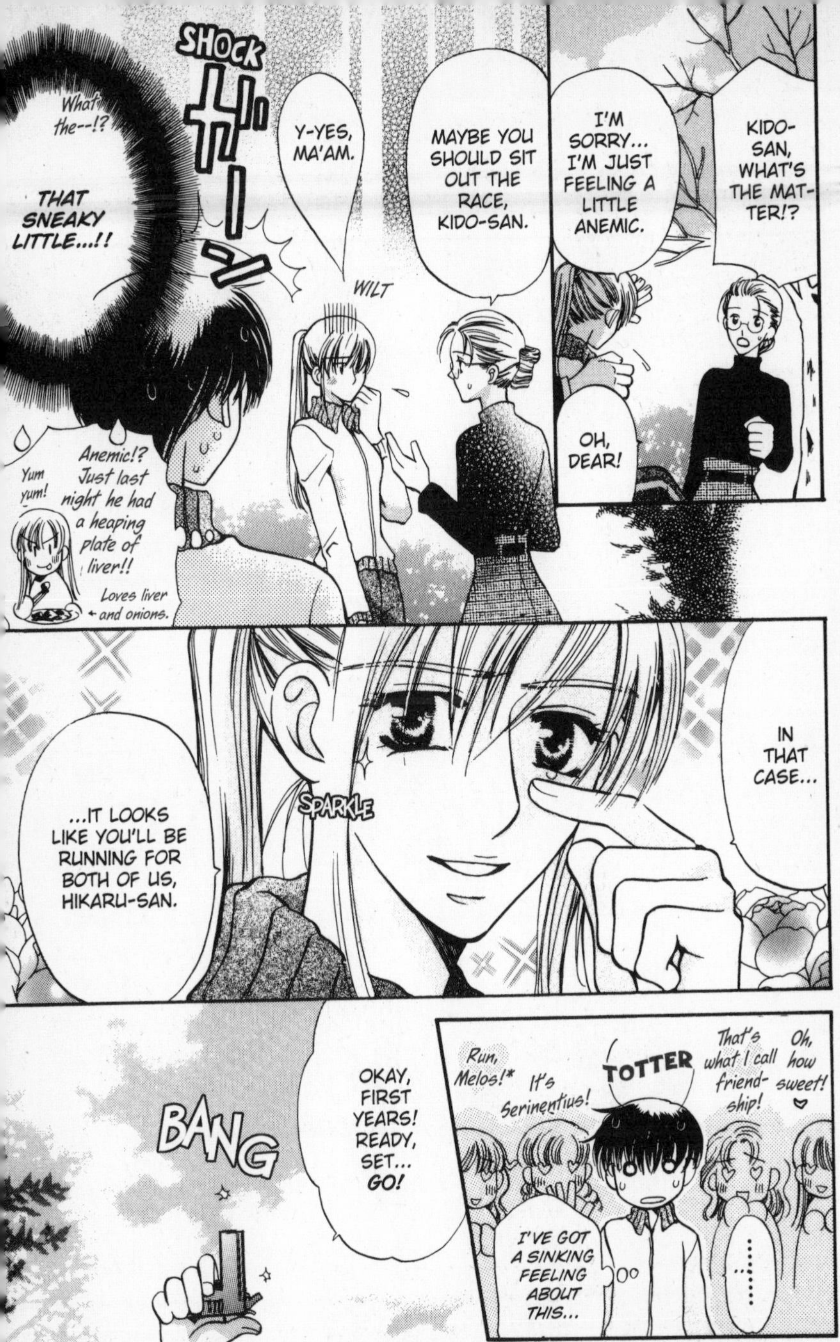
KIDO-SAN, WHAT'S THE MAT-TER!?
I'M SORRY... I'M JUST FEELING A LITTLE ANEMIC.
OH, DEAR!
MAYBE YOU SHOULD SIT OUT THE RACE, KIDO-SAN.
Y-YES, MA'AM.
WILT
SHOCK
What the--!?
THAT SNEAKY LITTLE...!!
Anemic!? Just last night he had a heaping plate of liver!!
Yum yum!
Loves liver and onions.
IN THAT CASE...
...IT LOOKS LIKE YOU'LL BE RUNNING FOR BOTH OF US, HIKARU-SAN.
SPARKLE
Oh, how sweet!
That's what I call friend-ship!
TOTTER
It's Serinentius!
Run, Melos!*
......
I'VE GOT A SINKING FEELING ABOUT THIS...
OKAY, FIRST YEARS! READY, SET... GO!
BANG

*See Translator's Notes at back of book.

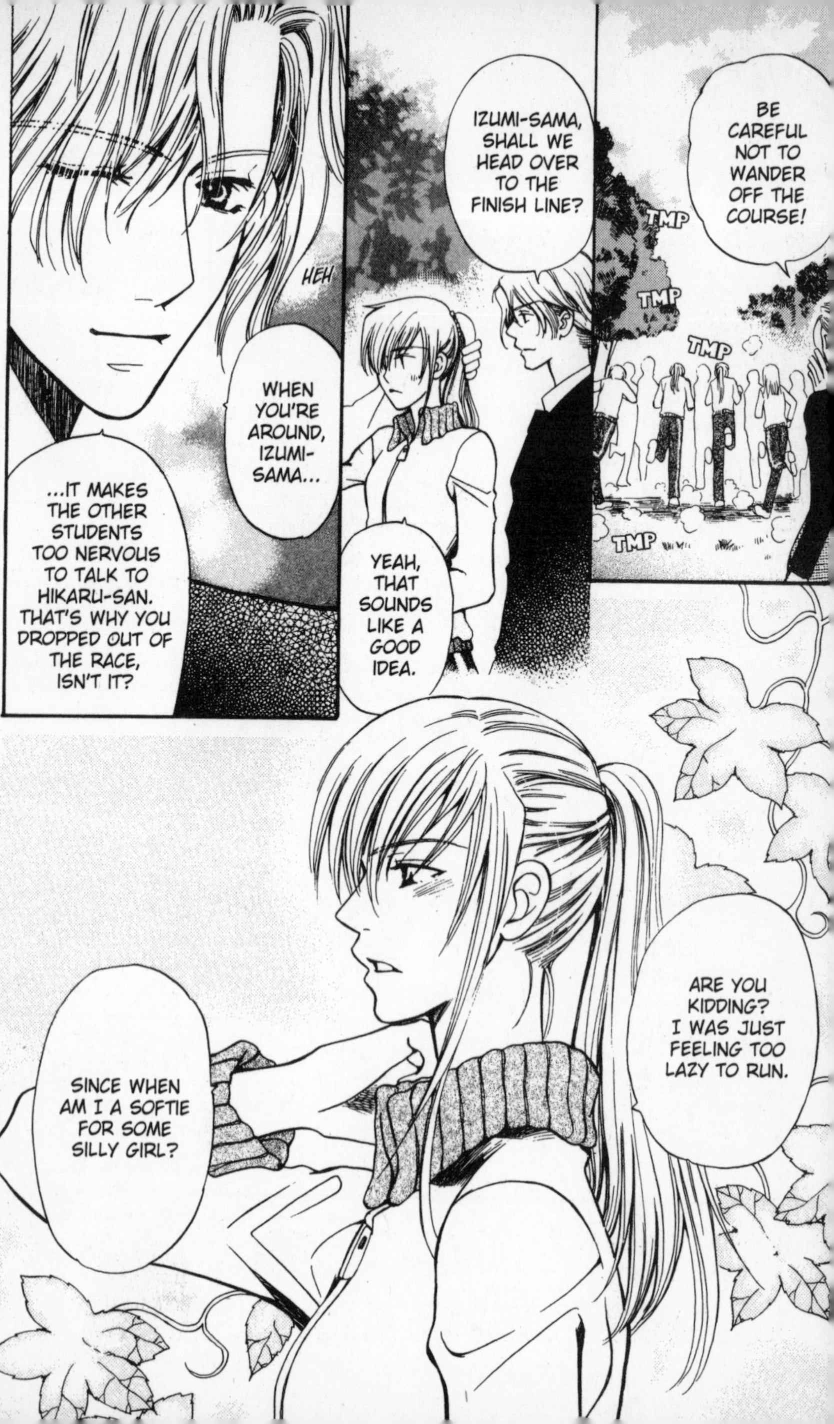
BE CAREFUL NOT TO WANDER OFF THE COURSE!
TMP
TMP
TMP
TMP
IZUMI-SAMA, SHALL WE HEAD OVER TO THE FINISH LINE?
YEAH, THAT SOUNDS LIKE A GOOD IDEA.
HEH
WHEN YOU'RE AROUND, IZUMI-SAMA...
...IT MAKES THE OTHER STUDENTS TOO NERVOUS TO TALK TO HIKARU-SAN. THAT'S WHY YOU DROPPED OUT OF THE RACE, ISN'T IT?
ARE YOU KIDDING? I WAS JUST FEELING TOO LAZY TO RUN.
SINCE WHEN AM I A SOFTIE FOR SOME SILLY GIRL?

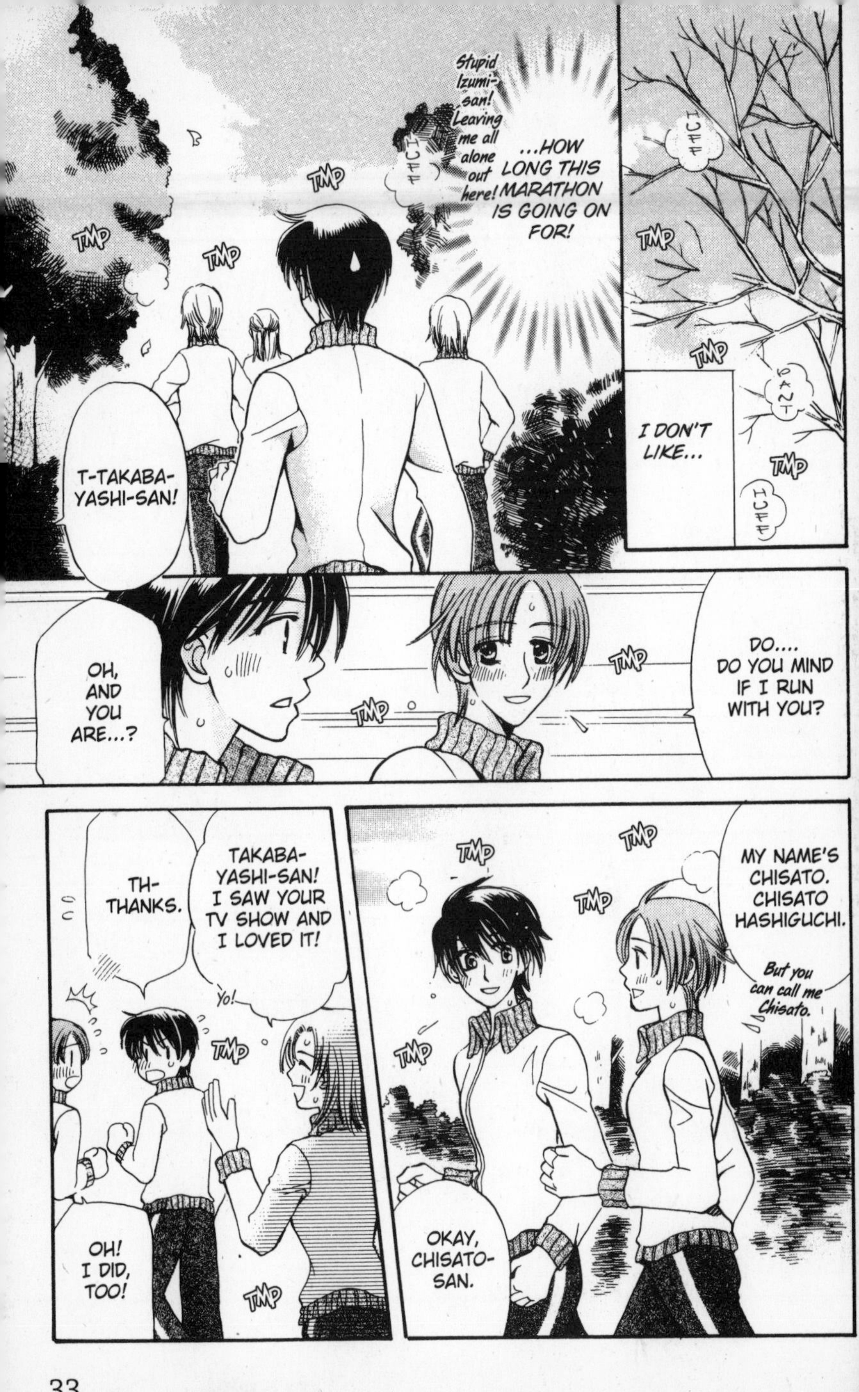
HUFF
TMP
TMP
PANT
I DON'T LIKE...
TMP
HUFF
Stupid Izumi-san! Leaving me all alone out here!
...HOW LONG THIS MARATHON IS GOING ON FOR!
HUFF
TMP
TMP
TMP
T-TAKABAYASHI-SAN!
DO.... DO YOU MIND IF I RUN WITH YOU?
TMP
TMP
OH, AND YOU ARE...?
MY NAME'S CHISATO. CHISATO HASHIGUCHI.
But you can call me Chisato.
TMP
TMP
TMP
TMP
OKAY, CHISATO-SAN.
TAKABAYASHI-SAN! I SAW YOUR TV SHOW AND I LOVED IT!
TH-THANKS.
Yo!
TMP
OH! I DID, TOO!
TMP

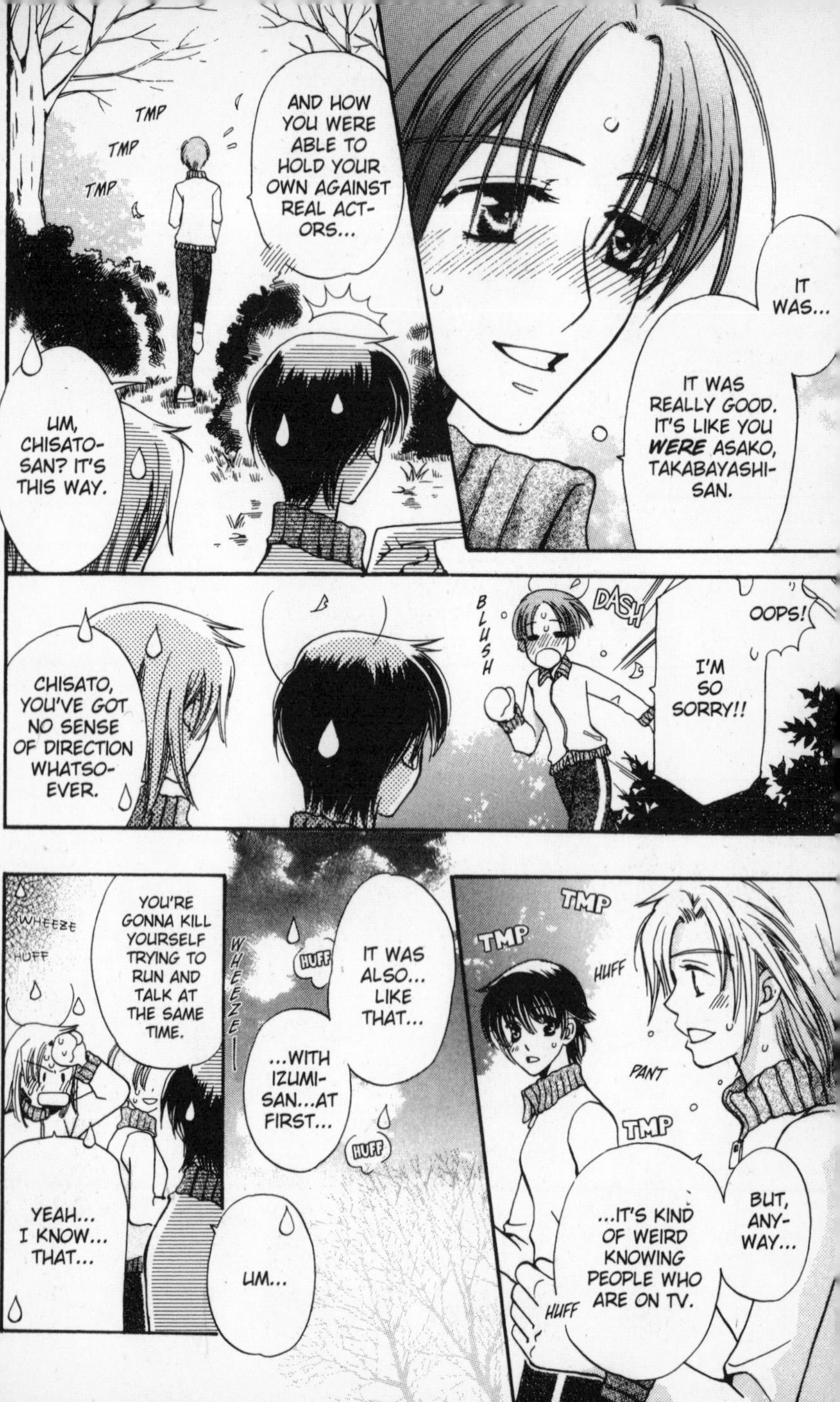
IT WAS...
IT WAS REALLY GOOD. IT'S LIKE YOU **WERE** ASAKO, TAKABAYASHI-SAN.
AND HOW YOU WERE ABLE TO HOLD YOUR OWN AGAINST REAL ACTORS...
TMP
TMP
TMP
UM, CHISATO-SAN? IT'S THIS WAY.
OOPS!
I'M SO SORRY!!
DASH
BLUSH
CHISATO, YOU'VE GOT NO SENSE OF DIRECTION WHATSOEVER.
TMP
TMP
HUFF
BUT, ANYWAY...
...IT'S KIND OF WEIRD KNOWING PEOPLE WHO ARE ON TV.
PANT
TMP
HUFF
IT WAS ALSO... LIKE THAT...
HUFF
WHEEZE
...WITH IZUMI-SAN...AT FIRST...
HUFF
UM...
YOU'RE GONNA KILL YOURSELF TRYING TO RUN AND TALK AT THE SAME TIME.
WHEEZE
HUFF
YEAH... I KNOW... THAT...

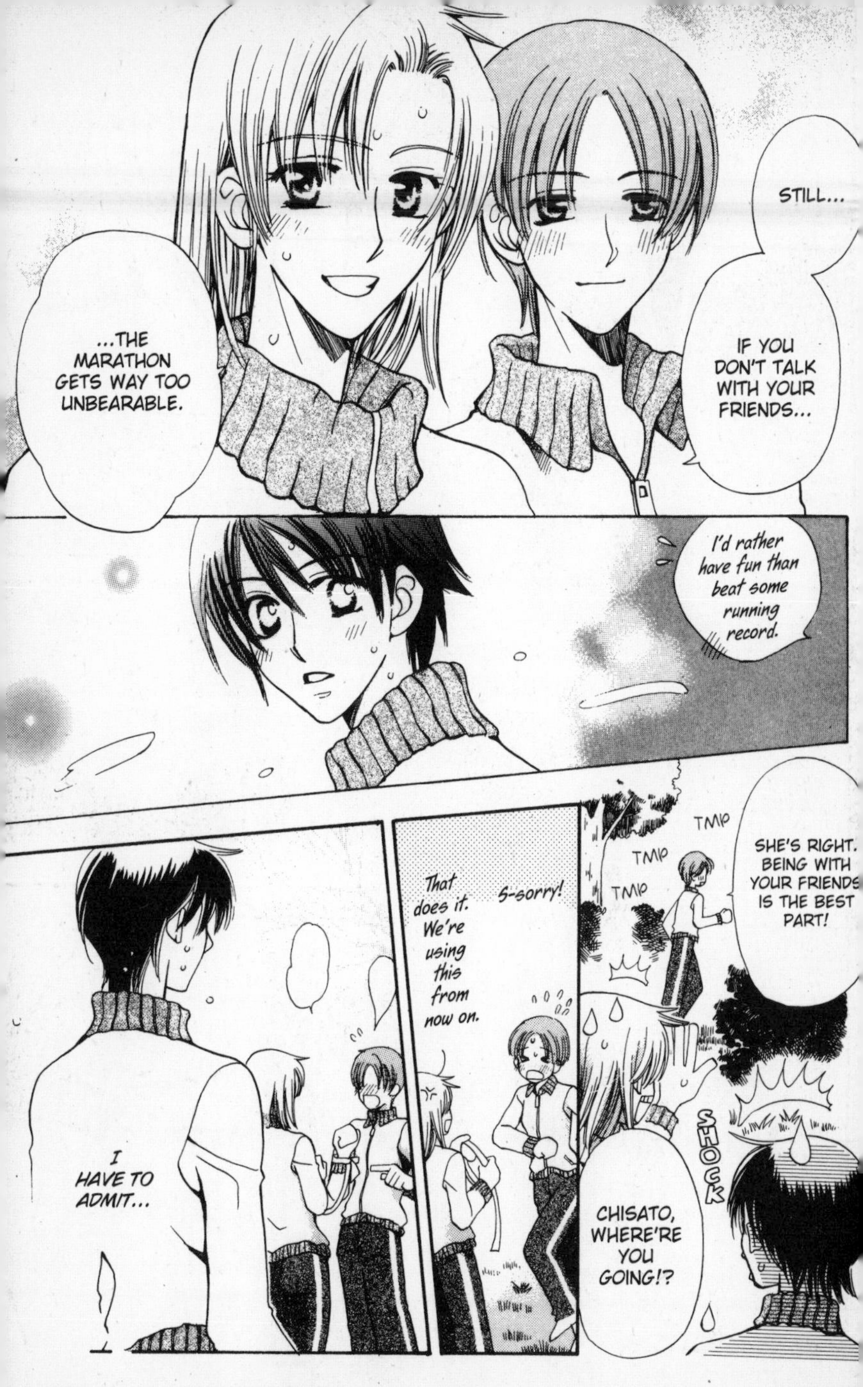
STILL...
IF YOU DON'T TALK WITH YOUR FRIENDS...
...THE MARATHON GETS WAY TOO UNBEARABLE.
I'd rather have fun than beat some running record.
SHE'S RIGHT. BEING WITH YOUR FRIENDS IS THE BEST PART!
TMP
TMP
TMP
SHOCK
CHISATO, WHERE'RE YOU GOING!?
S-sorry!
That does it. We're using this from now on.
I HAVE TO ADMIT...

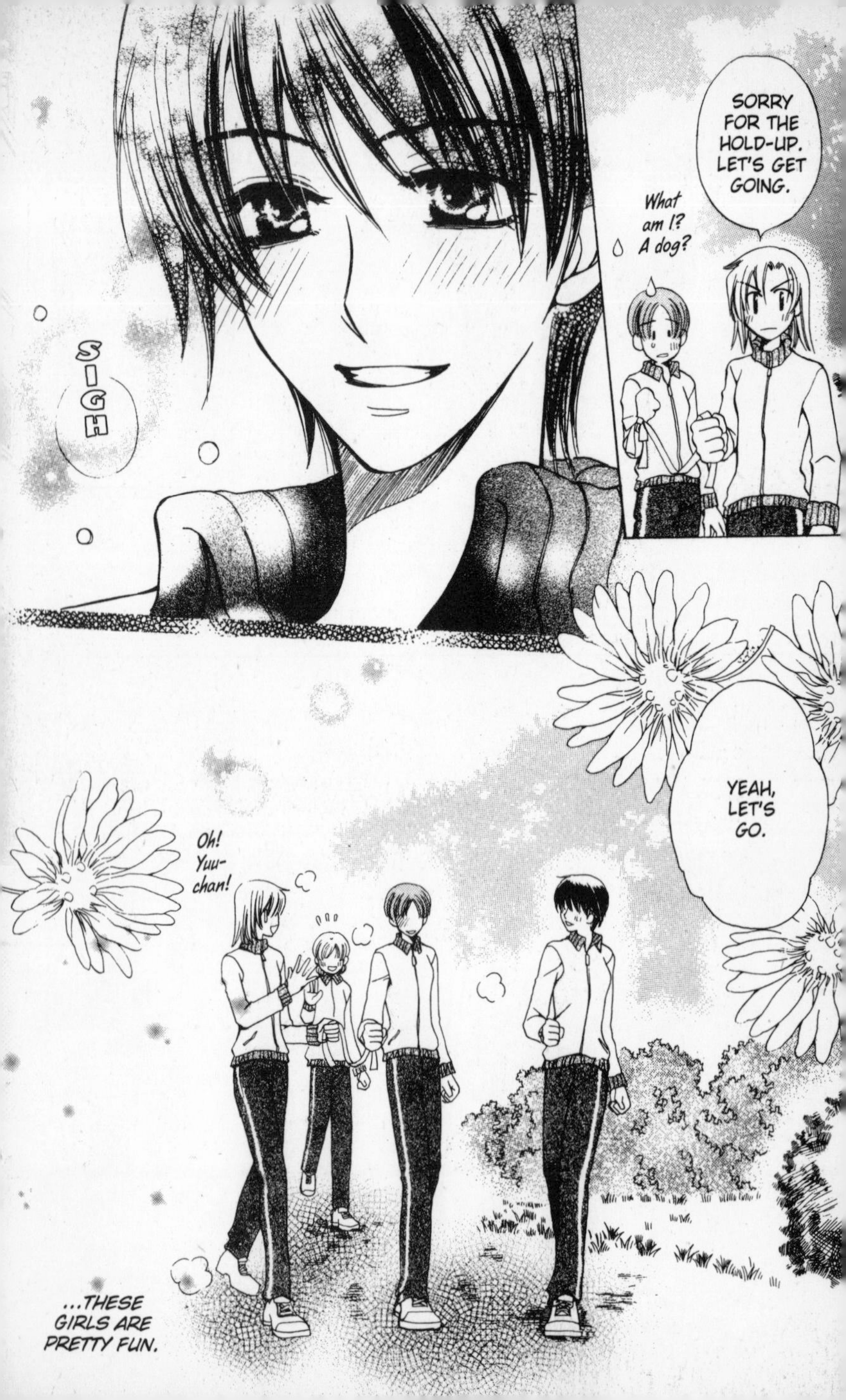
SORRY FOR THE HOLD-UP. LET'S GET GOING.
What am I? A dog?
SIGH
YEAH, LET'S GO.
Oh! Yuu-chan!
...THESE GIRLS ARE PRETTY FUN.

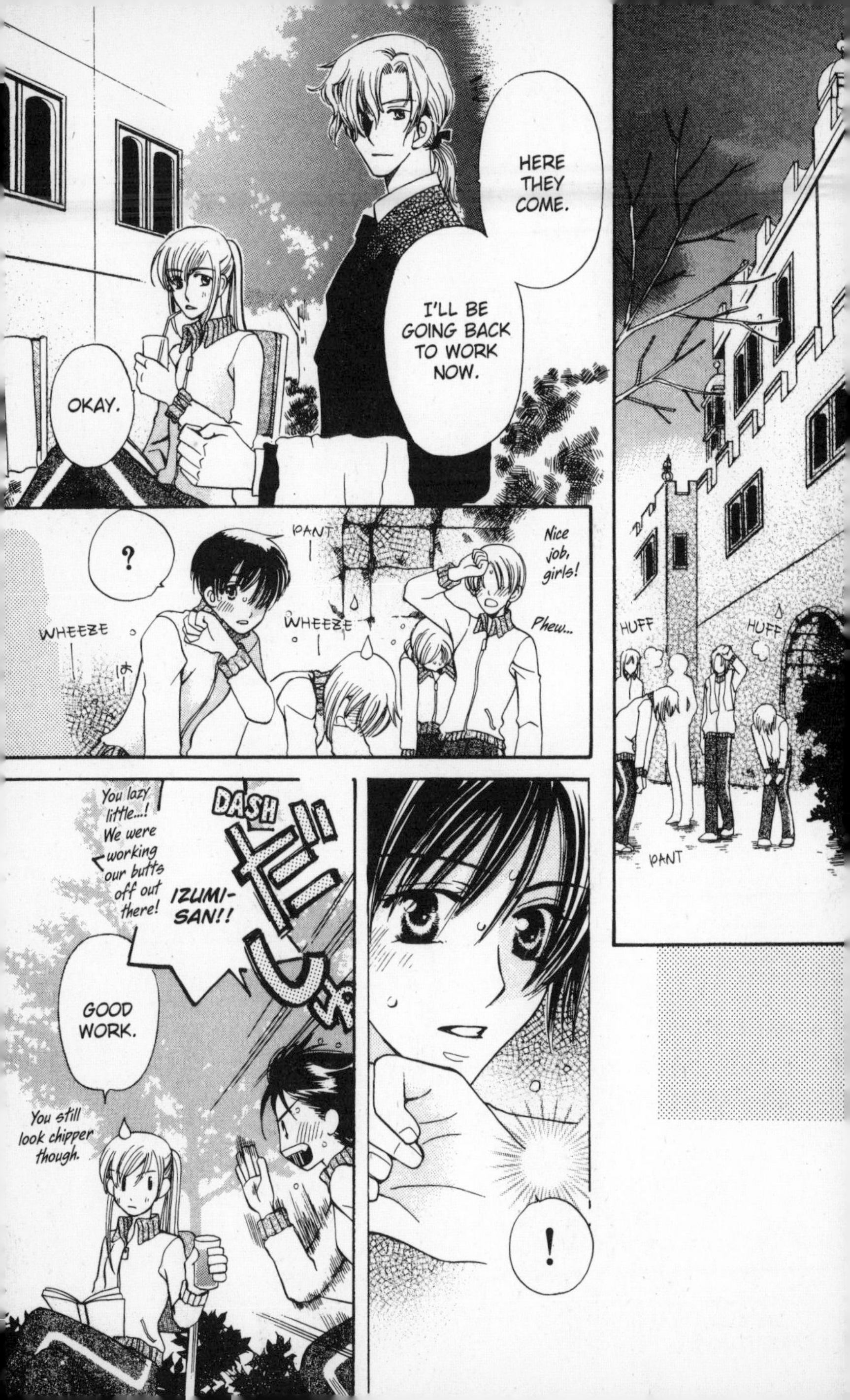

HUFF
HUFF
PANT
HERE THEY COME.
I'LL BE GOING BACK TO WORK NOW.
OKAY.
Nice job, girls!
PANT
?
Phew...
WHEEZE
WHEEZE
!
DASH
IZUMI-SAN!!
You lazy little...! We were working our butts off out there!
GOOD WORK.
You still look chipper though.

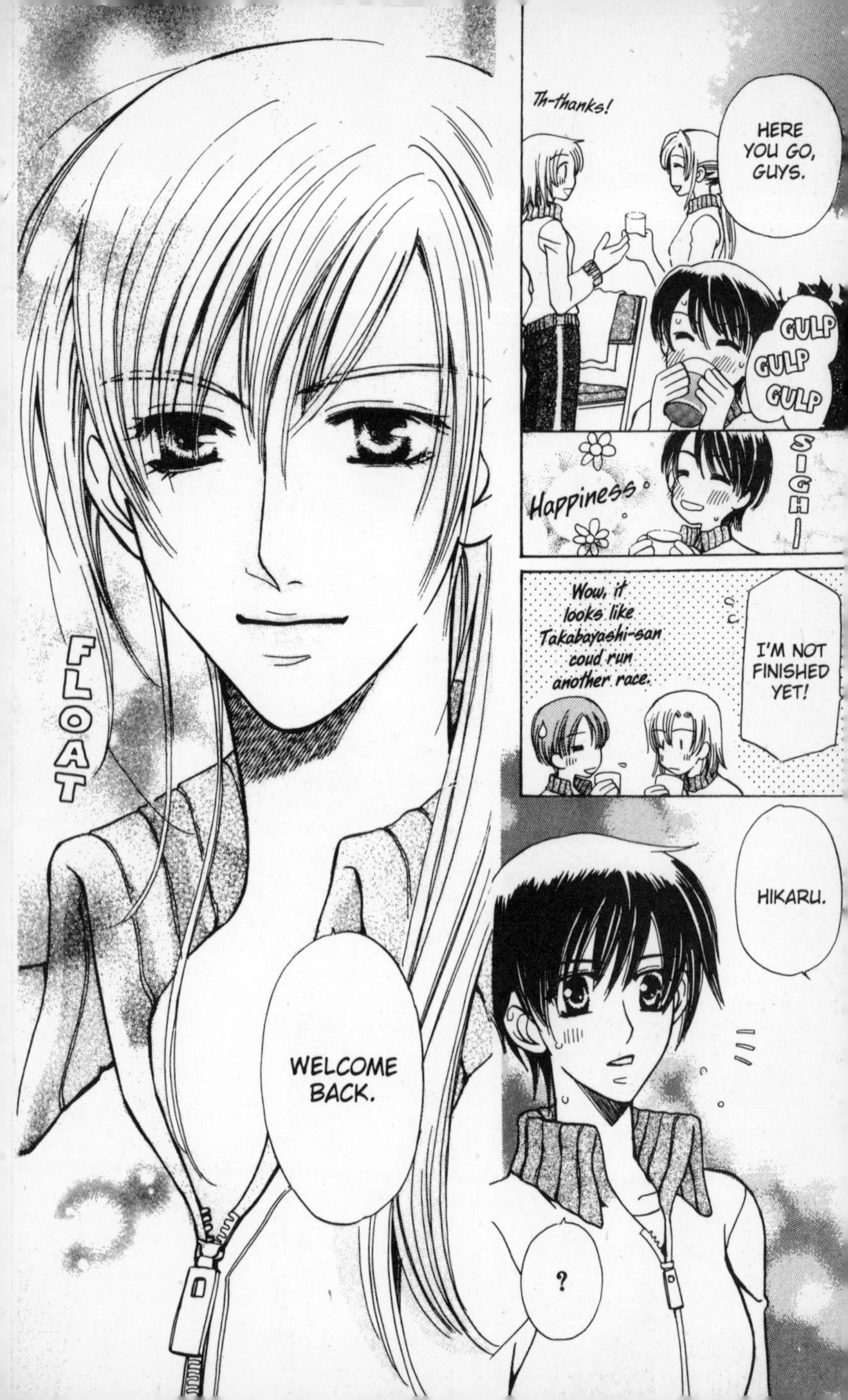
HERE YOU GO, GUYS.
Th-thanks!
GULP GULP GULP
SIGH!
Happiness
I'M NOT FINISHED YET!
Wow, it looks like Takabayashi-san coud run another race.
HIKARU.
?
FLOAT
WELCOME BACK.

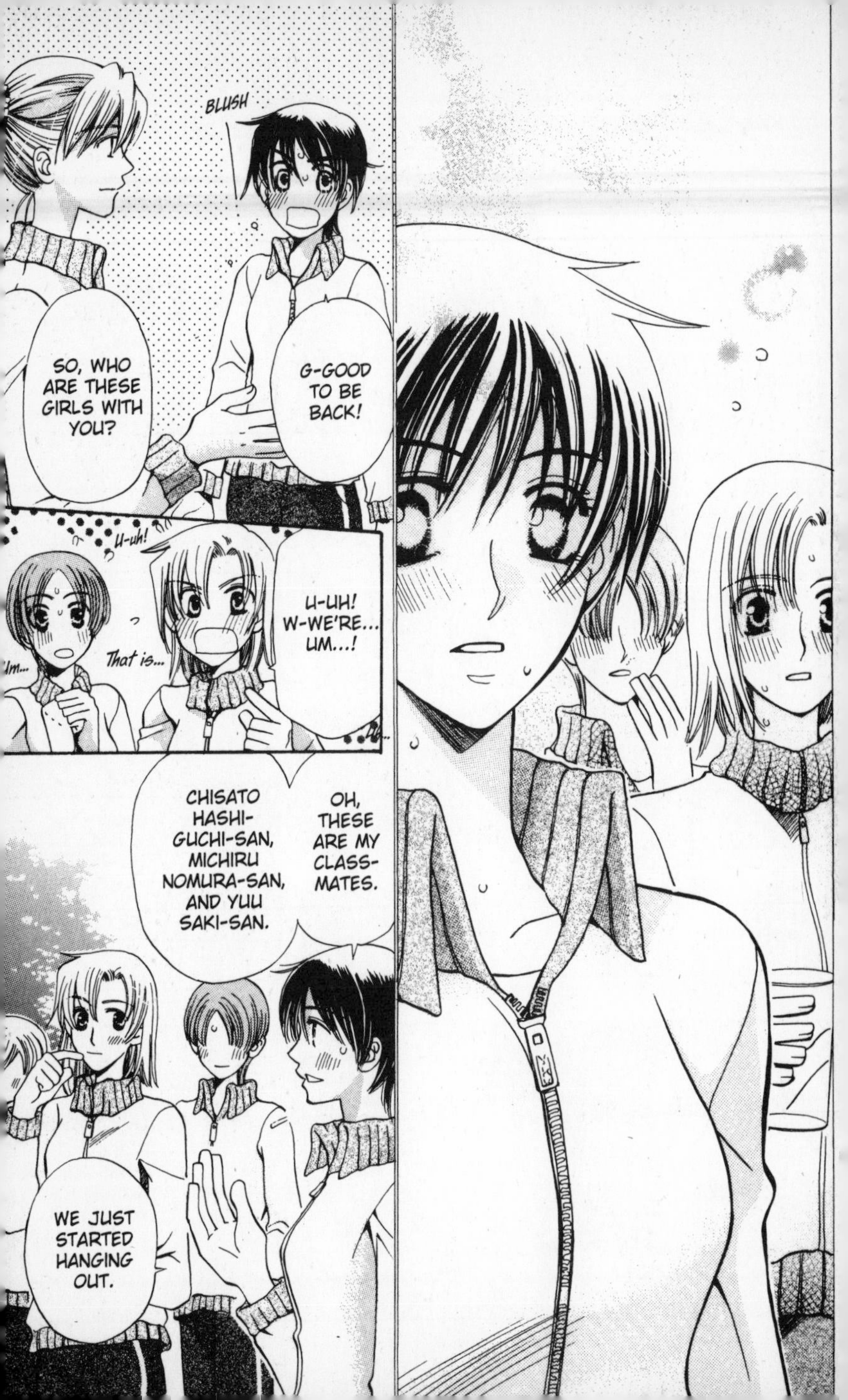
BLUSH
G-GOOD TO BE BACK!
SO, WHO ARE THESE GIRLS WITH YOU?
U-uh!
U-UH! W-WE'RE... UM...!
That is...
OH, THESE ARE MY CLASSMATES.
CHISATO HASHI-GUCHI-SAN, MICHIRU NOMURA-SAN, AND YUU SAKI-SAN.
WE JUST STARTED HANGING OUT.

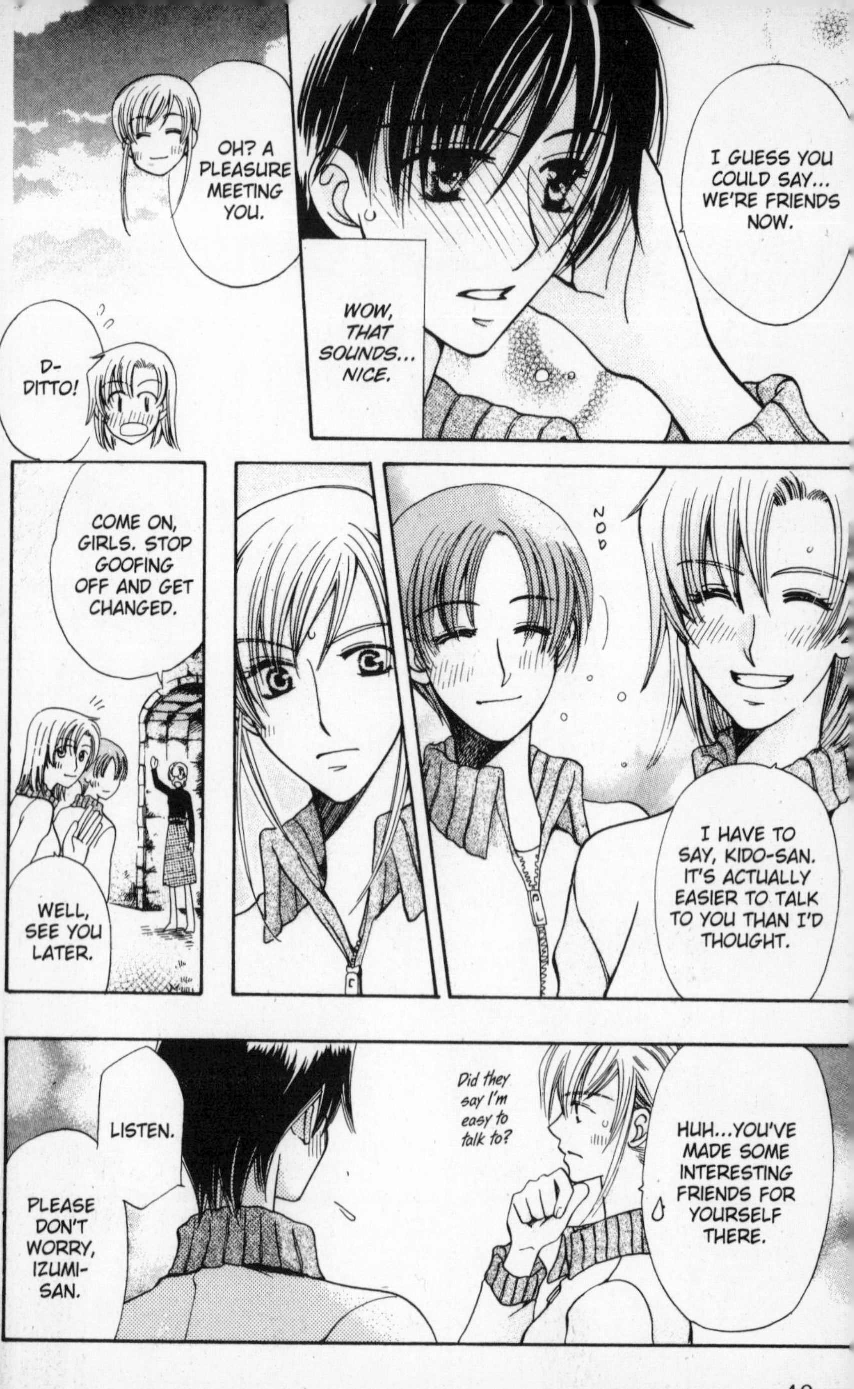

I GUESS YOU COULD SAY... WE'RE FRIENDS NOW.
WOW, THAT SOUNDS... NICE.
OH? A PLEASURE MEETING YOU.
D-DITTO!
NOD
I HAVE TO SAY, KIDO-SAN. IT'S ACTUALLY EASIER TO TALK TO YOU THAN I'D THOUGHT.
COME ON, GIRLS. STOP GOOFING OFF AND GET CHANGED.
WELL, SEE YOU LATER.
HUH...YOU'VE MADE SOME INTERESTING FRIENDS FOR YOURSELF THERE.
Did they say I'm easy to talk to?
LISTEN.
PLEASE DON'T WORRY, IZUMI-SAN.

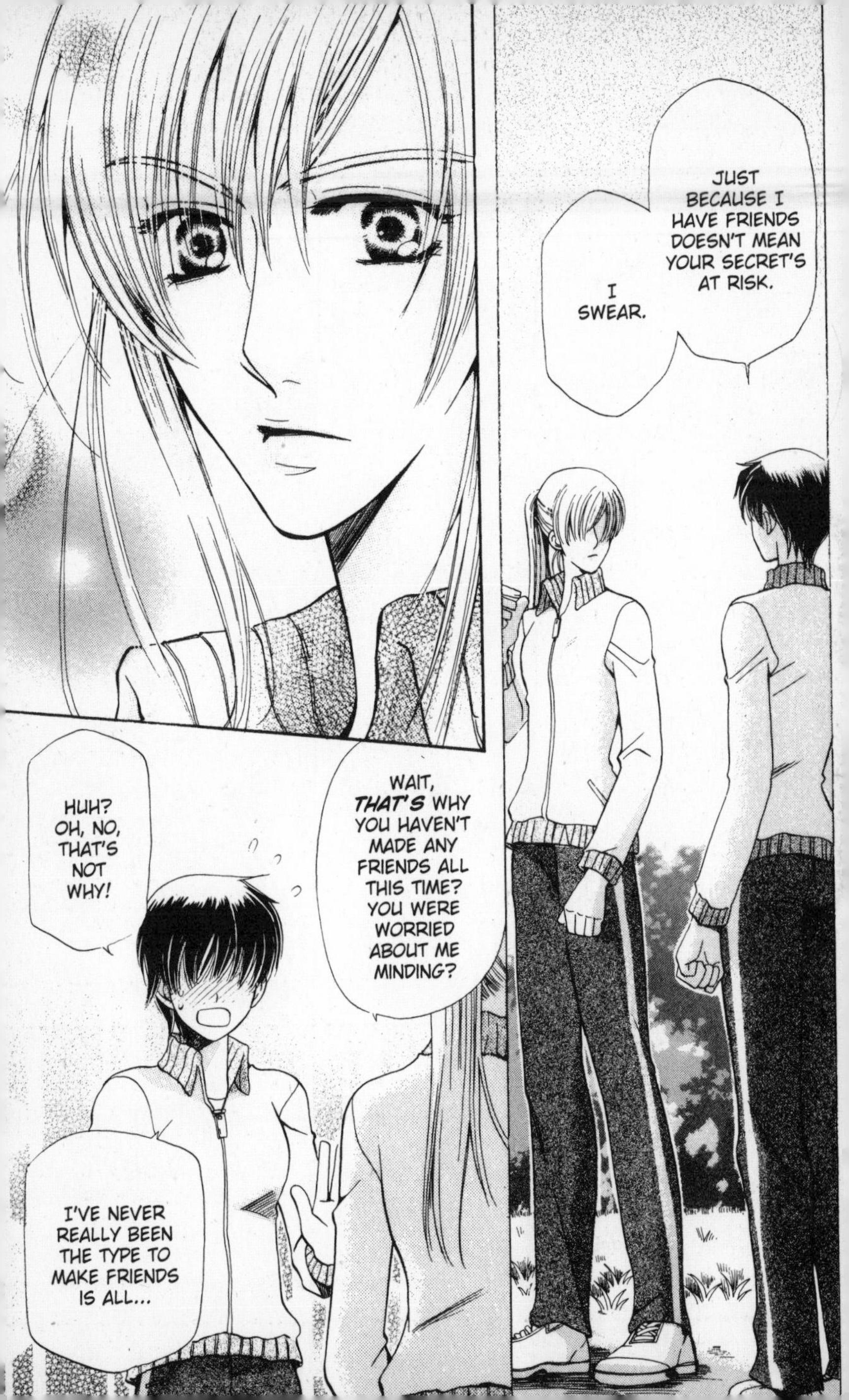
JUST BECAUSE I HAVE FRIENDS DOESN'T MEAN YOUR SECRET'S AT RISK.
I SWEAR.
WAIT, ***THAT'S*** WHY YOU HAVEN'T MADE ANY FRIENDS ALL THIS TIME? YOU WERE WORRIED ABOUT ME MINDING?
HUH? OH, NO, THAT'S NOT WHY!
I'VE NEVER REALLY BEEN THE TYPE TO MAKE FRIENDS IS ALL...

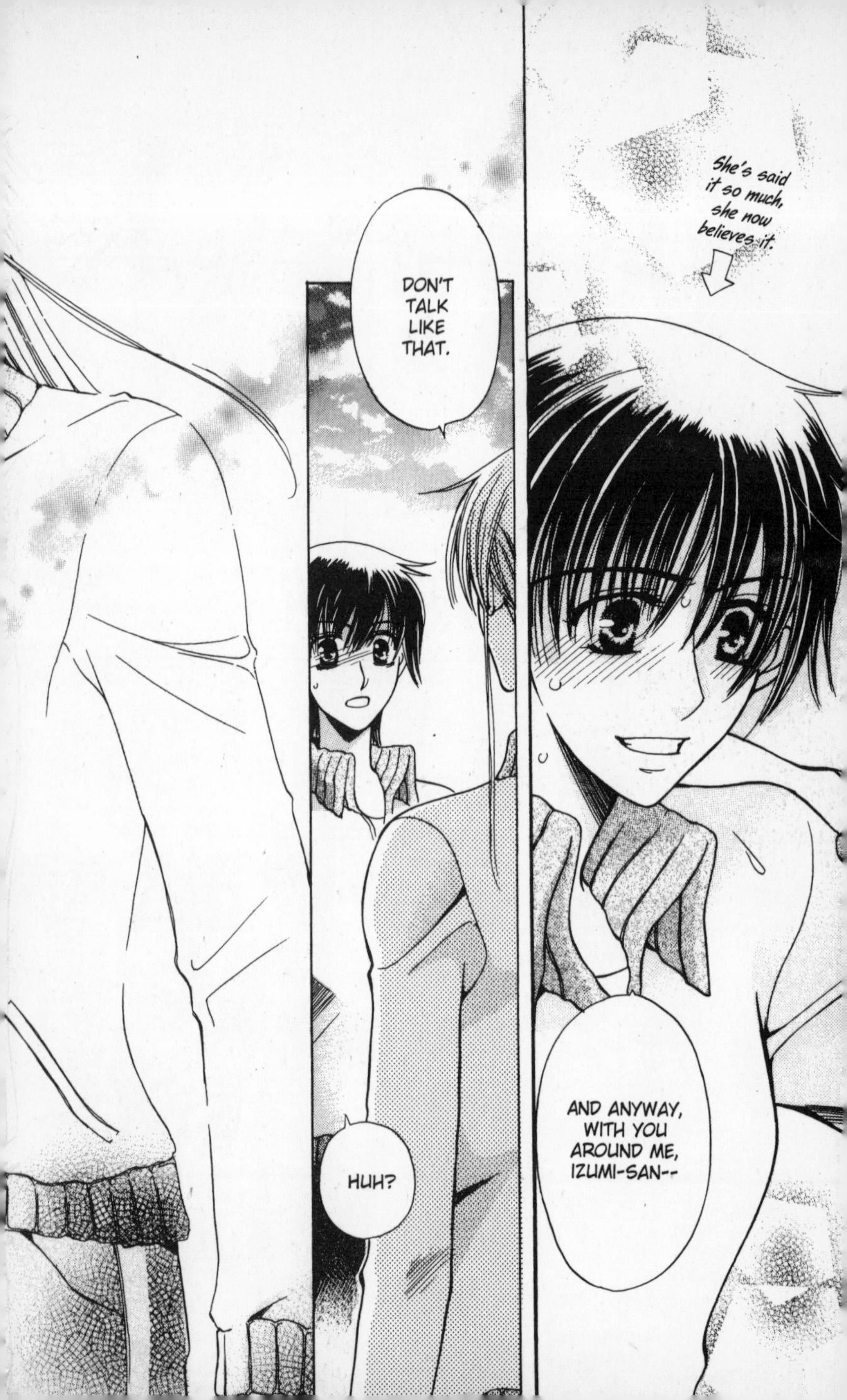
She's said it so much, she now believes it.
AND ANYWAY, WITH YOU AROUND ME, IZUMI-SAN--
DON'T TALK LIKE THAT.
HUH?

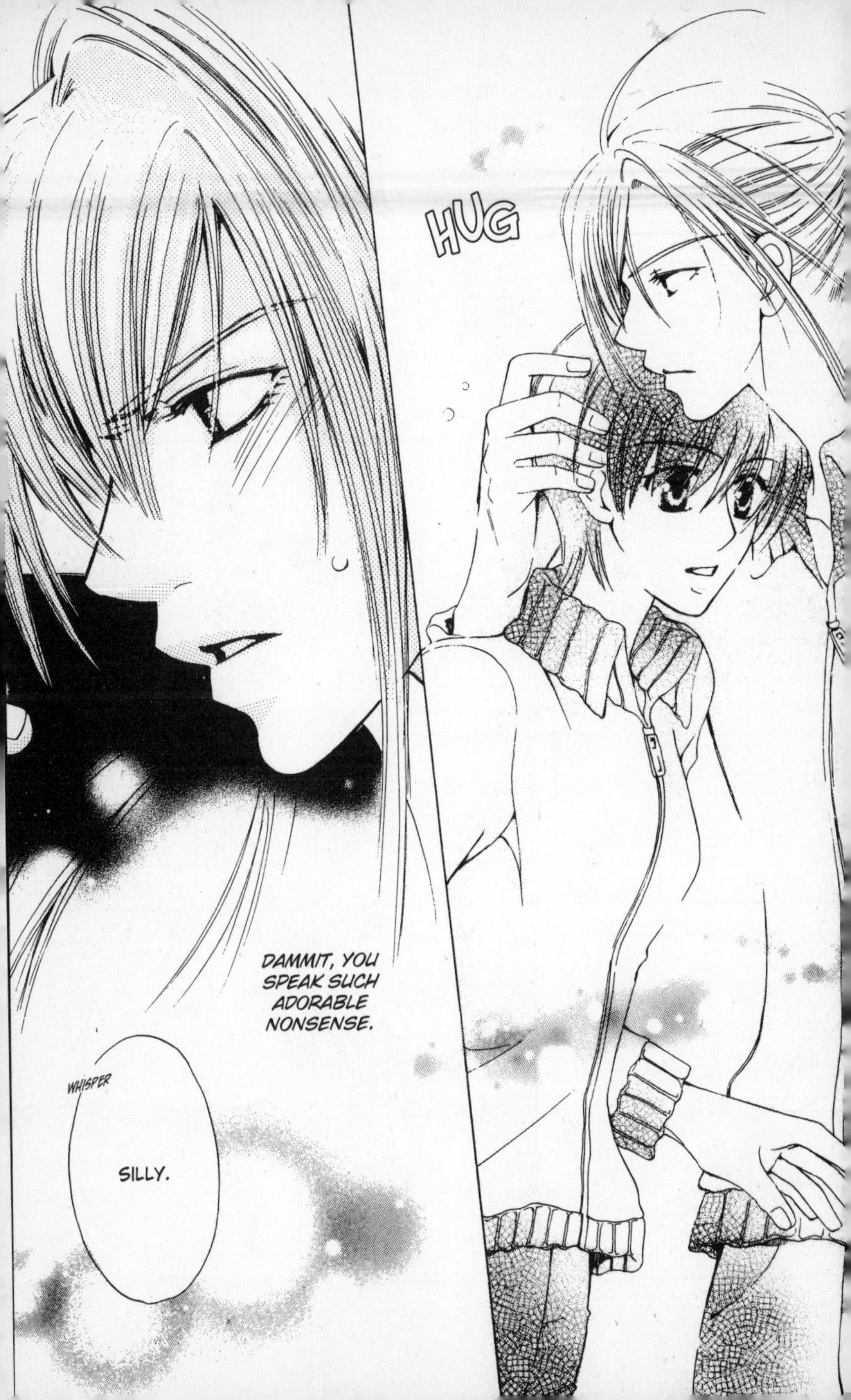
HUG
DAMMIT, YOU SPEAK SUCH ADORABLE NONSENSE.
WHISPER
SILLY.

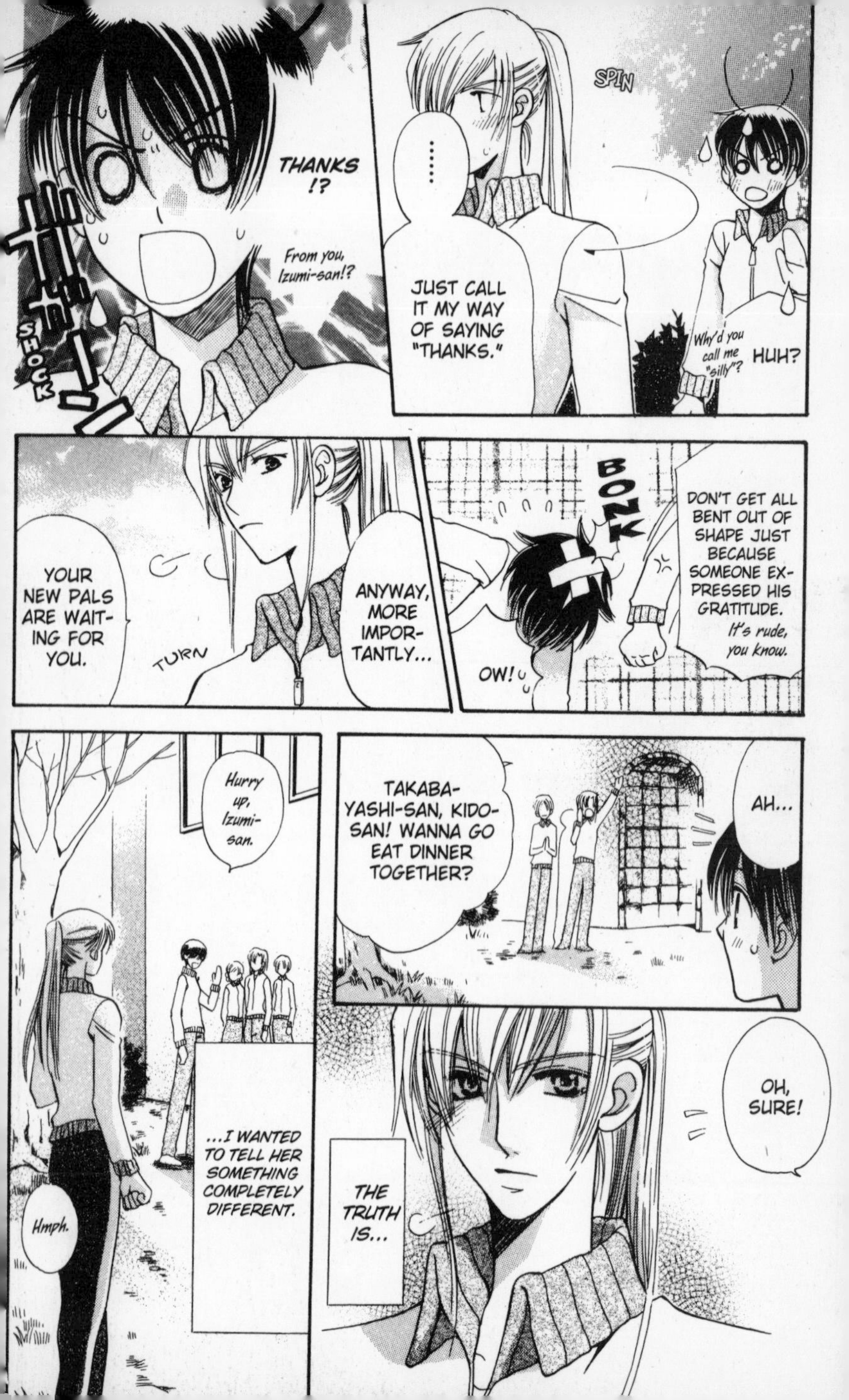
SPIN
HUH?
Why'd you call me "silly"?
......
JUST CALL IT MY WAY OF SAYING "THANKS."
THANKS!?
From you, Izumi-san!?
SHOCK
BONK
DON'T GET ALL BENT OUT OF SHAPE JUST BECAUSE SOMEONE EXPRESSED HIS GRATITUDE.
It's rude, you know.
OW!
ANYWAY, MORE IMPORTANTLY...
YOUR NEW PALS ARE WAITING FOR YOU.
TURN
AH...
TAKABAYASHI-SAN, KIDO-SAN! WANNA GO EAT DINNER TOGETHER?
OH, SURE!
THE TRUTH IS...
...I WANTED TO TELL HER SOMETHING COMPLETELY DIFFERENT.
Hurry up, Izumi-san.
Hmph.

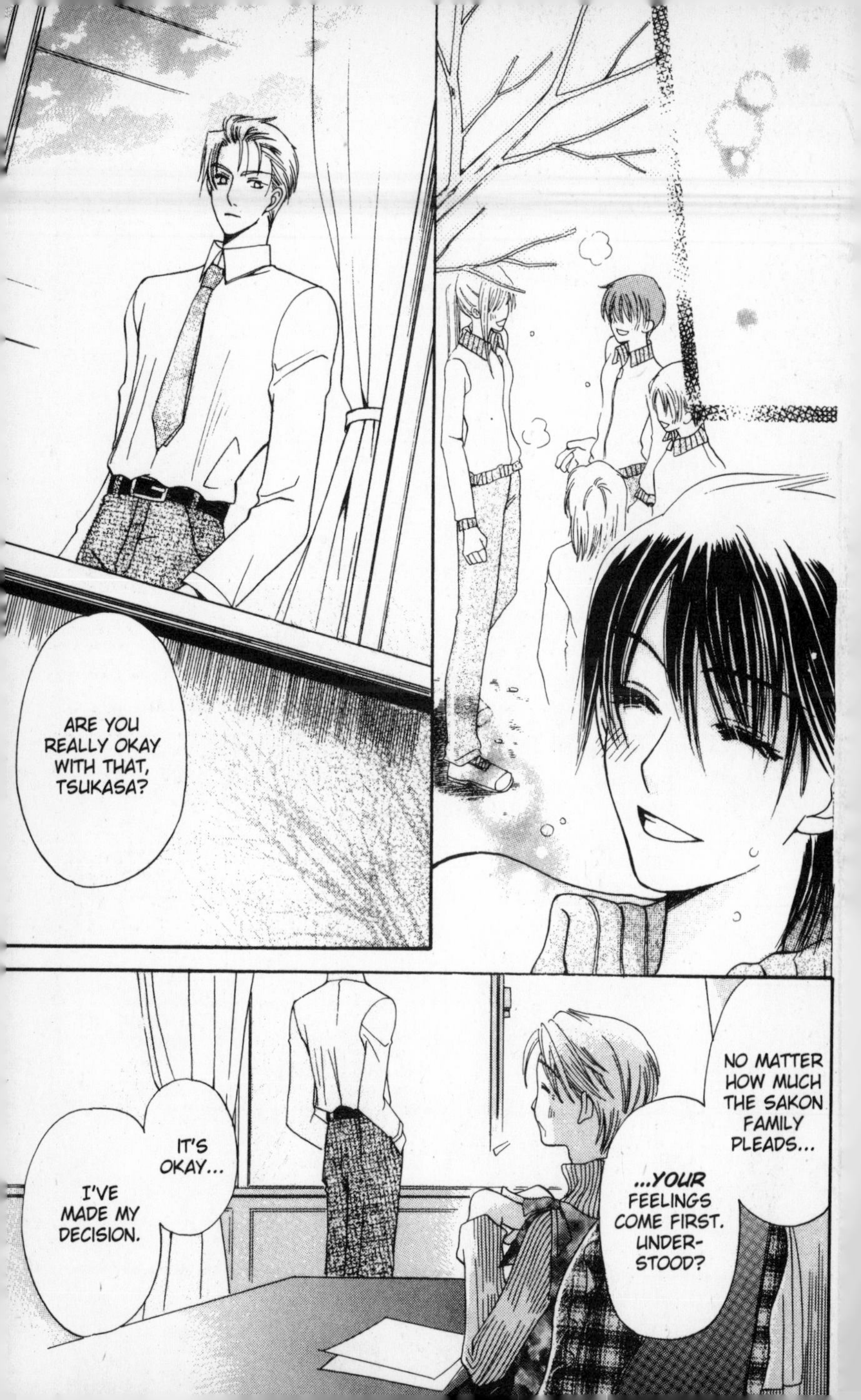
ARE YOU REALLY OKAY WITH THAT, TSUKASA?
NO MATTER HOW MUCH THE SAKON FAMILY PLEADS...
...YOUR FEELINGS COME FIRST. UNDERSTOOD?
IT'S OKAY...
I'VE MADE MY DECISION.

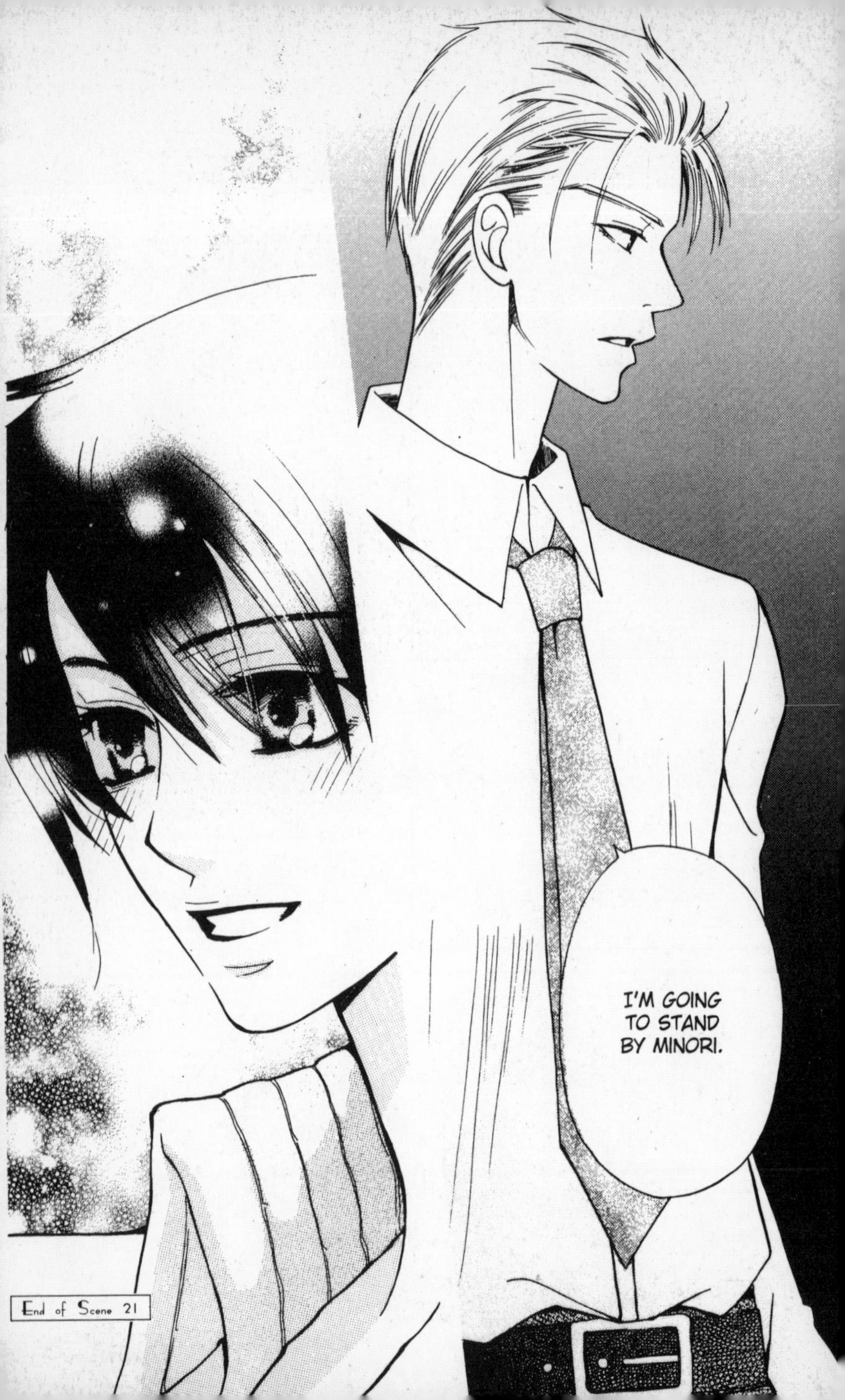
I'M GOING TO STAND BY MINORI.
End of Scene 21

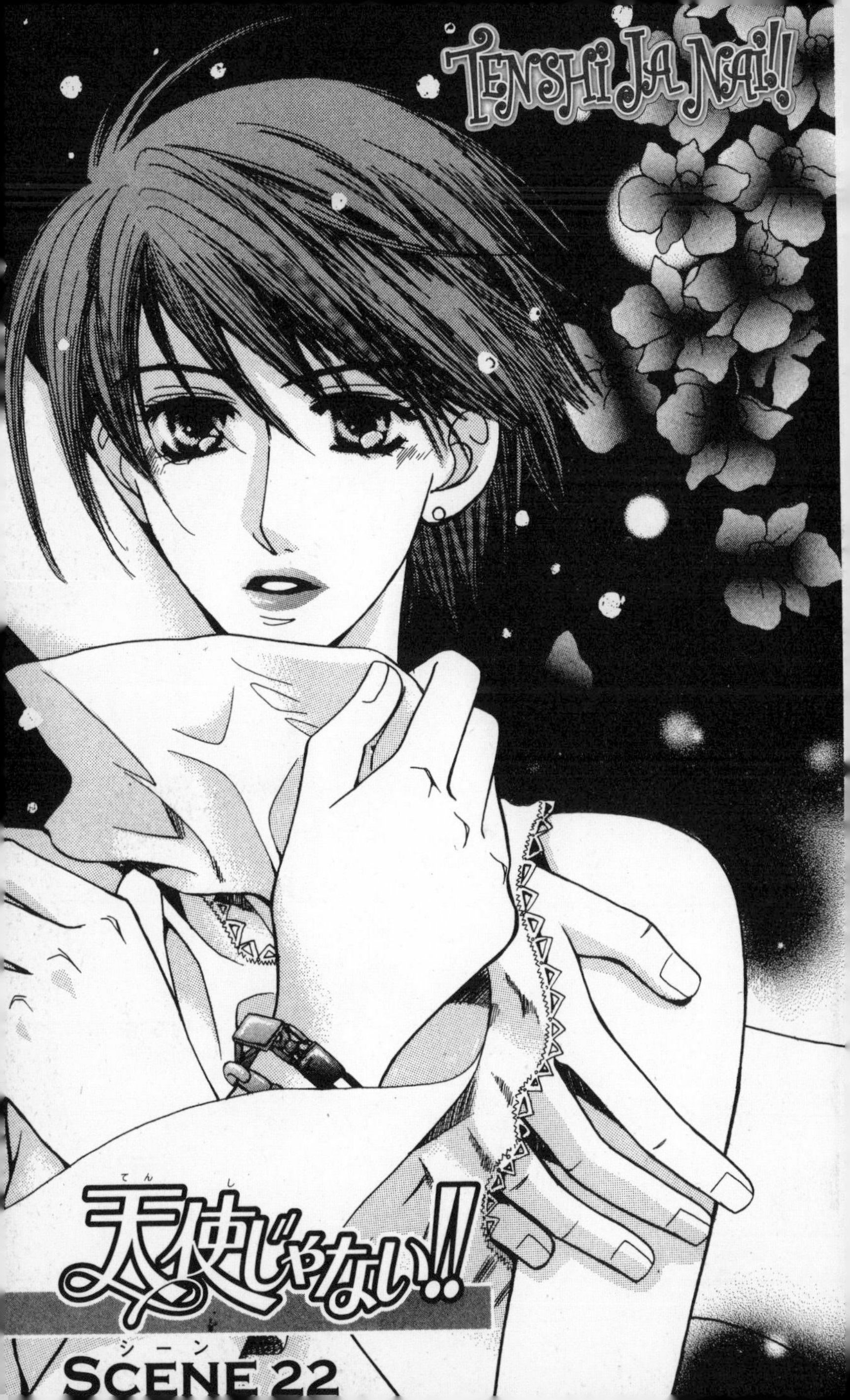
TENSHI JA NAI!!
天使じゃない!!
SCENE 22

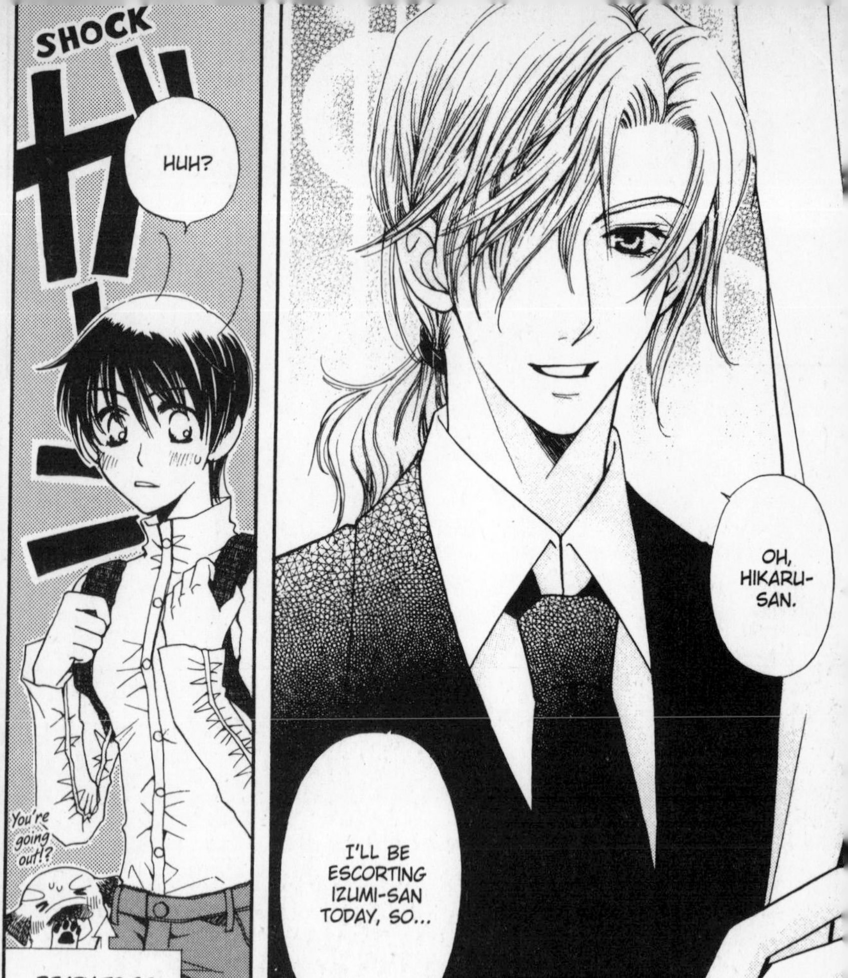
OH, HIKARU-SAN.
I'LL BE ESCORTING IZUMI-SAN TODAY, SO...
SHOCK
HUH?
You're going out!?
READY TO GO.

Chisato Hashiguchi (16 years old)
Born: June 30
Blood Type: A
Kind of a bubble-brain. Founding member of a Seika campus secret club known as the "Hikaru Takabayashi Unofficial Fan Club" (it seems...).

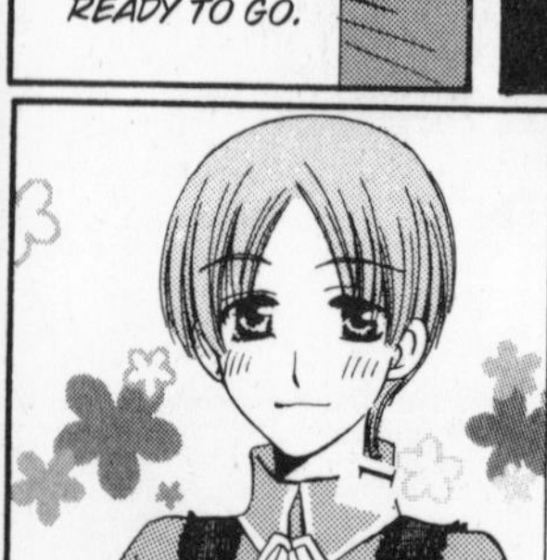

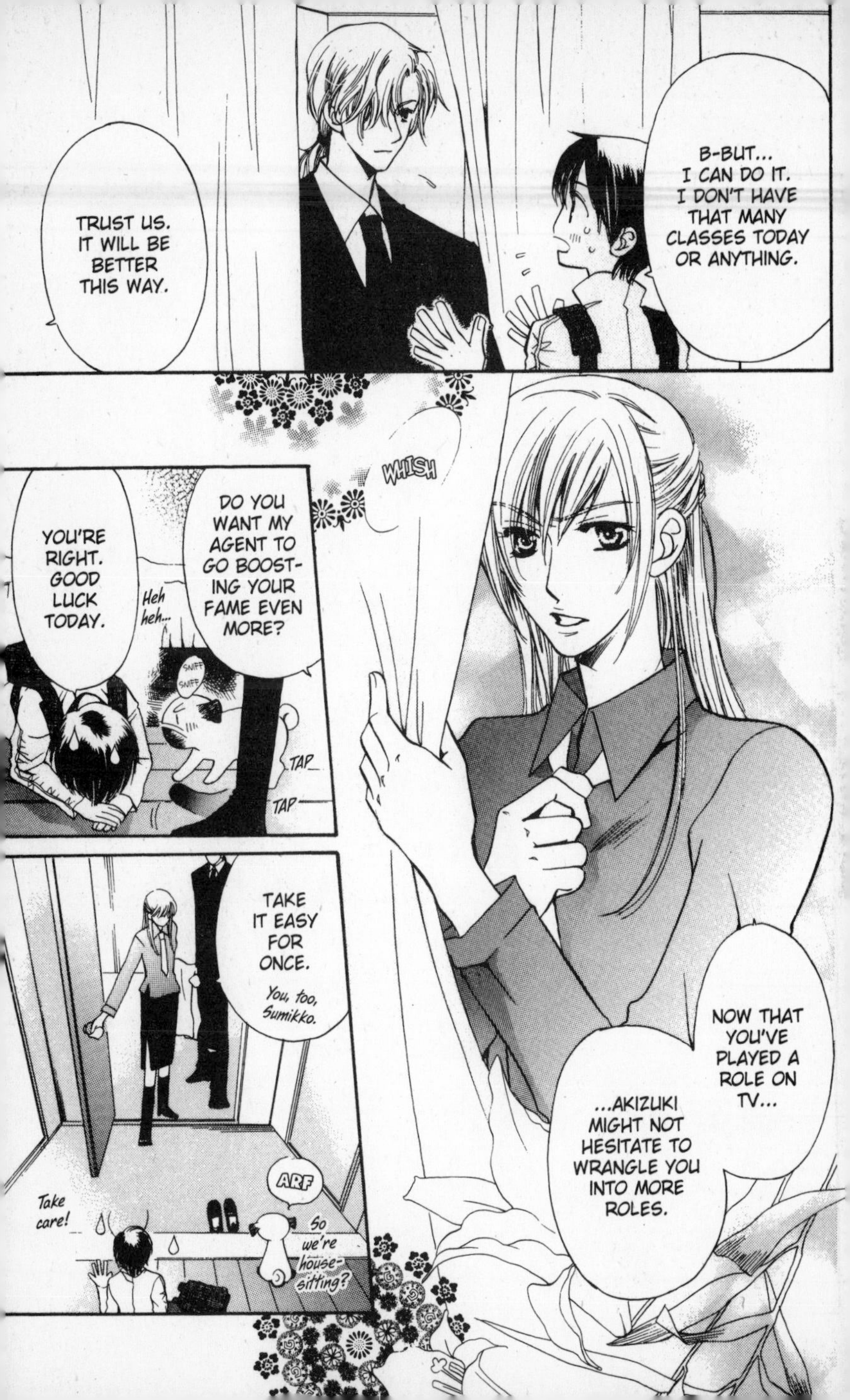
B-BUT... I CAN DO IT. I DON'T HAVE THAT MANY CLASSES TODAY OR ANYTHING.
TRUST US. IT WILL BE BETTER THIS WAY.
WHISH
NOW THAT YOU'VE PLAYED A ROLE ON TV...
...AKIZUKI MIGHT NOT HESITATE TO WRANGLE YOU INTO MORE ROLES.
DO YOU WANT MY AGENT TO GO BOOSTING YOUR FAME EVEN MORE?
Heh heh...
YOU'RE RIGHT. GOOD LUCK TODAY.
SNIFF SNIFF
TAP
TAP
TAKE IT EASY FOR ONCE.
You, too, Sumikko.
ARF
So we're house-sitting?
Take care!

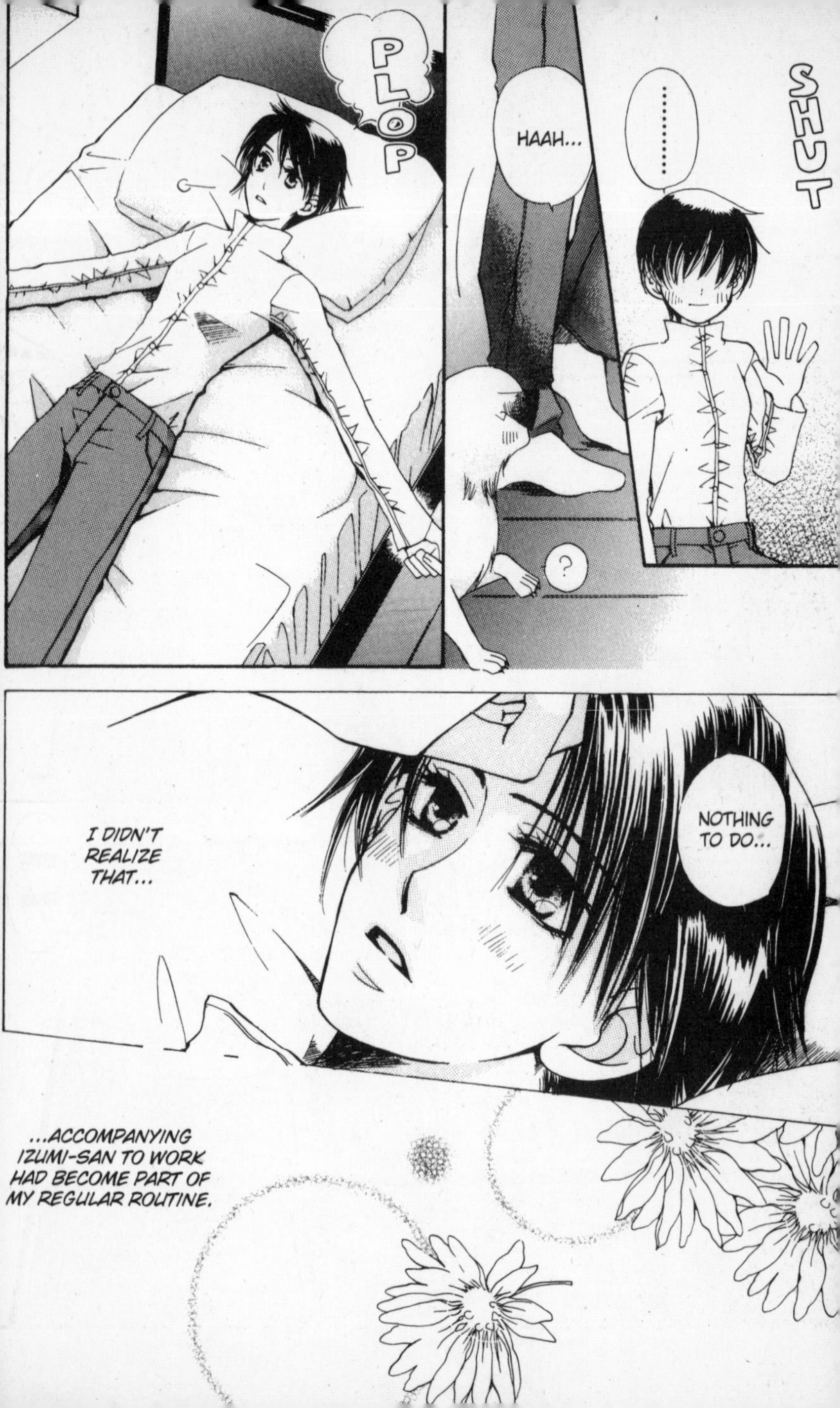
SHUT
......
HAAH...
?
PLOP
NOTHING TO DO...
I DIDN'T REALIZE THAT...
...ACCOMPANYING IZUMI-SAN TO WORK HAD BECOME PART OF MY REGULAR ROUTINE.

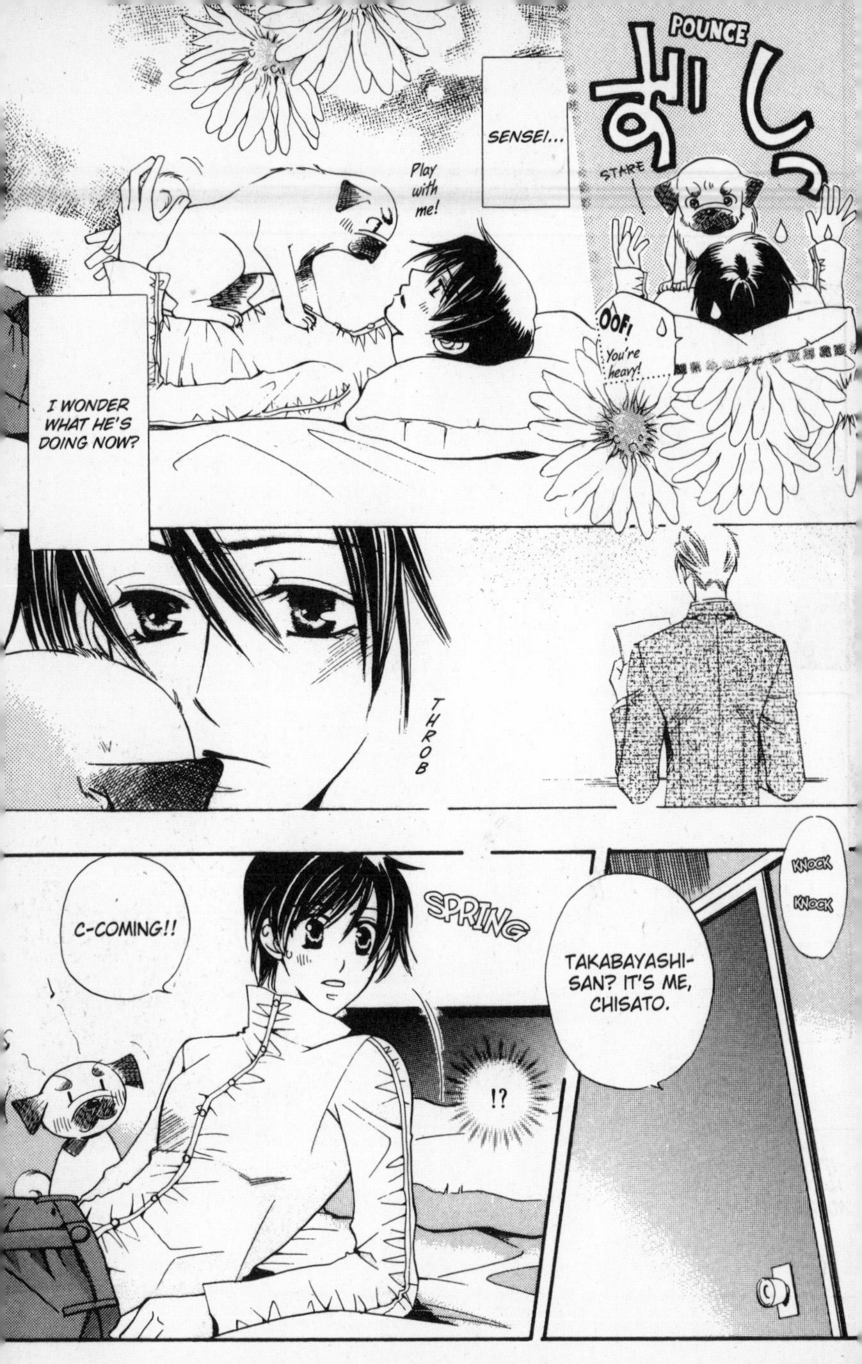
POUNCE
ずしっ
STARE
OOF!
You're heavy!
SENSEI...
Play with me!
I WONDER WHAT HE'S DOING NOW?
THROB
KNOCK
KNOCK
TAKABAYASHI-SAN? IT'S ME, CHISATO.
!?
SPRING
C-COMING!!

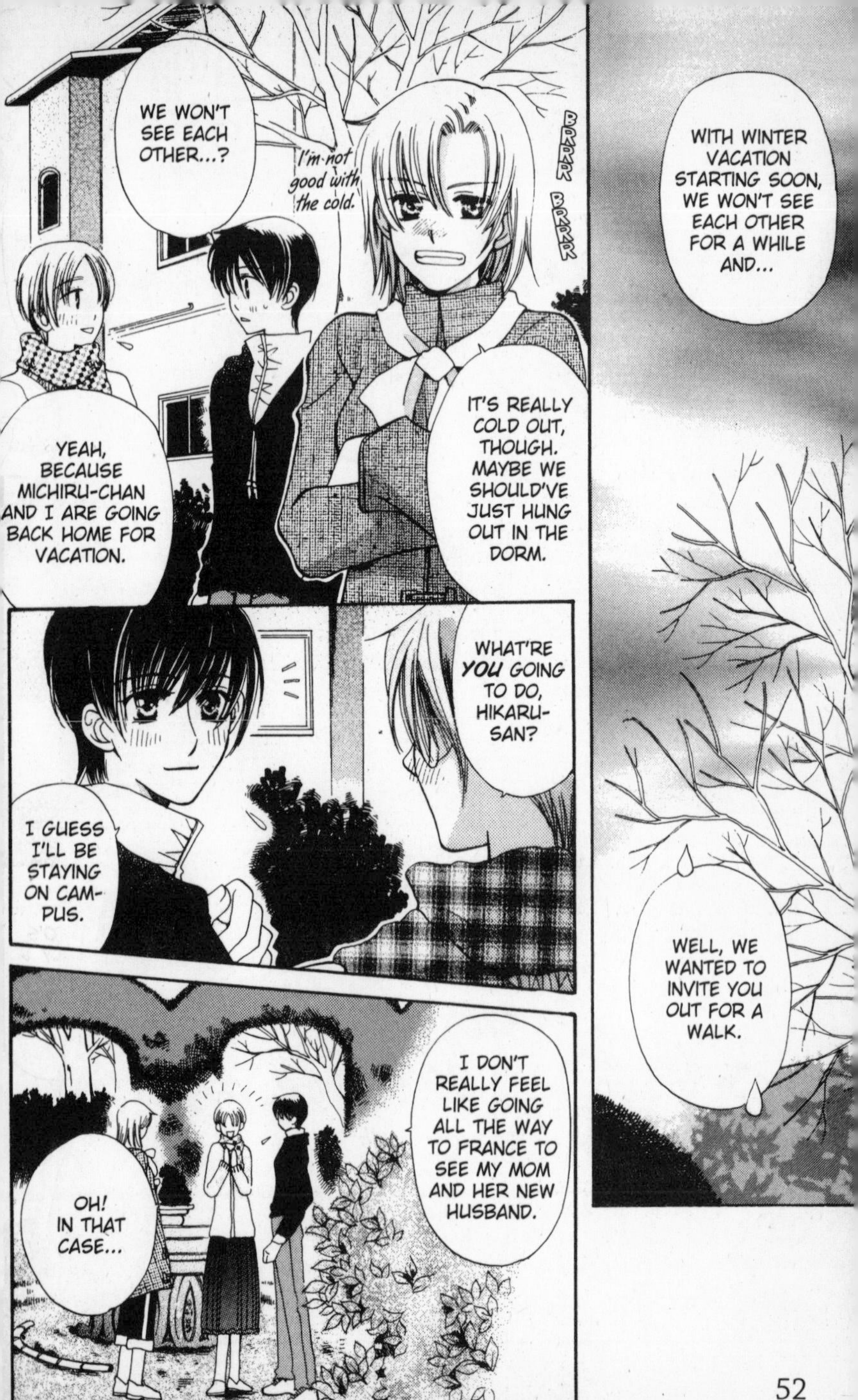
WITH WINTER VACATION STARTING SOON, WE WON'T SEE EACH OTHER FOR A WHILE AND...
WELL, WE WANTED TO INVITE YOU OUT FOR A WALK.
BRRRR BRRRR
I'm not good with the cold.
WE WON'T SEE EACH OTHER...?
IT'S REALLY COLD OUT, THOUGH. MAYBE WE SHOULD'VE JUST HUNG OUT IN THE DORM.
YEAH, BECAUSE MICHIRU-CHAN AND I ARE GOING BACK HOME FOR VACATION.
WHAT'RE *YOU* GOING TO DO, HIKARU-SAN?
I GUESS I'LL BE STAYING ON CAM-PUS.
I DON'T REALLY FEEL LIKE GOING ALL THE WAY TO FRANCE TO SEE MY MOM AND HER NEW HUSBAND.
OH! IN THAT CASE...

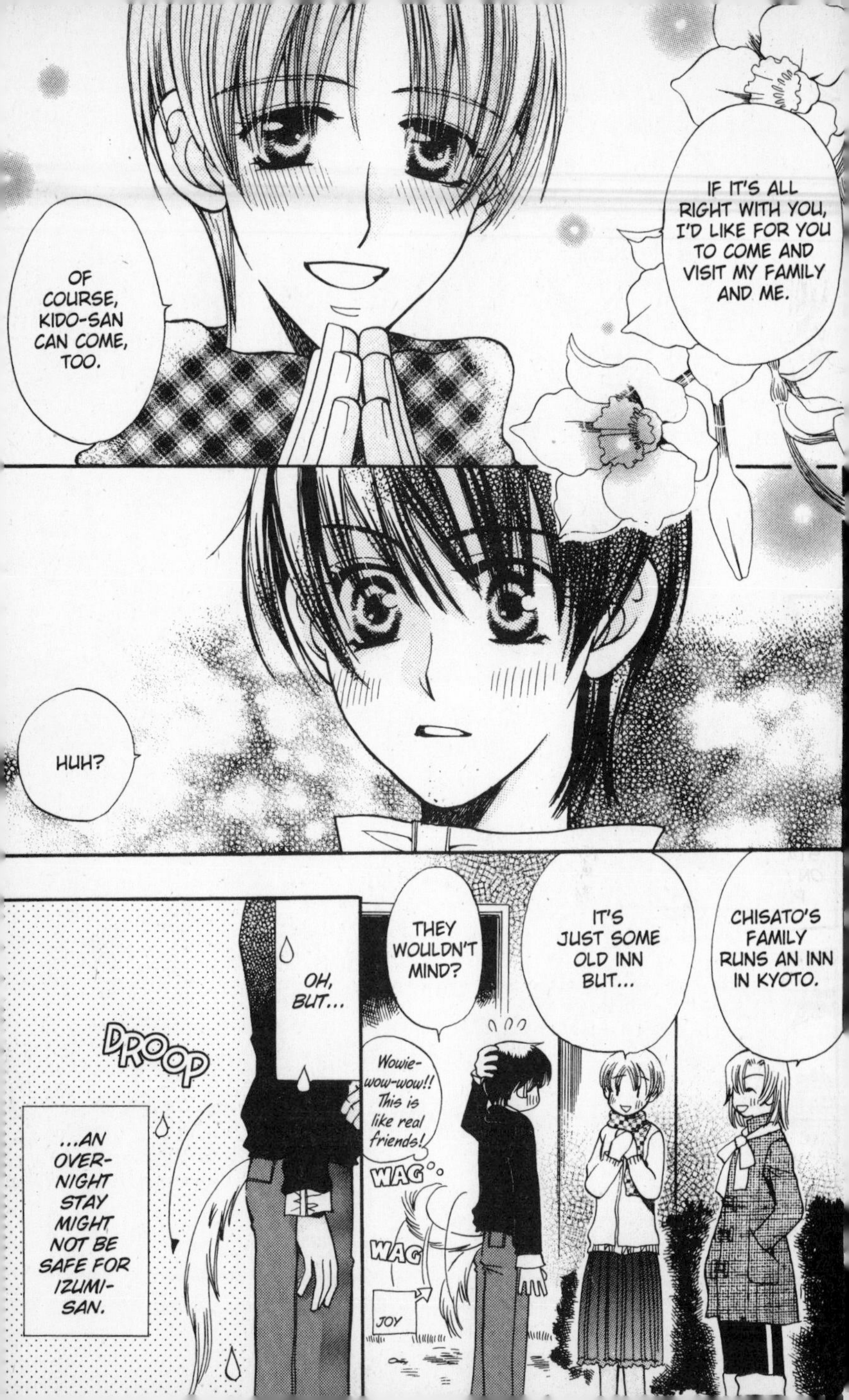
IF IT'S ALL RIGHT WITH YOU, I'D LIKE FOR YOU TO COME AND VISIT MY FAMILY AND ME.
OF COURSE, KIDO-SAN CAN COME, TOO.
HUH?
CHISATO'S FAMILY RUNS AN INN IN KYOTO.
IT'S JUST SOME OLD INN BUT...
THEY WOULDN'T MIND?
Wowie-wow-wow!! This is like real friends!
WAG
WAG
JOY
OH, BUT...
DROOP
...AN OVER-NIGHT STAY MIGHT NOT BE SAFE FOR IZUMI-SAN.

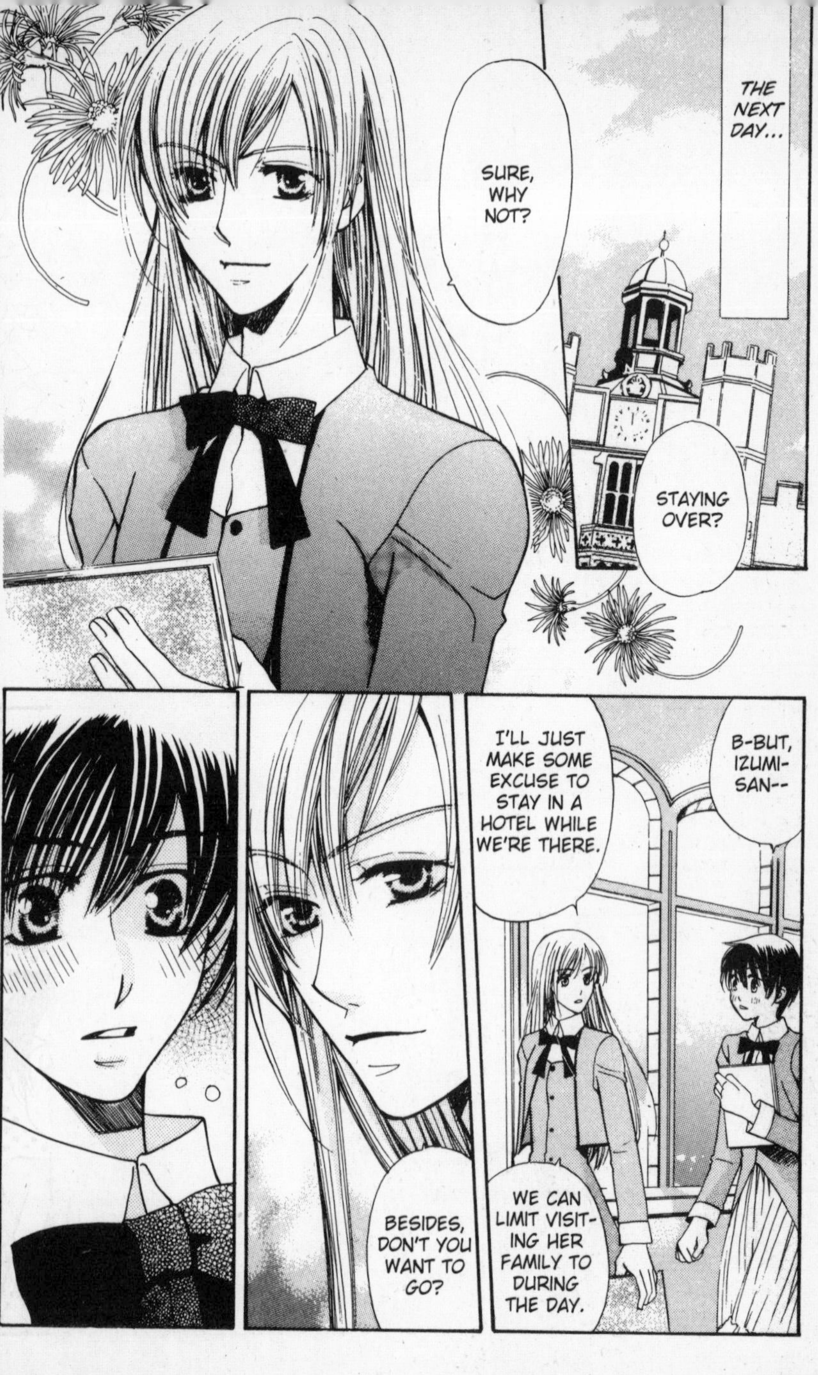
THE NEXT DAY...
STAYING OVER?
SURE, WHY NOT?
B-BUT, IZUMI-SAN--
I'LL JUST MAKE SOME EXCUSE TO STAY IN A HOTEL WHILE WE'RE THERE.
WE CAN LIMIT VISIT-ING HER FAMILY TO DURING THE DAY.
BESIDES, DON'T YOU WANT TO GO?

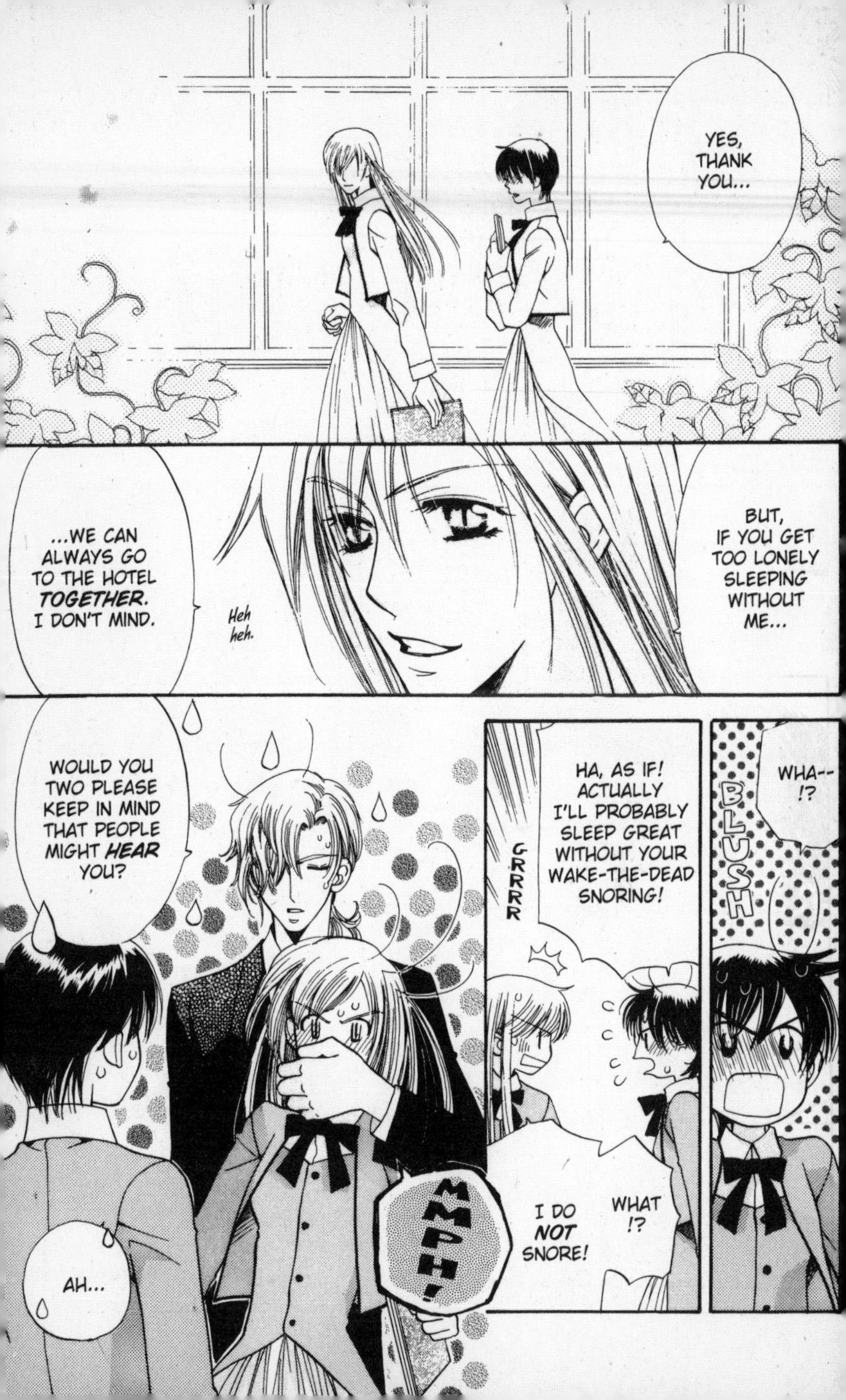
YES, THANK YOU...
BUT, IF YOU GET TOO LONELY SLEEPING WITHOUT ME...
Heh heh.
...WE CAN ALWAYS GO TO THE HOTEL *TOGETHER*. I DON'T MIND.
WHA-- !?
BLUSH
HA, AS IF! ACTUALLY I'LL PROBABLY SLEEP GREAT WITHOUT YOUR WAKE-THE-DEAD SNORING!
GRRRR
WHAT !?
I DO *NOT* SNORE!
WOULD YOU TWO PLEASE KEEP IN MIND THAT PEOPLE MIGHT *HEAR* YOU?
MMPH!
AH...

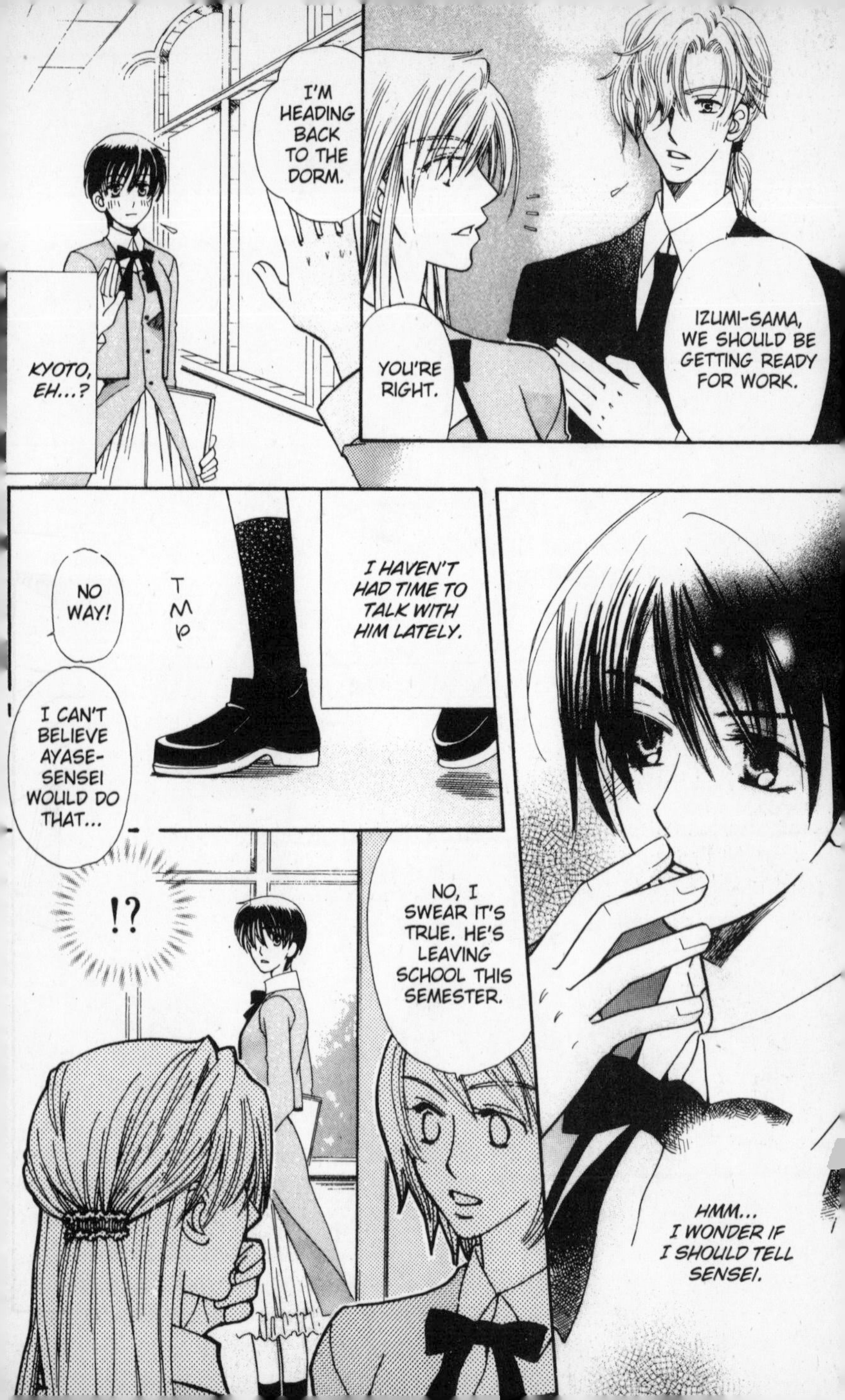
IZUMI-SAMA, WE SHOULD BE GETTING READY FOR WORK.
YOU'RE RIGHT.
I'M HEADING BACK TO THE DORM.
KYOTO, EH...?
HMM... I WONDER IF I SHOULD TELL SENSEI.
I HAVEN'T HAD TIME TO TALK WITH HIM LATELY.
TMP
NO WAY!
I CAN'T BELIEVE AYASE-SENSEI WOULD DO THAT...
NO, I SWEAR IT'S TRUE. HE'S LEAVING SCHOOL THIS SEMESTER.
!?

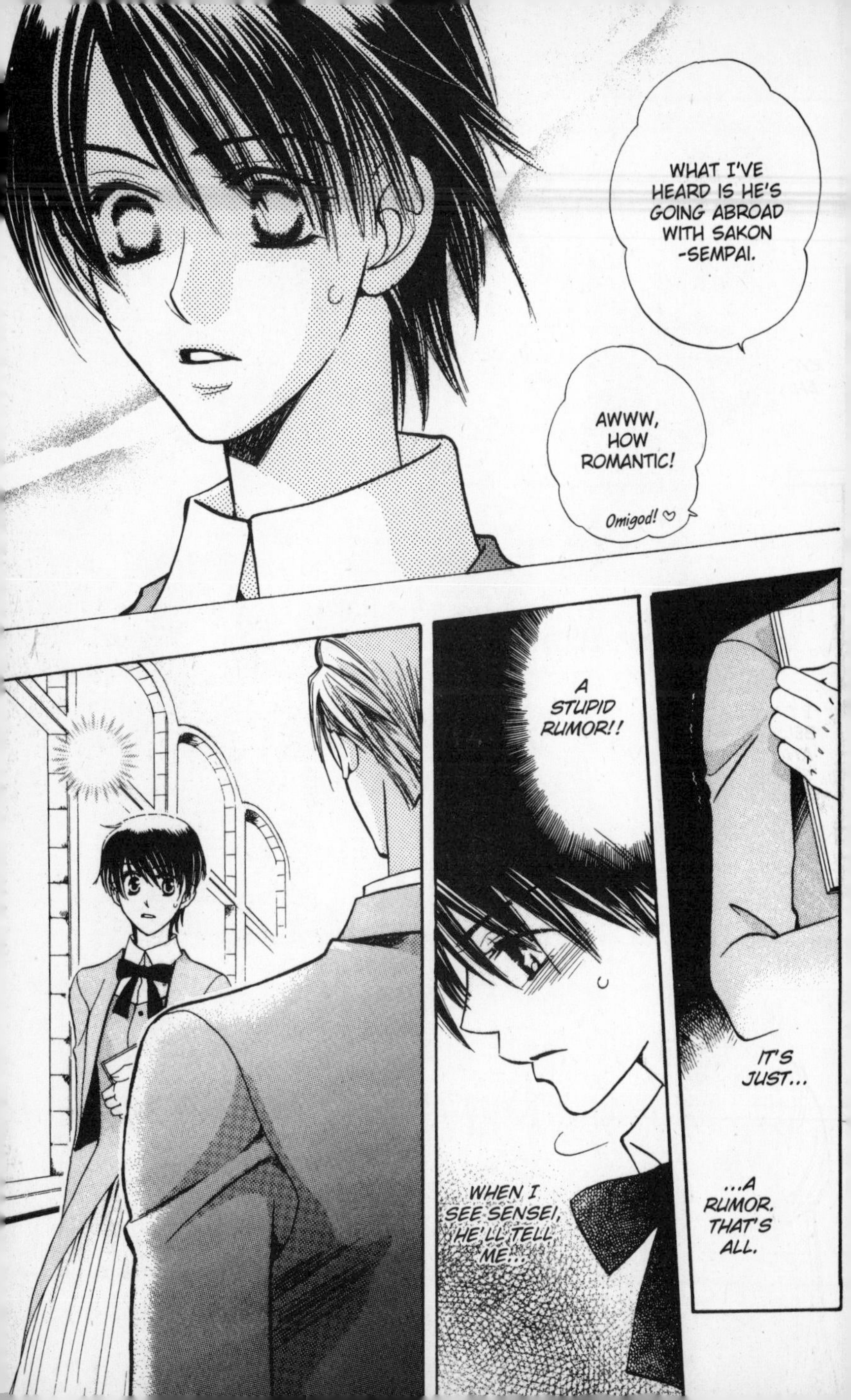
WHAT I'VE HEARD IS HE'S GOING ABROAD WITH SAKON -SEMPAI.
AWWW, HOW ROMANTIC!
Omigod! ♡
IT'S JUST...
...A RUMOR. THAT'S ALL.
A STUPID RUMOR!!
WHEN I SEE SENSEI, HE'LL TELL ME...

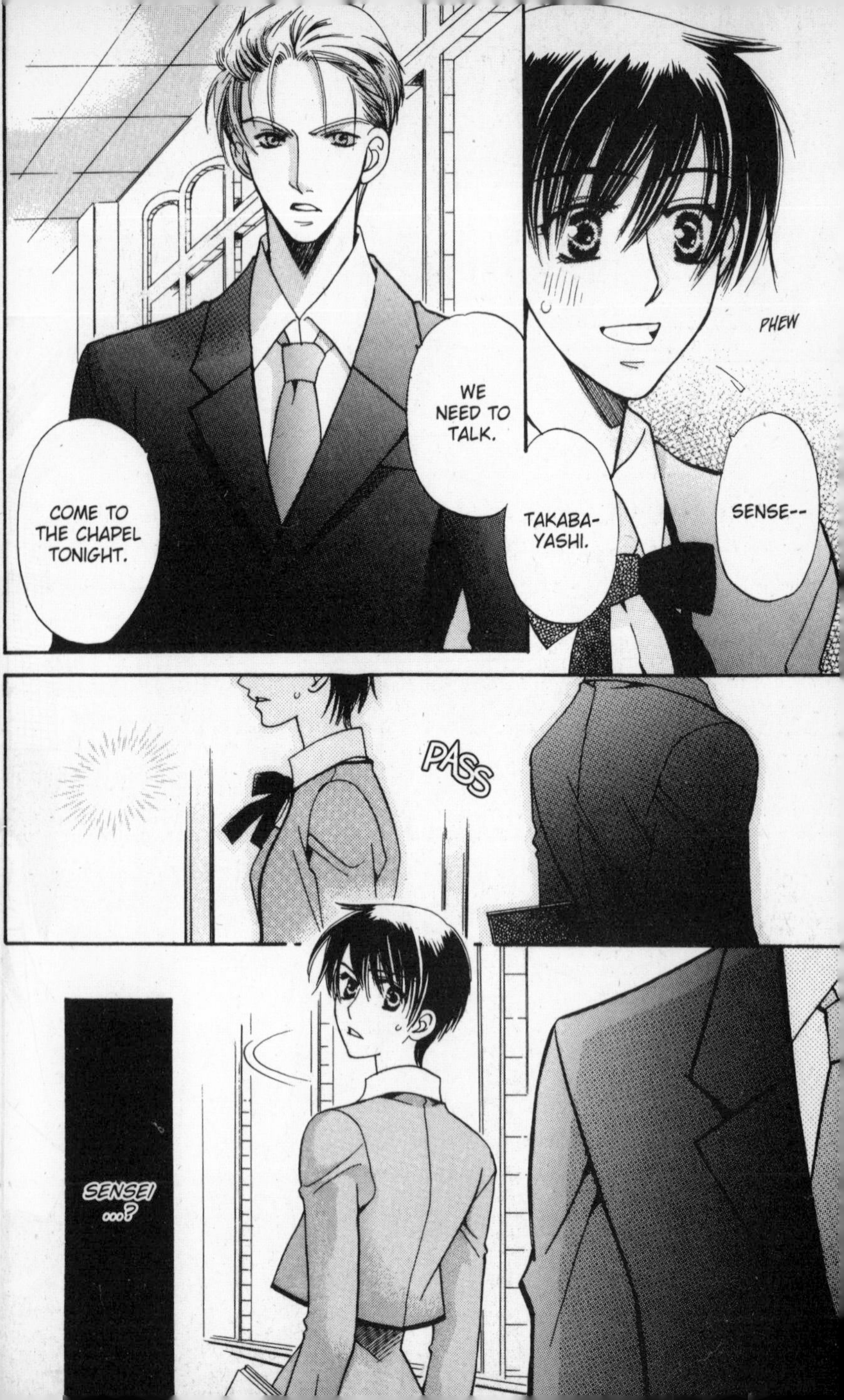
PHEW
SENSE--
TAKABA-YASHI.
WE NEED TO TALK.
COME TO THE CHAPEL TONIGHT.
PASS
SENSEI ...?

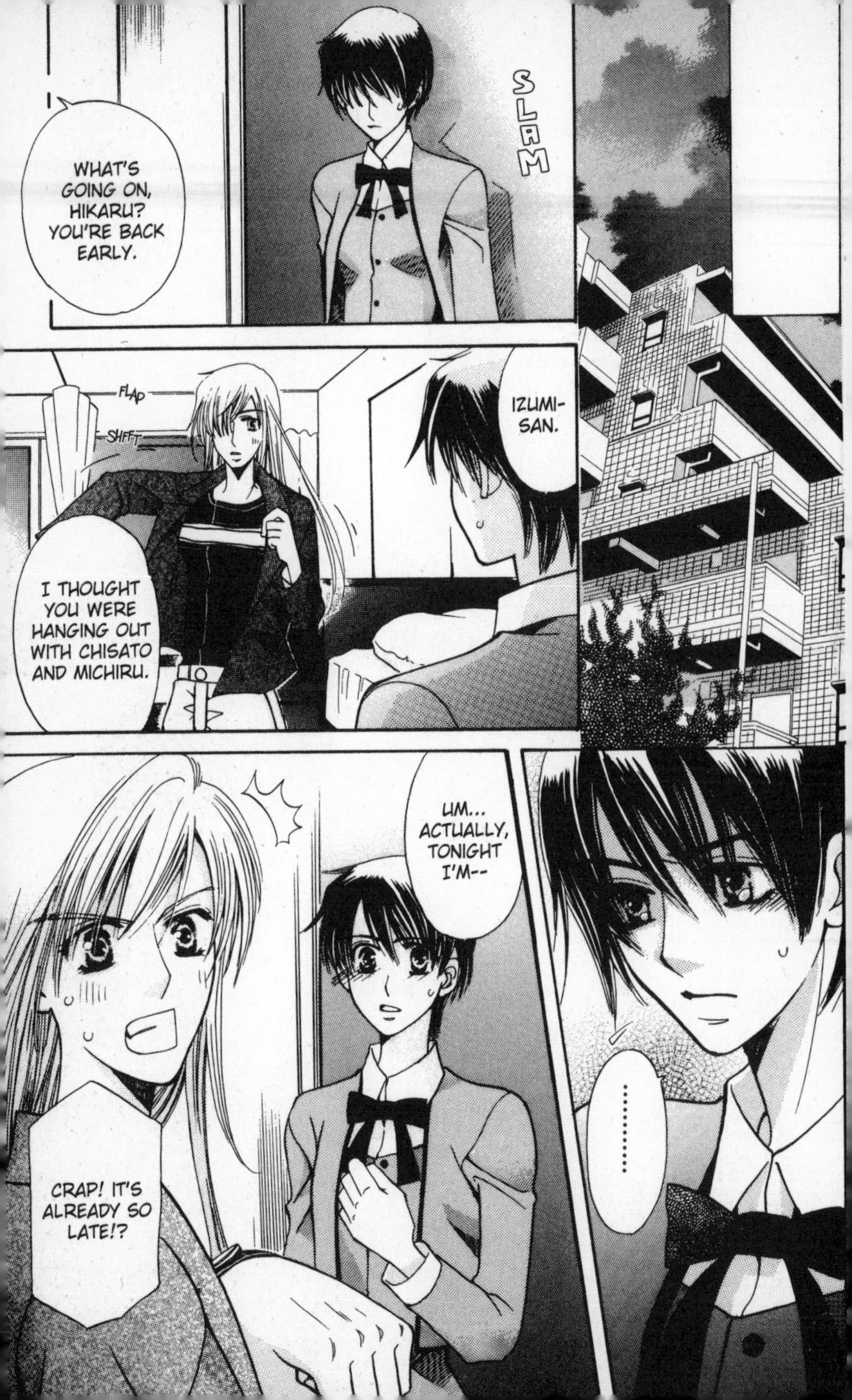
SLAM
WHAT'S GOING ON, HIKARU? YOU'RE BACK EARLY.
IZUMI-SAN.
FLAP
SHFFT
I THOUGHT YOU WERE HANGING OUT WITH CHISATO AND MICHIRU.
......
UM... ACTUALLY, TONIGHT I'M--
CRAP! IT'S ALREADY SO LATE!?

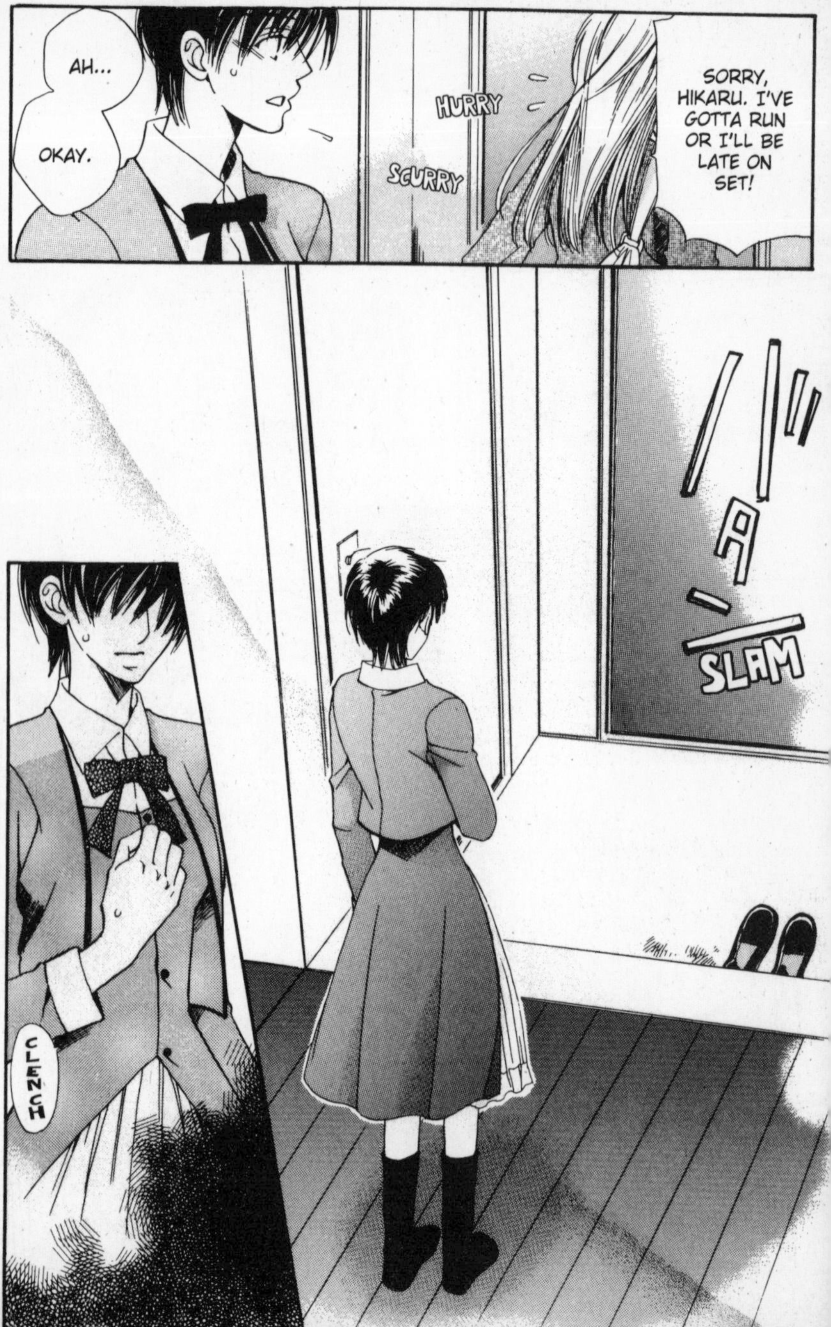
SORRY, HIKARU. I'VE GOTTA RUN OR I'LL BE LATE ON SET!
HURRY
SCURRY
AH...
OKAY.
SLAM
CLENCH

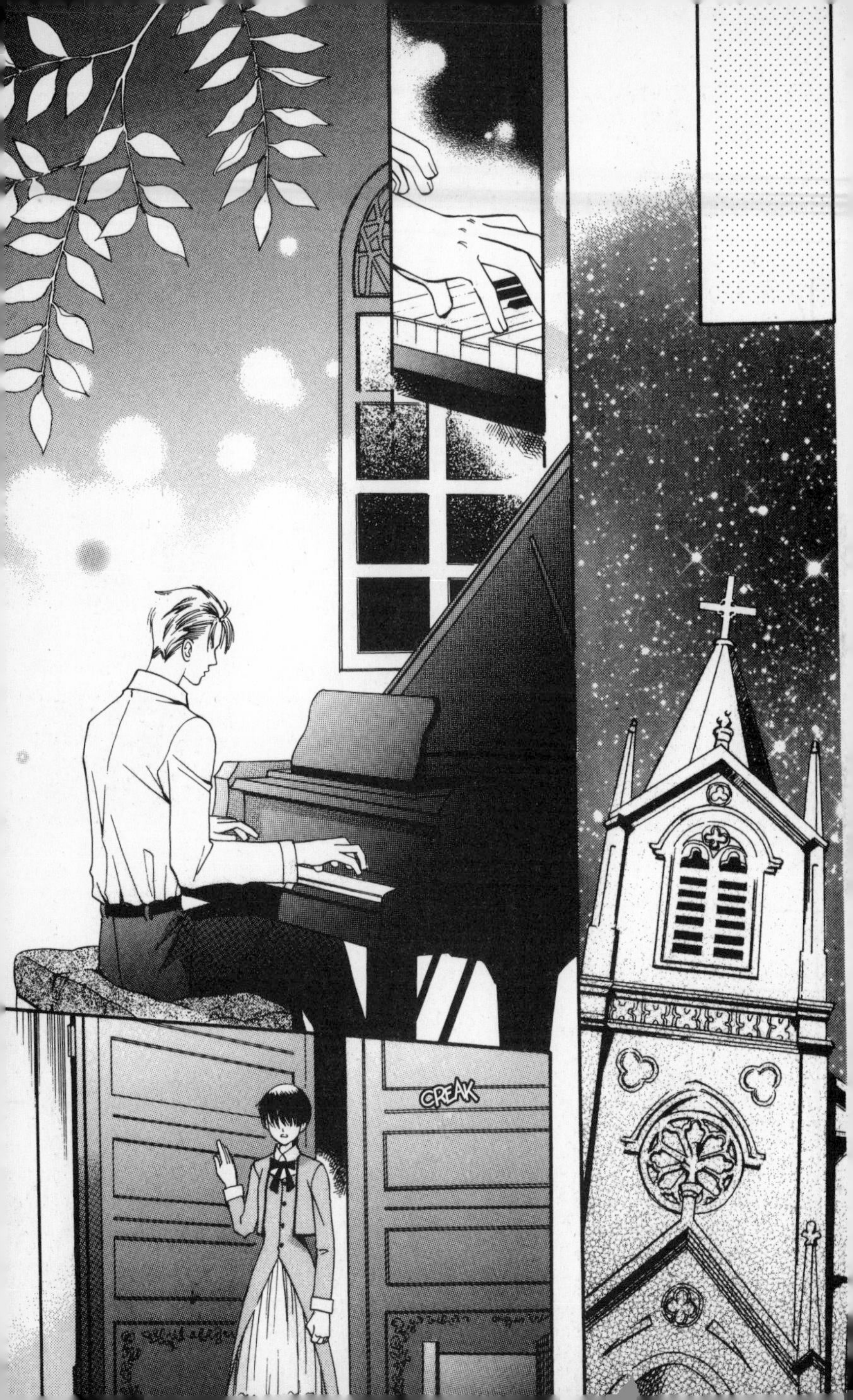
CREAK

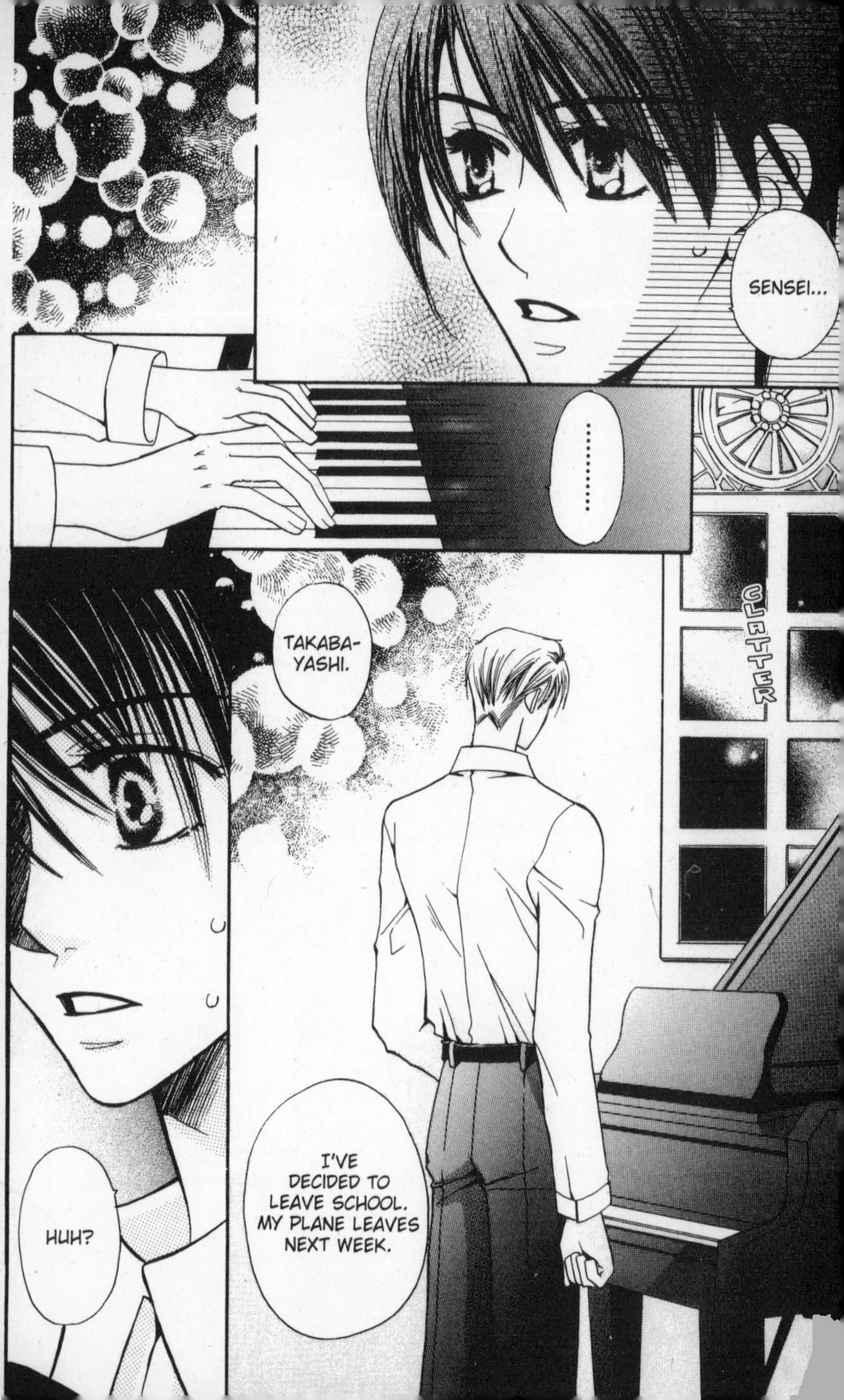
SENSEI...
......
CLATTER
TAKABA-YASHI.
I'VE DECIDED TO LEAVE SCHOOL. MY PLANE LEAVES NEXT WEEK.
HUH?

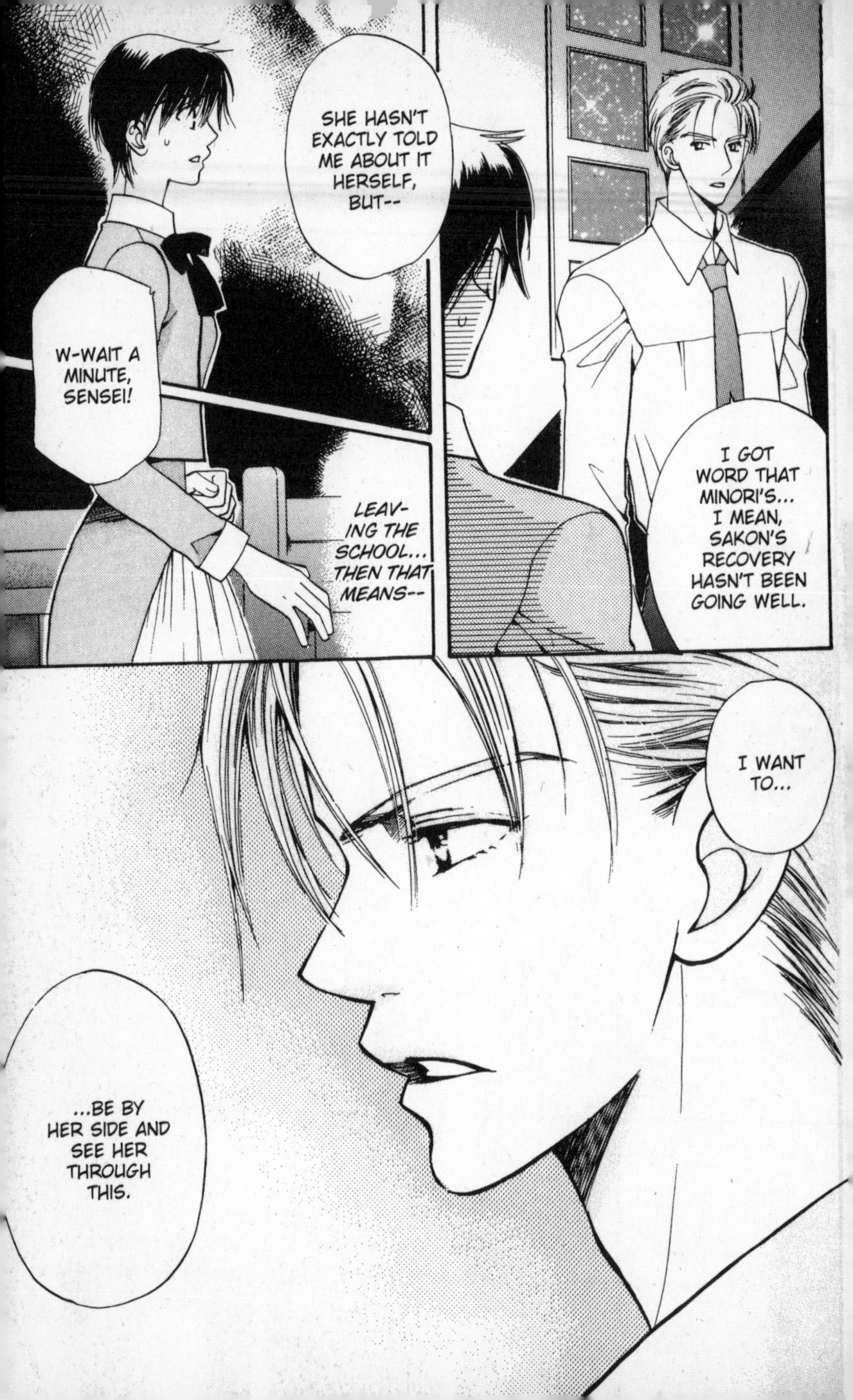
I GOT WORD THAT MINORI'S... I MEAN, SAKON'S RECOVERY HASN'T BEEN GOING WELL.
SHE HASN'T EXACTLY TOLD ME ABOUT IT HERSELF, BUT--
LEAVING THE SCHOOL... THEN THAT MEANS--
W-WAIT A MINUTE, SENSEI!
I WANT TO...
...BE BY HER SIDE AND SEE HER THROUGH THIS.

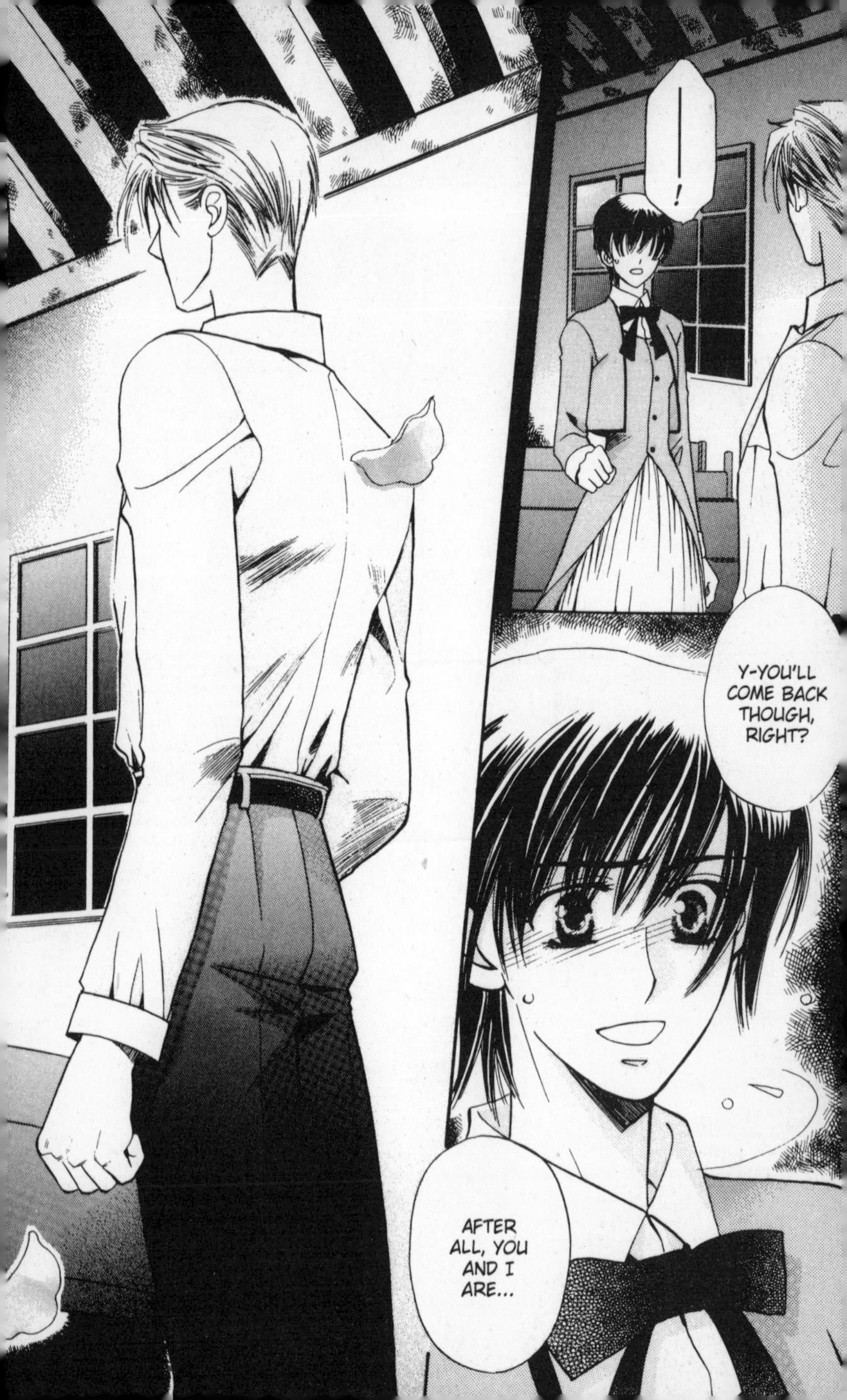
!!
Y-YOU'LL COME BACK THOUGH, RIGHT?
AFTER ALL, YOU AND I ARE...

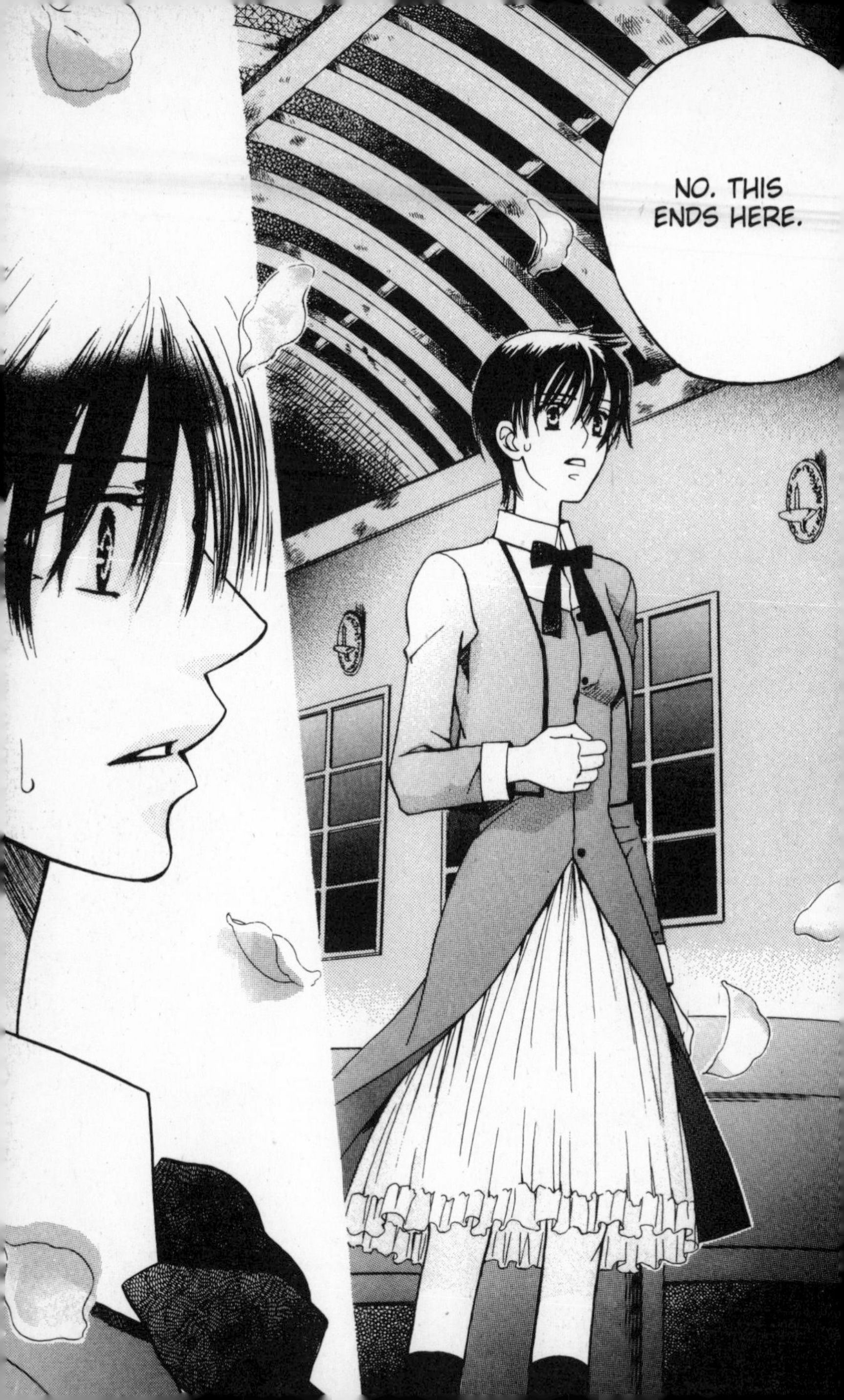
NO. THIS ENDS HERE.

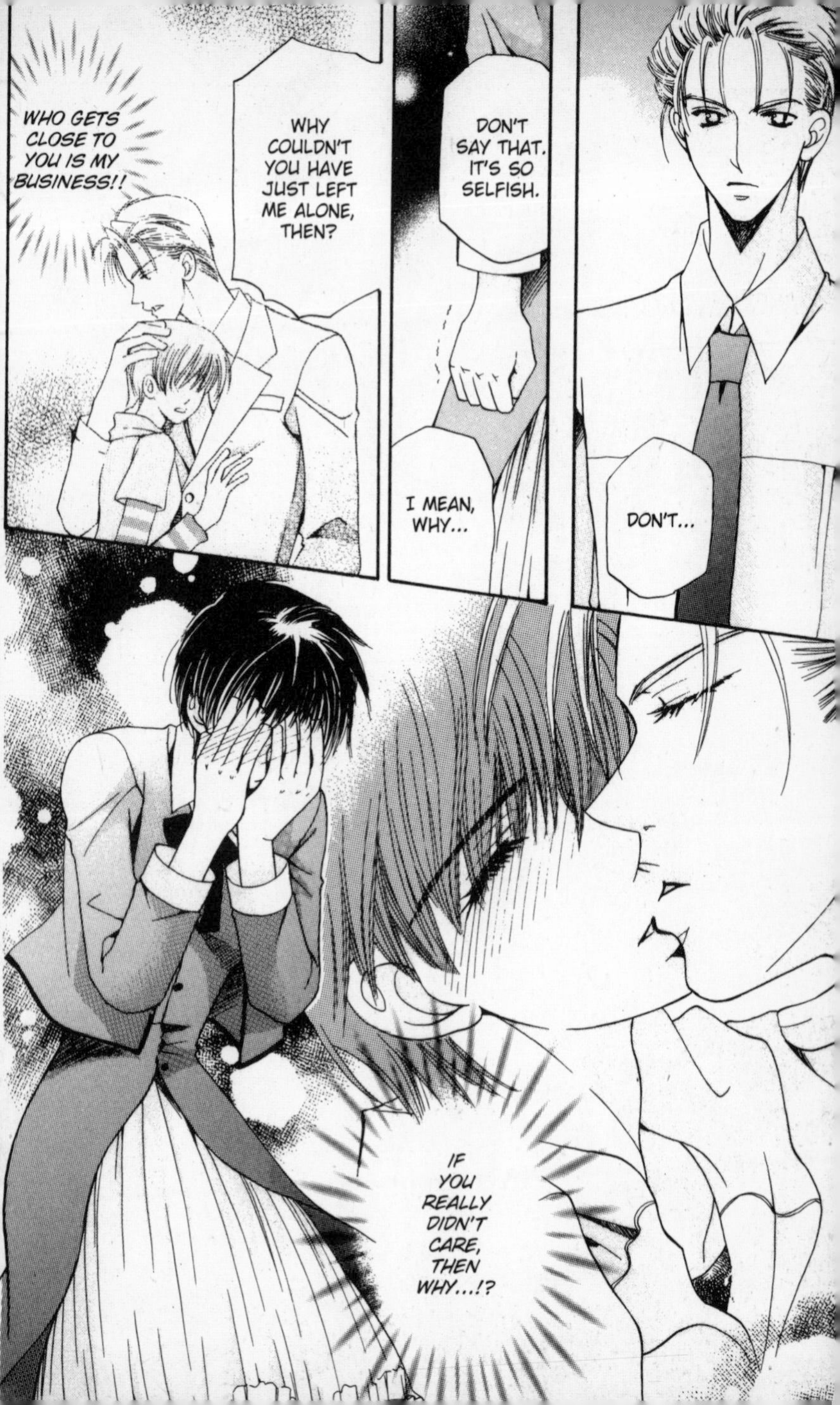
DON'T...
DON'T SAY THAT. IT'S SO SELFISH.
I MEAN, WHY...
WHY COULDN'T YOU HAVE JUST LEFT ME ALONE, THEN?
WHO GETS CLOSE TO YOU IS MY BUSINESS!!
IF YOU REALLY DIDN'T CARE, THEN WHY...!?

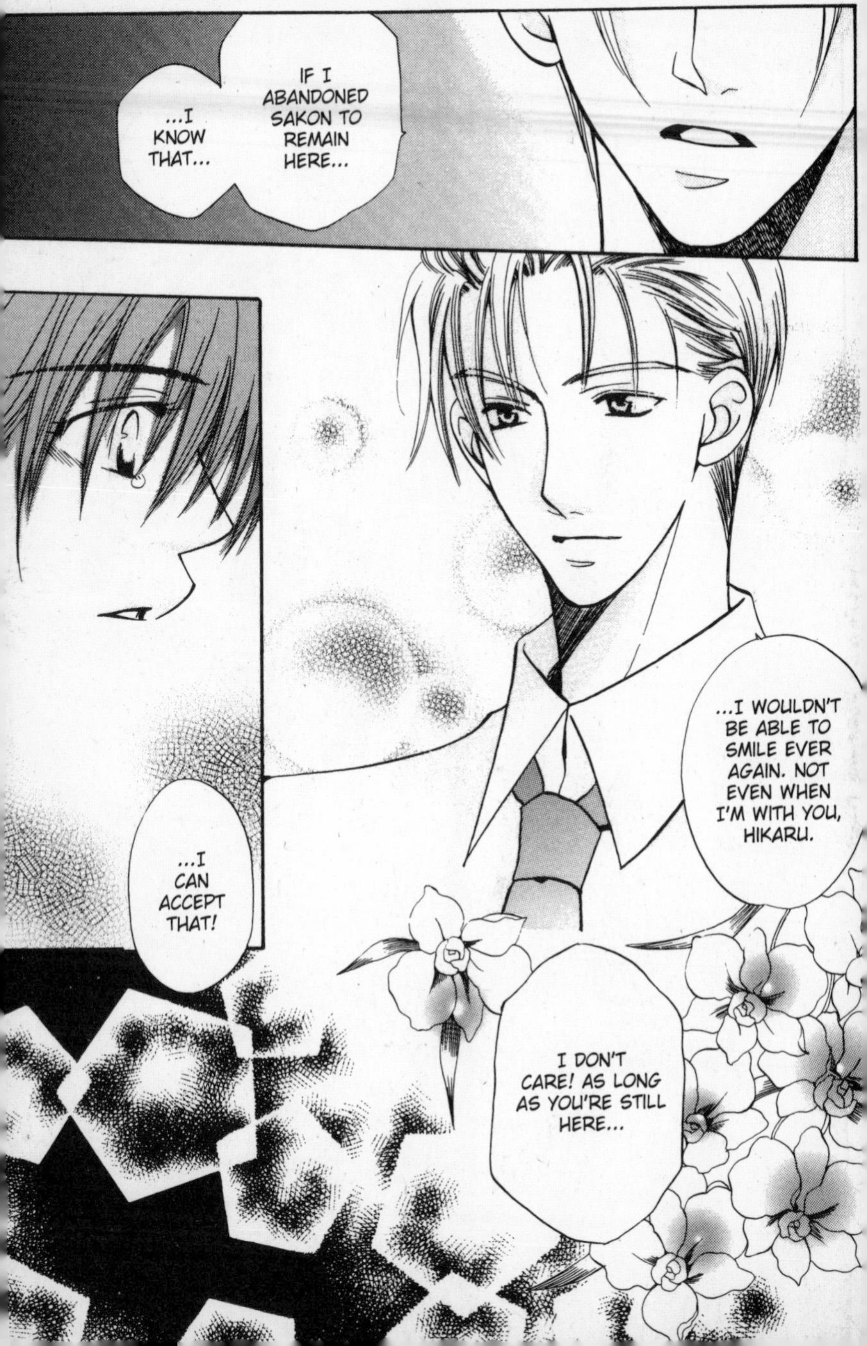
IF I ABANDONED SAKON TO REMAIN HERE...
...I KNOW THAT...
...I WOULDN'T BE ABLE TO SMILE EVER AGAIN. NOT EVEN WHEN I'M WITH YOU, HIKARU.
...I CAN ACCEPT THAT!
I DON'T CARE! AS LONG AS YOU'RE STILL HERE...

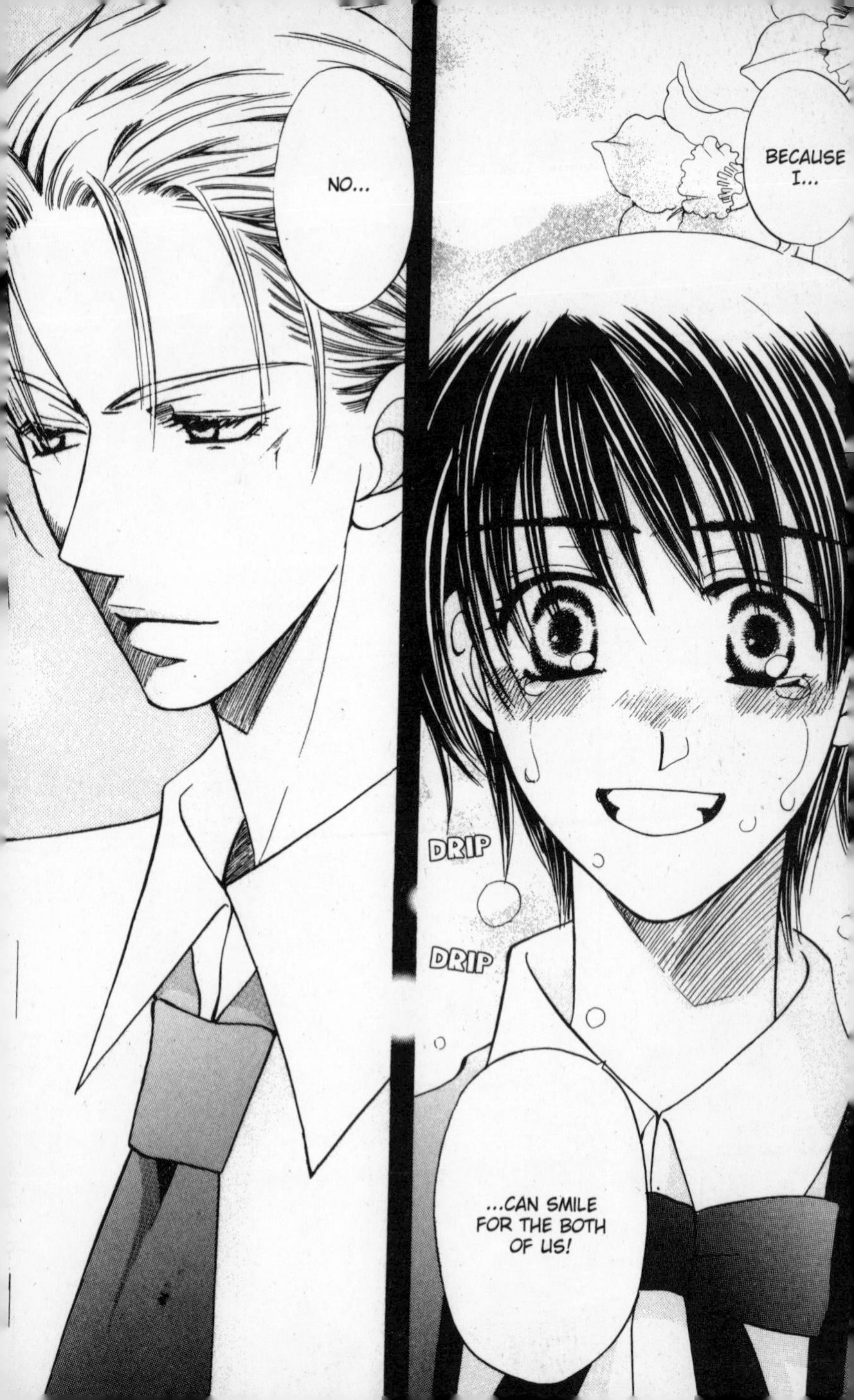
BECAUSE I...
DRIP
DRIP
...CAN SMILE FOR THE BOTH OF US!
NO...

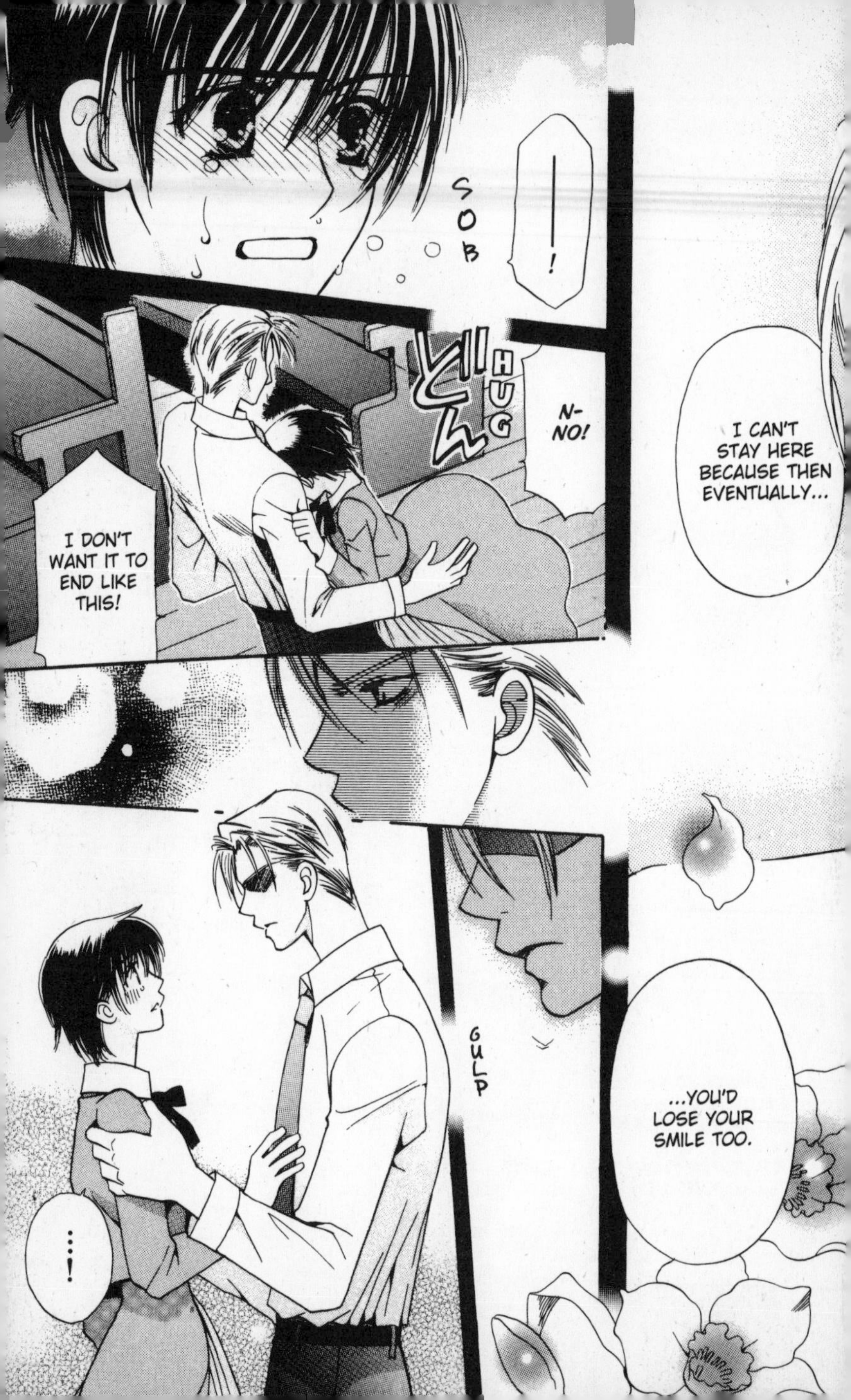
I CAN'T STAY HERE BECAUSE THEN EVENTUALLY...
—!
SOB
HUG
N-NO!
I DON'T WANT IT TO END LIKE THIS!
...YOU'D LOSE YOUR SMILE TOO.
GULP
...!

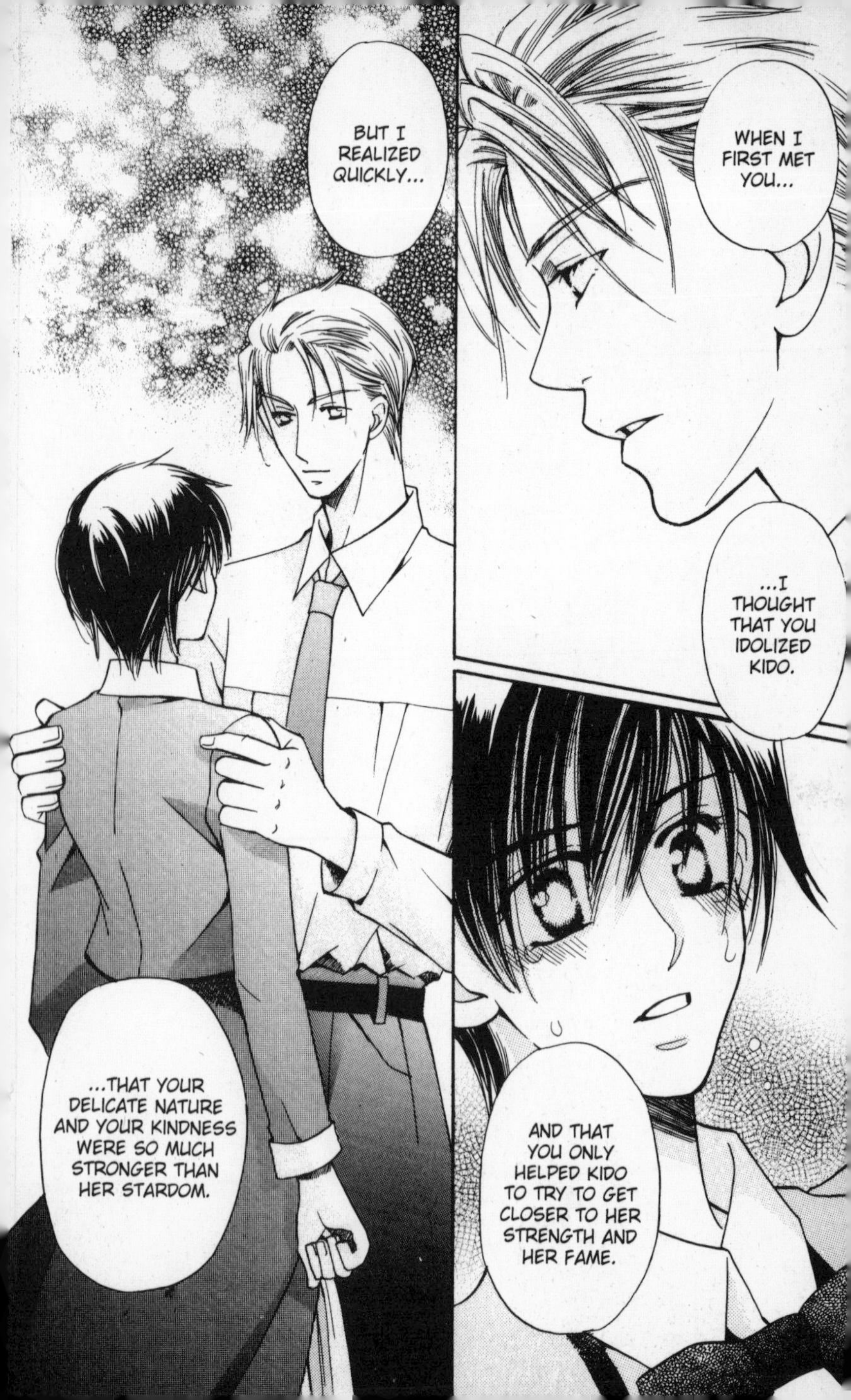
WHEN I FIRST MET YOU...
...I THOUGHT THAT YOU IDOLIZED KIDO.
AND THAT YOU ONLY HELPED KIDO TO TRY TO GET CLOSER TO HER STRENGTH AND HER FAME.
BUT I REALIZED QUICKLY...
...THAT YOUR DELICATE NATURE AND YOUR KINDNESS WERE SO MUCH STRONGER THAN HER STARDOM.

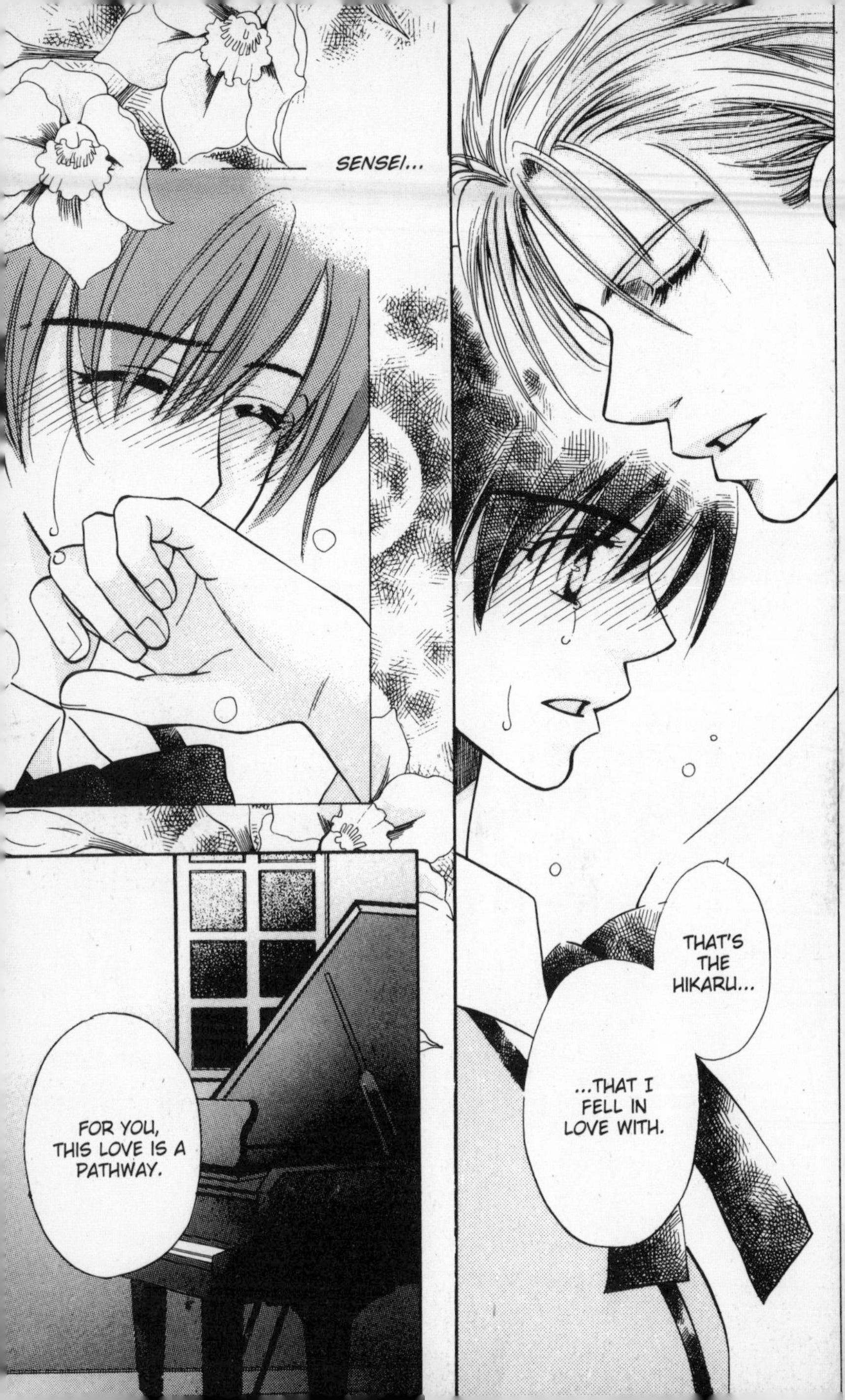
THAT'S THE HIKARU...
...THAT I FELL IN LOVE WITH.
SENSEI...
FOR YOU, THIS LOVE IS A PATHWAY.

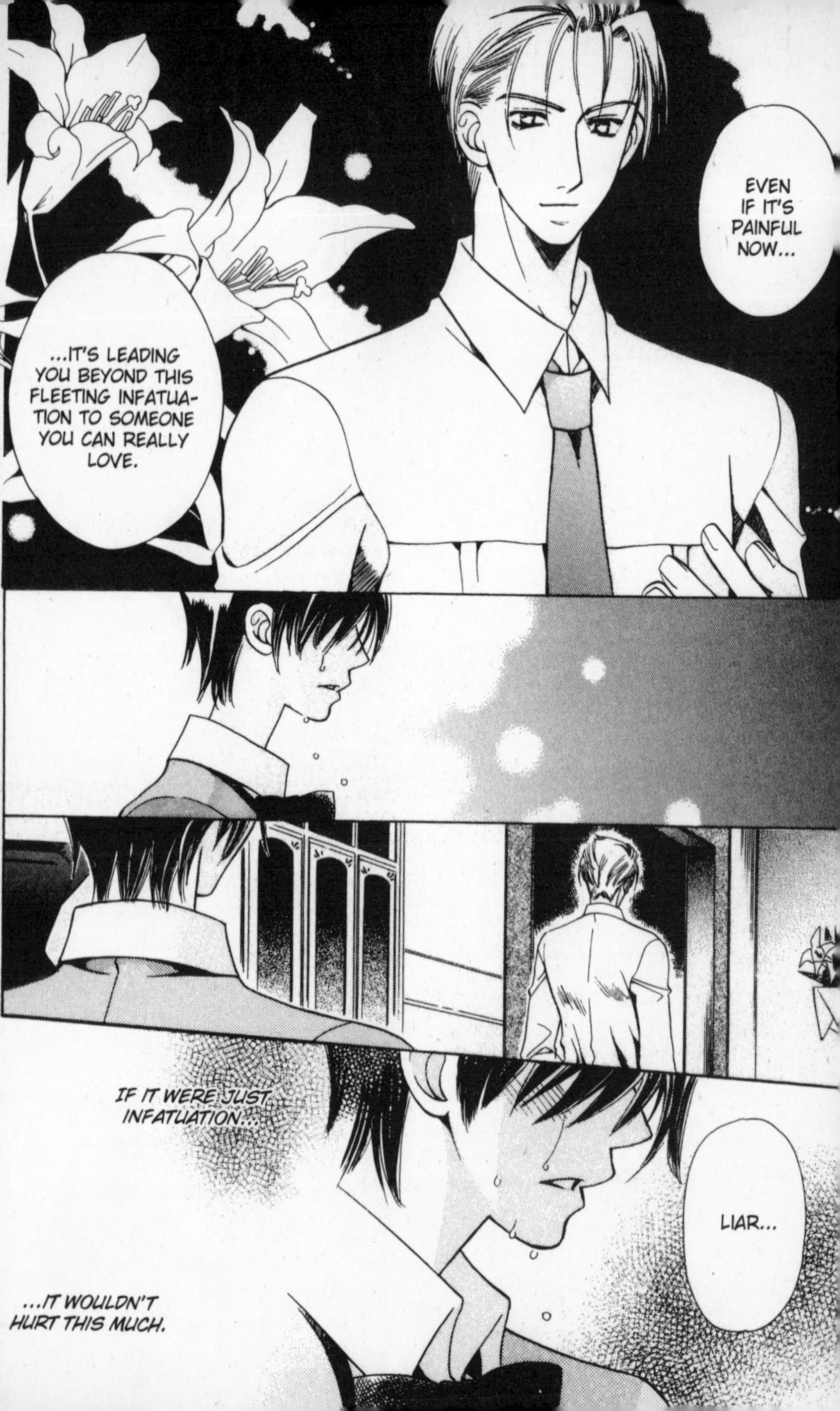
EVEN IF IT'S PAINFUL NOW...
...IT'S LEADING YOU BEYOND THIS FLEETING INFATUATION TO SOMEONE YOU CAN REALLY LOVE.
LIAR...
IF IT WERE JUST INFATUATION...
...IT WOULDN'T HURT THIS MUCH.

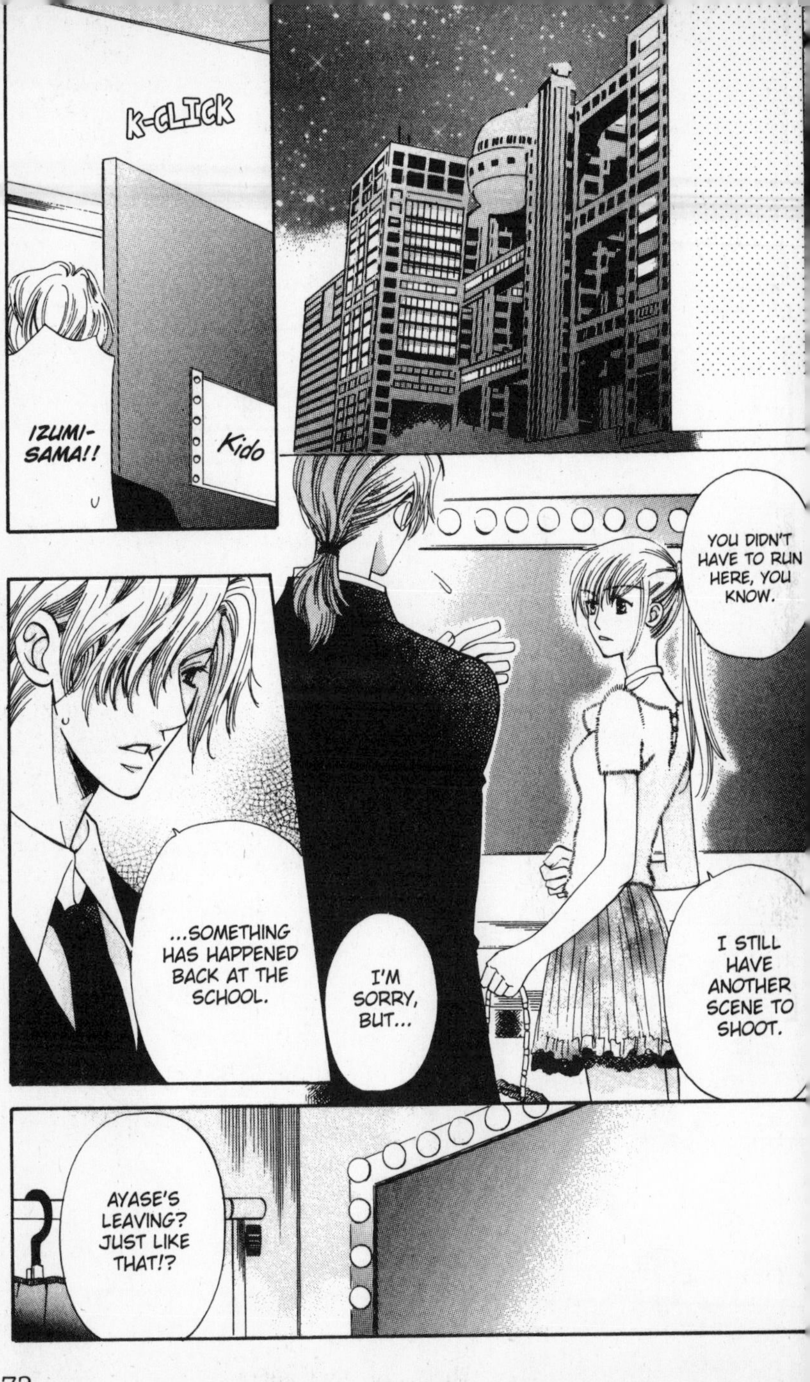
K-CLICK
Kido
IZUMI-SAMA!!
YOU DIDN'T HAVE TO RUN HERE, YOU KNOW.
I STILL HAVE ANOTHER SCENE TO SHOOT.
I'M SORRY, BUT...
...SOMETHING HAS HAPPENED BACK AT THE SCHOOL.
AYASE'S LEAVING? JUST LIKE THAT!?

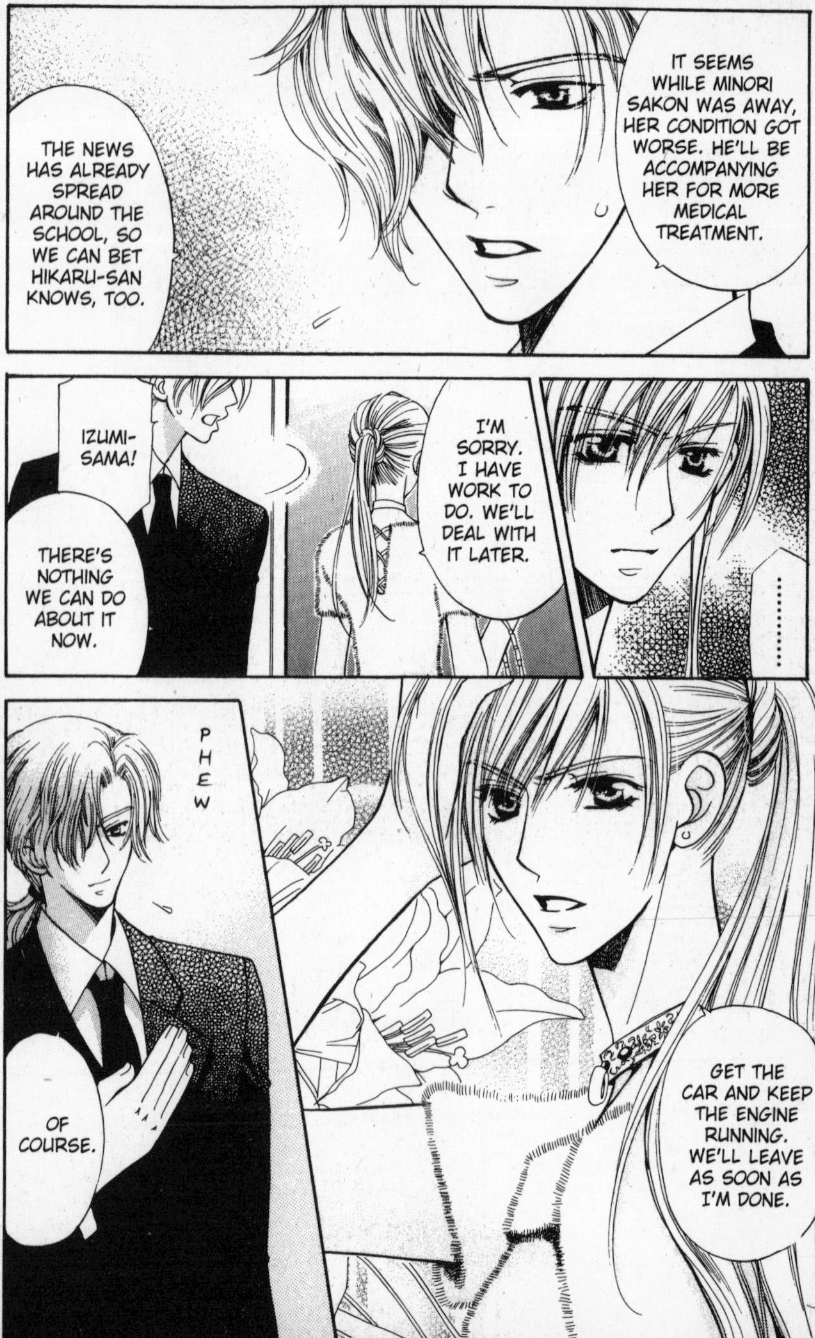
IT SEEMS WHILE MINORI SAKON WAS AWAY, HER CONDITION GOT WORSE. HE'LL BE ACCOMPANYING HER FOR MORE MEDICAL TREATMENT.
THE NEWS HAS ALREADY SPREAD AROUND THE SCHOOL, SO WE CAN BET HIKARU-SAN KNOWS, TOO.
....
I'M SORRY. I HAVE WORK TO DO. WE'LL DEAL WITH IT LATER.
IZUMI-SAMA!
THERE'S NOTHING WE CAN DO ABOUT IT NOW.
GET THE CAR AND KEEP THE ENGINE RUNNING. WE'LL LEAVE AS SOON AS I'M DONE.
PHEW
OF COURSE.

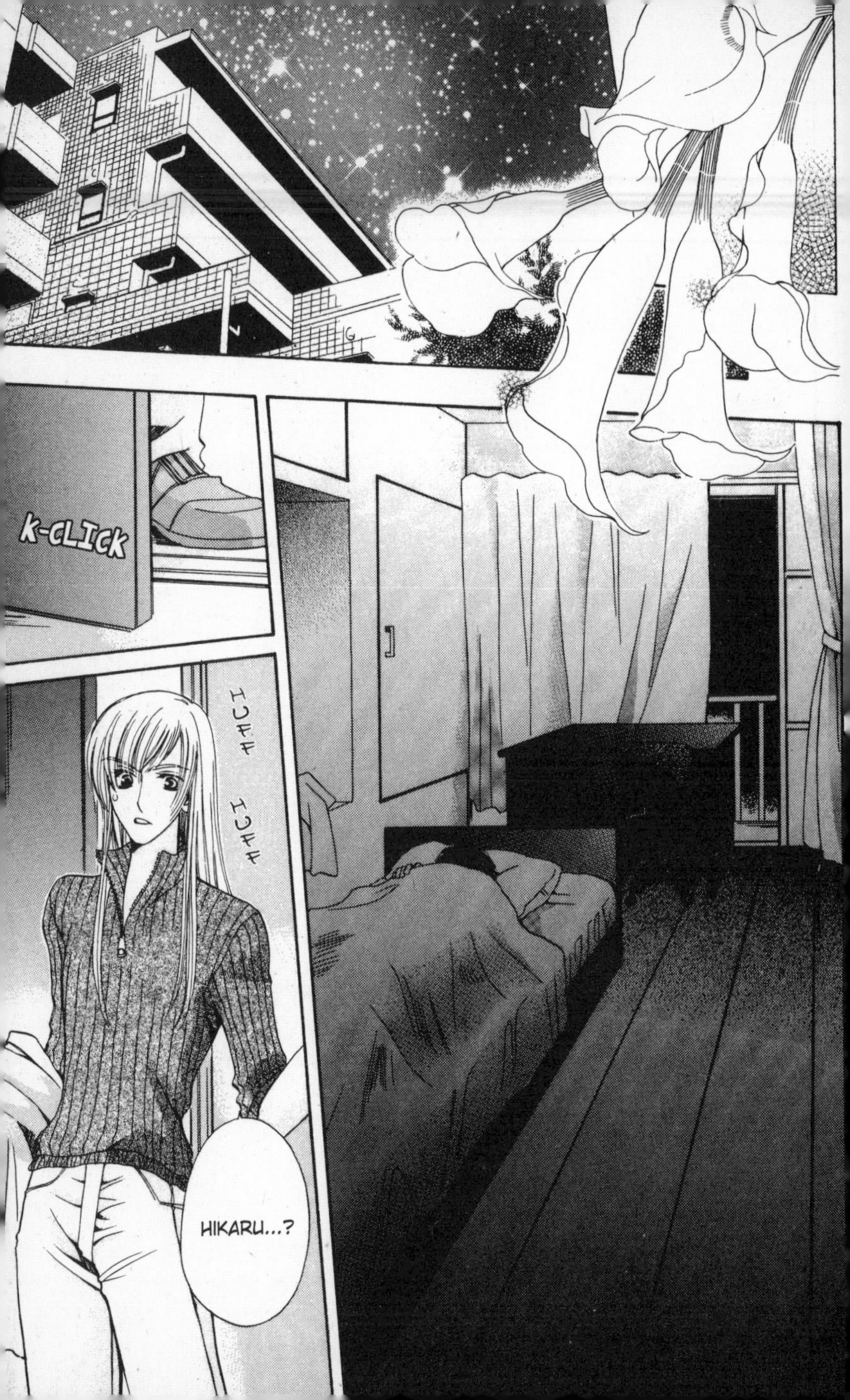
K-CLICK
HUFF HUFF
HIKARU...?

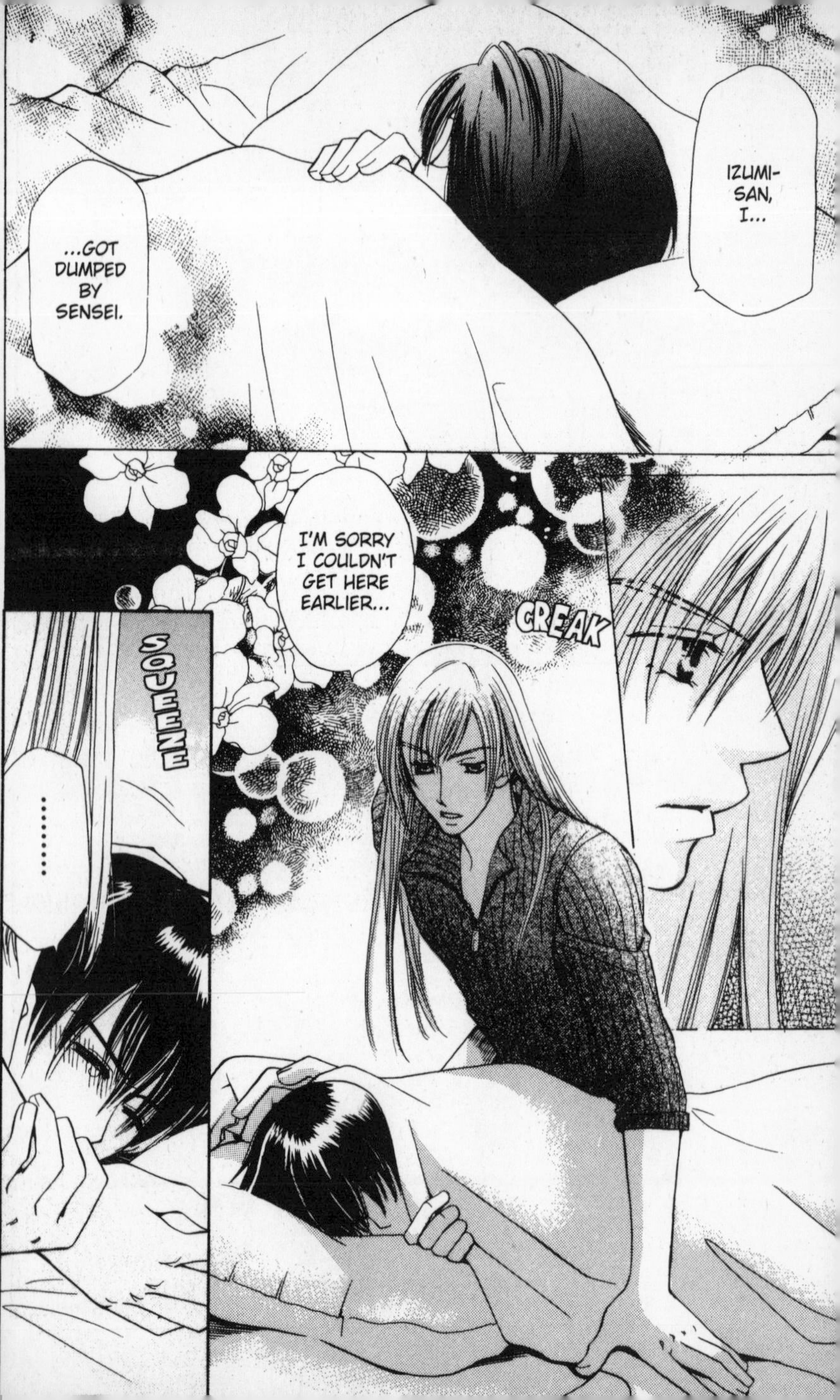
IZUMI-SAN, I...
...GOT DUMPED BY SENSEI.
I'M SORRY I COULDN'T GET HERE EARLIER...
CREAK
SQUEEZE
......

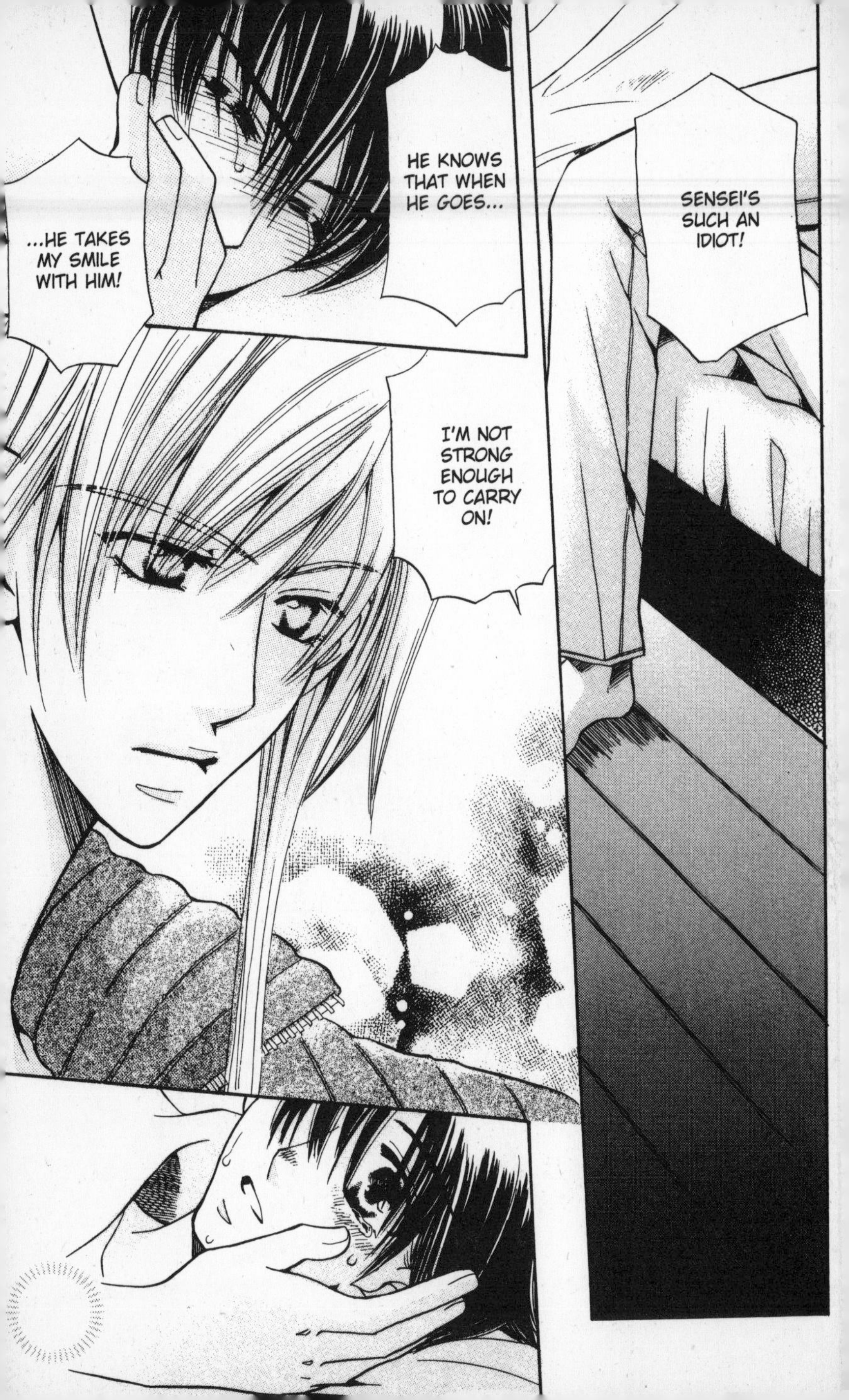
SENSEI'S SUCH AN IDIOT!
HE KNOWS THAT WHEN HE GOES...
...HE TAKES MY SMILE WITH HIM!
I'M NOT STRONG ENOUGH TO CARRY ON!

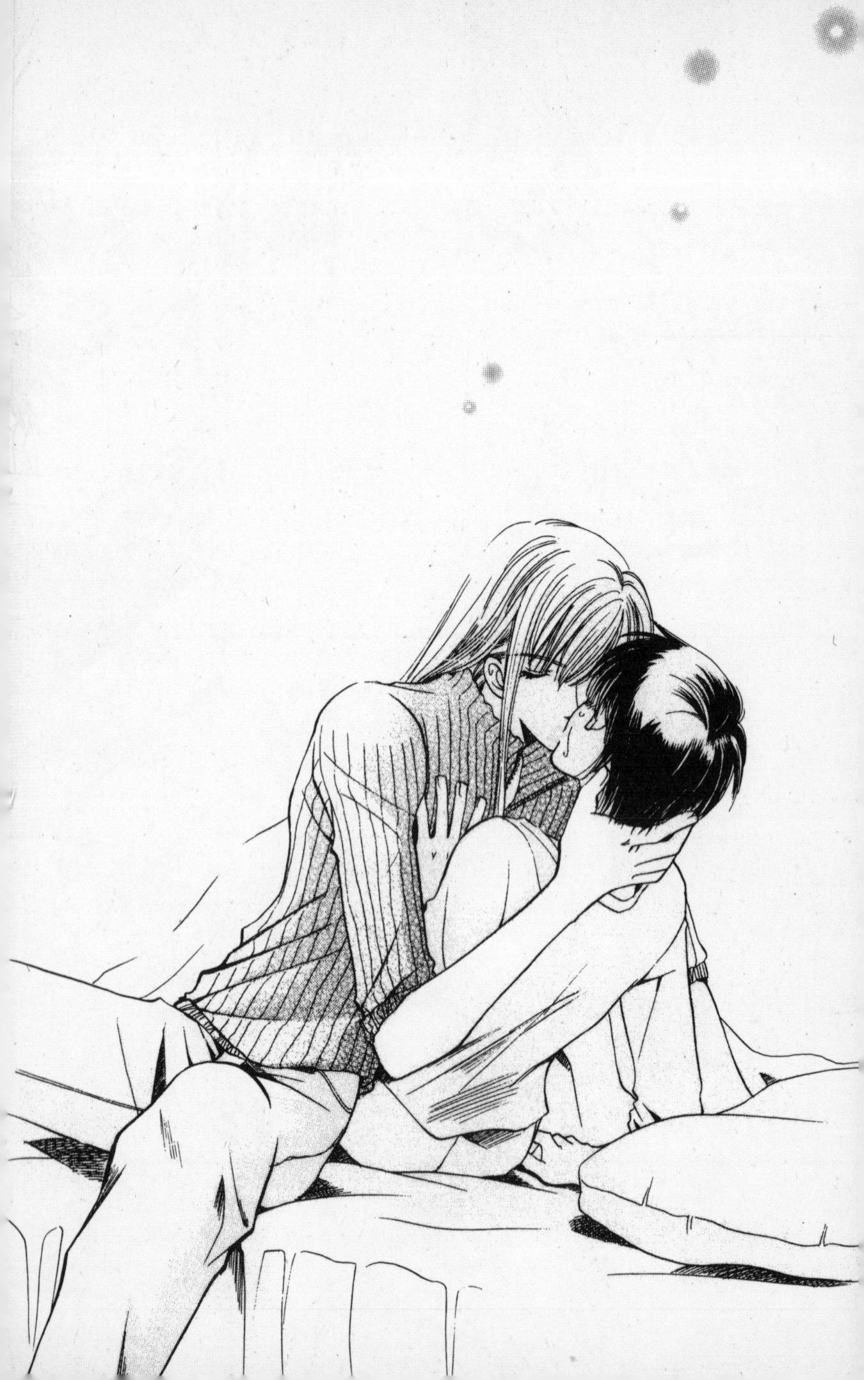

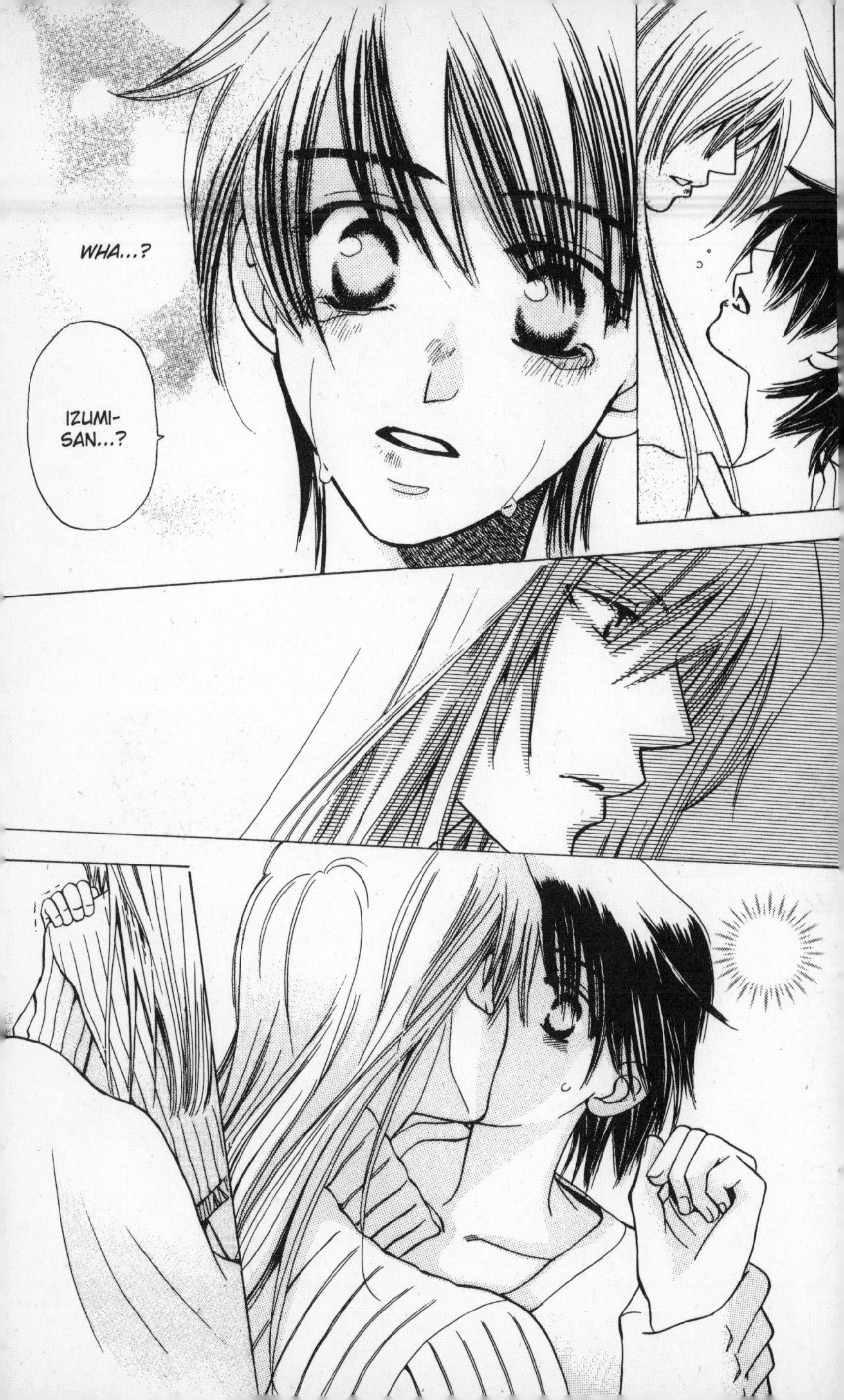
WHA...?
IZUMI-SAN...?

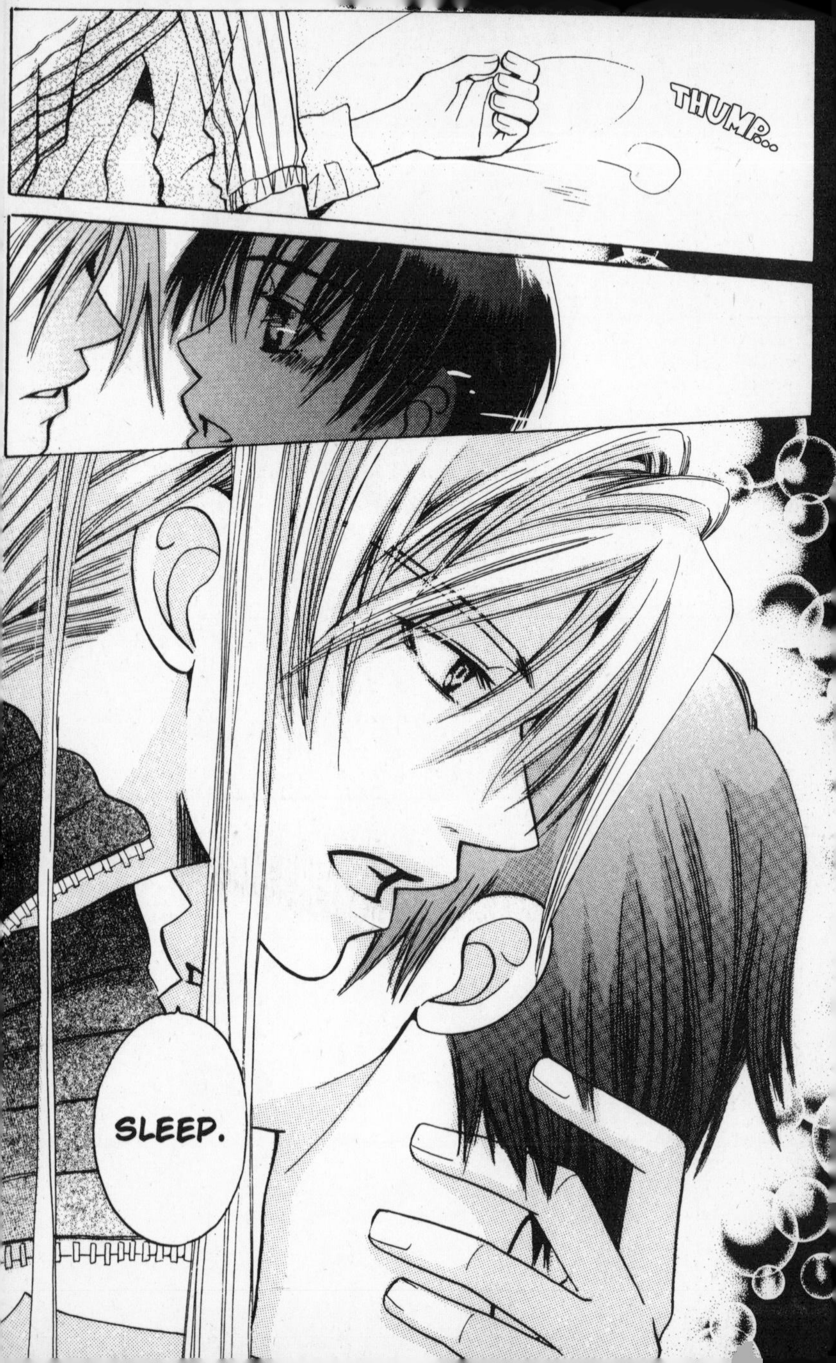
THUMP...
SLEEP.

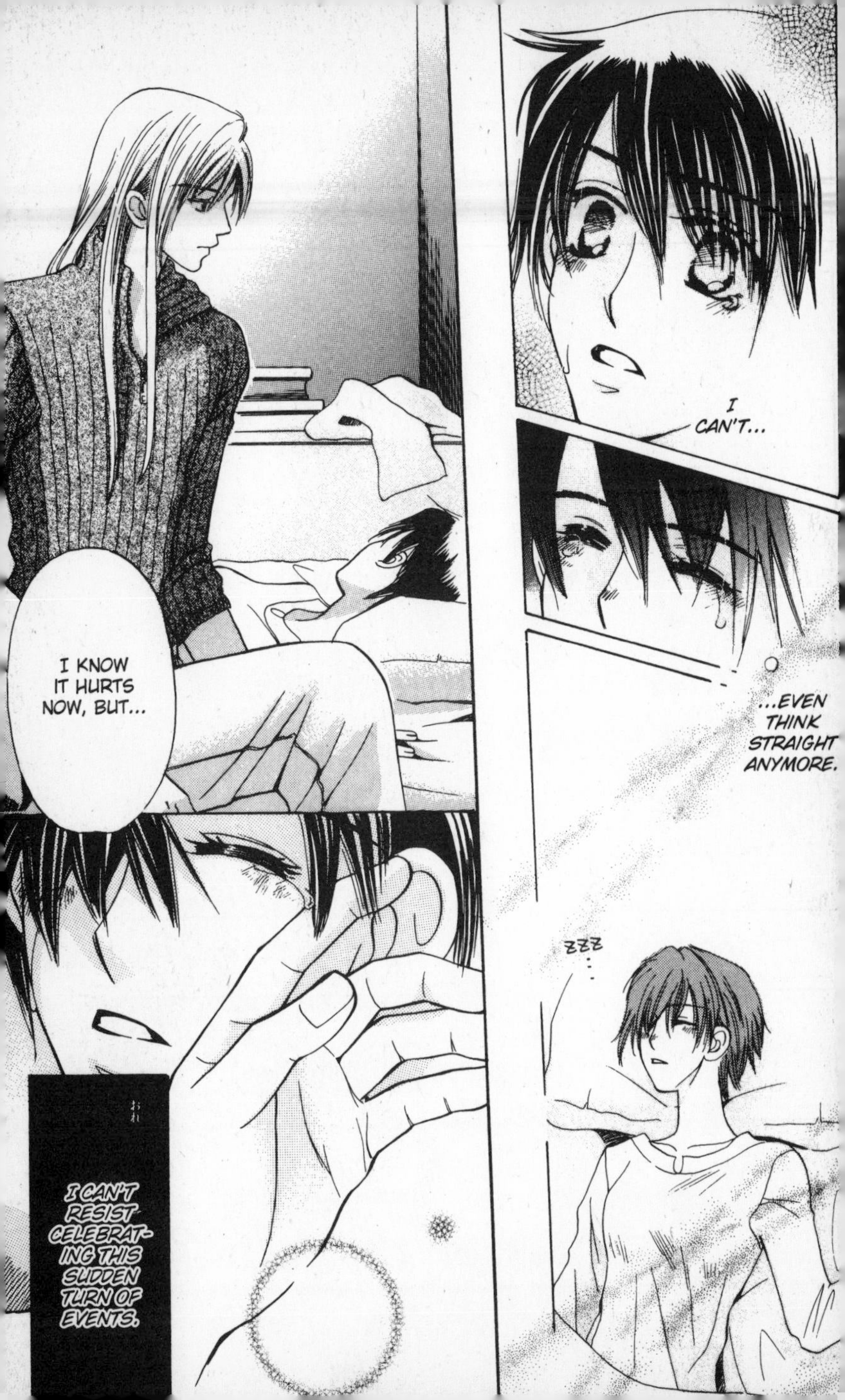
I CAN'T...
...EVEN THINK STRAIGHT ANYMORE.
ZZZ...
I KNOW IT HURTS NOW, BUT...
I CAN'T RESIST CELEBRATING THIS SUDDEN TURN OF EVENTS.

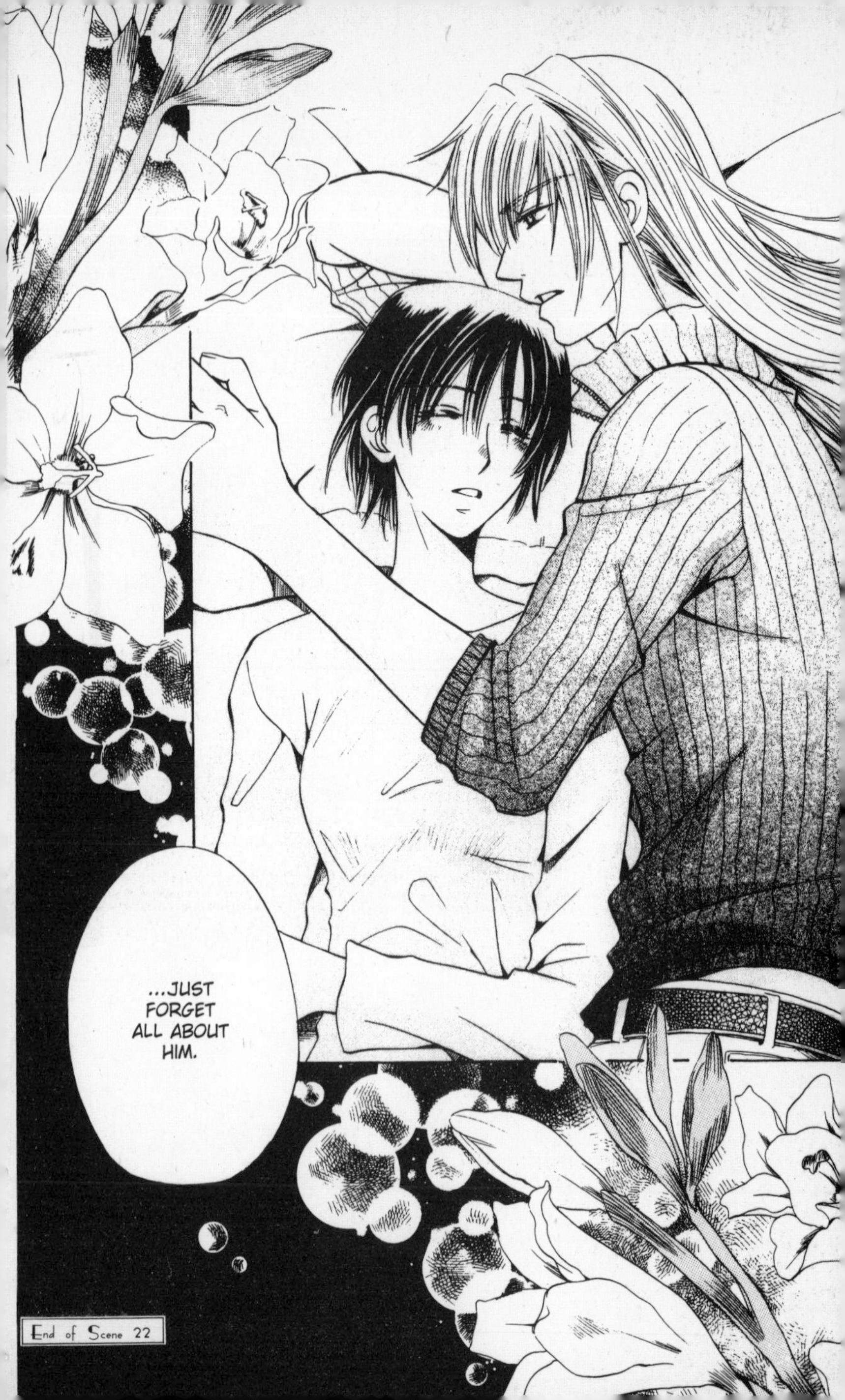
...JUST FORGET ALL ABOUT HIM.
End of Scene 22

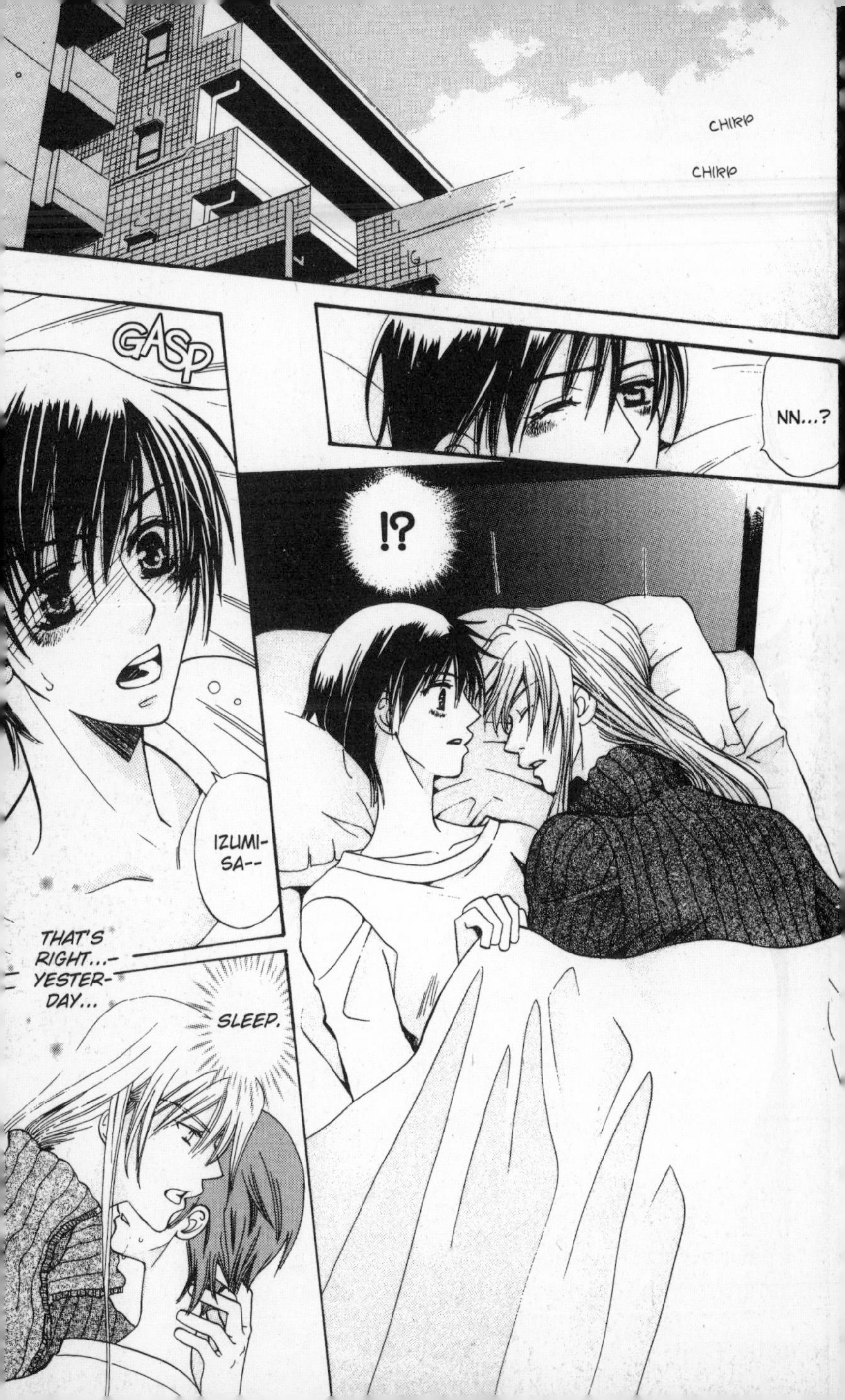
CHIRP
CHIRP
NN...?
!?
GASP
IZUMI-SA--
THAT'S RIGHT...-YESTER-DAY...
SLEEP.

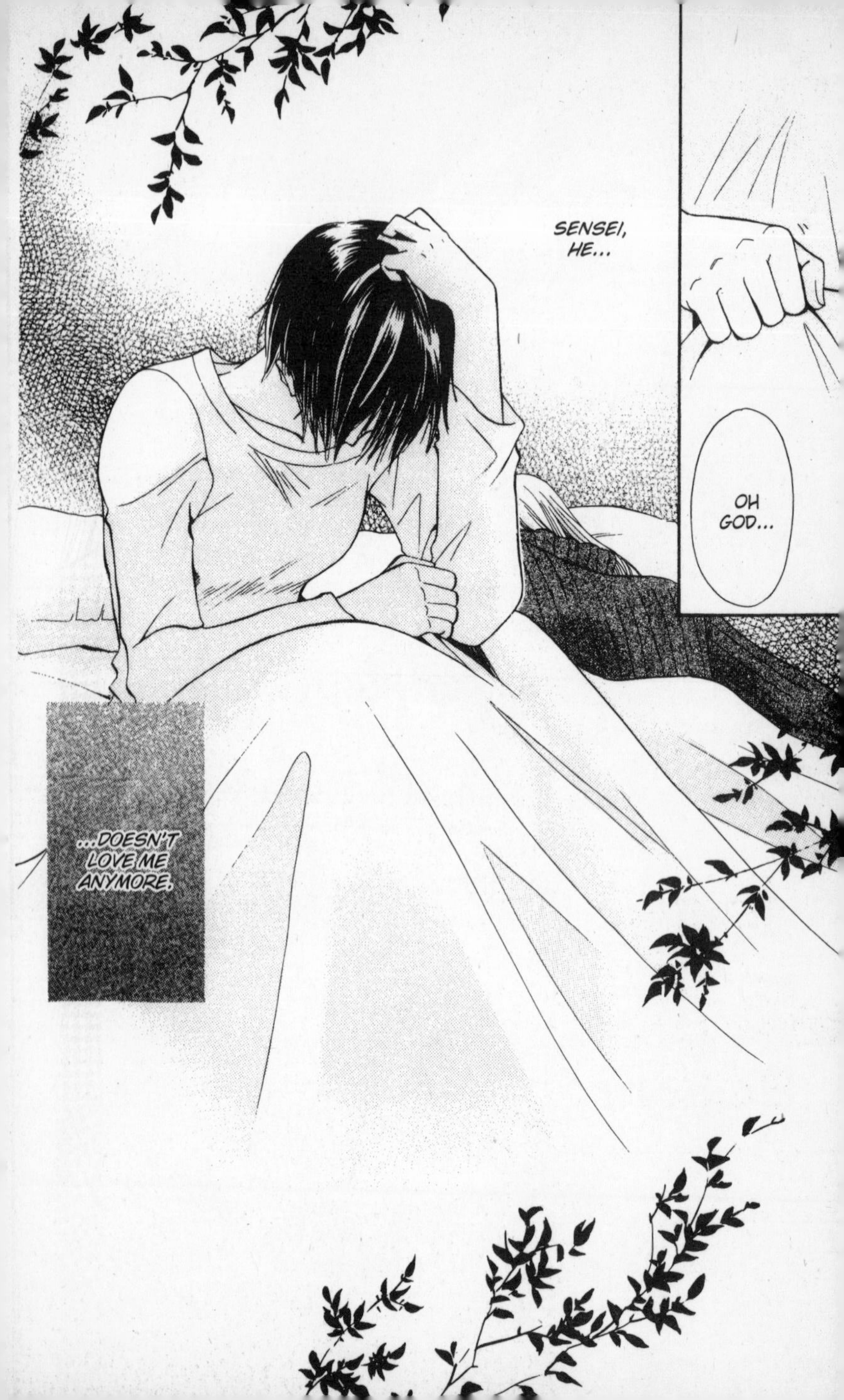
OH GOD...
SENSEI, HE...
...DOESN'T LOVE ME ANYMORE.

TENSHI JA NAI!!

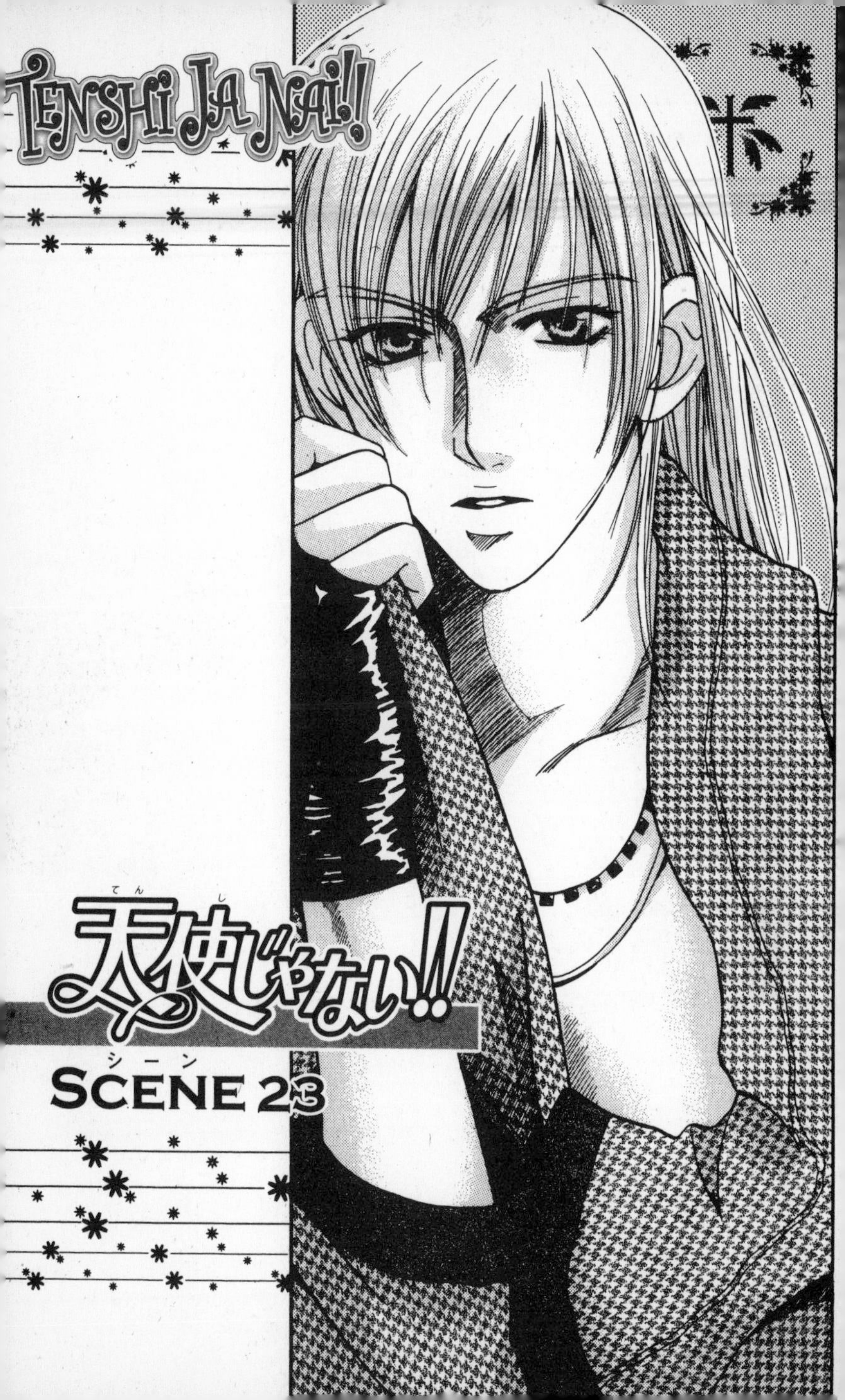

天使(てんし)じゃない!!

SCENE(シーン) 23

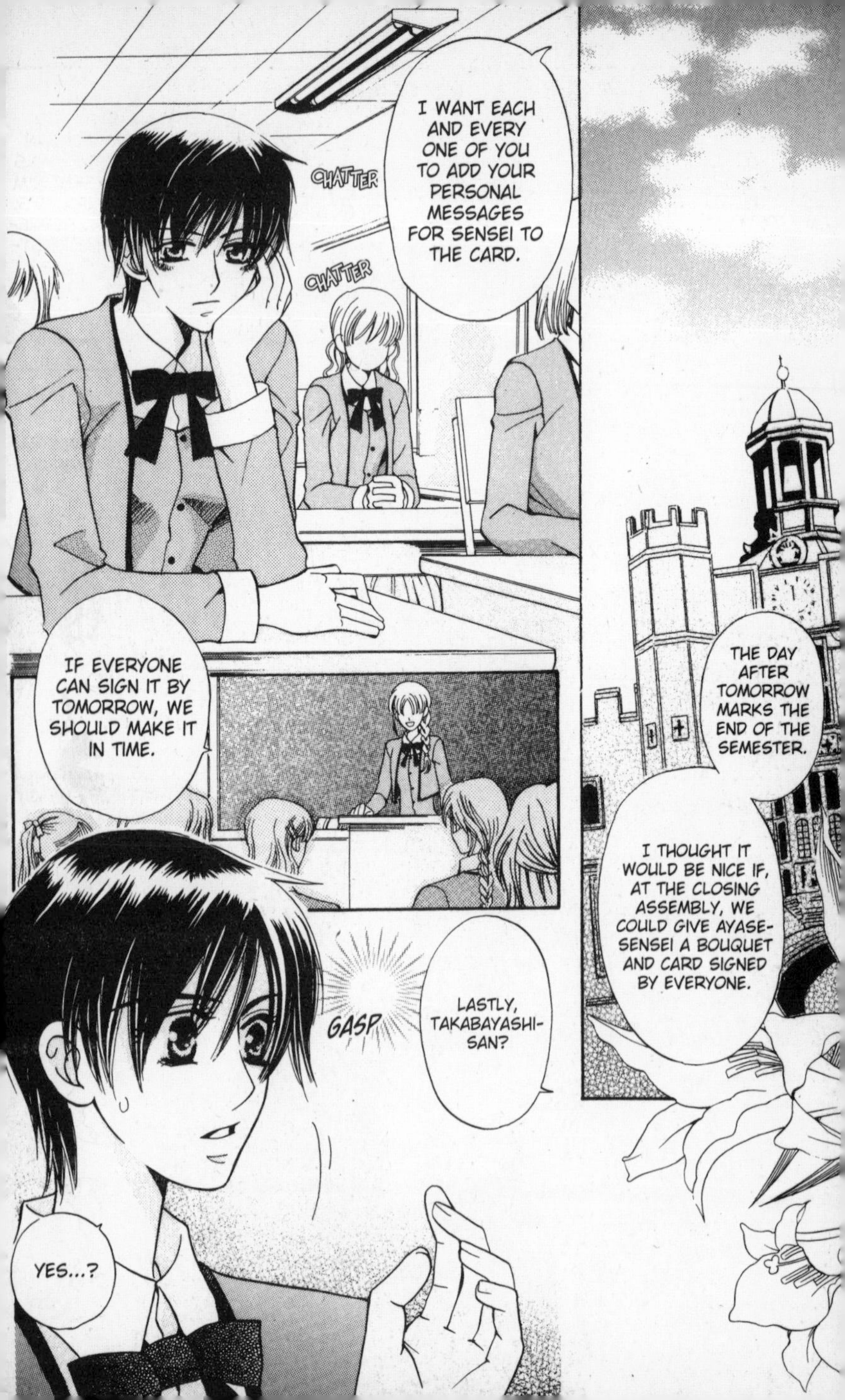
THE DAY AFTER TOMORROW MARKS THE END OF THE SEMESTER.
I THOUGHT IT WOULD BE NICE IF, AT THE CLOSING ASSEMBLY, WE COULD GIVE AYASE-SENSEI A BOUQUET AND CARD SIGNED BY EVERYONE.
I WANT EACH AND EVERY ONE OF YOU TO ADD YOUR PERSONAL MESSAGES FOR SENSEI TO THE CARD.
CHATTER
CHATTER
IF EVERYONE CAN SIGN IT BY TOMORROW, WE SHOULD MAKE IT IN TIME.
LASTLY, TAKABAYASHI-SAN?
GASP
YES...?

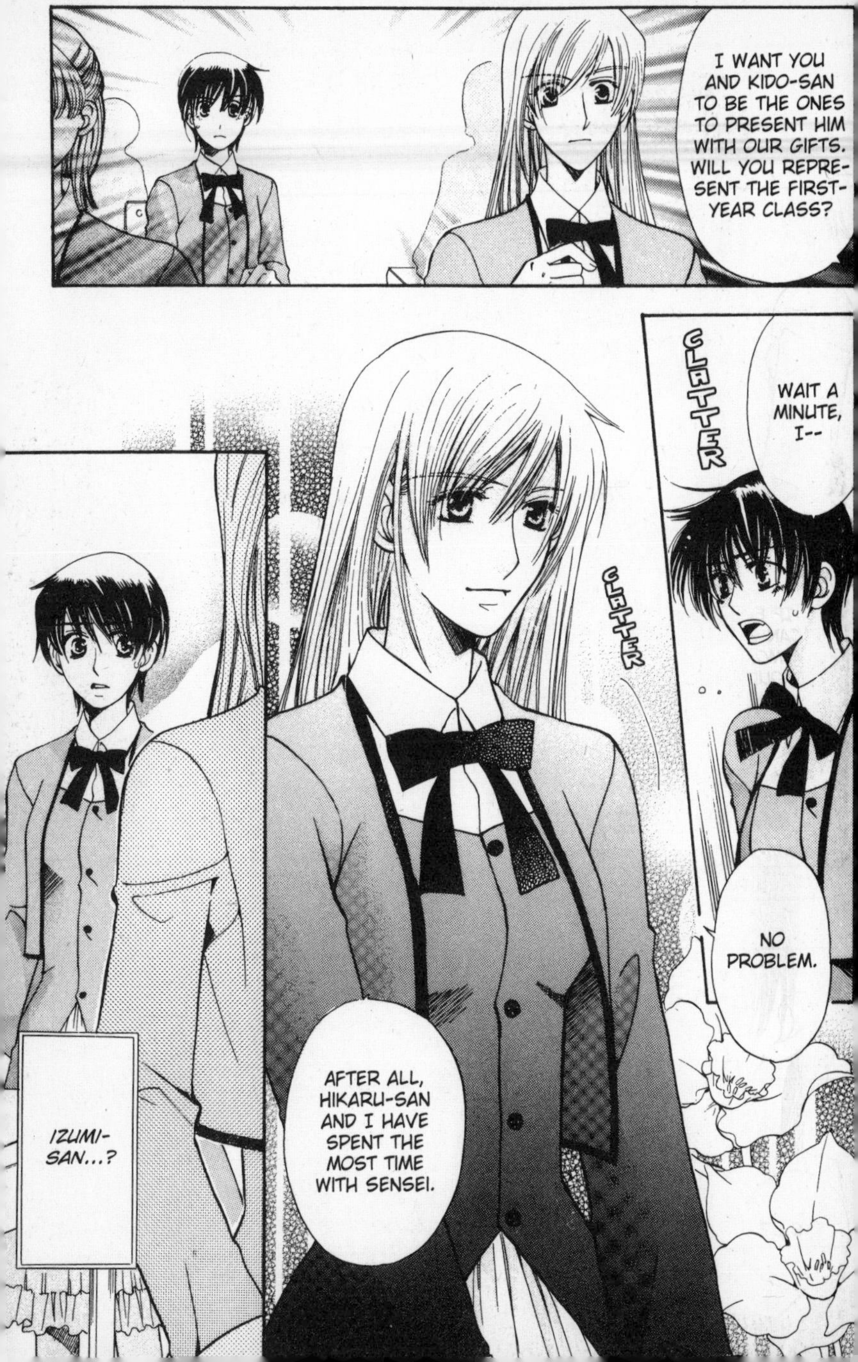
I WANT YOU AND KIDO-SAN TO BE THE ONES TO PRESENT HIM WITH OUR GIFTS. WILL YOU REPRESENT THE FIRST-YEAR CLASS?
CLATTER
WAIT A MINUTE, I--
CLATTER
NO PROBLEM.
AFTER ALL, HIKARU-SAN AND I HAVE SPENT THE MOST TIME WITH SENSEI.
IZUMI-SAN...?

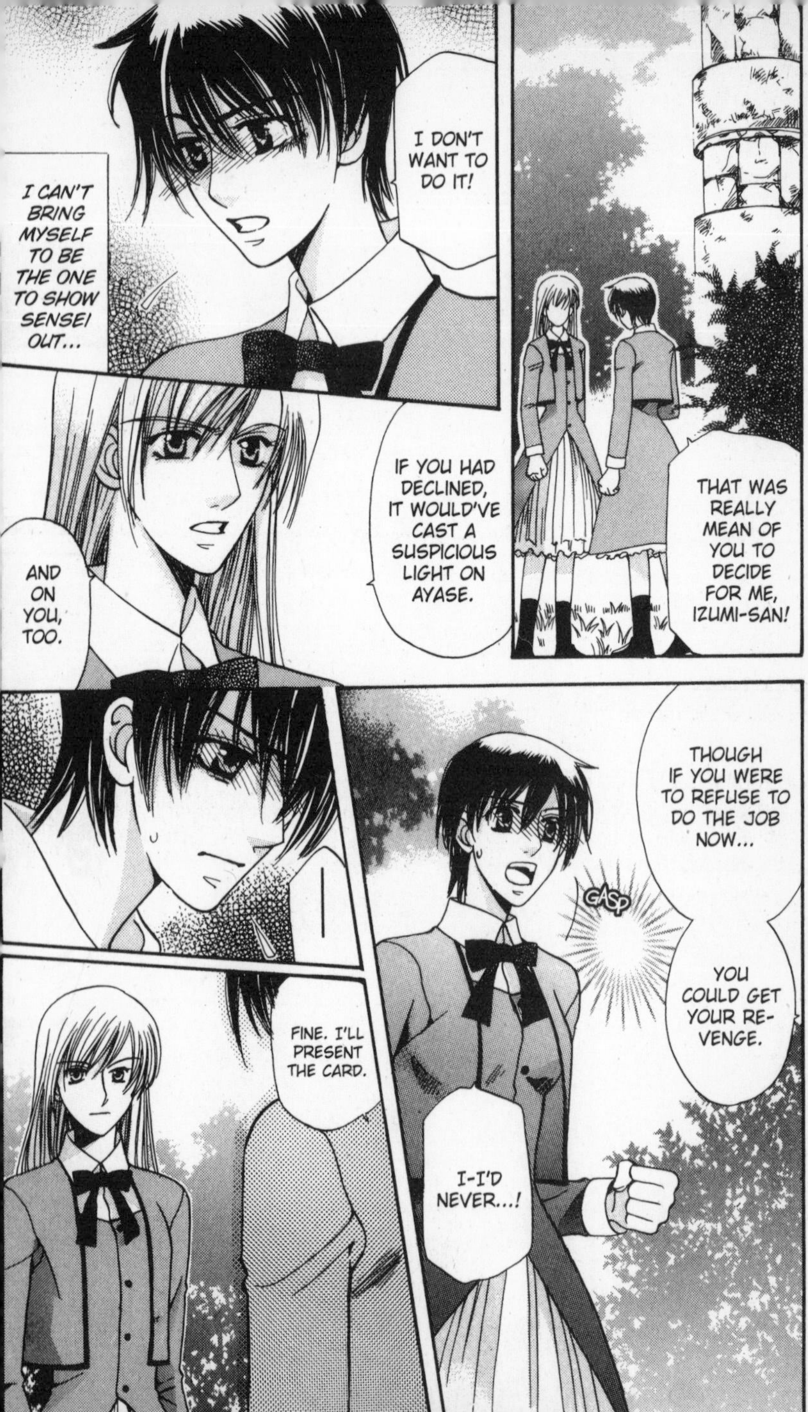
THAT WAS REALLY MEAN OF YOU TO DECIDE FOR ME, IZUMI-SAN!
I DON'T WANT TO DO IT!
I CAN'T BRING MYSELF TO BE THE ONE TO SHOW SENSEI OUT...
IF YOU HAD DECLINED, IT WOULD'VE CAST A SUSPICIOUS LIGHT ON AYASE.
AND ON YOU, TOO.
THOUGH IF YOU WERE TO REFUSE TO DO THE JOB NOW...
YOU COULD GET YOUR RE-VENGE.
GASP
I-I'D NEVER...!
FINE. I'LL PRESENT THE CARD.

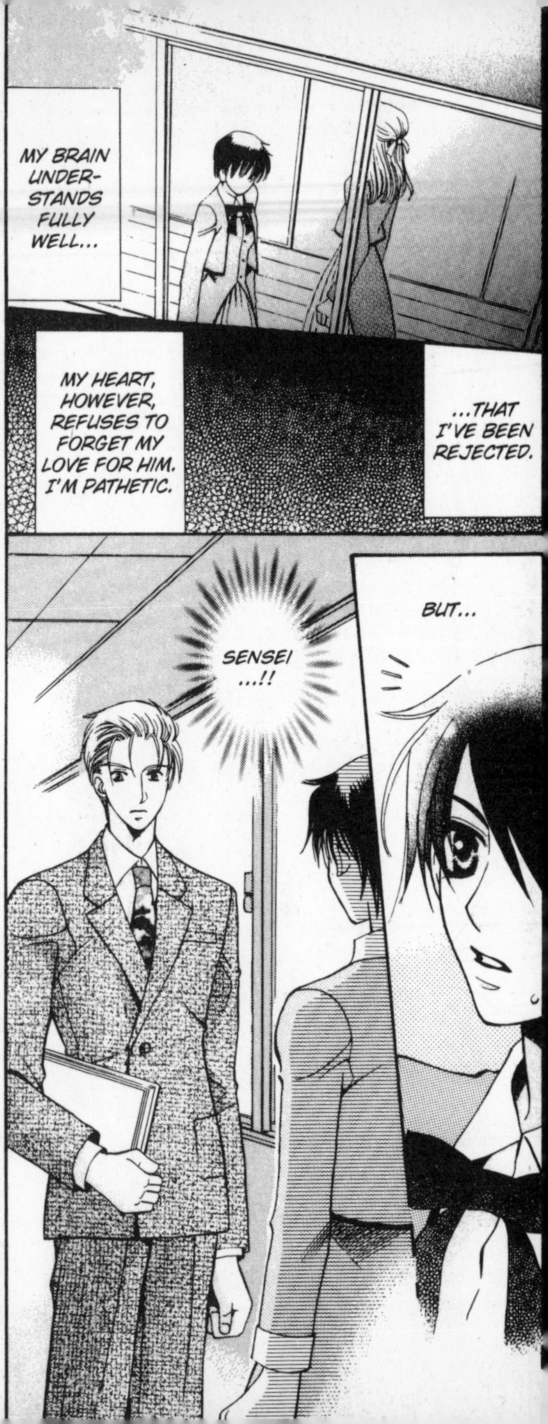
MY BRAIN UNDER-STANDS FULLY WELL...
...THAT I'VE BEEN REJECTED.
MY HEART, HOWEVER, REFUSES TO FORGET MY LOVE FOR HIM. I'M PATHETIC.
BUT...
SENSEI ...!!

My Current Addictions

I just realized recently that it seems my addictions come in waves...

I got into ROMANCE NOVELS →
(that's all I read for one month)

→ A CERTAIN NINJA ANIME →
(only on DVD)

→ GOURMET FOOD
(I tried to withstand temptation)

→ GAMING →
(like an infatuated monkey)

→ THE INTERNET →
(that bewitching box makes you lose track of time)...

→ ...and then I got back into romance novels...
(endless)

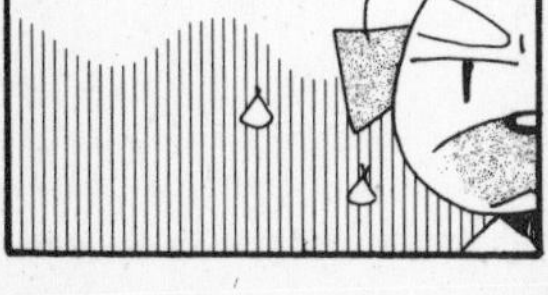

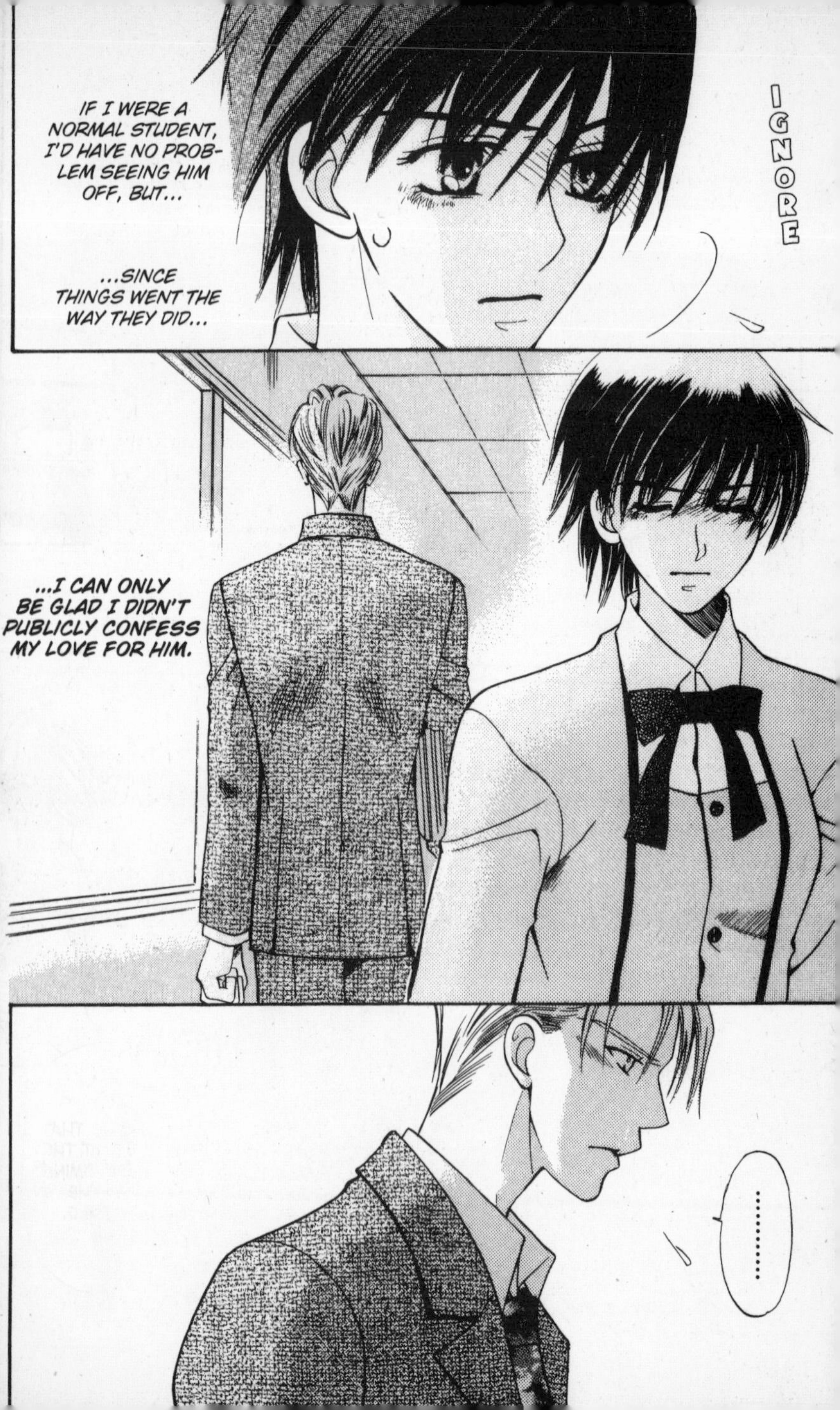
IF I WERE A NORMAL STUDENT, I'D HAVE NO PROB-LEM SEEING HIM OFF, BUT...
IGNORE
...SINCE THINGS WENT THE WAY THEY DID...
...I CAN ONLY BE GLAD I DIDN'T PUBLICLY CONFESS MY LOVE FOR HIM.
......

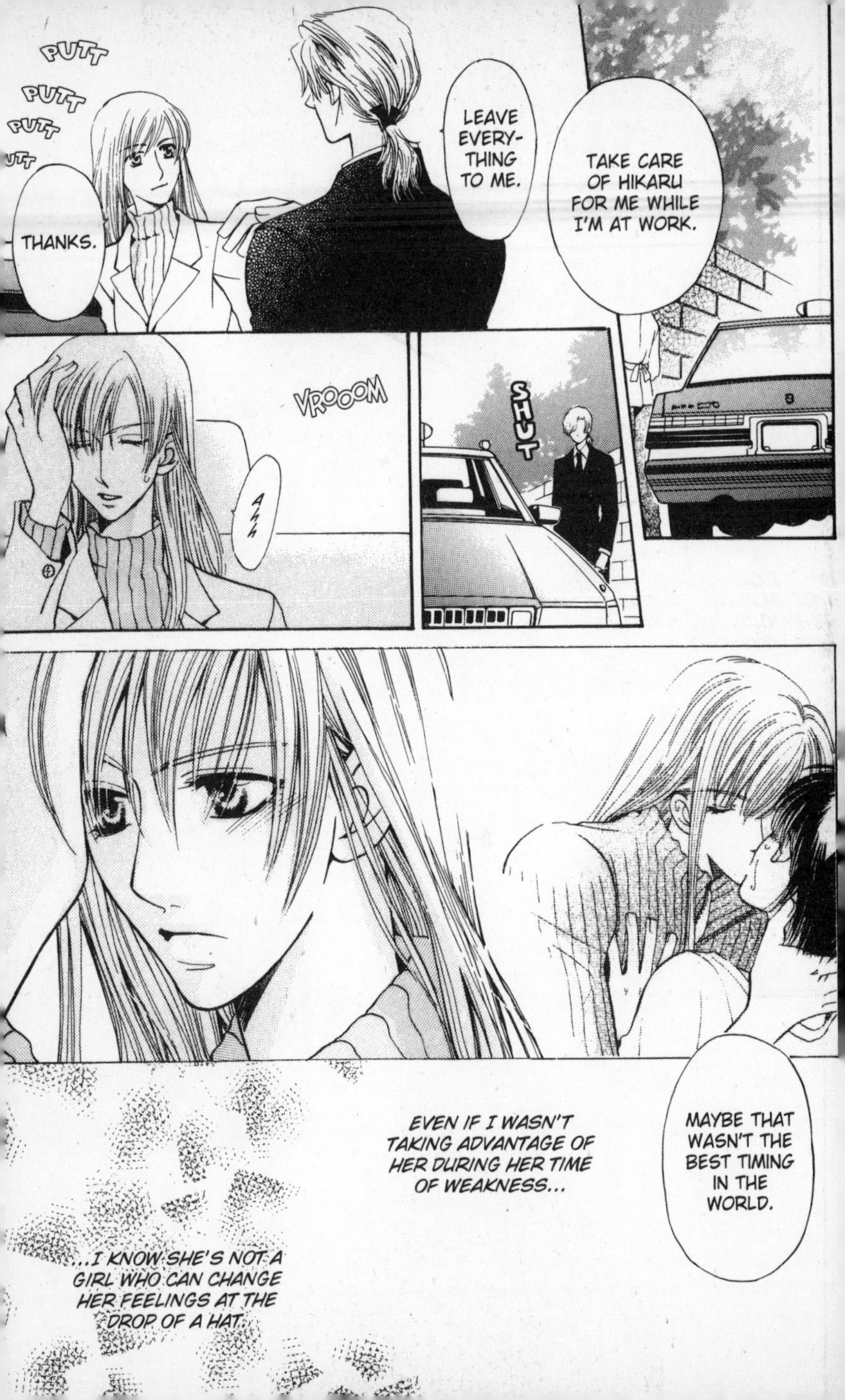
TAKE CARE OF HIKARU FOR ME WHILE I'M AT WORK.
LEAVE EVERY-THING TO ME.
PUTT PUTT PUTT
THANKS.
SHUT
VROOOM
AHH
MAYBE THAT WASN'T THE BEST TIMING IN THE WORLD.
EVEN IF I WASN'T TAKING ADVANTAGE OF HER DURING HER TIME OF WEAKNESS...
...I KNOW SHE'S NOT A GIRL WHO CAN CHANGE HER FEELINGS AT THE DROP OF A HAT.

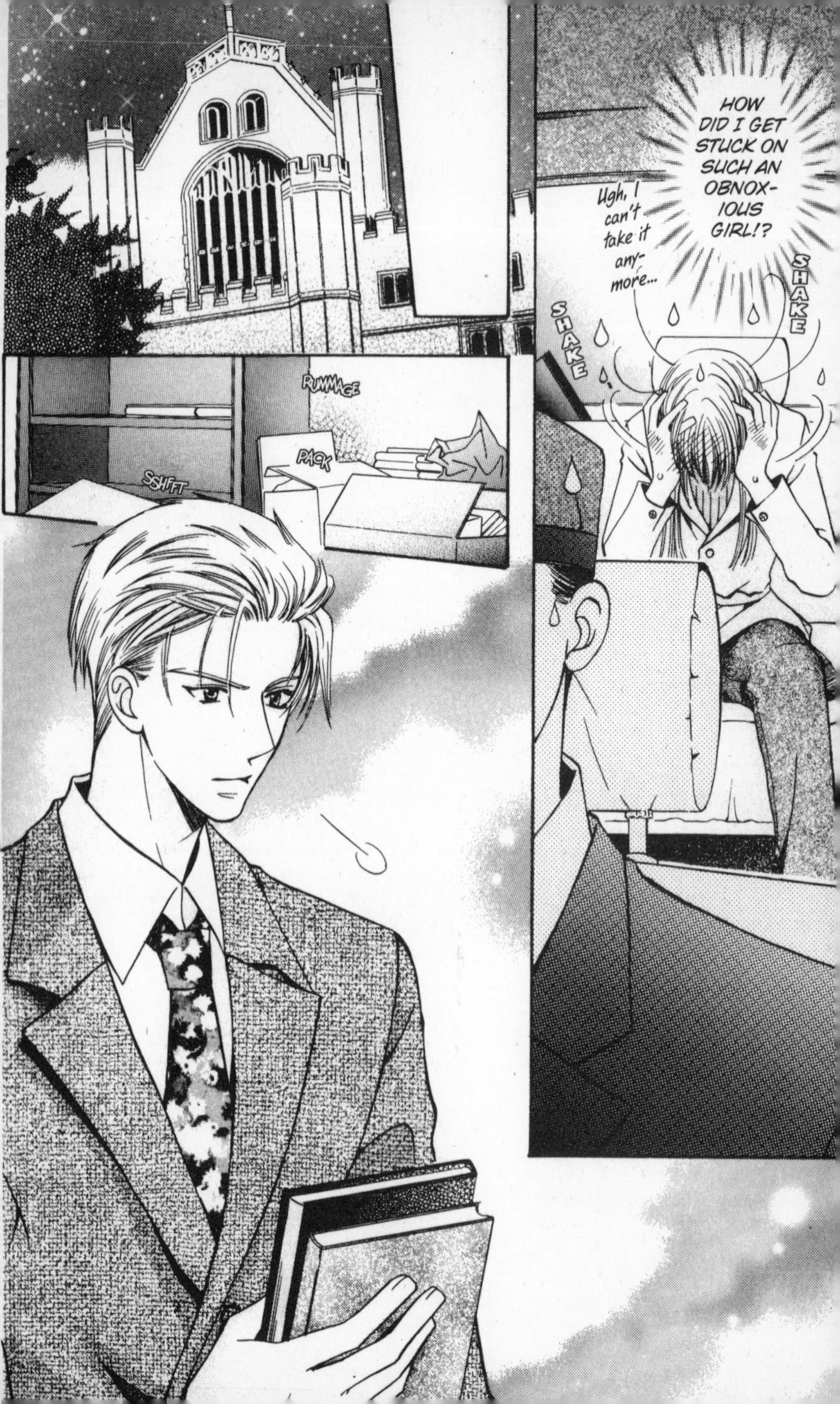
HOW DID I GET STUCK ON SUCH AN OBNOX-IOUS GIRL!?
Ugh, I can't take it any-more...
SHAKE
SHAKE
RUMMAGE
PACK
SSHFFT

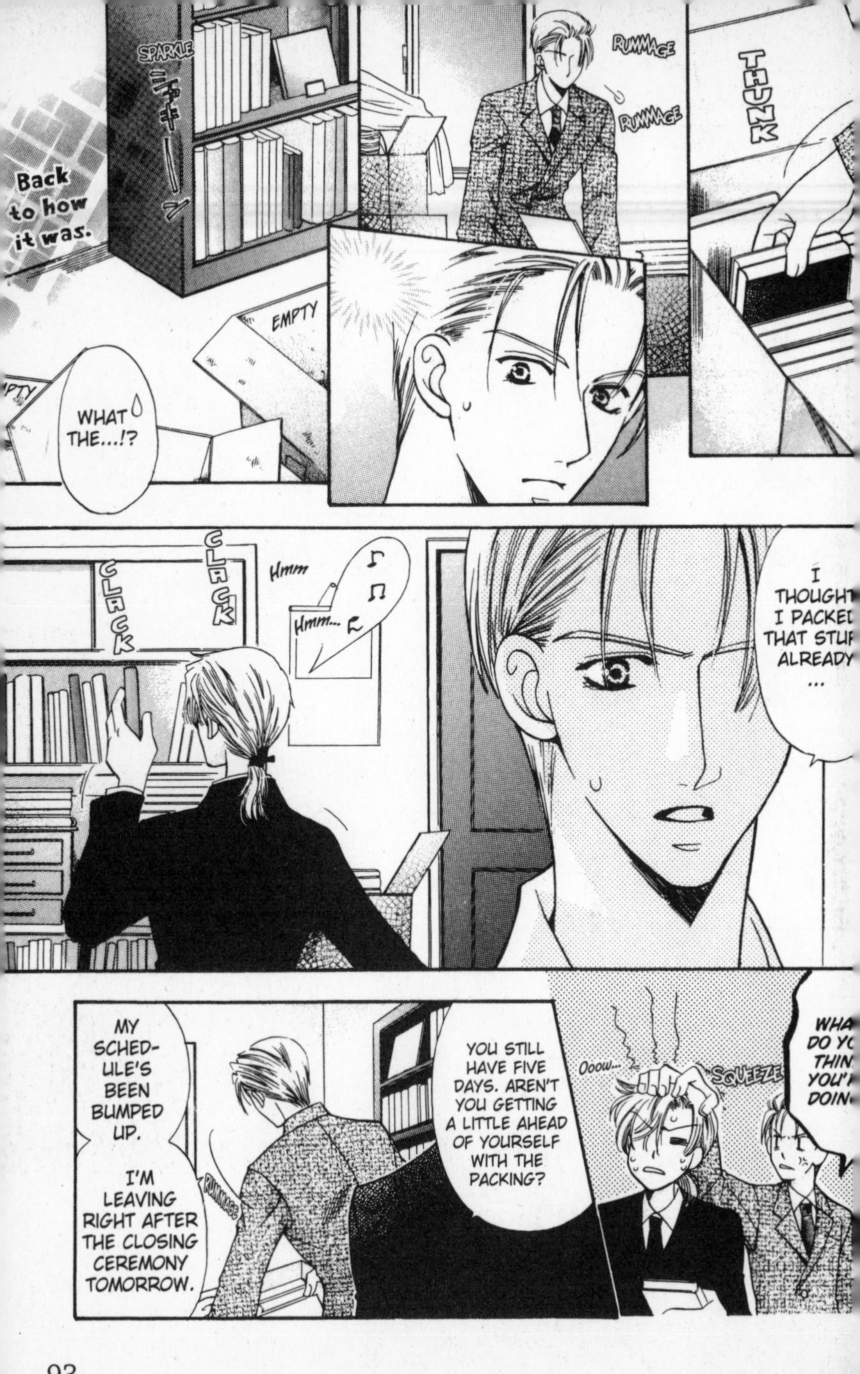
THUNK
RUMMAGE
RUMMAGE
SPARKLE
Back to how it was.
EMPTY
EMPTY
WHAT THE...!?
I THOUGHT I PACKED THAT STUF ALREADY ...
Hmm
Hmm...
CLACK
CLACK
WHA DO YO THIN YOU'I DOIN
SQUEEZE
Ooow...
YOU STILL HAVE FIVE DAYS. AREN'T YOU GETTING A LITTLE AHEAD OF YOURSELF WITH THE PACKING?
MY SCHED-ULE'S BEEN BUMPED UP.
RUMMAGE
I'M LEAVING RIGHT AFTER THE CLOSING CEREMONY TOMORROW.

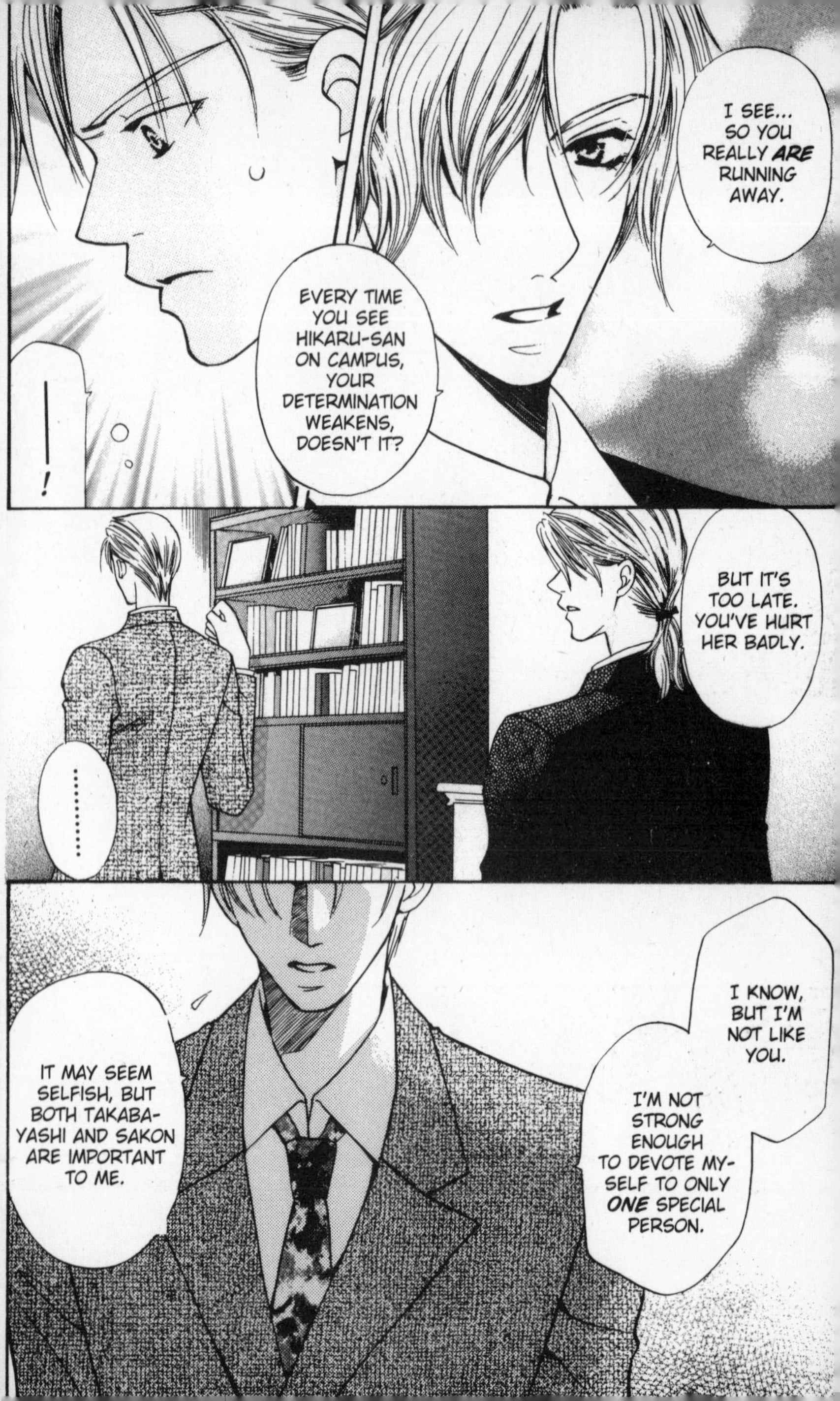
I SEE... SO YOU REALLY ARE RUNNING AWAY.
EVERY TIME YOU SEE HIKARU-SAN ON CAMPUS, YOUR DETERMINATION WEAKENS, DOESN'T IT?
!
BUT IT'S TOO LATE. YOU'VE HURT HER BADLY.
......
I KNOW, BUT I'M NOT LIKE YOU.
I'M NOT STRONG ENOUGH TO DEVOTE MY-SELF TO ONLY ONE SPECIAL PERSON.
IT MAY SEEM SELFISH, BUT BOTH TAKABA-YASHI AND SAKON ARE IMPORTANT TO ME.

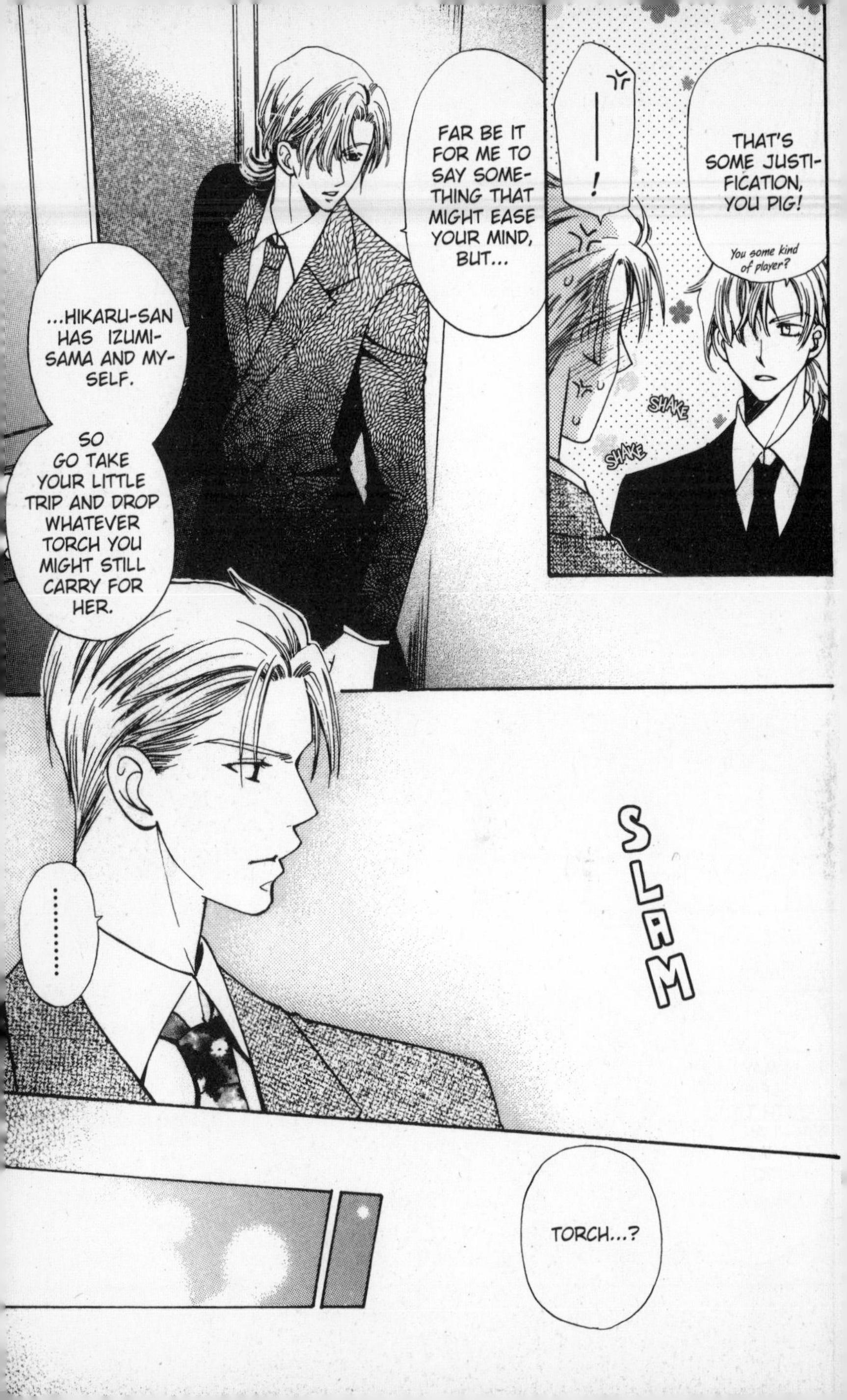
THAT'S SOME JUSTI-FICATION, YOU PIG!
You some kind of player?
—!
SHAKE
SHAKE
FAR BE IT FOR ME TO SAY SOME-THING THAT MIGHT EASE YOUR MIND, BUT...
...HIKARU-SAN HAS IZUMI-SAMA AND MY-SELF.
SO GO TAKE YOUR LITTLE TRIP AND DROP WHATEVER TORCH YOU MIGHT STILL CARRY FOR HER.
SLAM
....
TORCH...?

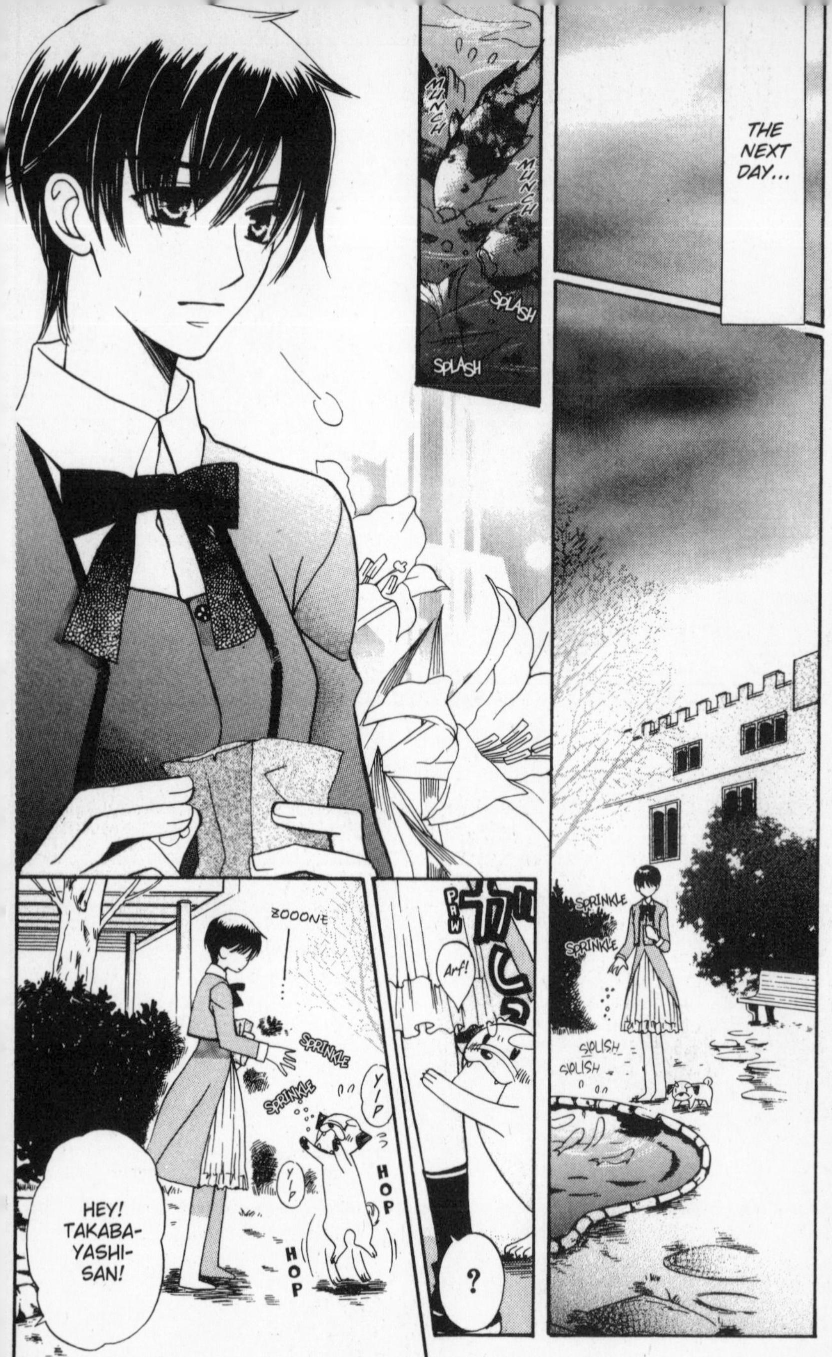
THE NEXT DAY...
SPRINKLE
SPRINKLE
SPLISH
SPLISH
MUNCH
MUNCH
SPLASH
SPLASH
PAW
Arf!
?
ZOOONE
SPRINKLE
SPRINKLE
YIP
YIP
HOP
HOP
HEY! TAKABA-YASHI-SAN!

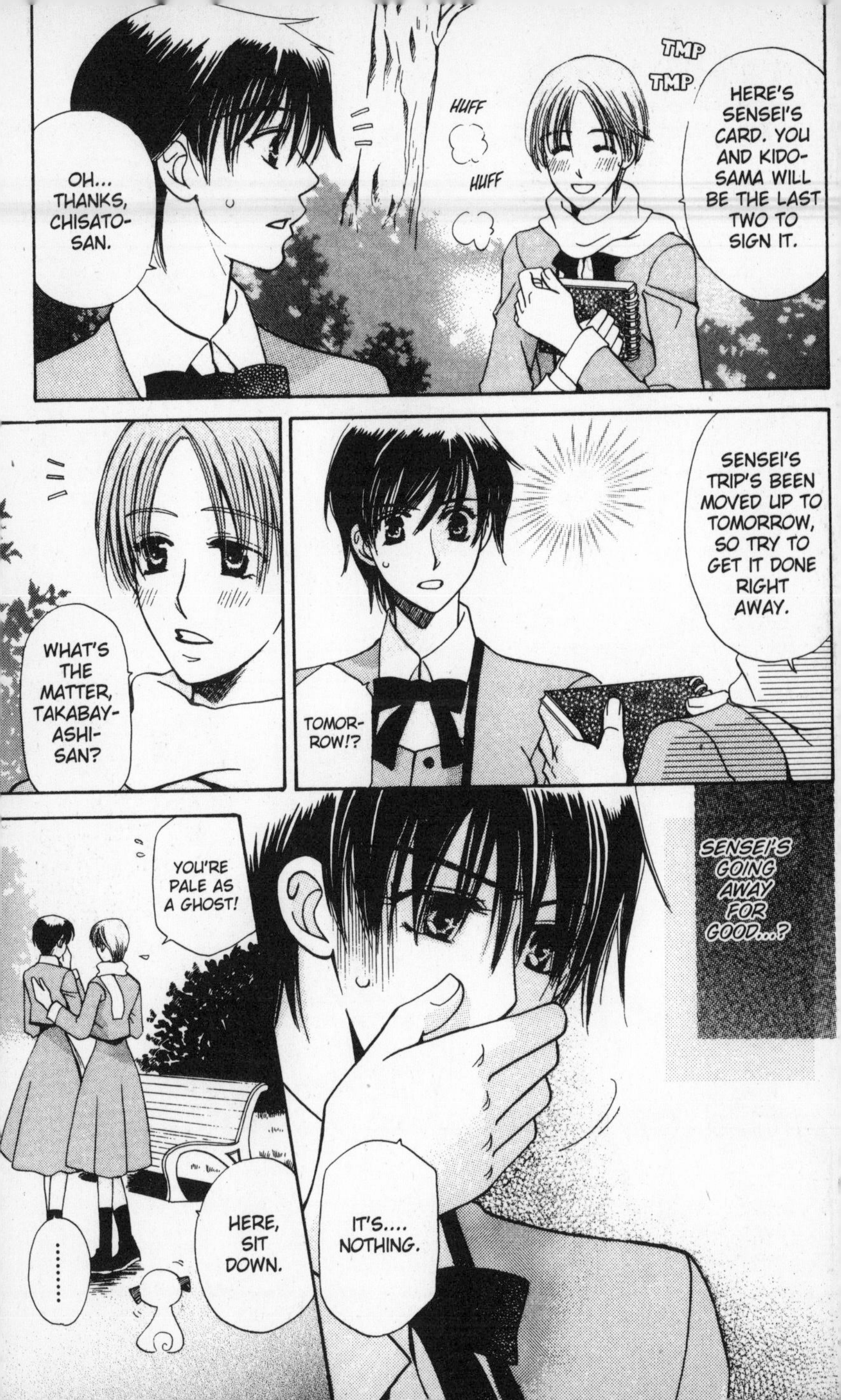
TMP
TMP
HERE'S SENSEI'S CARD. YOU AND KIDO-SAMA WILL BE THE LAST TWO TO SIGN IT.
HUFF
HUFF
OH... THANKS, CHISATO-SAN.
SENSEI'S TRIP'S BEEN MOVED UP TO TOMORROW, SO TRY TO GET IT DONE RIGHT AWAY.
TOMOR-ROW!?
WHAT'S THE MATTER, TAKABAY-ASHI-SAN?
SENSEI'S GOING AWAY FOR GOOD...?
YOU'RE PALE AS A GHOST!
IT'S.... NOTHING.
HERE, SIT DOWN.
......

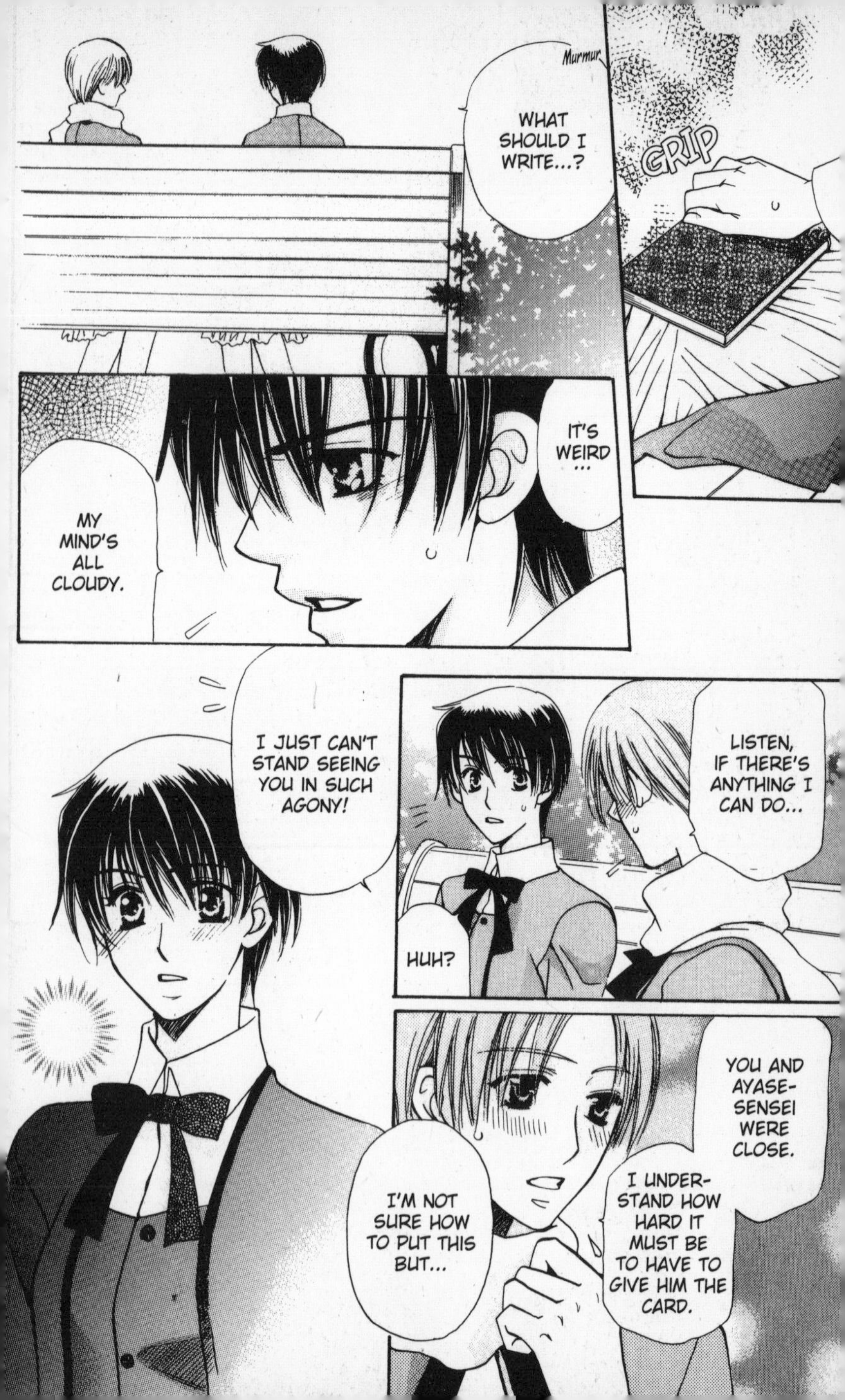
GRIP
Murmur
WHAT SHOULD I WRITE...?
IT'S WEIRD...
MY MIND'S ALL CLOUDY.
LISTEN, IF THERE'S ANYTHING I CAN DO...
HUH?
YOU AND AYASE-SENSEI WERE CLOSE.
I UNDER-STAND HOW HARD IT MUST BE TO HAVE TO GIVE HIM THE CARD.
I'M NOT SURE HOW TO PUT THIS BUT...
I JUST CAN'T STAND SEEING YOU IN SUCH AGONY!

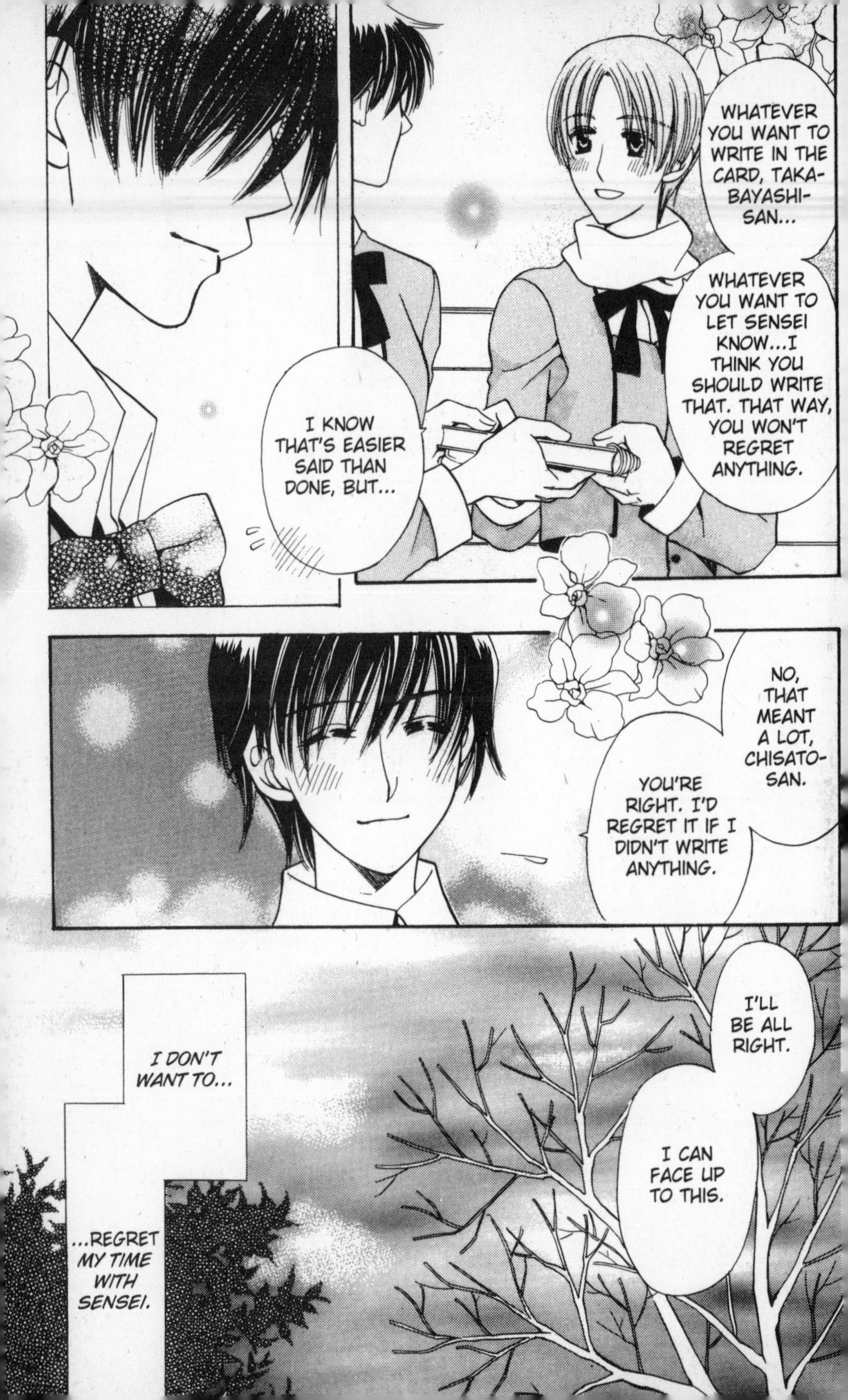
WHATEVER YOU WANT TO WRITE IN THE CARD, TAKA-BAYASHI-SAN...
WHATEVER YOU WANT TO LET SENSEI KNOW...I THINK YOU SHOULD WRITE THAT. THAT WAY, YOU WON'T REGRET ANYTHING.
I KNOW THAT'S EASIER SAID THAN DONE, BUT...
NO, THAT MEANT A LOT, CHISATO-SAN.
YOU'RE RIGHT. I'D REGRET IT IF I DIDN'T WRITE ANYTHING.
I'LL BE ALL RIGHT.
I CAN FACE UP TO THIS.
I DON'T WANT TO...
...REGRET MY TIME WITH SENSEI.

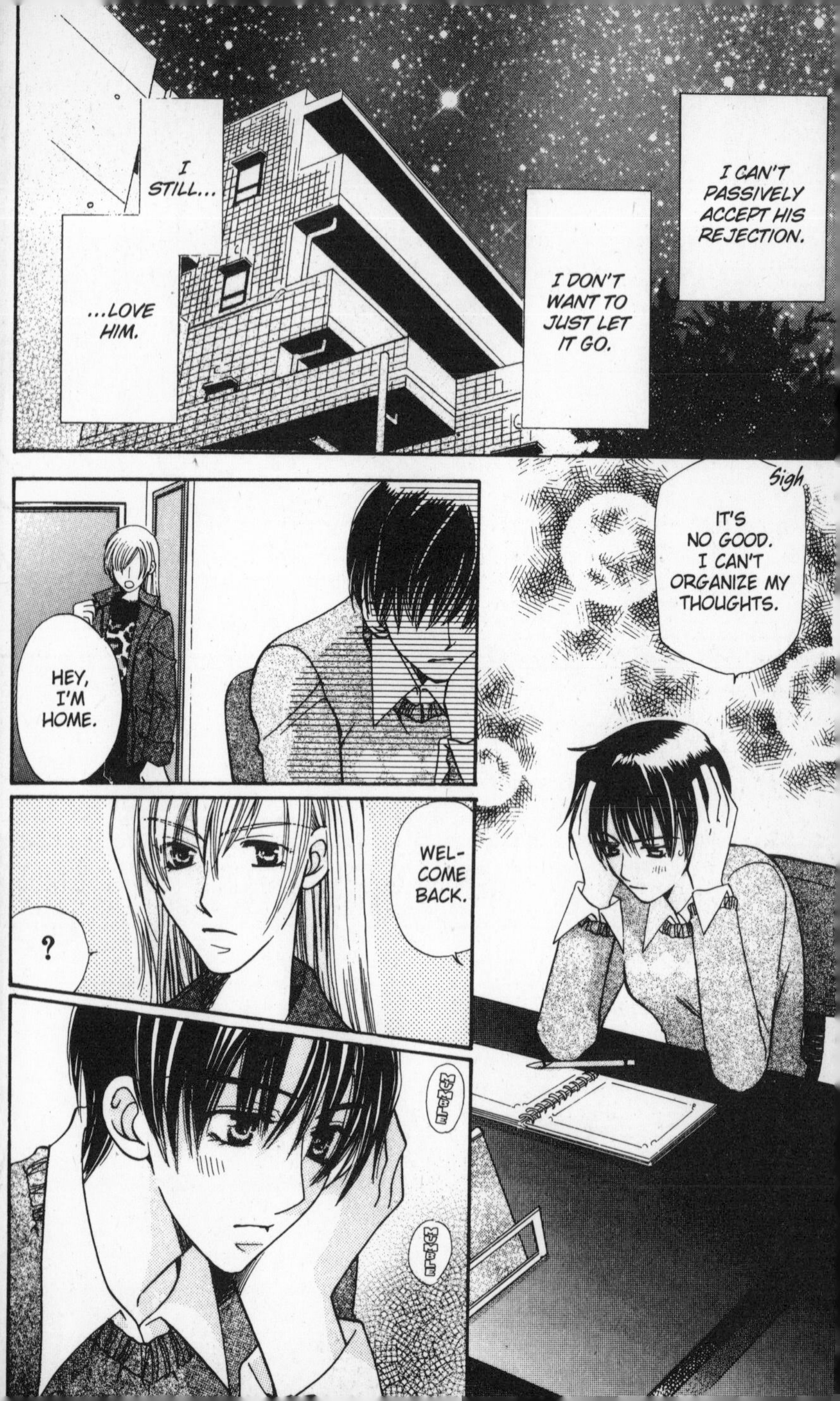
I CAN'T PASSIVELY ACCEPT HIS REJECTION.
I DON'T WANT TO JUST LET IT GO.
I STILL...
...LOVE HIM.
Sigh
IT'S NO GOOD. I CAN'T ORGANIZE MY THOUGHTS.
HEY, I'M HOME.
WEL-COME BACK.
?
MUMBLE
MUMBLE

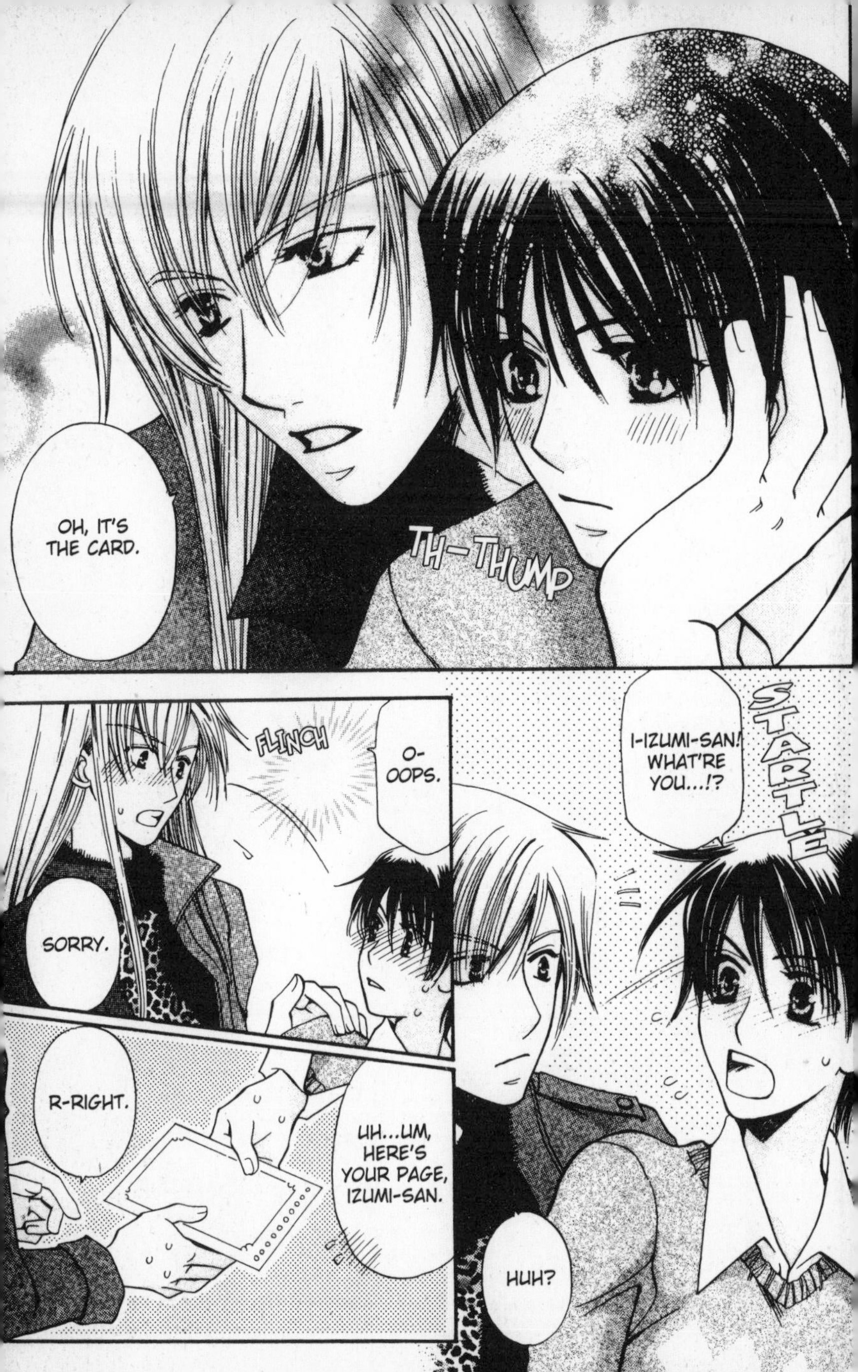
OH, IT'S THE CARD.
TH-THUMP
I-IZUMI-SAN! WHAT'RE YOU...!?
STARTLE
HUH?
O-OOPS.
FLINCH
SORRY.
UH...UM, HERE'S YOUR PAGE, IZUMI-SAN.
R-RIGHT.

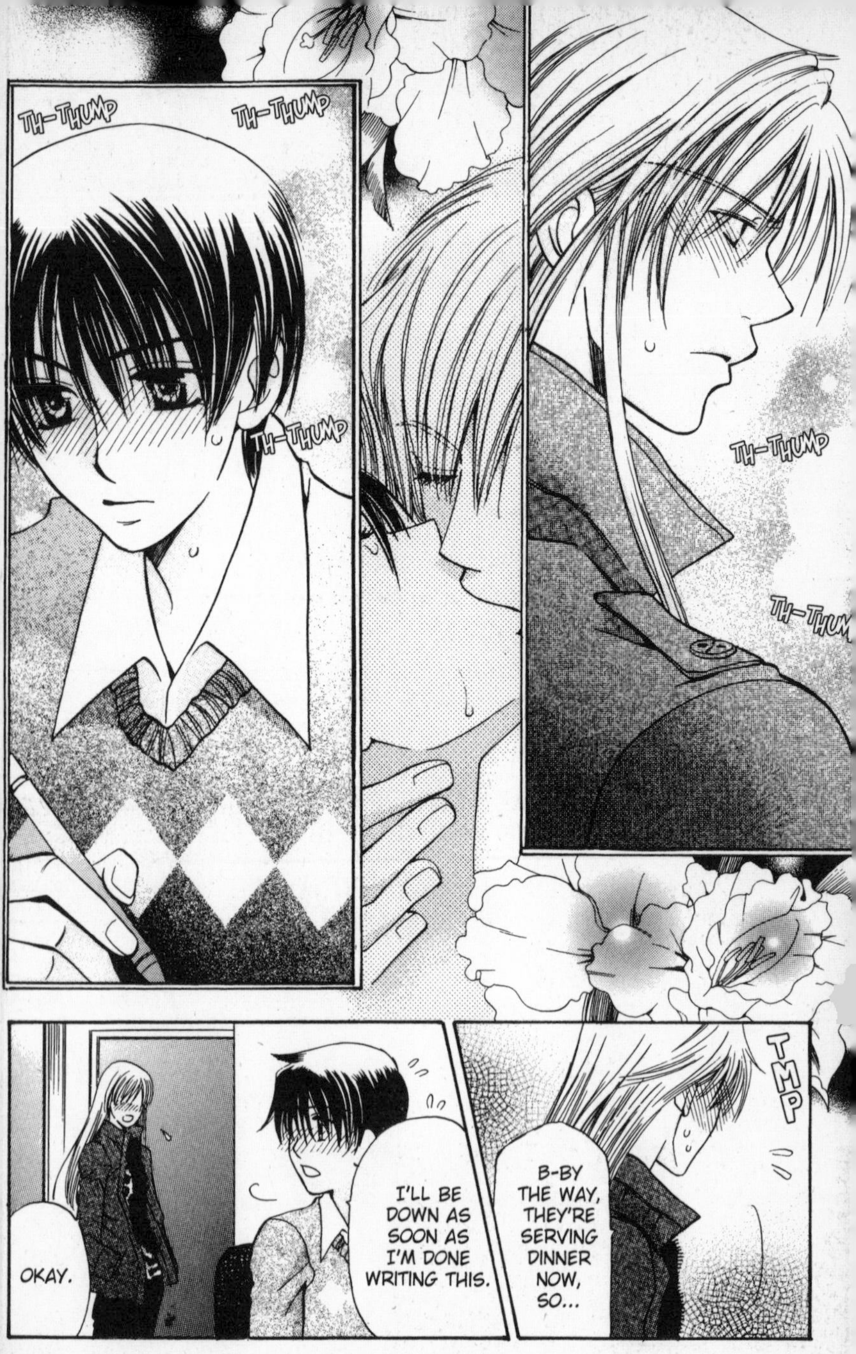
TH-THUMP
TH-THUM
TH-THUMP
TH-THUMP
TH-THUMP
TMP
B-BY THE WAY, THEY'RE SERVING DINNER NOW, SO...
I'LL BE DOWN AS SOON AS I'M DONE WRITING THIS.
OKAY.

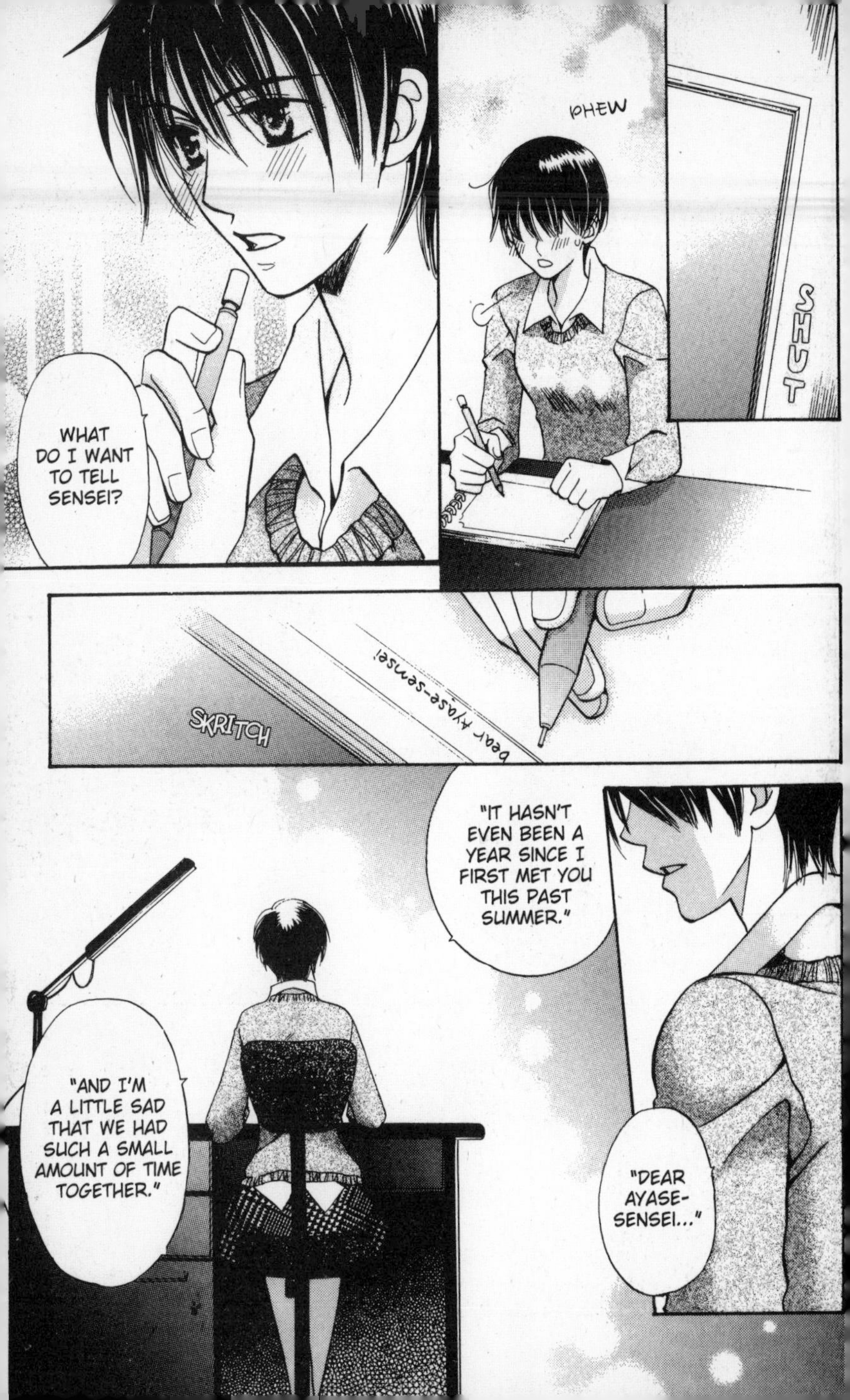
SHUT
PHEW
WHAT DO I WANT TO TELL SENSEI?
SKRITCH
Dear Ayase-sensei!
"DEAR AYASE-SENSEI..."
"IT HASN'T EVEN BEEN A YEAR SINCE I FIRST MET YOU THIS PAST SUMMER."
"AND I'M A LITTLE SAD THAT WE HAD SUCH A SMALL AMOUNT OF TIME TOGETHER."

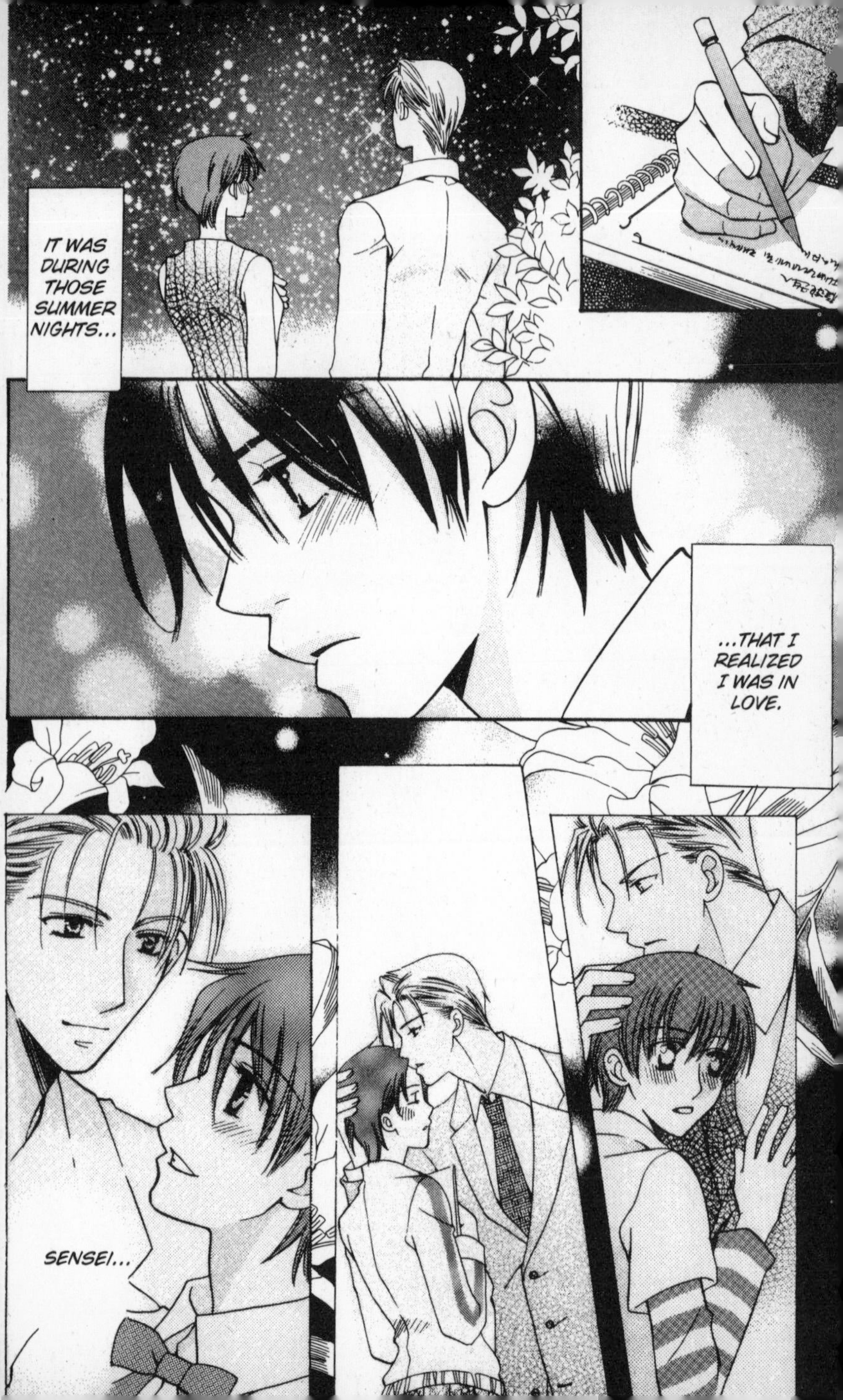
IT WAS DURING THOSE SUMMER NIGHTS...
...THAT I REALIZED I WAS IN LOVE.
SENSEI...

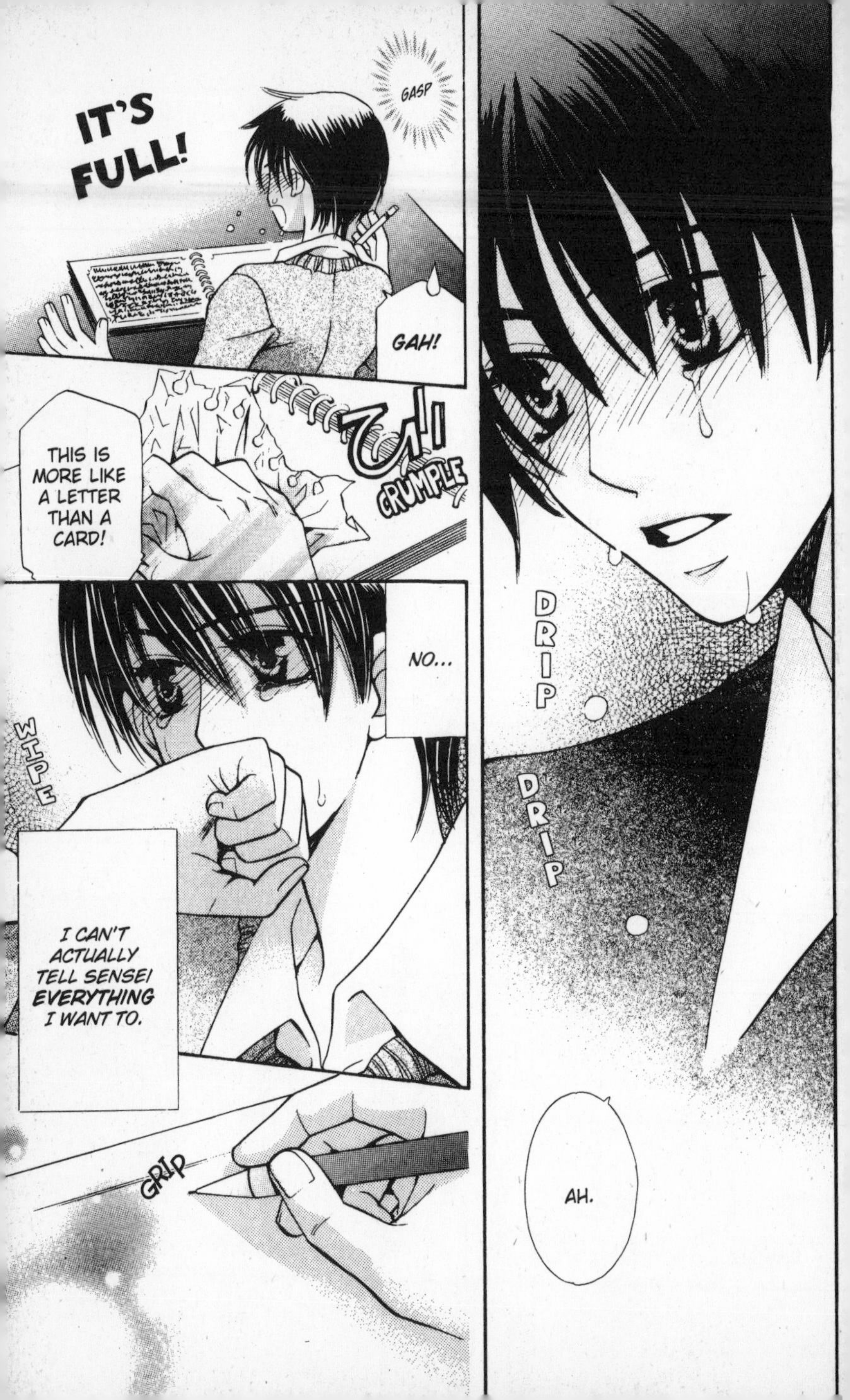
DRIP
DRIP
DRIP
DRIP
AH.
GASP
IT'S FULL!
GAH!
CRUMPLE
THIS IS MORE LIKE A LETTER THAN A CARD!
NO...
WIPE
I CAN'T ACTUALLY TELL SENSEI **EVERYTHING** I WANT TO.
GRIP

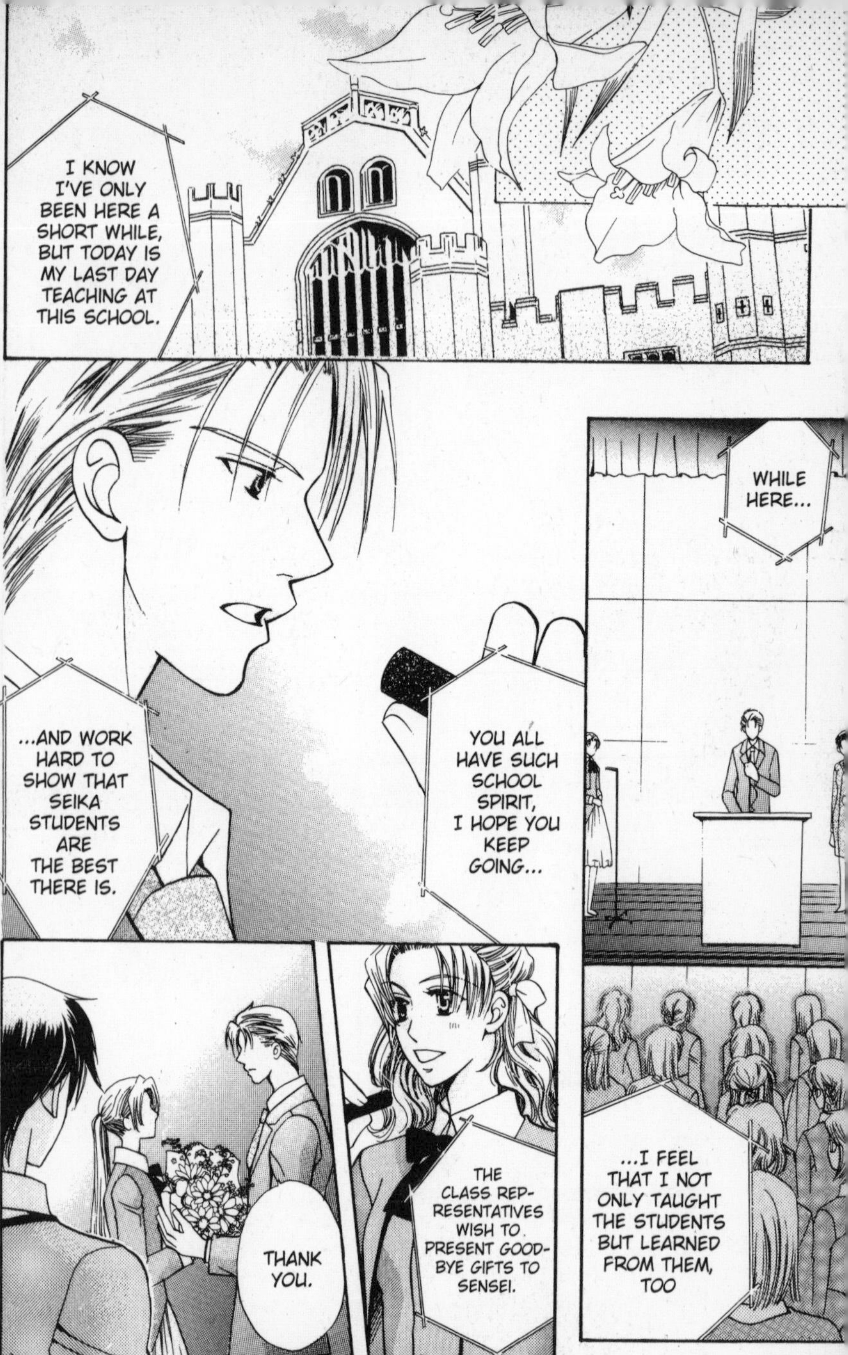
I KNOW I'VE ONLY BEEN HERE A SHORT WHILE, BUT TODAY IS MY LAST DAY TEACHING AT THIS SCHOOL.
WHILE HERE...
...I FEEL THAT I NOT ONLY TAUGHT THE STUDENTS BUT LEARNED FROM THEM, TOO
YOU ALL HAVE SUCH SCHOOL SPIRIT, I HOPE YOU KEEP GOING...
...AND WORK HARD TO SHOW THAT SEIKA STUDENTS ARE THE BEST THERE IS.
THE CLASS REP-RESENTATIVES WISH TO PRESENT GOOD-BYE GIFTS TO SENSEI.
THANK YOU.

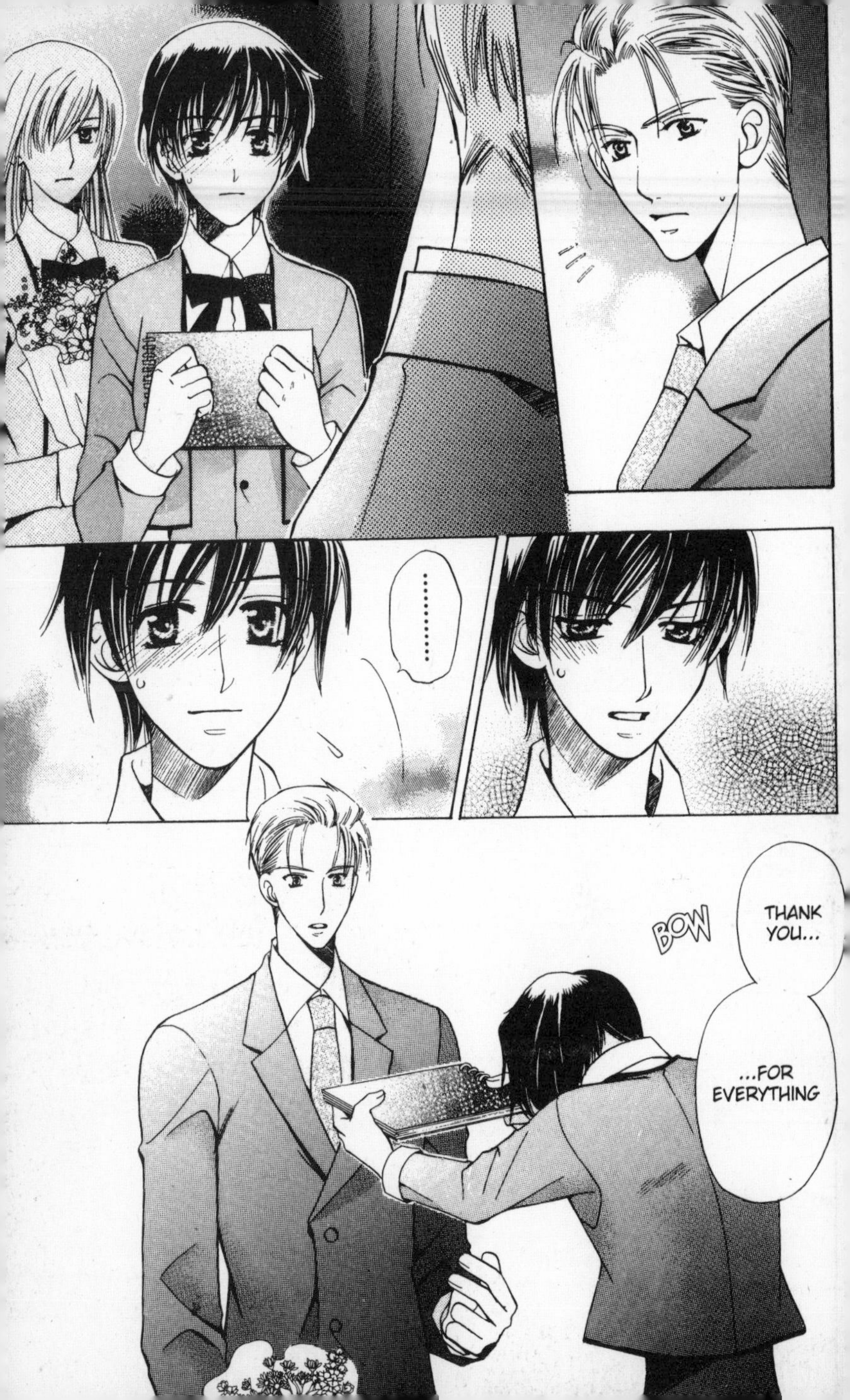

......
BOW
THANK YOU...
...FOR EVERYTHING

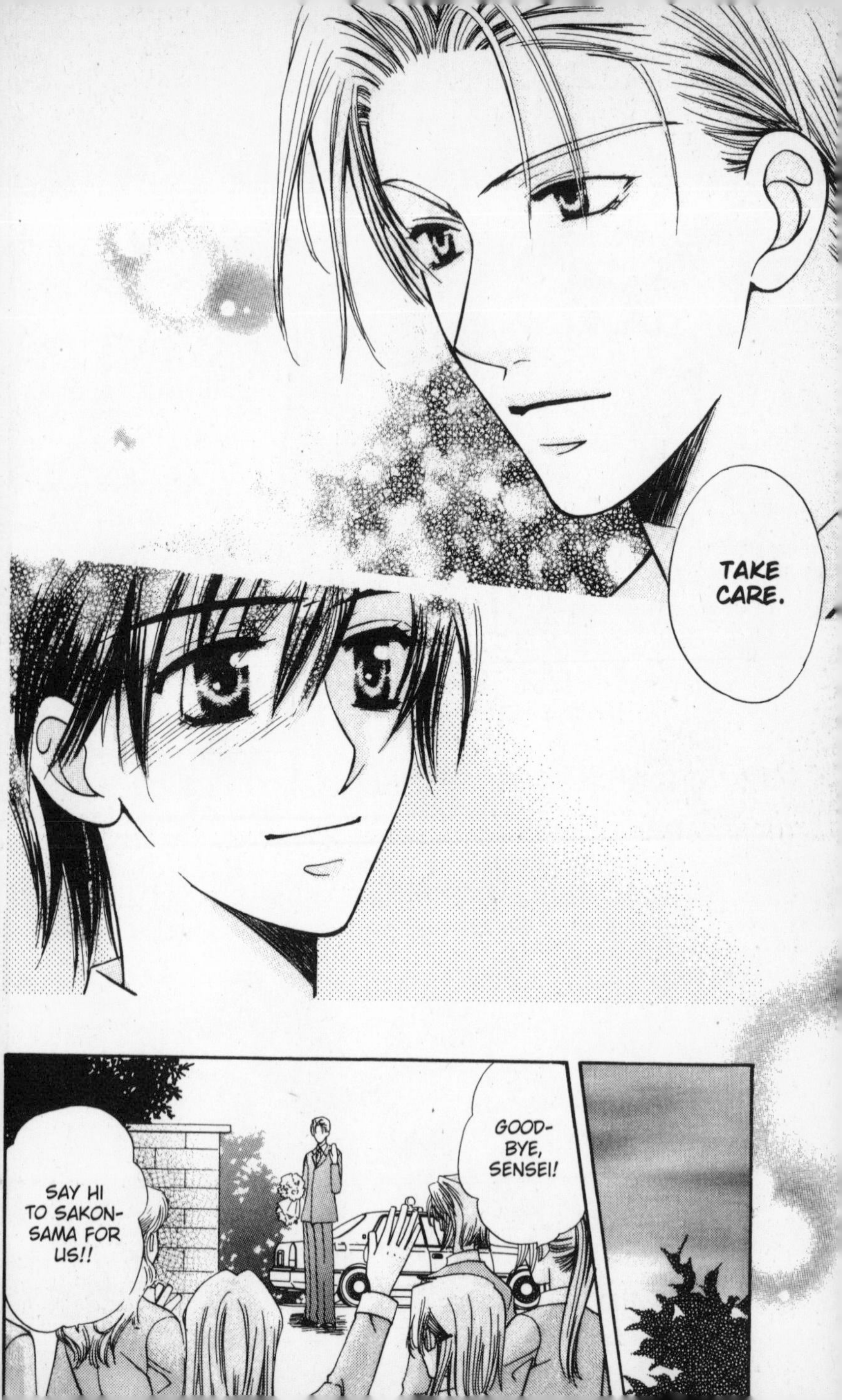
TAKE CARE.
GOOD-BYE, SENSEI!
SAY HI TO SAKON-SAMA FOR US!!

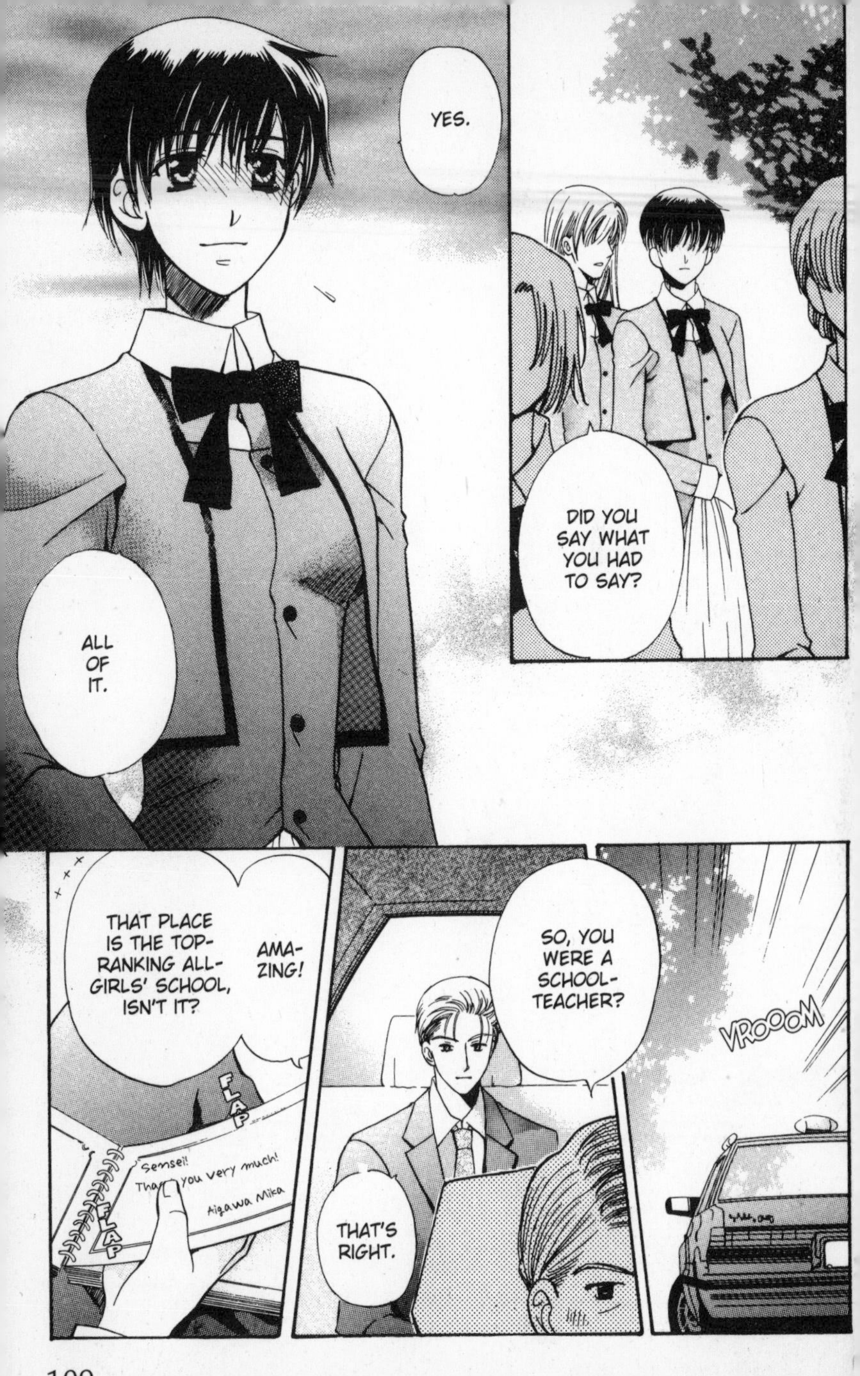
DID YOU SAY WHAT YOU HAD TO SAY?
YES.
ALL OF IT.
VROOOM
SO, YOU WERE A SCHOOL-TEACHER?
THAT'S RIGHT.
AMA-ZING!
THAT PLACE IS THE TOP-RANKING ALL-GIRLS' SCHOOL, ISN'T IT?
FLAP
FLAP
Sensei!
Tha you very much!
Aigawa Mika

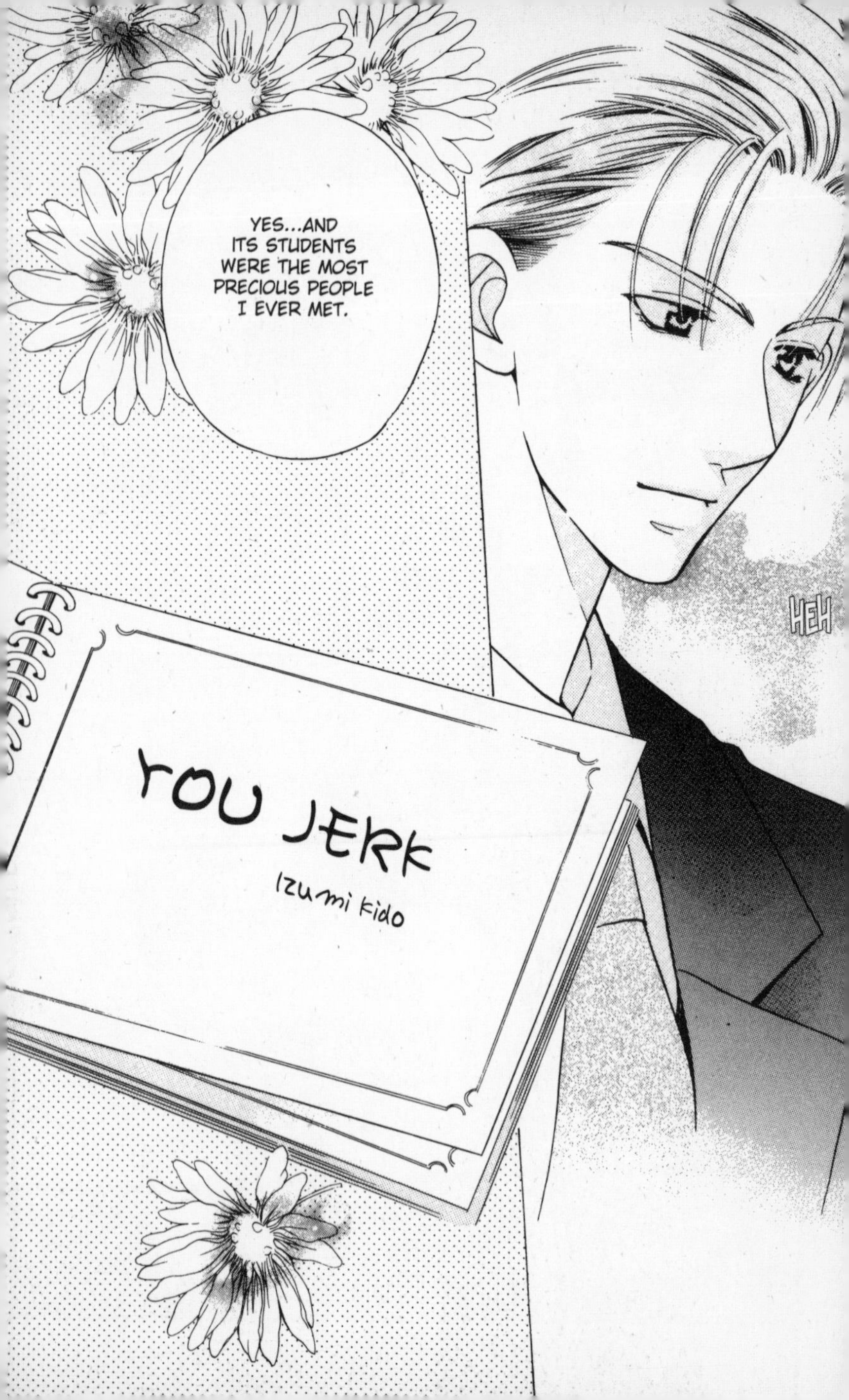
YES...AND ITS STUDENTS WERE THE MOST PRECIOUS PEOPLE I EVER MET.
HEH
YOU JERK
Izumi Kido

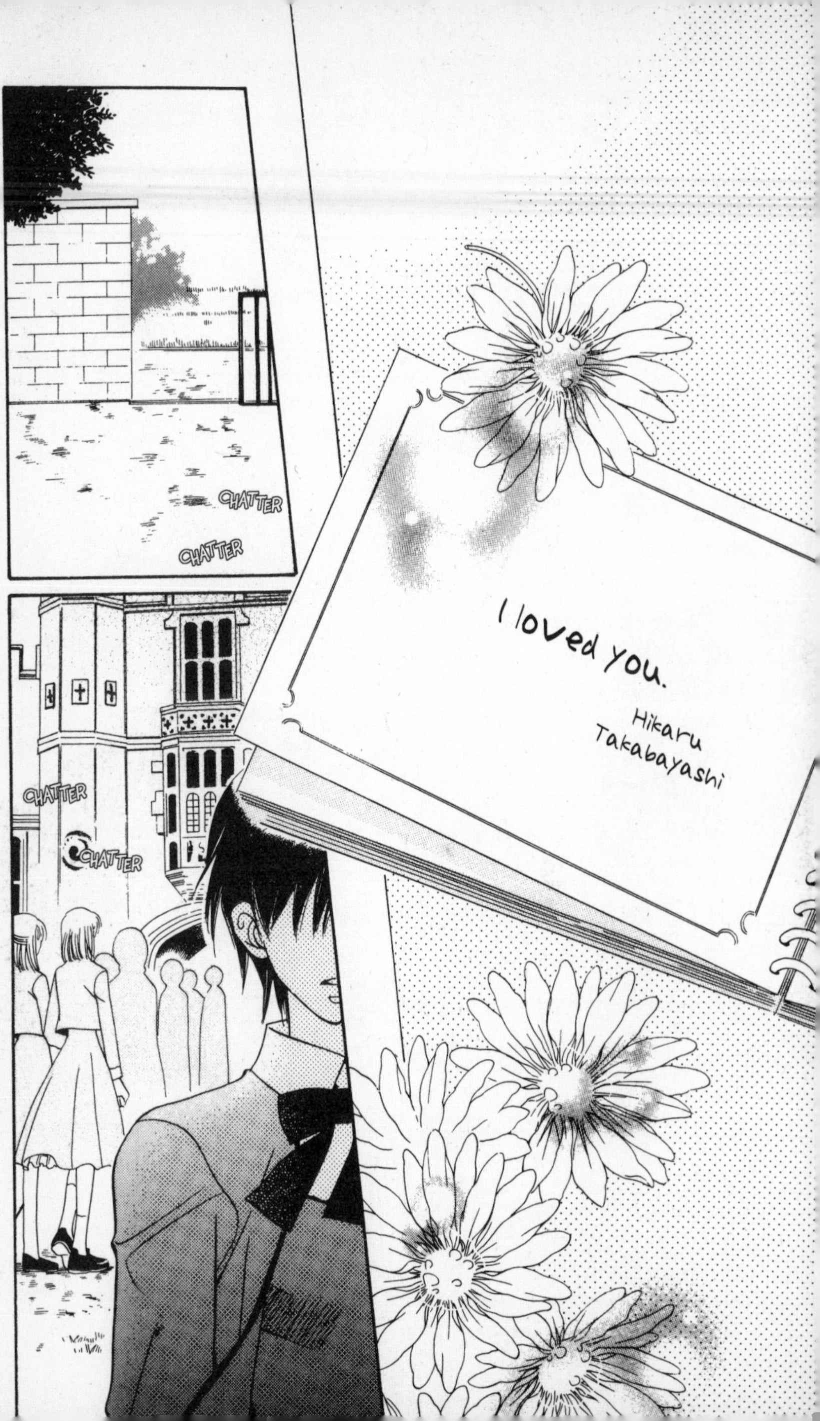
I loved you.
Hikaru Takabayashi
CHATTER
CHATTER
CHATTER
CHATTER

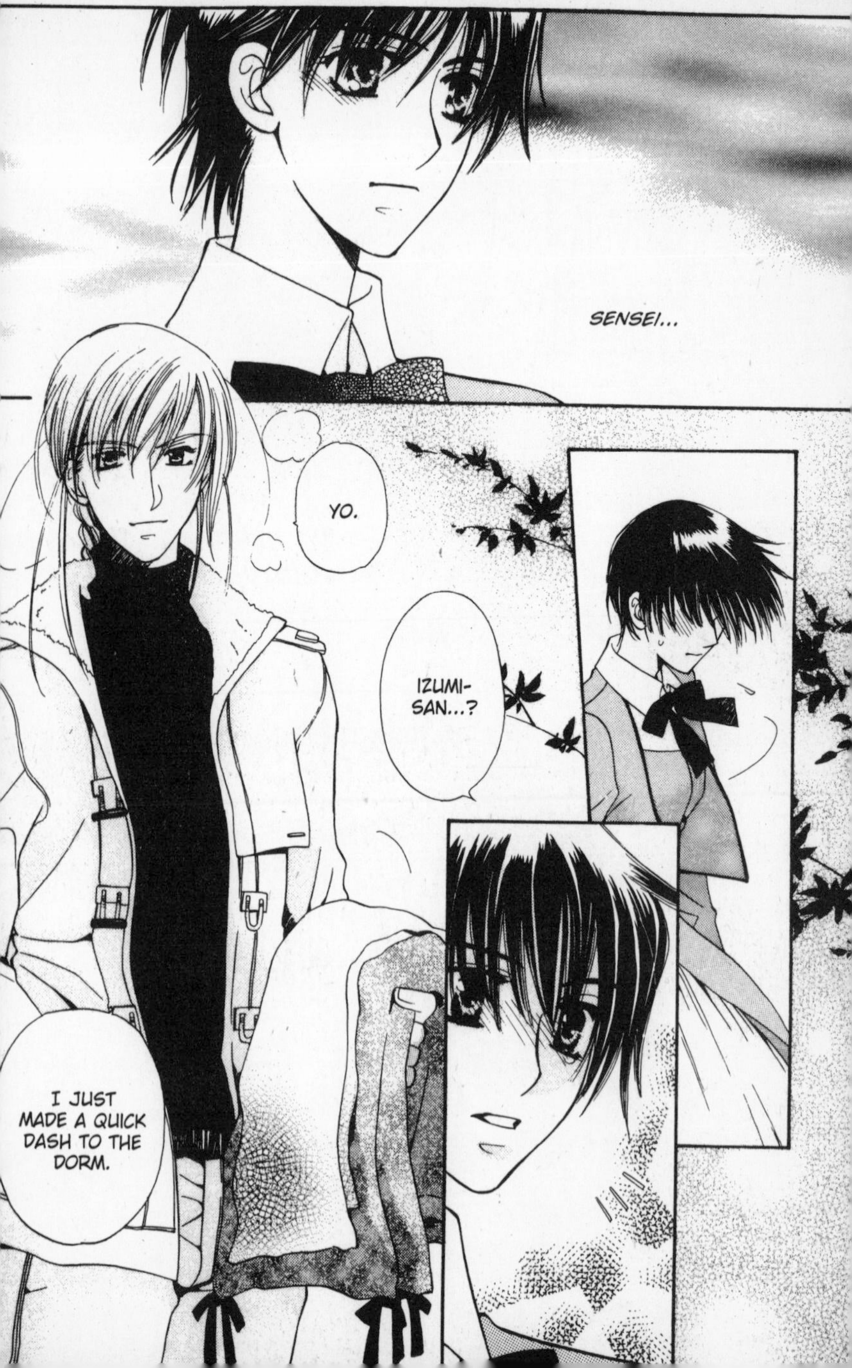
SENSEI...
YO.
IZUMI-SAN...?
I JUST MADE A QUICK DASH TO THE DORM.

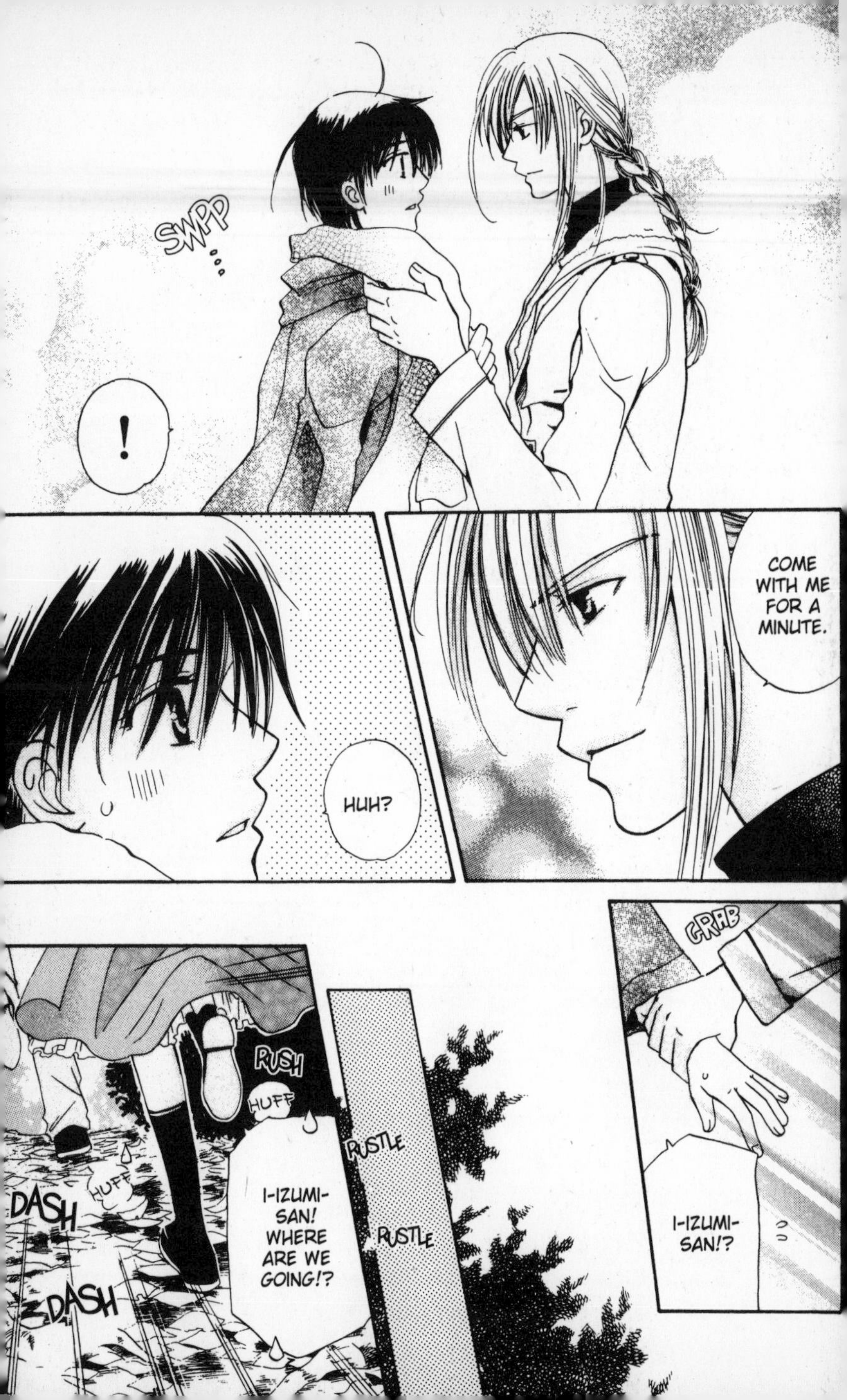
SWPP
!
COME WITH ME FOR A MINUTE.
HUH?
GRAB
I-IZUMI-SAN!?
RUSTLE
RUSTLE
RUSH
HUFF
I-IZUMI-SAN! WHERE ARE WE GOING!?
HUFF
DASH
DASH

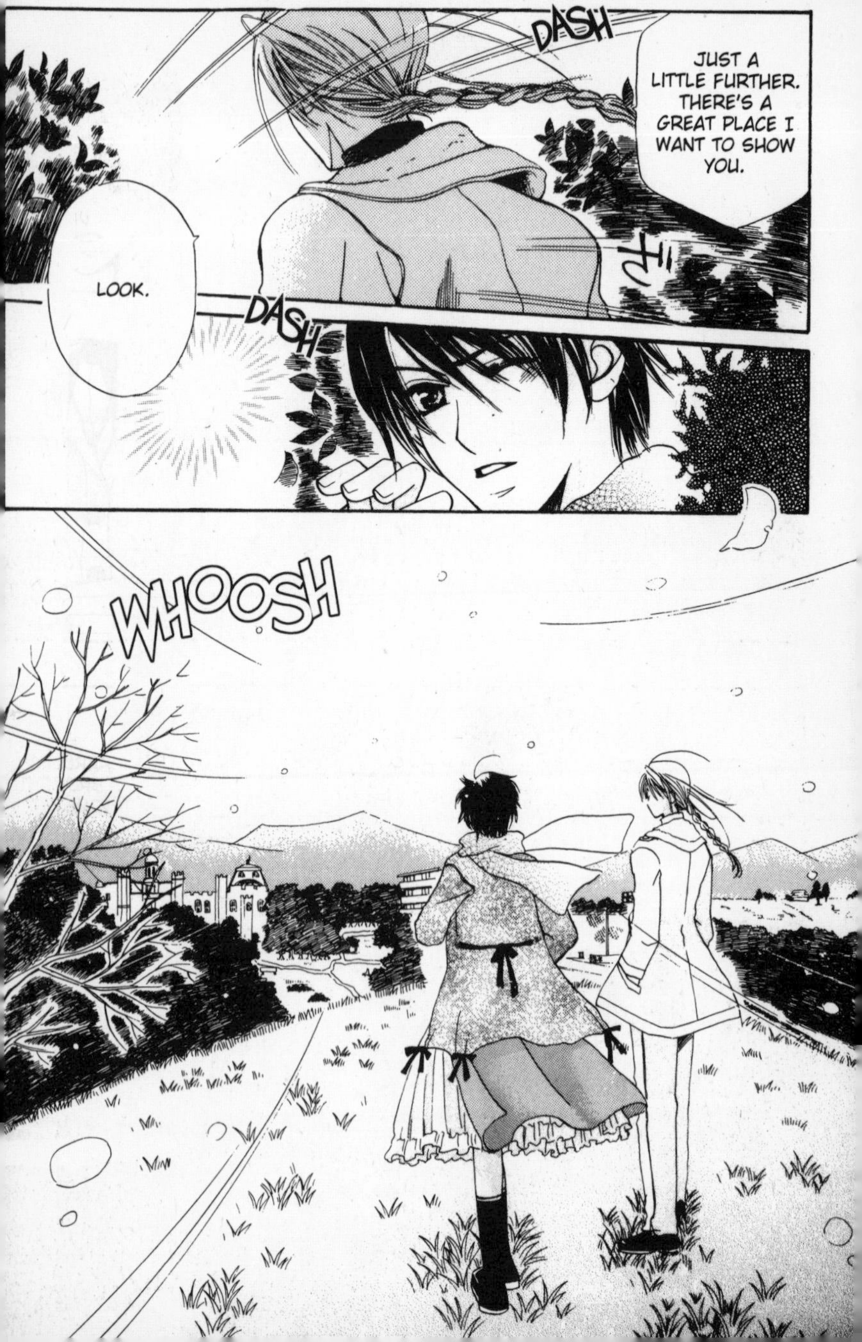
DASH
JUST A LITTLE FURTHER. THERE'S A GREAT PLACE I WANT TO SHOW YOU.
DASH
LOOK.
WHOOSH

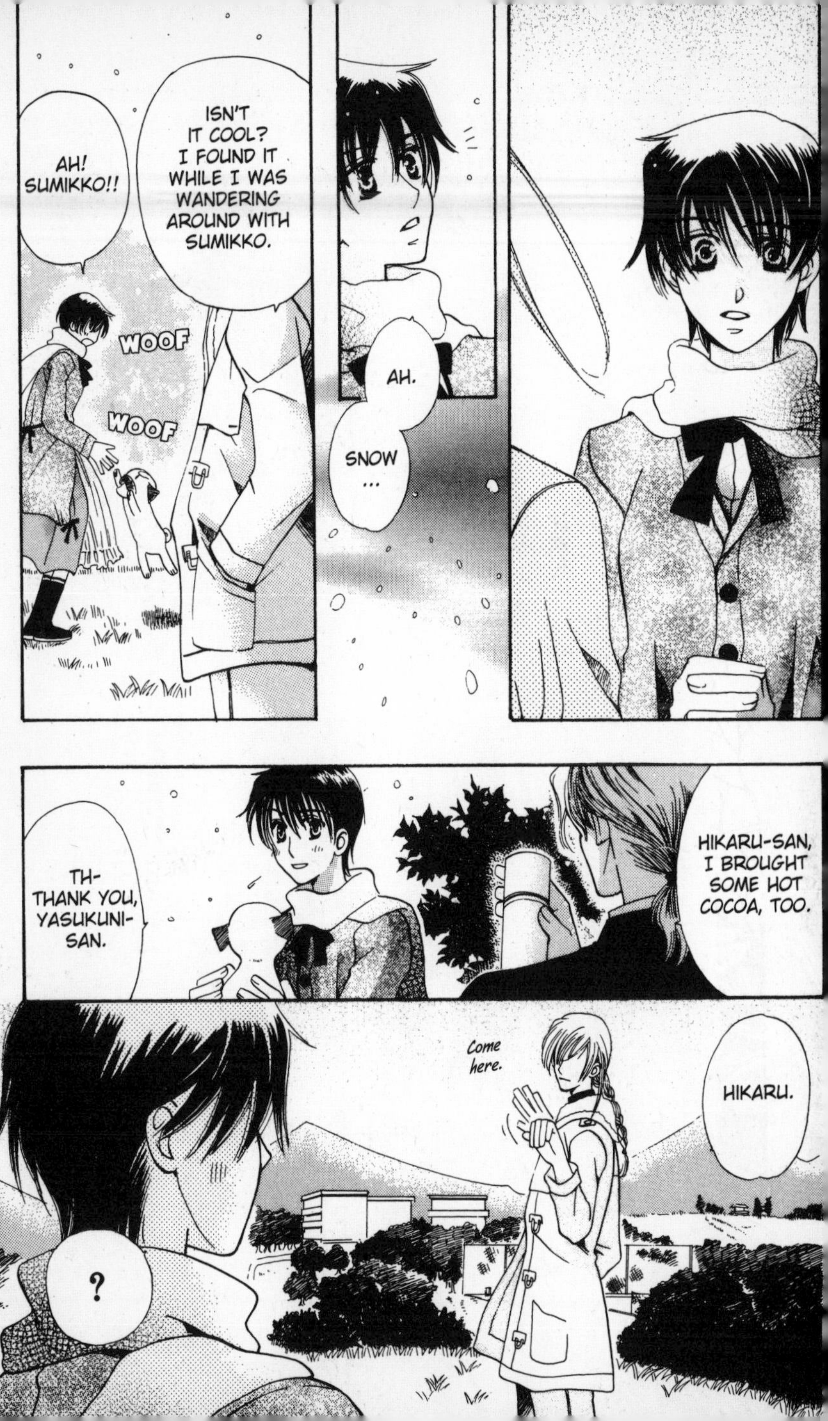
AH.
SNOW ...
ISN'T IT COOL? I FOUND IT WHILE I WAS WANDERING AROUND WITH SUMIKKO.
AH! SUMIKKO!!
WOOF
WOOF
HIKARU-SAN, I BROUGHT SOME HOT COCOA, TOO.
TH-THANK YOU, YASUKUNI-SAN.
HIKARU.
Come here.
?

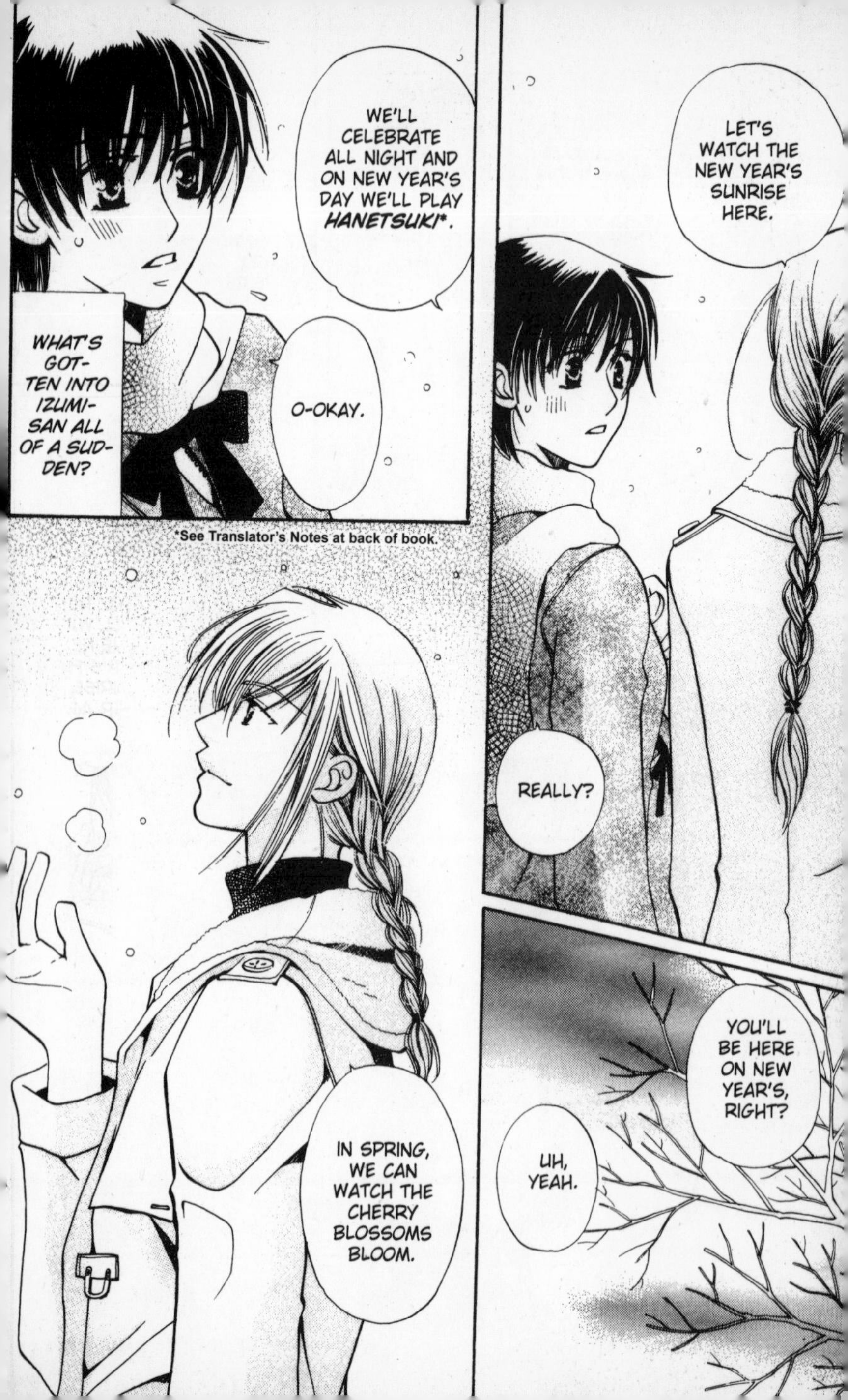
LET'S WATCH THE NEW YEAR'S SUNRISE HERE.
REALLY?
YOU'LL BE HERE ON NEW YEAR'S, RIGHT?
UH, YEAH.
WE'LL CELEBRATE ALL NIGHT AND ON NEW YEAR'S DAY WE'LL PLAY *HANETSUKI**.
O-OKAY.
WHAT'S GOT-TEN INTO IZUMI-SAN ALL OF A SUD-DEN?
IN SPRING, WE CAN WATCH THE CHERRY BLOSSOMS BLOOM.

*See Translator's Notes at back of book.

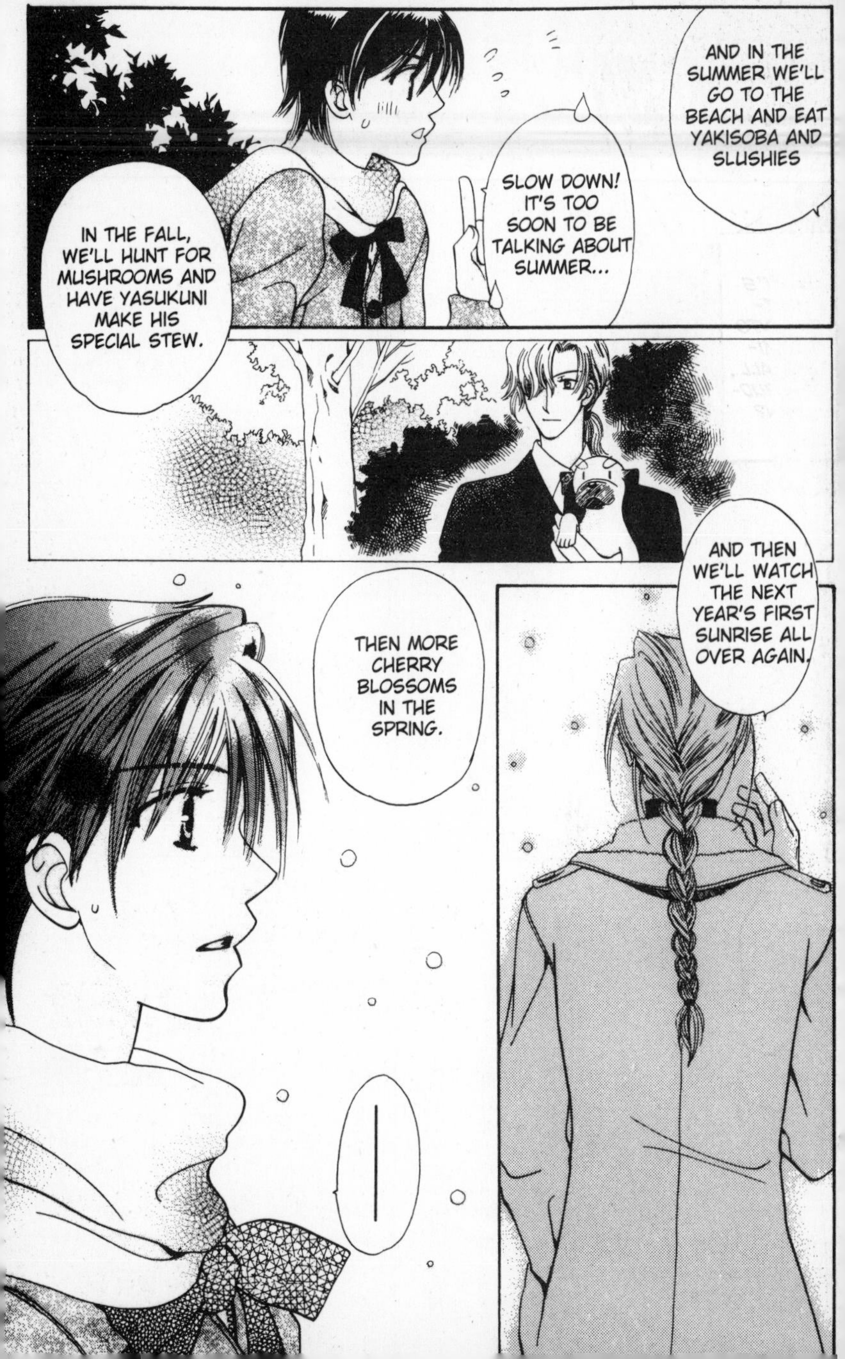
AND IN THE SUMMER WE'LL GO TO THE BEACH AND EAT YAKISOBA AND SLUSHIES
SLOW DOWN! IT'S TOO SOON TO BE TALKING ABOUT SUMMER...
IN THE FALL, WE'LL HUNT FOR MUSHROOMS AND HAVE YASUKUNI MAKE HIS SPECIAL STEW.
AND THEN WE'LL WATCH THE NEXT YEAR'S FIRST SUNRISE ALL OVER AGAIN.
THEN MORE CHERRY BLOSSOMS IN THE SPRING.

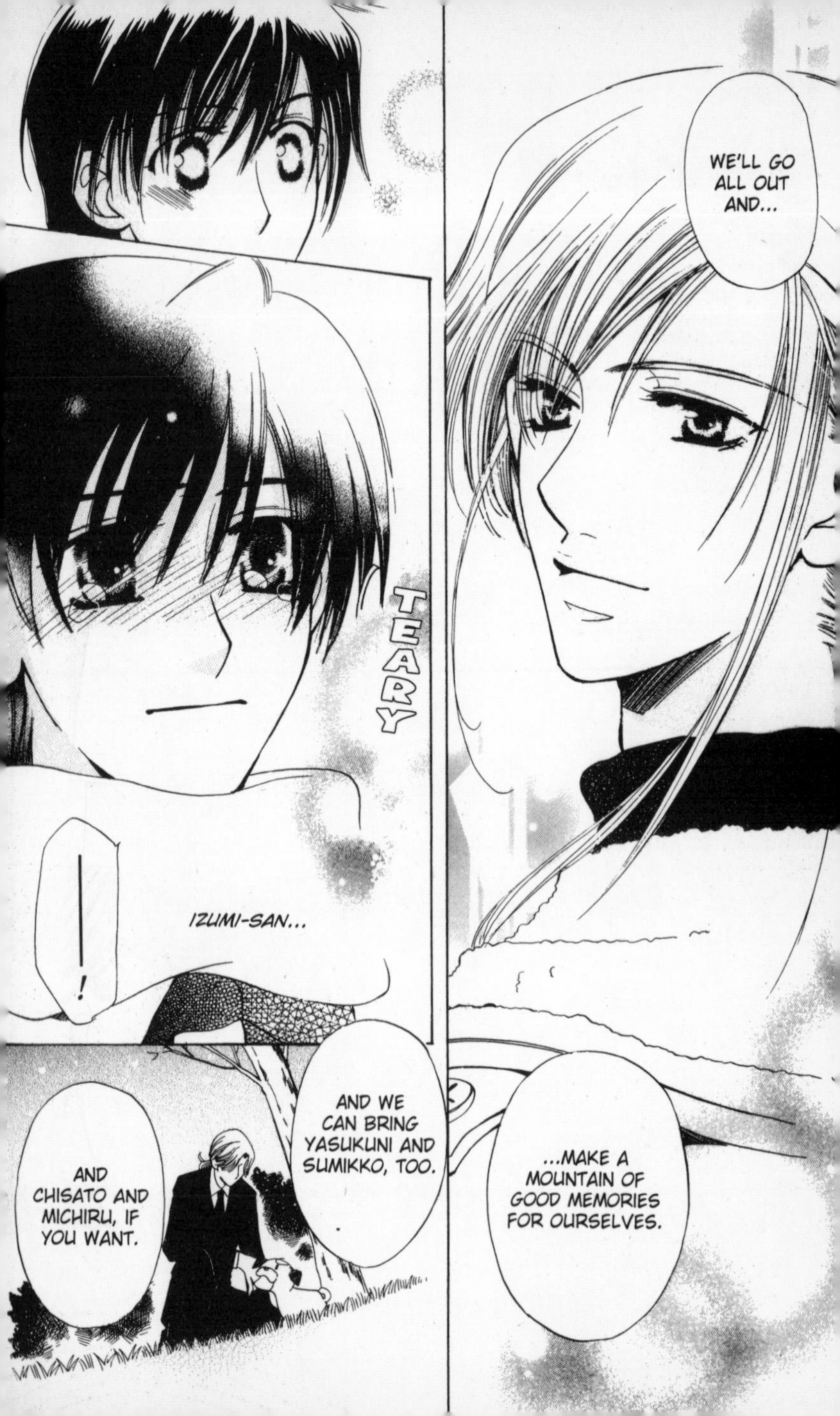
WE'LL GO ALL OUT AND...
...MAKE A MOUNTAIN OF GOOD MEMORIES FOR OURSELVES.
TEARY
IZUMI-SAN...
—!
AND WE CAN BRING YASUKUNI AND SUMIKKO, TOO.
AND CHISATO AND MICHIRU, IF YOU WANT.

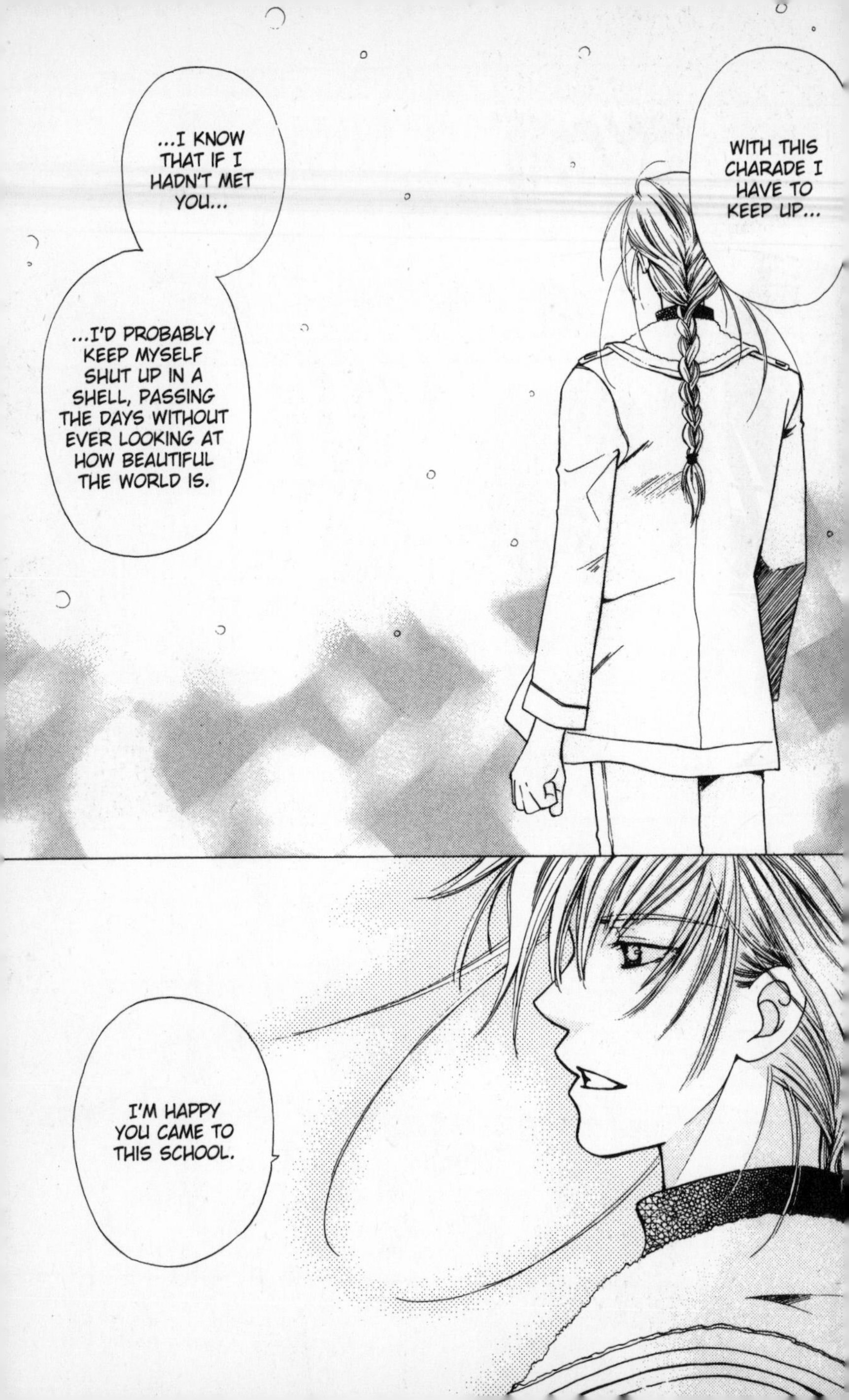
WITH THIS CHARADE I HAVE TO KEEP UP...
...I KNOW THAT IF I HADN'T MET YOU...
...I'D PROBABLY KEEP MYSELF SHUT UP IN A SHELL, PASSING THE DAYS WITHOUT EVER LOOKING AT HOW BEAUTIFUL THE WORLD IS.
I'M HAPPY YOU CAME TO THIS SCHOOL.

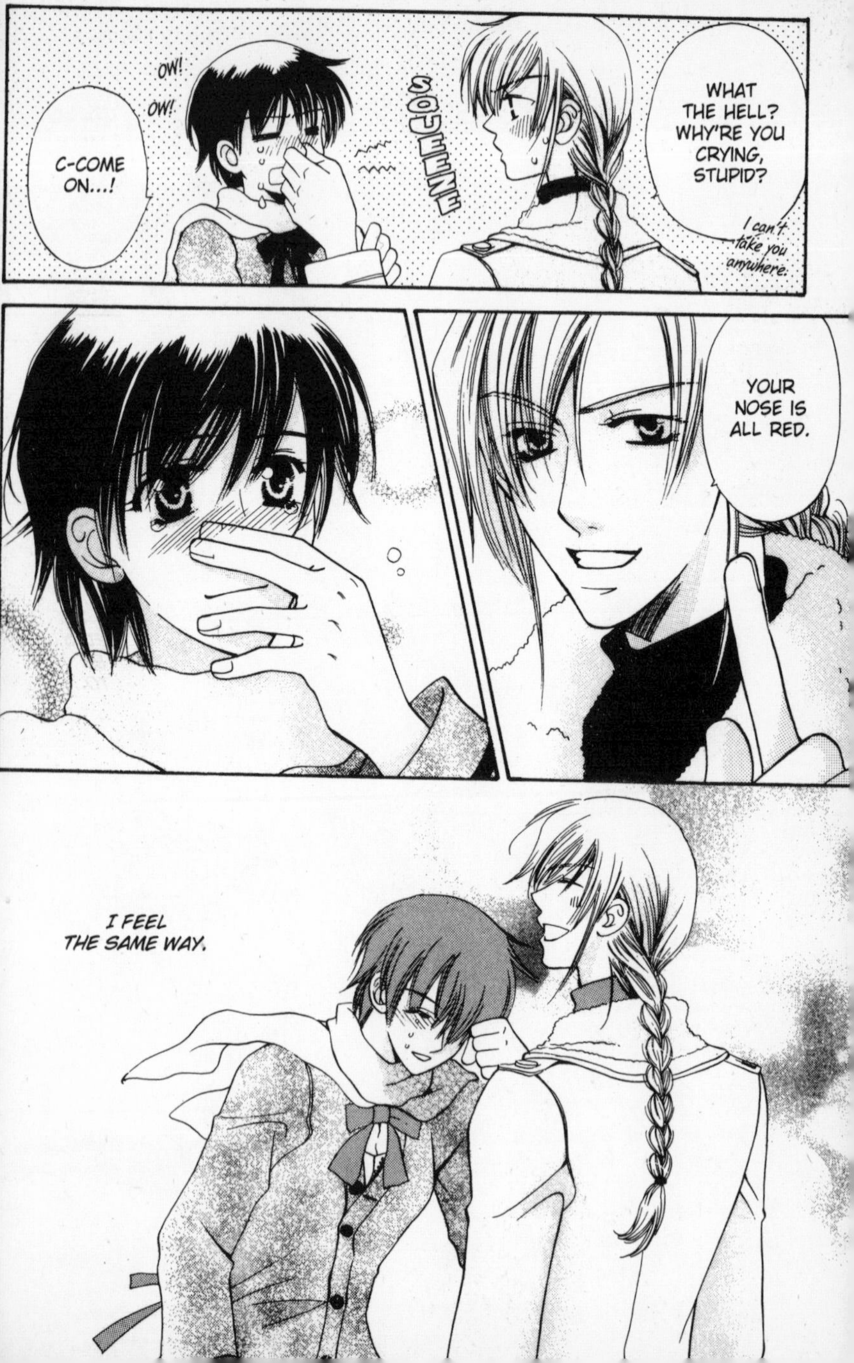
WHAT THE HELL? WHY'RE YOU CRYING, STUPID?
I can't take you anywhere.
SQUEEZE
OW!
OW!
C-COME ON...!
YOUR NOSE IS ALL RED.
I FEEL THE SAME WAY.

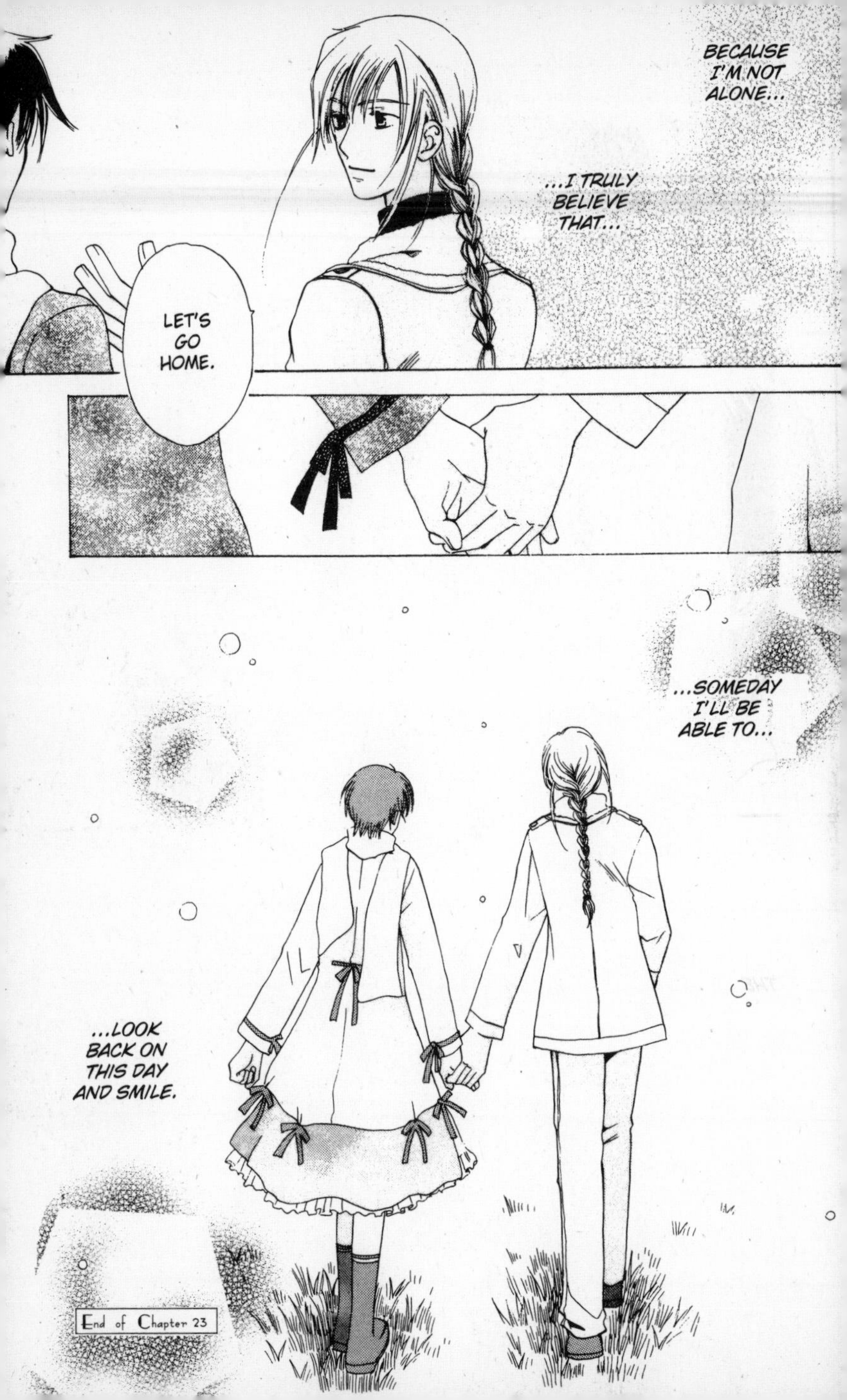
BECAUSE I'M NOT ALONE...
...I TRULY BELIEVE THAT...
LET'S GO HOME.
...SOMEDAY I'LL BE ABLE TO...
...LOOK BACK ON THIS DAY AND SMILE.
End of Chapter 23

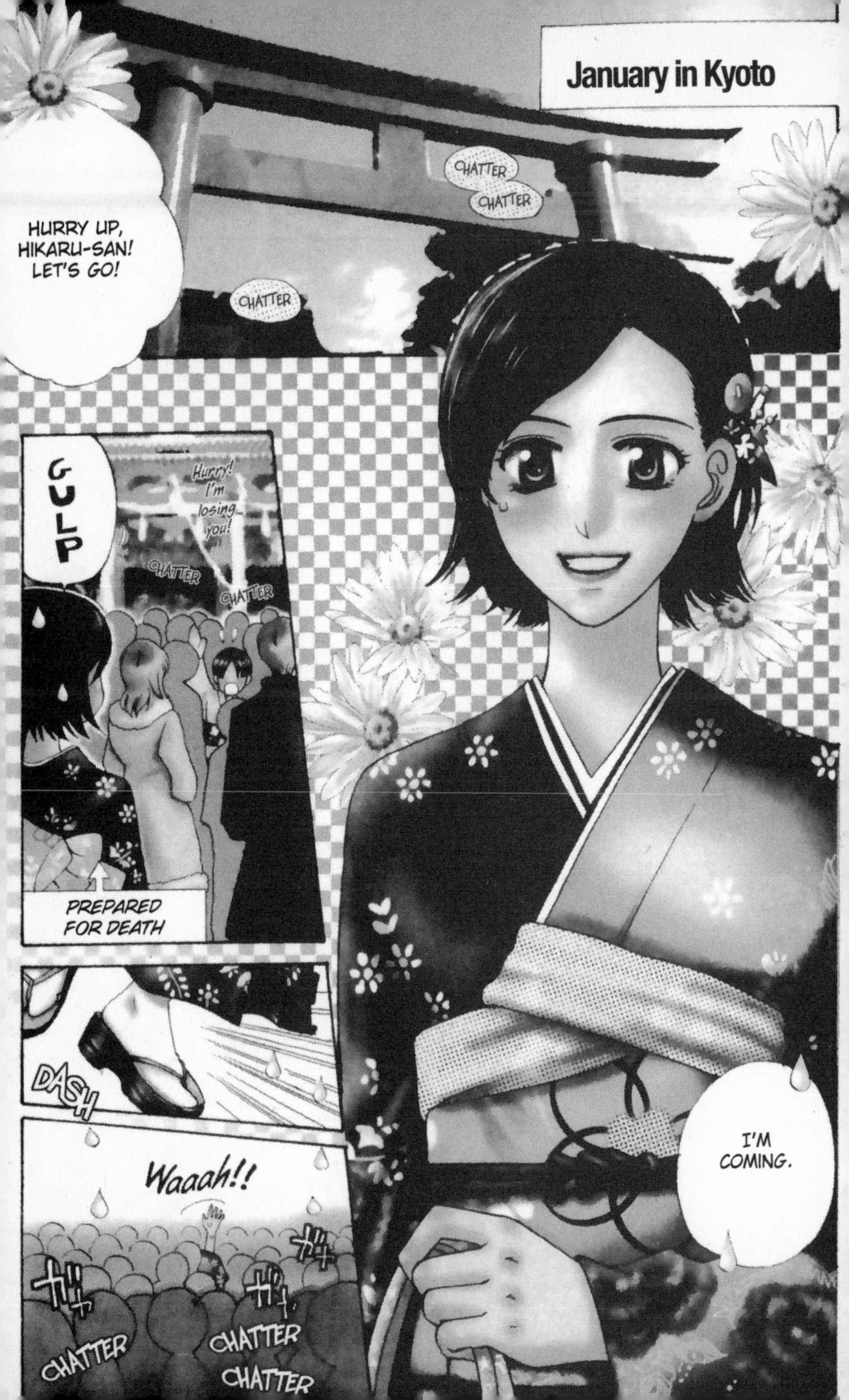
January in Kyoto
CHATTER
CHATTER
CHATTER
HURRY UP, HIKARU-SAN! LET'S GO!
I'M COMING.
GULP
Hurry! I'm losing you!
CHATTER
CHATTER
PREPARED FOR DEATH
DASH
Waaah!!
CHATTER
CHATTER
CHATTER

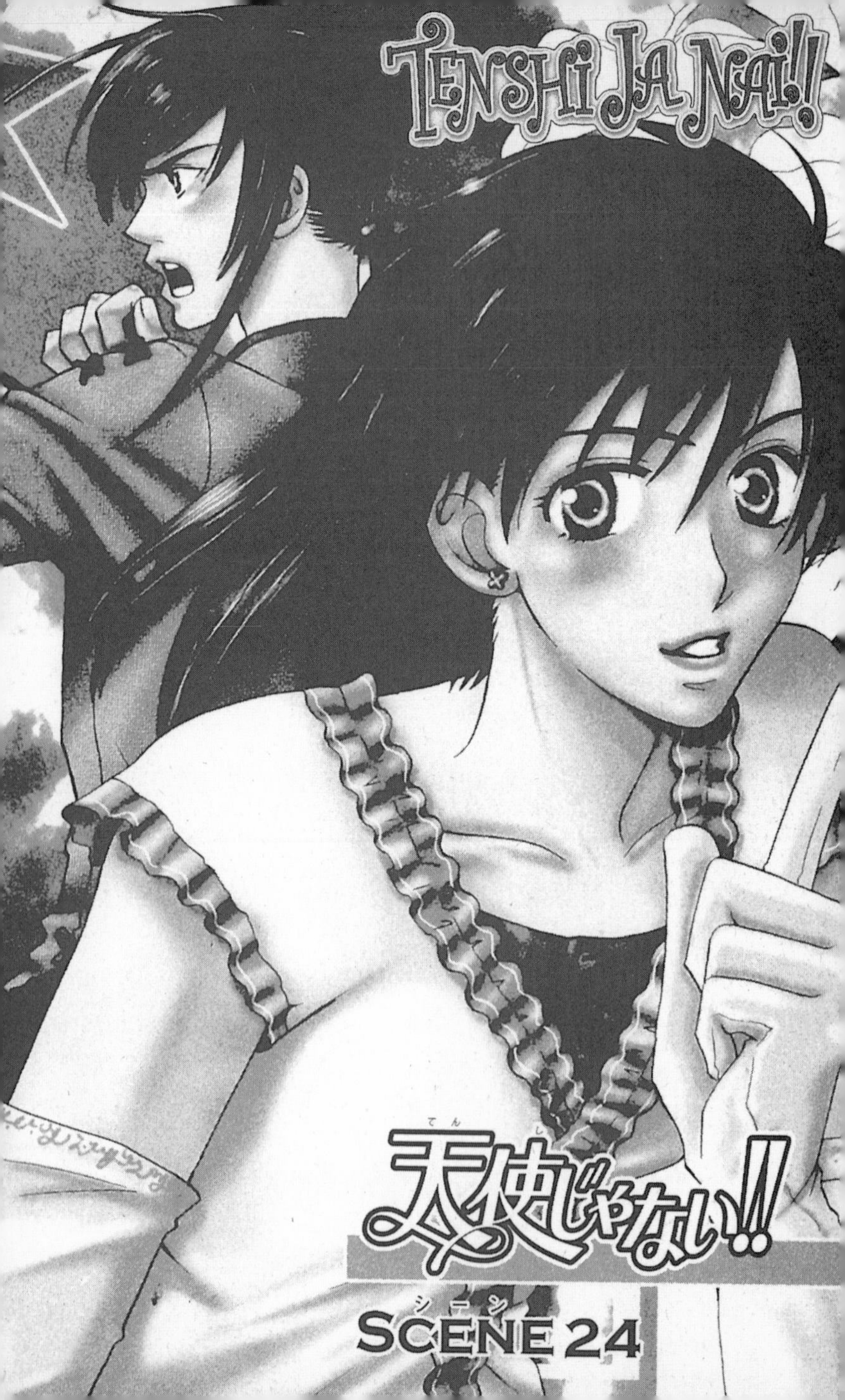
TENSHI JA NAI!!
天使じゃない!!
SCENE 24

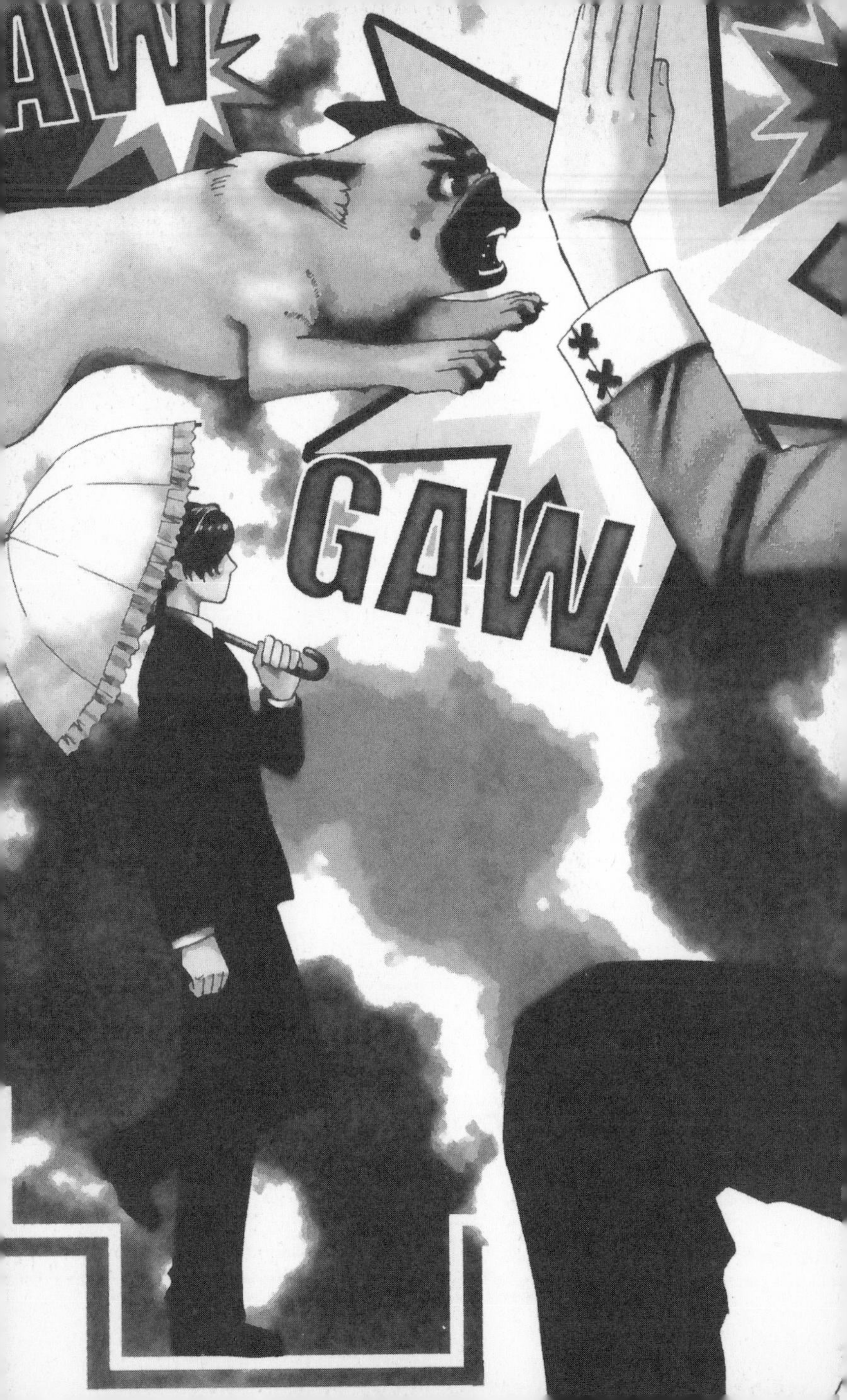
AW
GAW

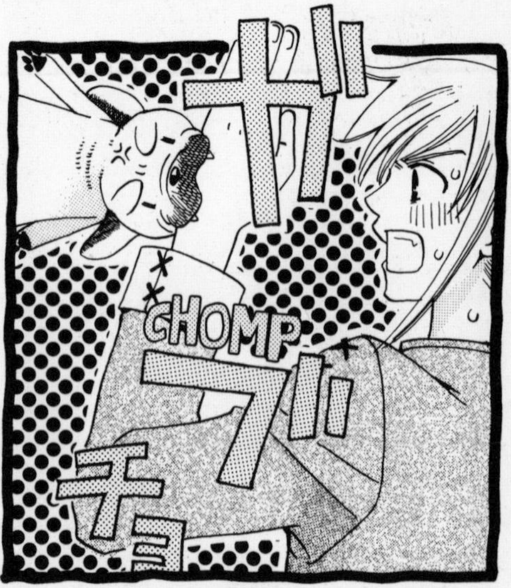
ガブ
CHOMP
チョ

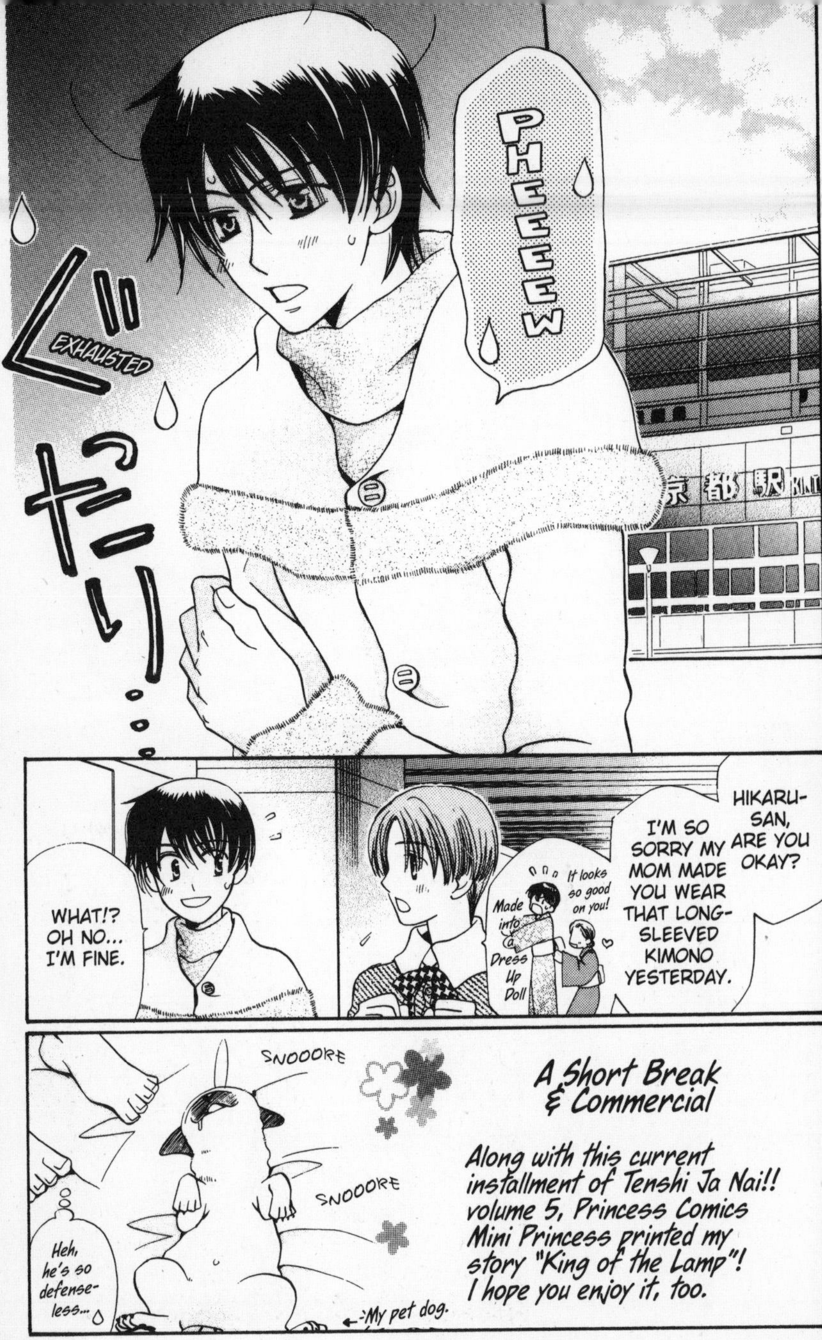
PHEEEEW
ぐったり
EXHAUSTED
京都駅
HIKARU-SAN, ARE YOU OKAY?
I'M SO SORRY MY MOM MADE YOU WEAR THAT LONG-SLEEVED KIMONO YESTERDAY.
It looks so good on you!
Made into a Dress Up Doll
WHAT!? OH NO... I'M FINE.
A Short Break & Commercial
Along with this current installment of Tenshi Ja Nai!! volume 5, Princess Comics Mini Princess printed my story "King of the Lamp"! I hope you enjoy it, too.
SNOOORE
SNOOORE
Heh, he's so defense-less...
My pet dog.

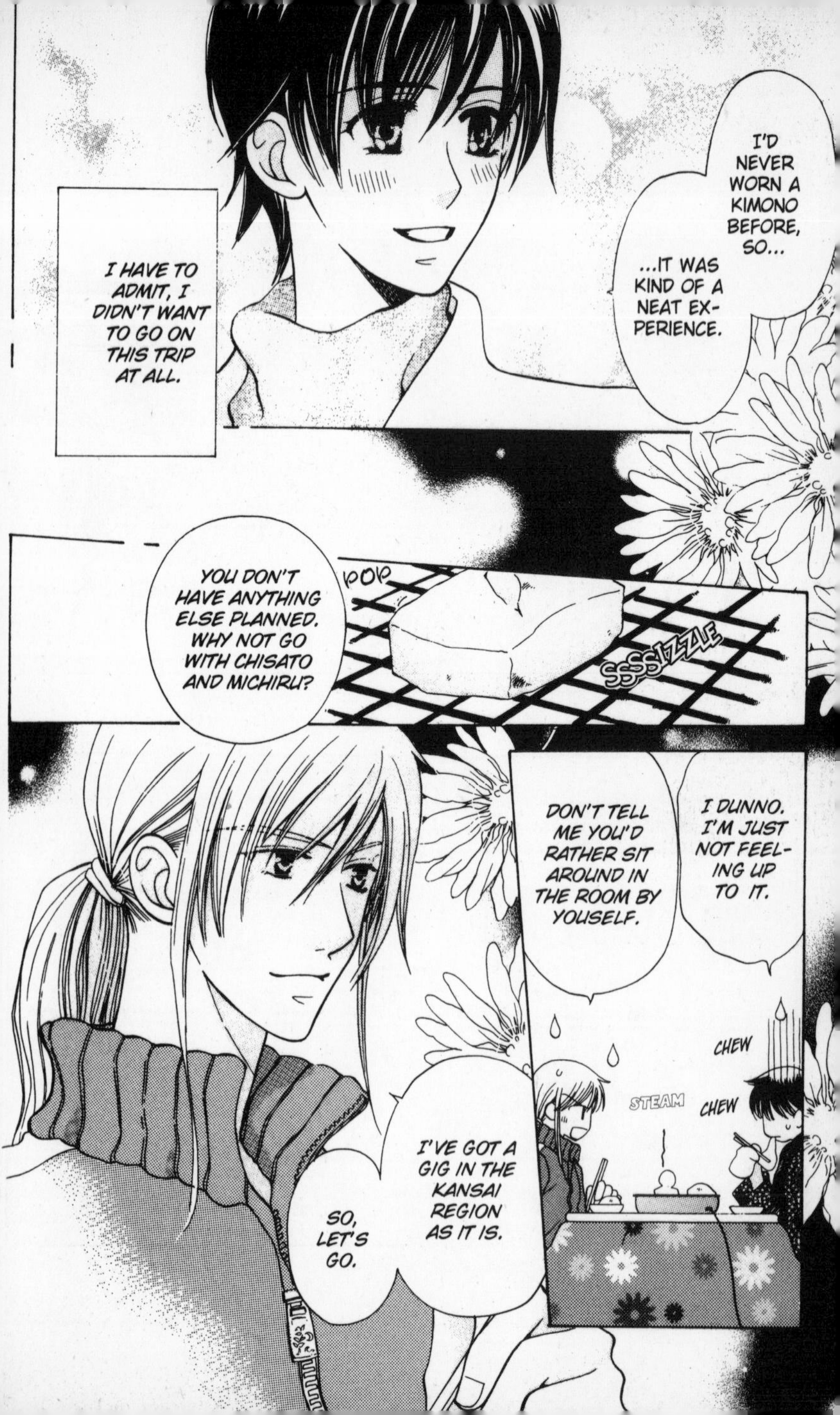
I'D NEVER WORN A KIMONO BEFORE, SO...
...IT WAS KIND OF A NEAT EXPERIENCE.
I HAVE TO ADMIT, I DIDN'T WANT TO GO ON THIS TRIP AT ALL.
POP
SSSSIZZLE
YOU DON'T HAVE ANYTHING ELSE PLANNED. WHY NOT GO WITH CHISATO AND MICHIRU?
I DUNNO. I'M JUST NOT FEELING UP TO IT.
DON'T TELL ME YOU'D RATHER SIT AROUND IN THE ROOM BY YOUSELF.
CHEW
CHEW
STEAM
I'VE GOT A GIG IN THE KANSAI REGION AS IT IS.
SO, LET'S GO.

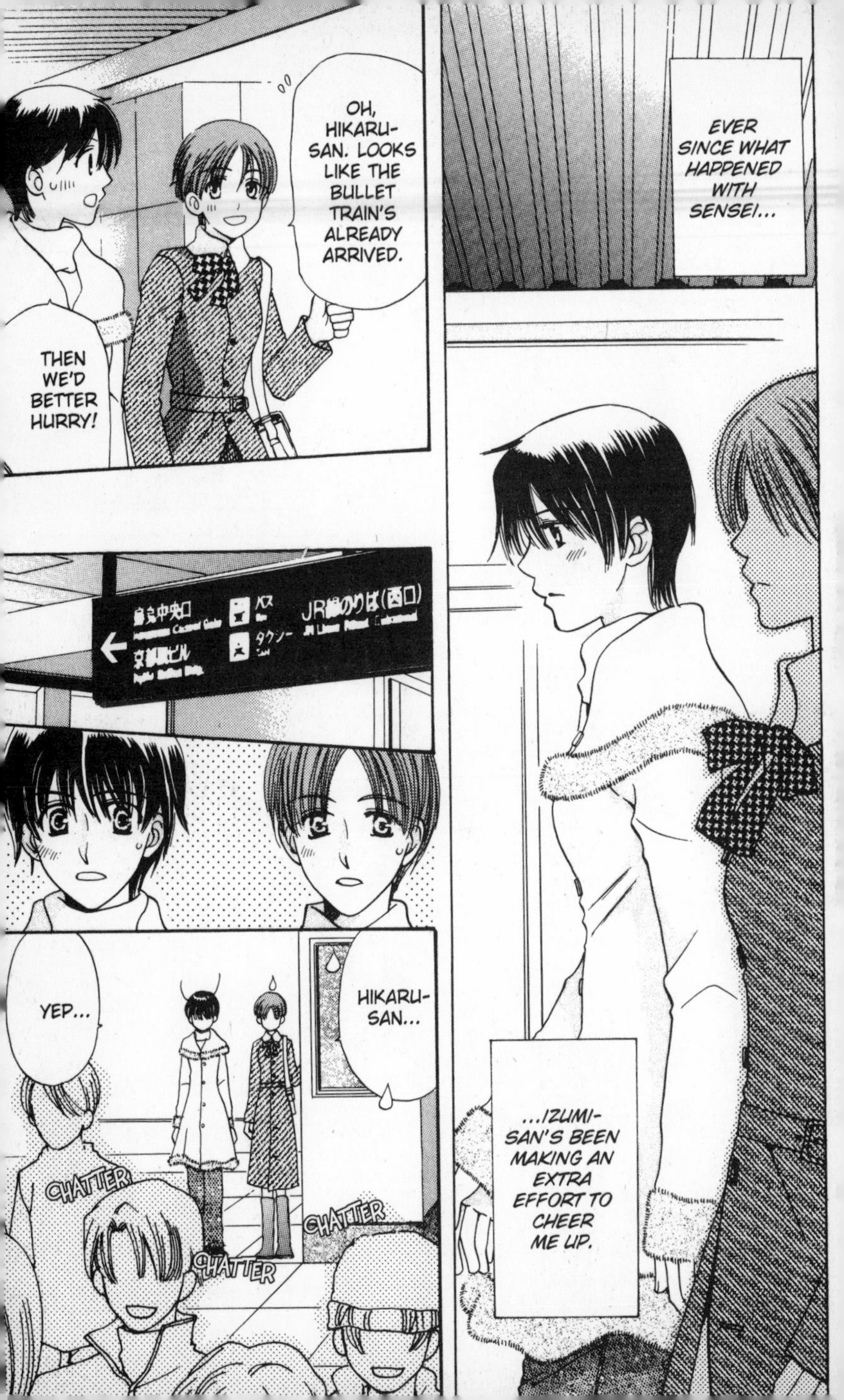
EVER SINCE WHAT HAPPENED WITH SENSEI...
...IZUMI-SAN'S BEEN MAKING AN EXTRA EFFORT TO CHEER ME UP.
OH, HIKARU-SAN. LOOKS LIKE THE BULLET TRAIN'S ALREADY ARRIVED.
THEN WE'D BETTER HURRY!
バス
タクシー
JR線のりば(西口)
HIKARU-SAN...
YEP...
CHATTER
CHATTER
CHATTER

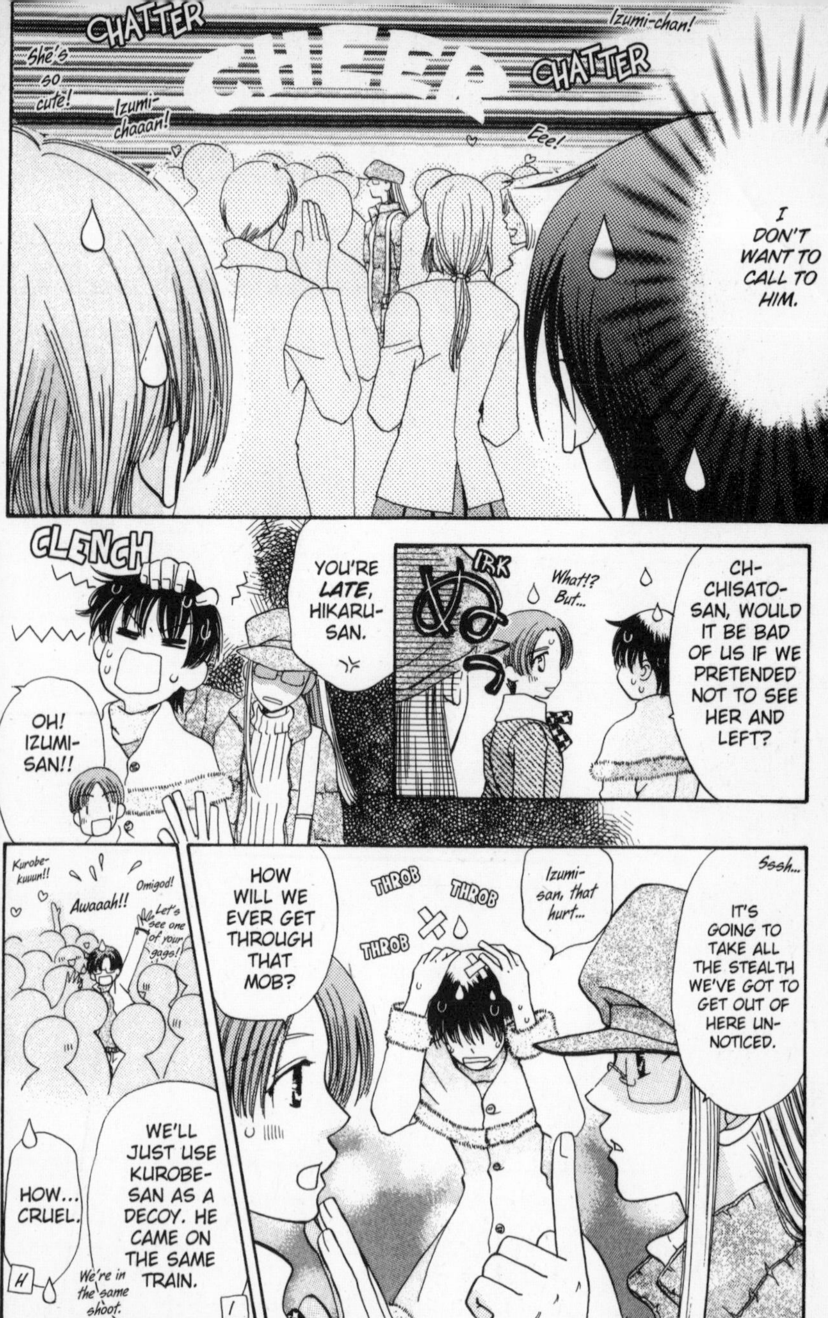
Izumi-chan!
CHATTER
CHEER
Eee!
Izumi-chaaan!
She's so cute!
CHATTER
I DON'T WANT TO CALL TO HIM.
CH-CHISATO-SAN, WOULD IT BE BAD OF US IF WE PRETENDED NOT TO SEE HER AND LEFT?
What!? But...
IRK
ぬっ
YOU'RE LATE, HIKARU-SAN.
CLENCH
OH! IZUMI-SAN!!
Sssh...
IT'S GOING TO TAKE ALL THE STEALTH WE'VE GOT TO GET OUT OF HERE UN-NOTICED.
Izumi-san, that hurt...
THROB
THROB
THROB
HOW WILL WE EVER GET THROUGH THAT MOB?
WE'LL JUST USE KUROBE-SAN AS A DECOY. HE CAME ON THE SAME TRAIN.
Omigod!
Let's see one of your gags!
Awaaah!!
Kurobe-kuuun!!
HOW... CRUEL.
We're in the same shoot.

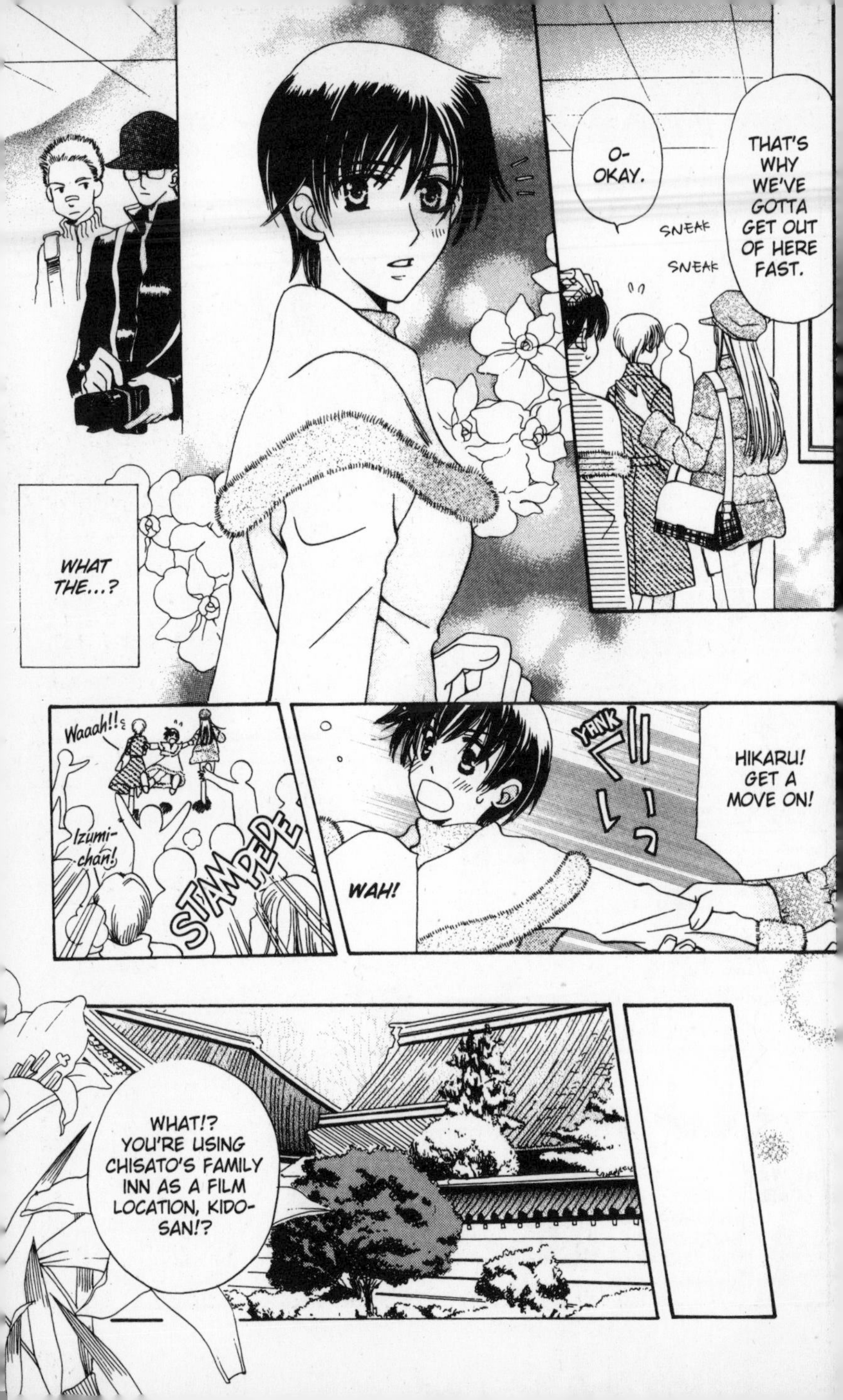
THAT'S WHY WE'VE GOTTA GET OUT OF HERE FAST.
O-OKAY.
SNEAK
SNEAK
WHAT THE...?
HIKARU! GET A MOVE ON!
YANK
WAH!
Waaah!!
Izumi-chan!
STAMPEDE
WHAT!? YOU'RE USING CHISATO'S FAMILY INN AS A FILM LOCATION, KIDO-SAN!?

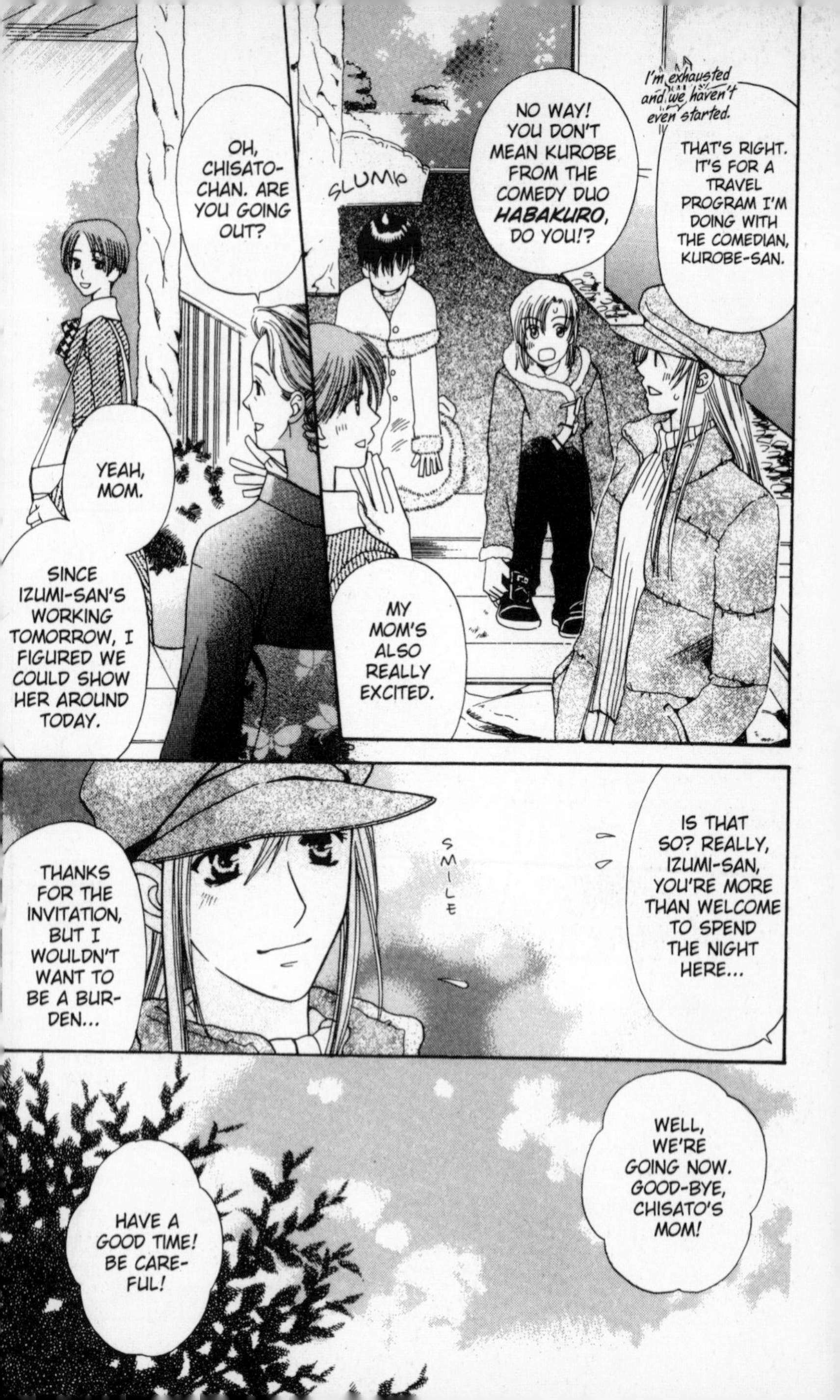
I'm exhausted and we haven't even started.
THAT'S RIGHT. IT'S FOR A TRAVEL PROGRAM I'M DOING WITH THE COMEDIAN, KUROBE-SAN.
NO WAY! YOU DON'T MEAN KUROBE FROM THE COMEDY DUO HABAKURO, DO YOU!?
SLUMP
MY MOM'S ALSO REALLY EXCITED.
OH, CHISATO-CHAN. ARE YOU GOING OUT?
YEAH, MOM.
SINCE IZUMI-SAN'S WORKING TOMORROW, I FIGURED WE COULD SHOW HER AROUND TODAY.
IS THAT SO? REALLY, IZUMI-SAN, YOU'RE MORE THAN WELCOME TO SPEND THE NIGHT HERE...
SMILE
THANKS FOR THE INVITATION, BUT I WOULDN'T WANT TO BE A BURDEN...
WELL, WE'RE GOING NOW. GOOD-BYE, CHISATO'S MOM!
HAVE A GOOD TIME! BE CAREFUL!

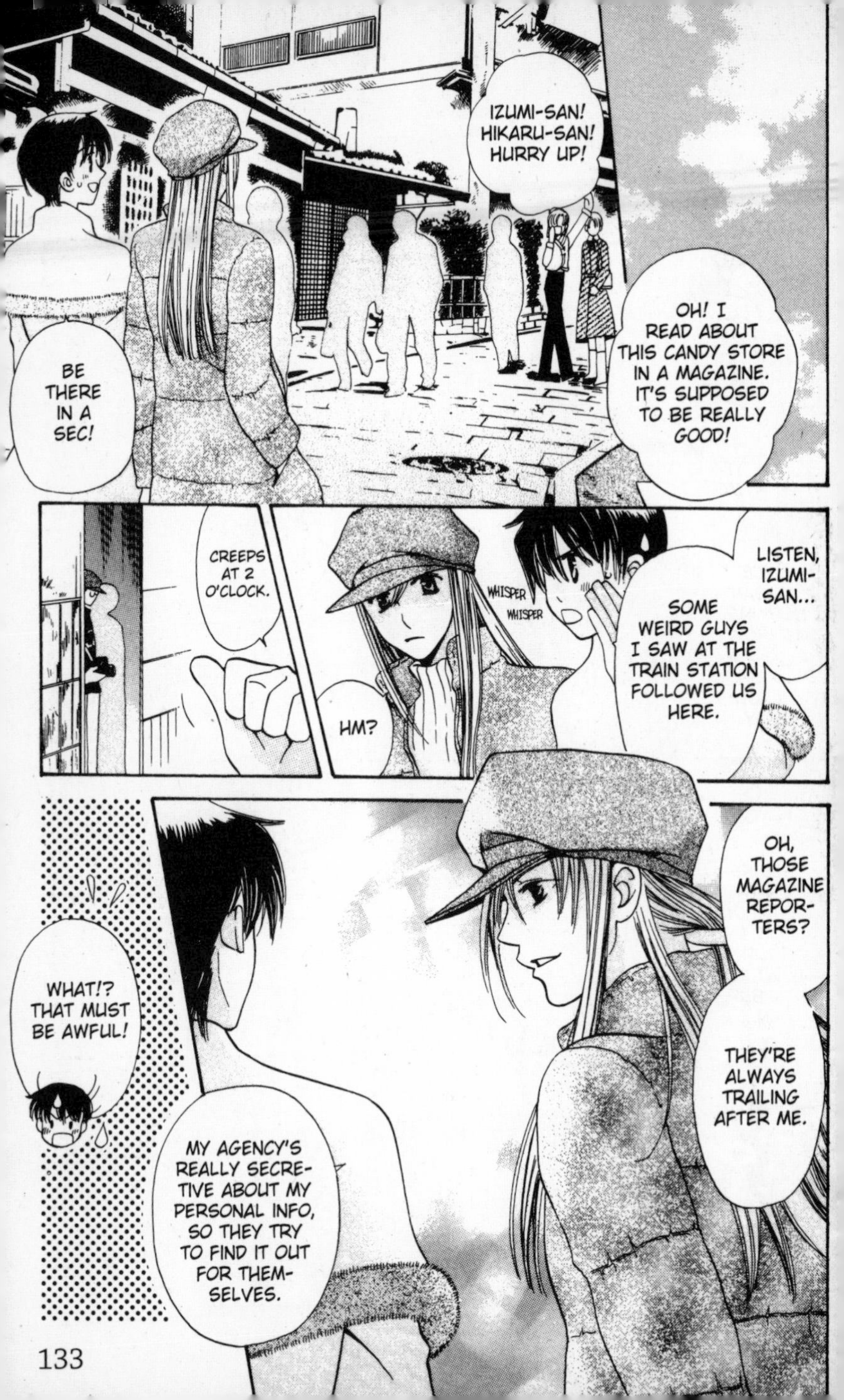
IZUMI-SAN! HIKARU-SAN! HURRY UP!
OH! I READ ABOUT THIS CANDY STORE IN A MAGAZINE. IT'S SUPPOSED TO BE REALLY GOOD!
BE THERE IN A SEC!
LISTEN, IZUMI-SAN...
SOME WEIRD GUYS I SAW AT THE TRAIN STATION FOLLOWED US HERE.
WHISPER
WHISPER
HM?
CREEPS AT 2 O'CLOCK.
OH, THOSE MAGAZINE REPOR-TERS?
THEY'RE ALWAYS TRAILING AFTER ME.
MY AGENCY'S REALLY SECRE-TIVE ABOUT MY PERSONAL INFO, SO THEY TRY TO FIND IT OUT FOR THEM-SELVES.
WHAT!? THAT MUST BE AWFUL!

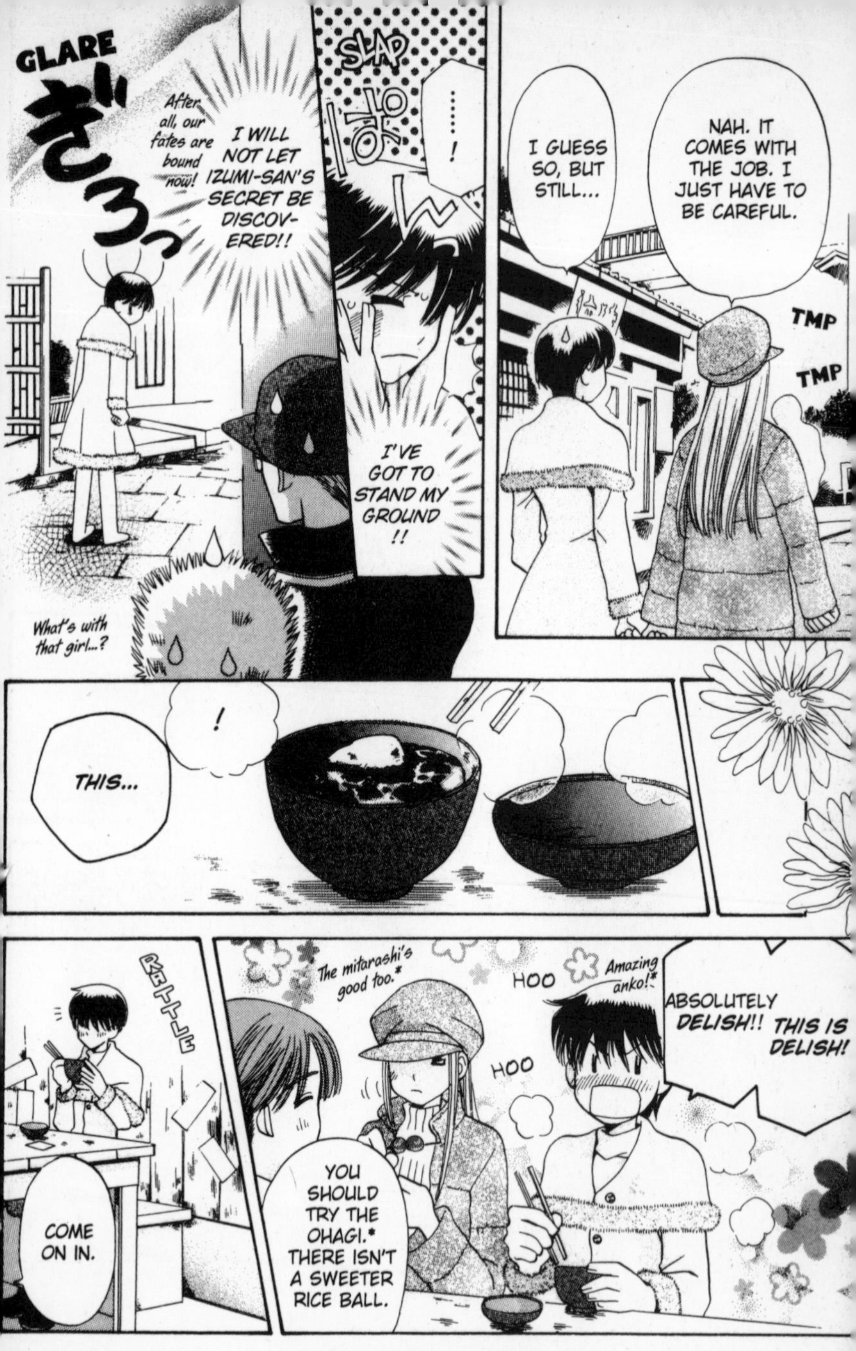
NAH. IT COMES WITH THE JOB. I JUST HAVE TO BE CAREFUL.
I GUESS SO, BUT STILL...
TMP
TMP
SLAP
......!
I'VE GOT TO STAND MY GROUND!!
GLARE
ぎろっ
I WILL NOT LET IZUMI-SAN'S SECRET BE DISCOVERED!!
After all, our fates are bound now!
What's with that girl...?
!
THIS...
ABSOLUTELY DELISH!!
THIS IS DELISH!
Amazing anko!*
HOO
HOO
The mitarashi's good too.*
YOU SHOULD TRY THE OHAGI.* THERE ISN'T A SWEETER RICE BALL.
RATTLE
COME ON IN.

*See Translator's Notes at back of book.

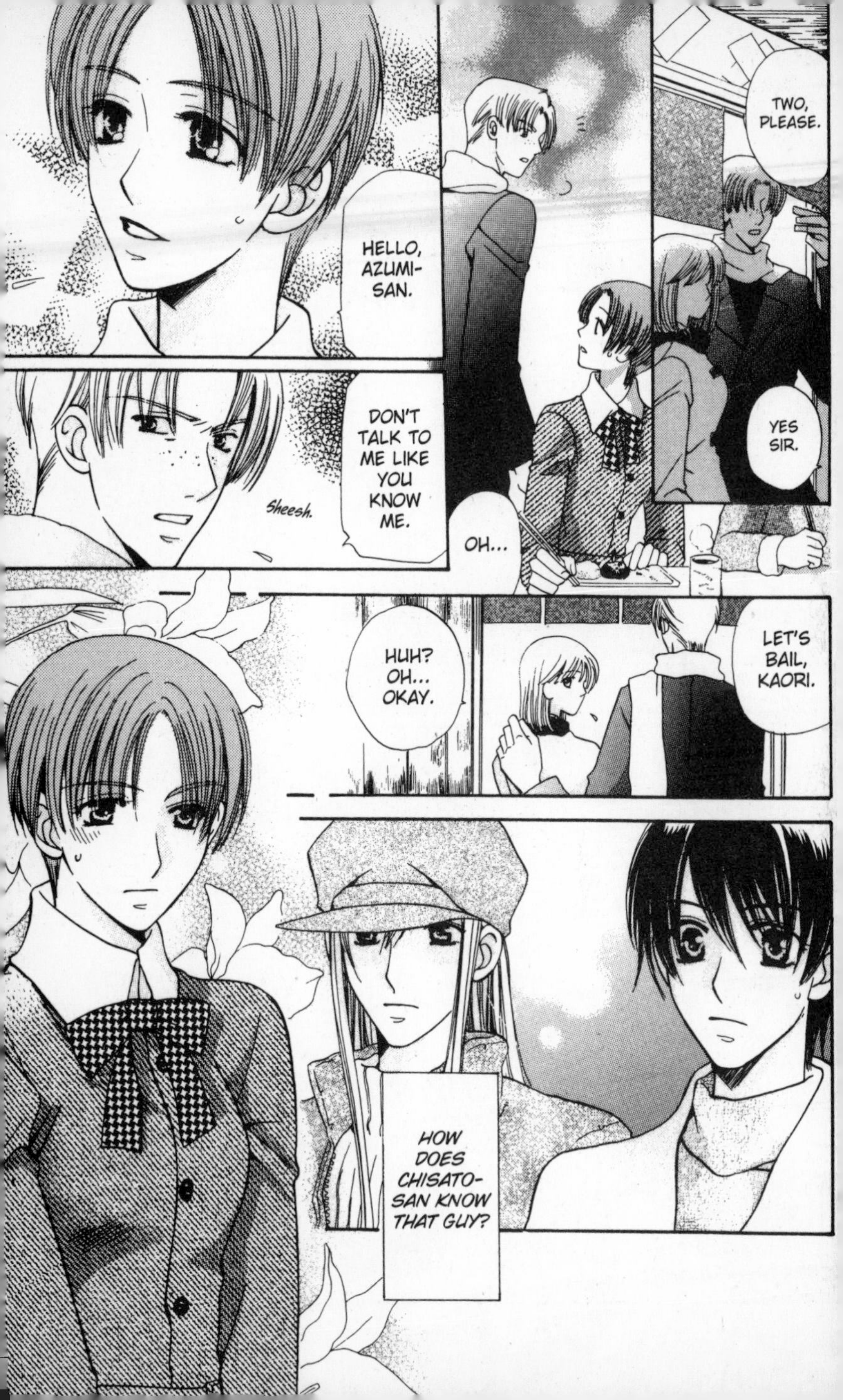
TWO, PLEASE.
YES SIR.
HELLO, AZUMI-SAN.
DON'T TALK TO ME LIKE YOU KNOW ME.
Sheesh.
OH...
LET'S BAIL, KAORI.
HUH? OH... OKAY.
HOW DOES CHISATO-SAN KNOW THAT GUY?

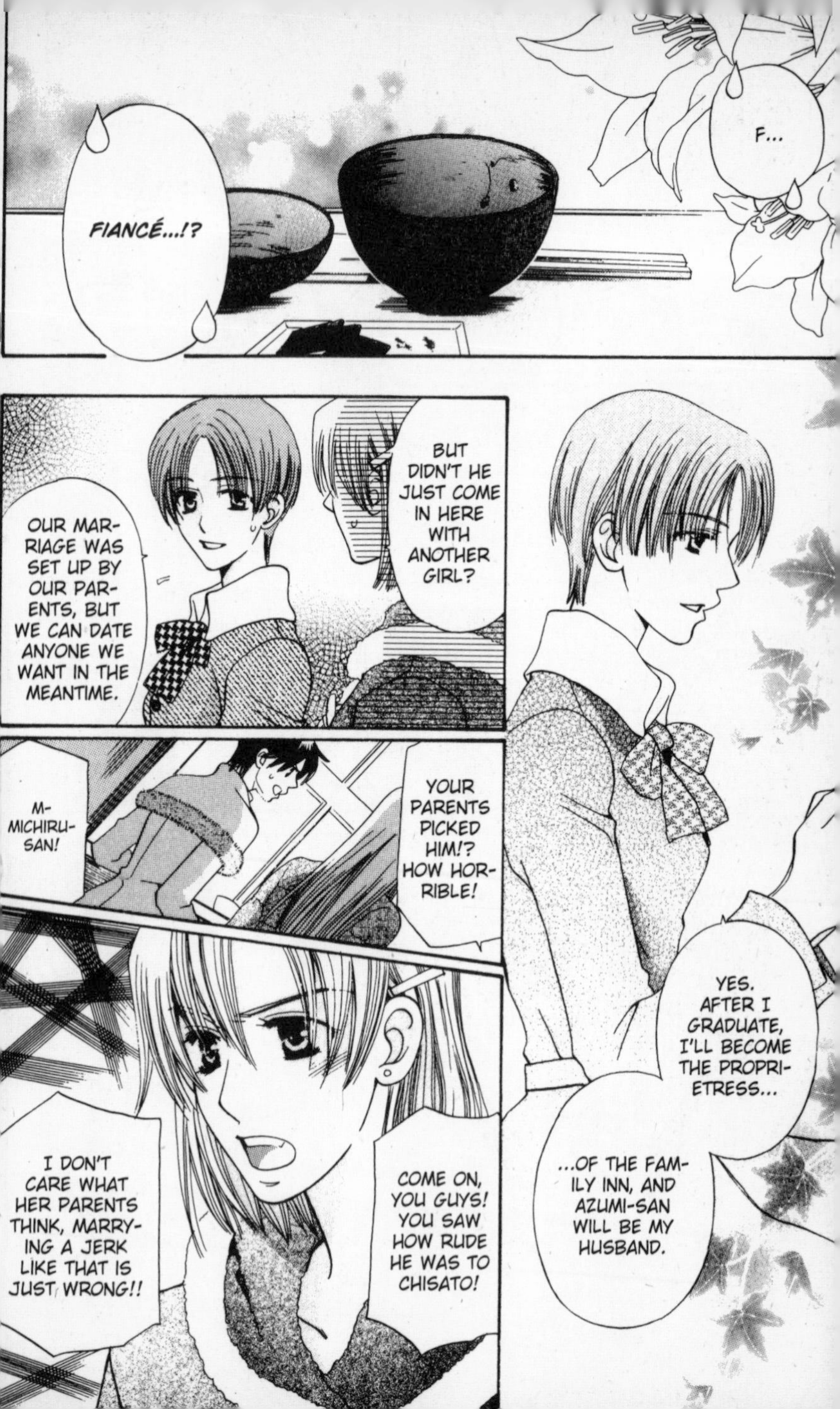
F...
FIANCÉ...!?
YES. AFTER I GRADUATE, I'LL BECOME THE PROPRIETRESS...
...OF THE FAMILY INN, AND AZUMI-SAN WILL BE MY HUSBAND.
BUT DIDN'T HE JUST COME IN HERE WITH ANOTHER GIRL?
OUR MARRIAGE WAS SET UP BY OUR PARENTS, BUT WE CAN DATE ANYONE WE WANT IN THE MEANTIME.
YOUR PARENTS PICKED HIM!? HOW HORRIBLE!
M-MICHIRU-SAN!
COME ON, YOU GUYS! YOU SAW HOW RUDE HE WAS TO CHISATO!
I DON'T CARE WHAT HER PARENTS THINK, MARRYING A JERK LIKE THAT IS JUST WRONG!!

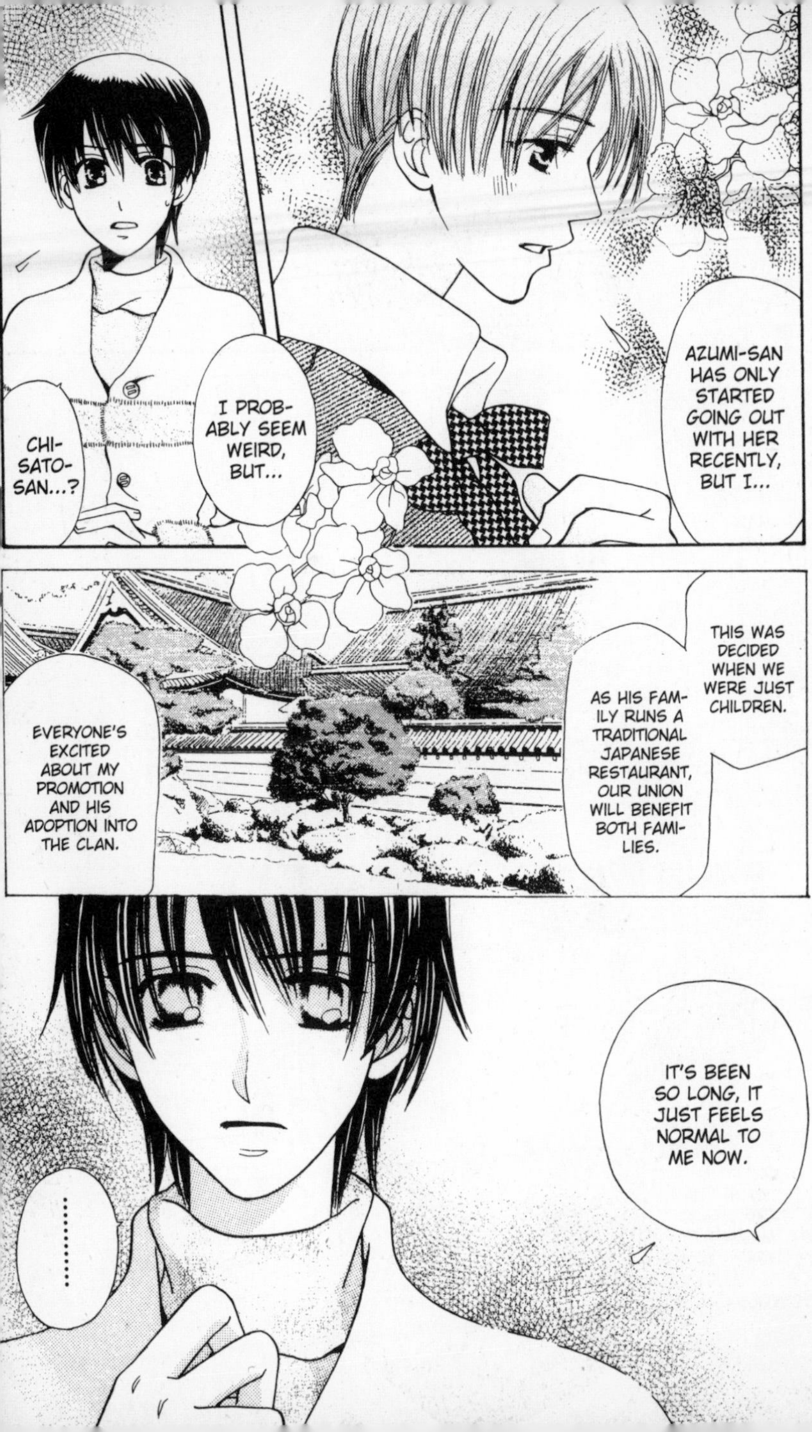

AZUMI-SAN HAS ONLY STARTED GOING OUT WITH HER RECENTLY, BUT I...
I PROB-ABLY SEEM WEIRD, BUT...
CHI-SATO-SAN...?
THIS WAS DECIDED WHEN WE WERE JUST CHILDREN.
AS HIS FAM-ILY RUNS A TRADITIONAL JAPANESE RESTAURANT, OUR UNION WILL BENEFIT BOTH FAMI-LIES.
EVERYONE'S EXCITED ABOUT MY PROMOTION AND HIS ADOPTION INTO THE CLAN.
IT'S BEEN SO LONG, IT JUST FEELS NORMAL TO ME NOW.
......

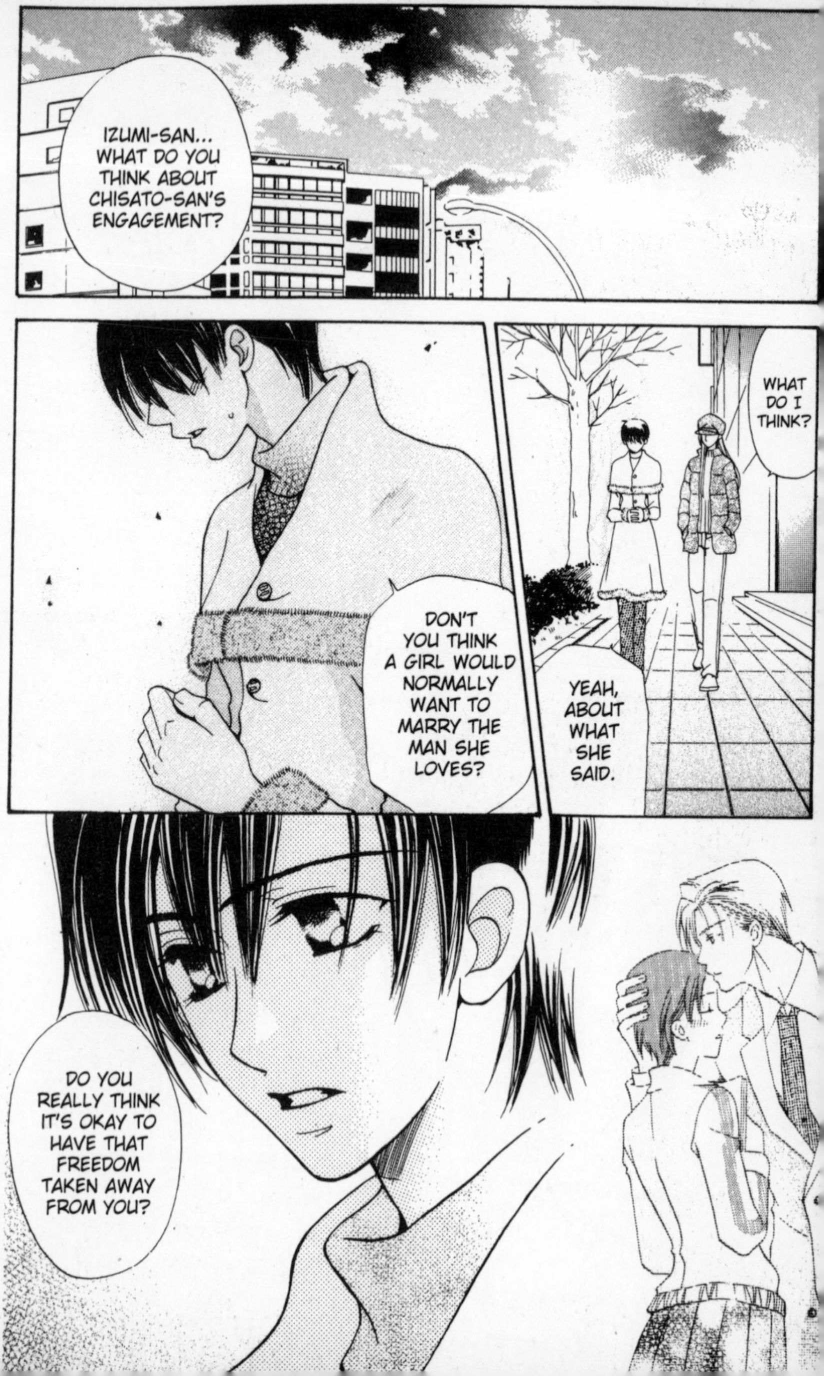
IZUMI-SAN... WHAT DO YOU THINK ABOUT CHISATO-SAN'S ENGAGEMENT?
WHAT DO I THINK?
YEAH, ABOUT WHAT SHE SAID.
DON'T YOU THINK A GIRL WOULD NORMALLY WANT TO MARRY THE MAN SHE LOVES?
DO YOU REALLY THINK IT'S OKAY TO HAVE THAT FREEDOM TAKEN AWAY FROM YOU?

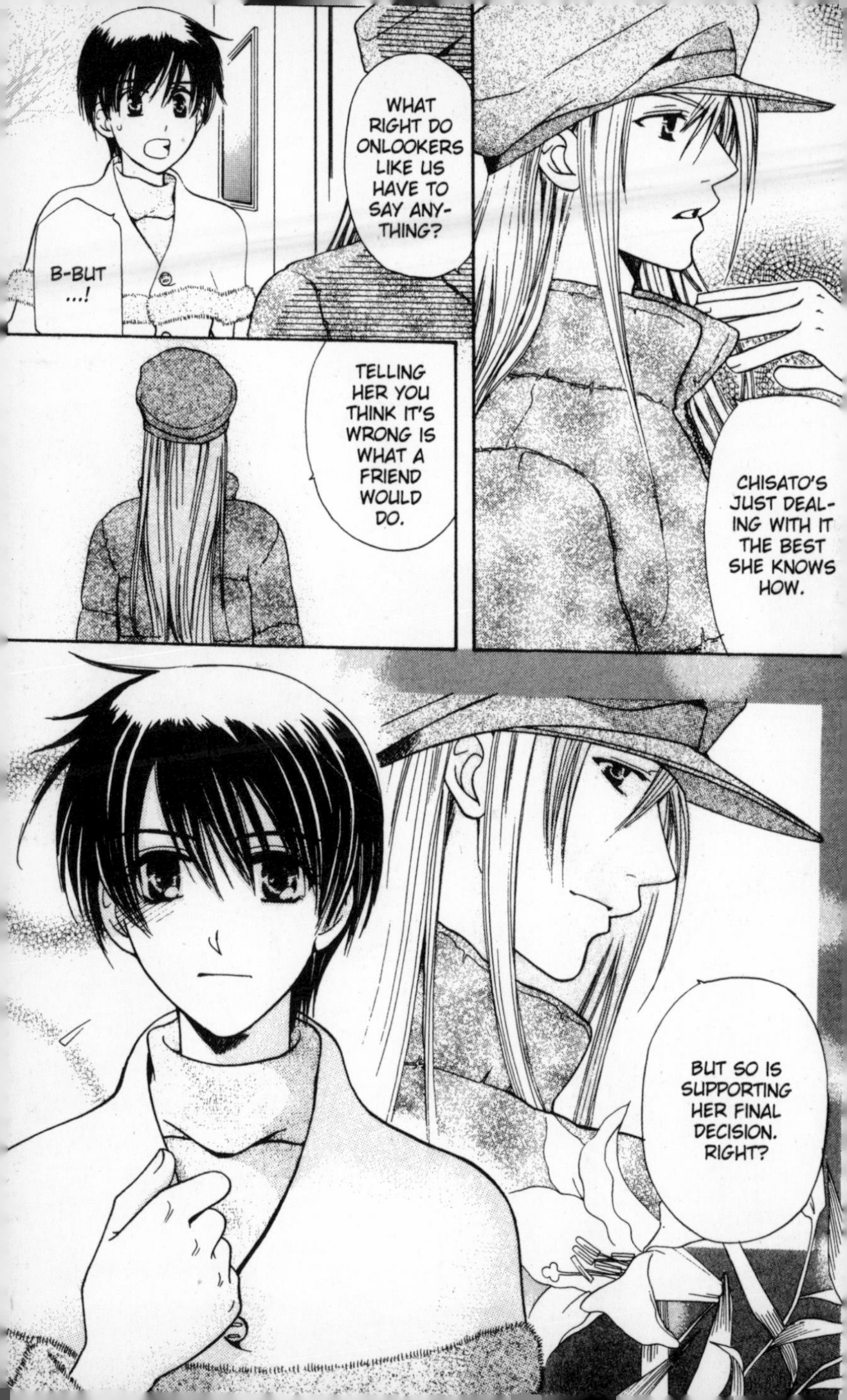
CHISATO'S JUST DEALING WITH IT THE BEST SHE KNOWS HOW.
WHAT RIGHT DO ONLOOKERS LIKE US HAVE TO SAY ANY-THING?
B-BUT ...!
TELLING HER YOU THINK IT'S WRONG IS WHAT A FRIEND WOULD DO.
BUT SO IS SUPPORTING HER FINAL DECISION. RIGHT?

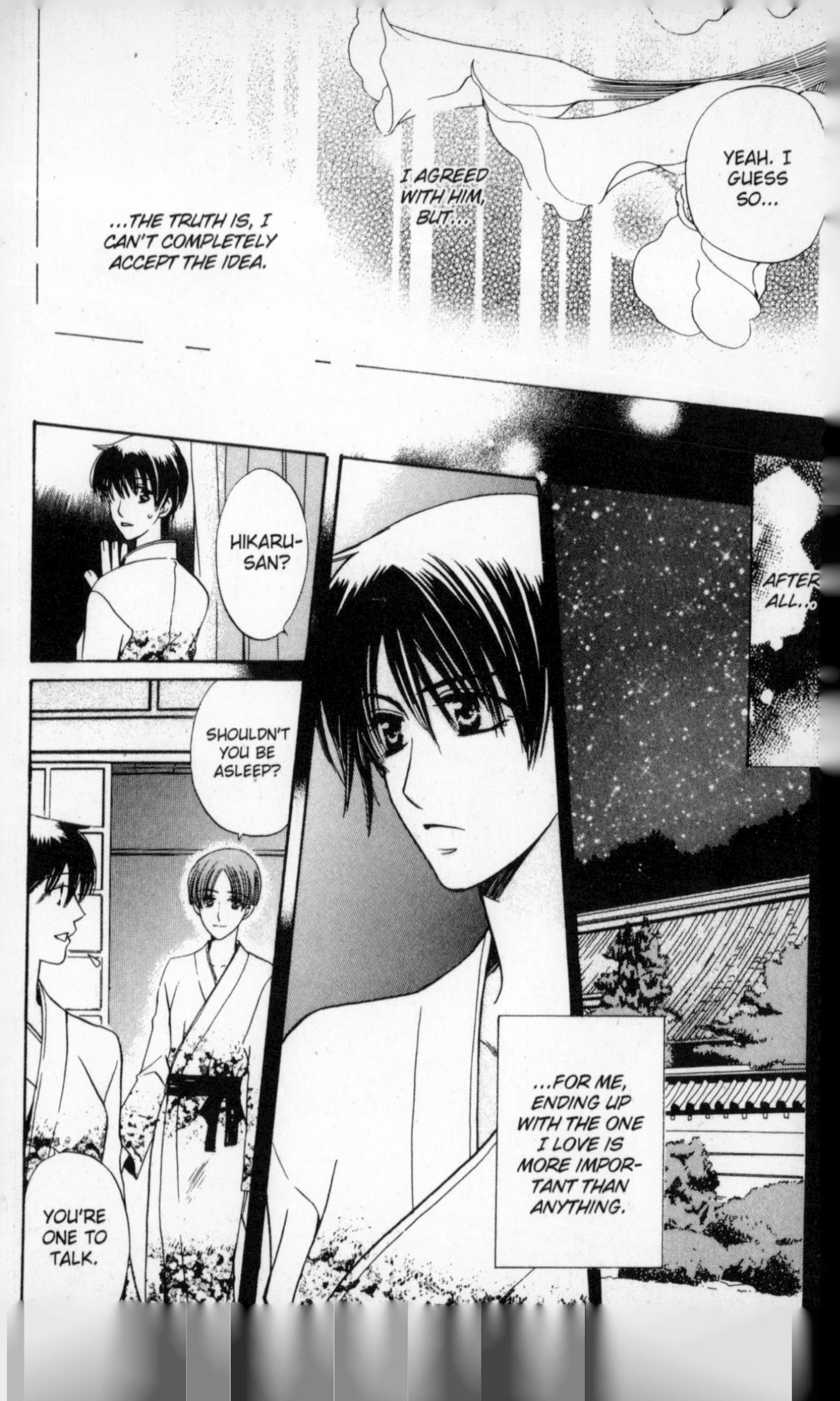
YEAH. I GUESS SO...
I AGREED WITH HIM, BUT...
...THE TRUTH IS, I CAN'T COMPLETELY ACCEPT THE IDEA.
AFTER ALL...
...FOR ME, ENDING UP WITH THE ONE I LOVE IS MORE IMPORTANT THAN ANYTHING.
HIKARU-SAN?
SHOULDN'T YOU BE ASLEEP?
YOU'RE ONE TO TALK.

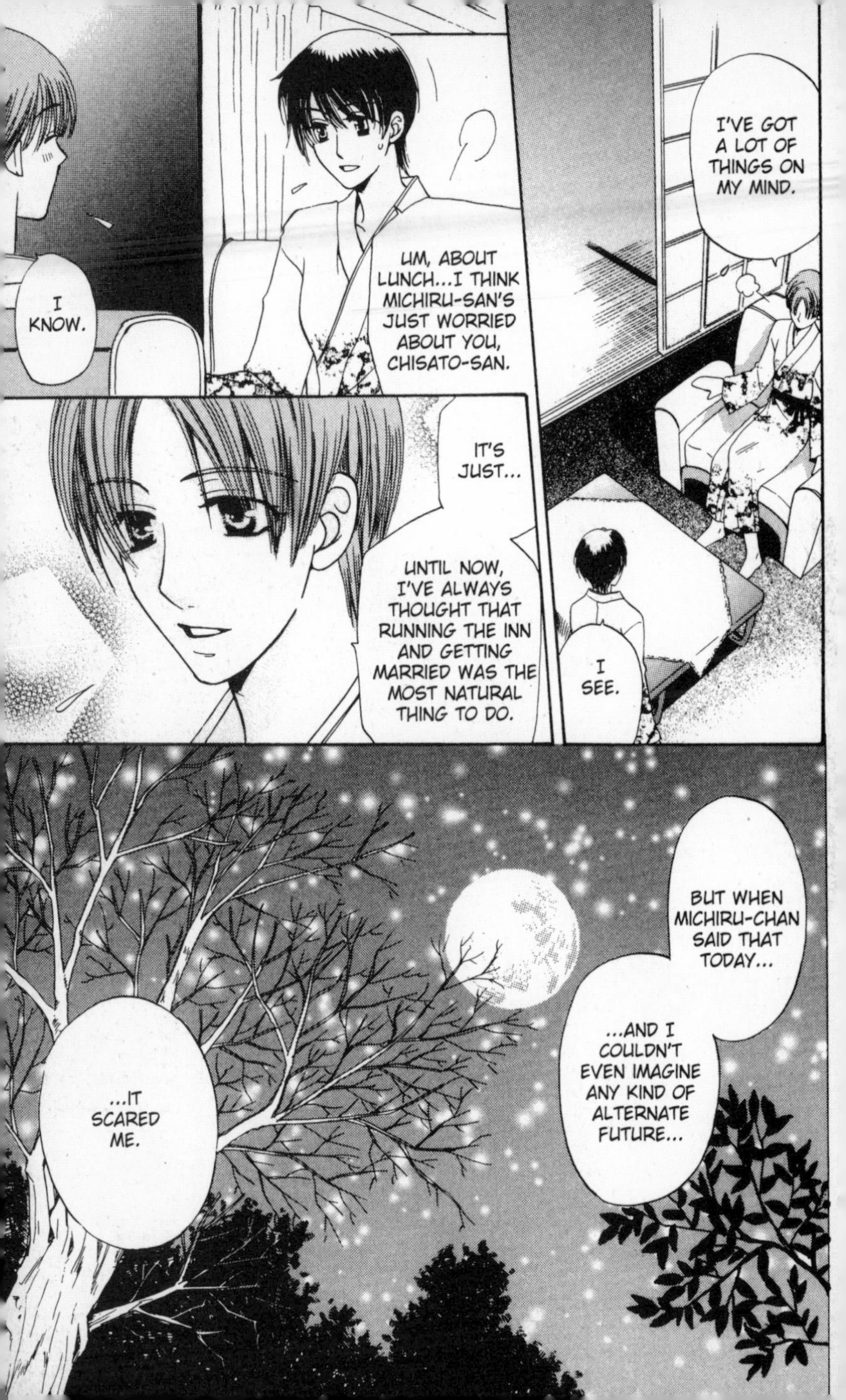
I'VE GOT A LOT OF THINGS ON MY MIND.
I SEE.
UM, ABOUT LUNCH...I THINK MICHIRU-SAN'S JUST WORRIED ABOUT YOU, CHISATO-SAN.
I KNOW.
IT'S JUST...
UNTIL NOW, I'VE ALWAYS THOUGHT THAT RUNNING THE INN AND GETTING MARRIED WAS THE MOST NATURAL THING TO DO.
BUT WHEN MICHIRU-CHAN SAID THAT TODAY...
...AND I COULDN'T EVEN IMAGINE ANY KIND OF ALTERNATE FUTURE...
...IT SCARED ME.

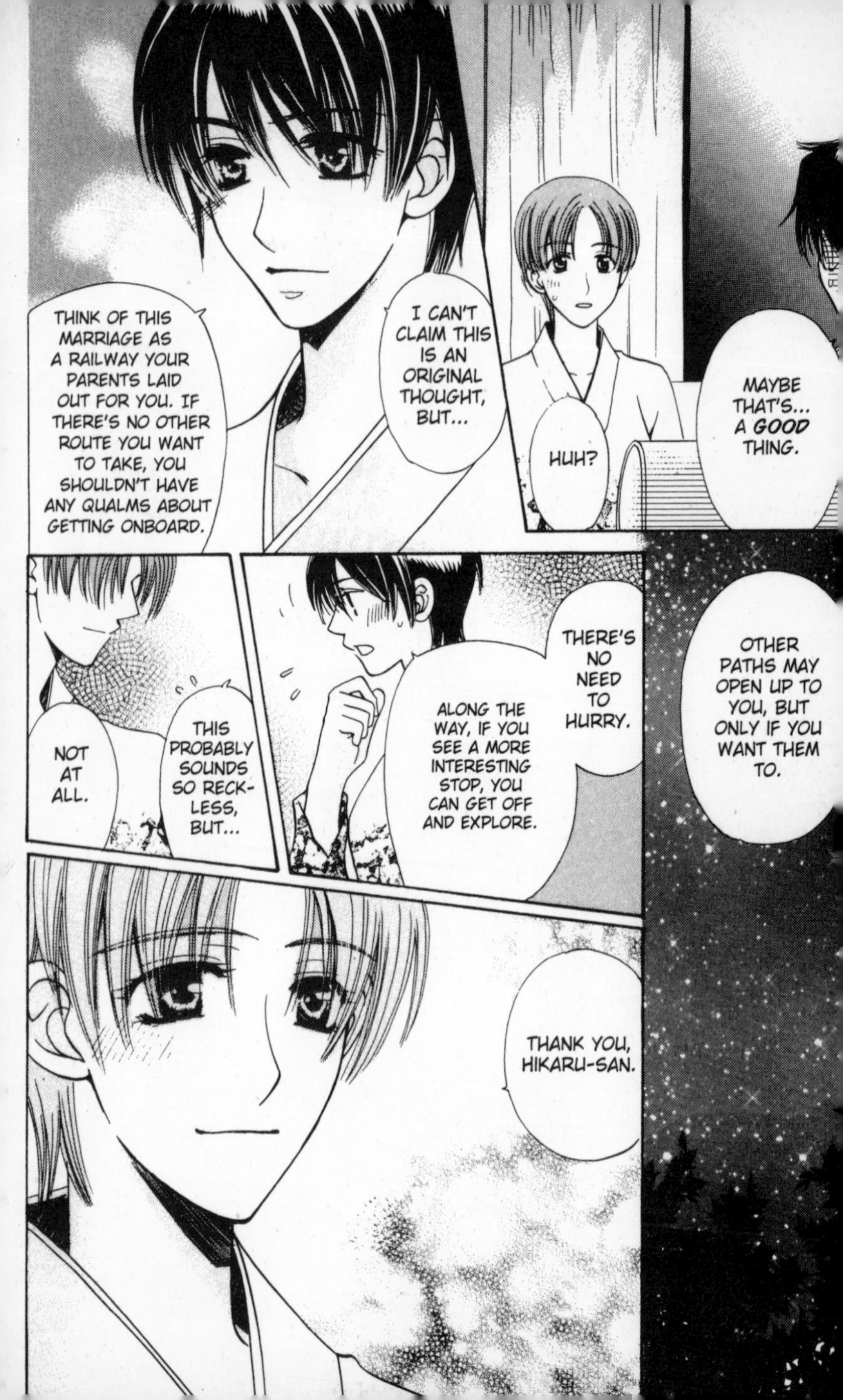
MAYBE THAT'S... A GOOD THING.
HUH?
I CAN'T CLAIM THIS IS AN ORIGINAL THOUGHT, BUT...
THINK OF THIS MARRIAGE AS A RAILWAY YOUR PARENTS LAID OUT FOR YOU. IF THERE'S NO OTHER ROUTE YOU WANT TO TAKE, YOU SHOULDN'T HAVE ANY QUALMS ABOUT GETTING ONBOARD.
OTHER PATHS MAY OPEN UP TO YOU, BUT ONLY IF YOU WANT THEM TO.
THERE'S NO NEED TO HURRY.
ALONG THE WAY, IF YOU SEE A MORE INTERESTING STOP, YOU CAN GET OFF AND EXPLORE.
THIS PROBABLY SOUNDS SO RECK-LESS, BUT...
NOT AT ALL.
THANK YOU, HIKARU-SAN.

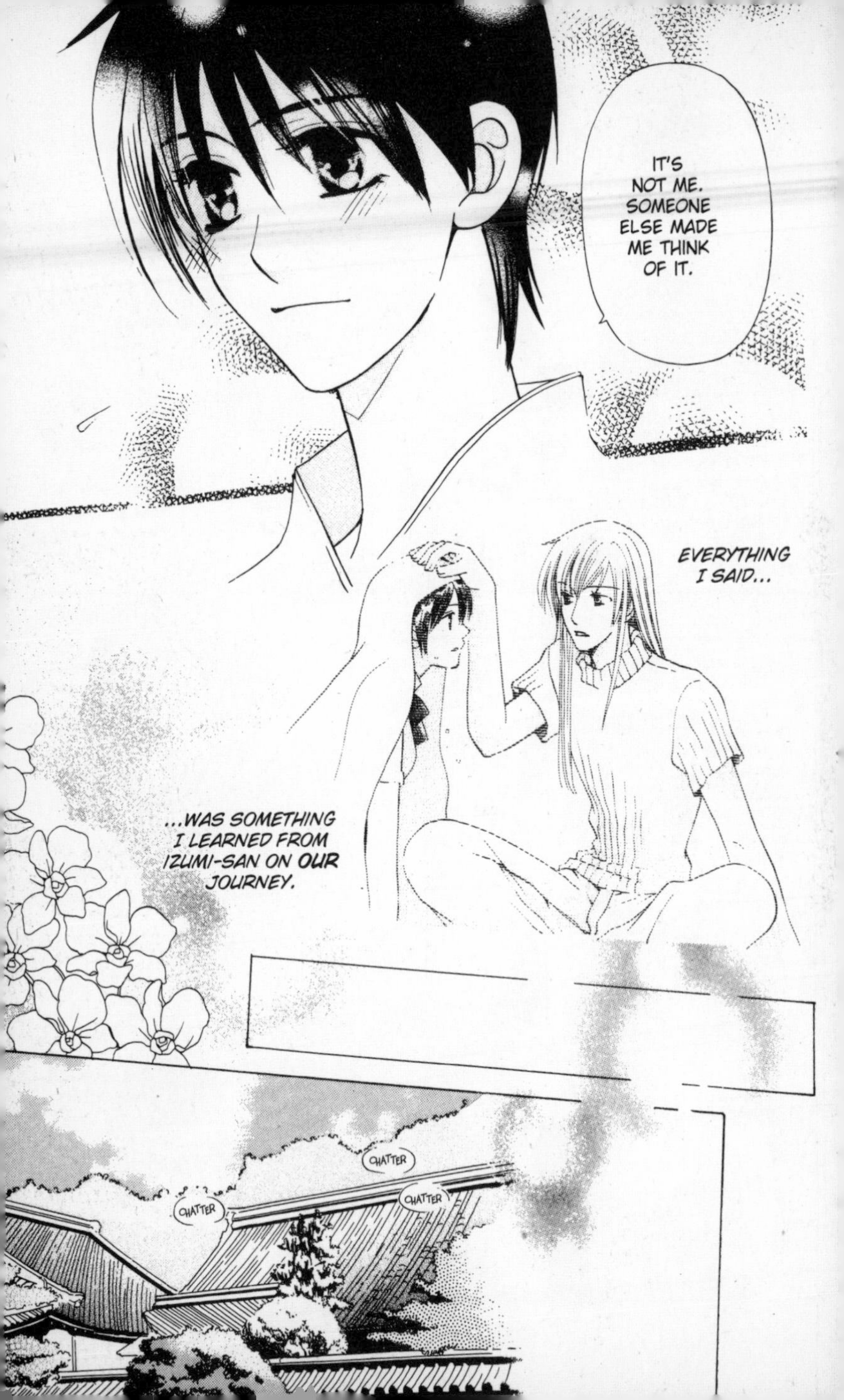
IT'S NOT ME. SOMEONE ELSE MADE ME THINK OF IT.
EVERYTHING I SAID...
...WAS SOMETHING I LEARNED FROM IZUMI-SAN ON OUR JOURNEY.
CHATTER
CHATTER
CHATTER

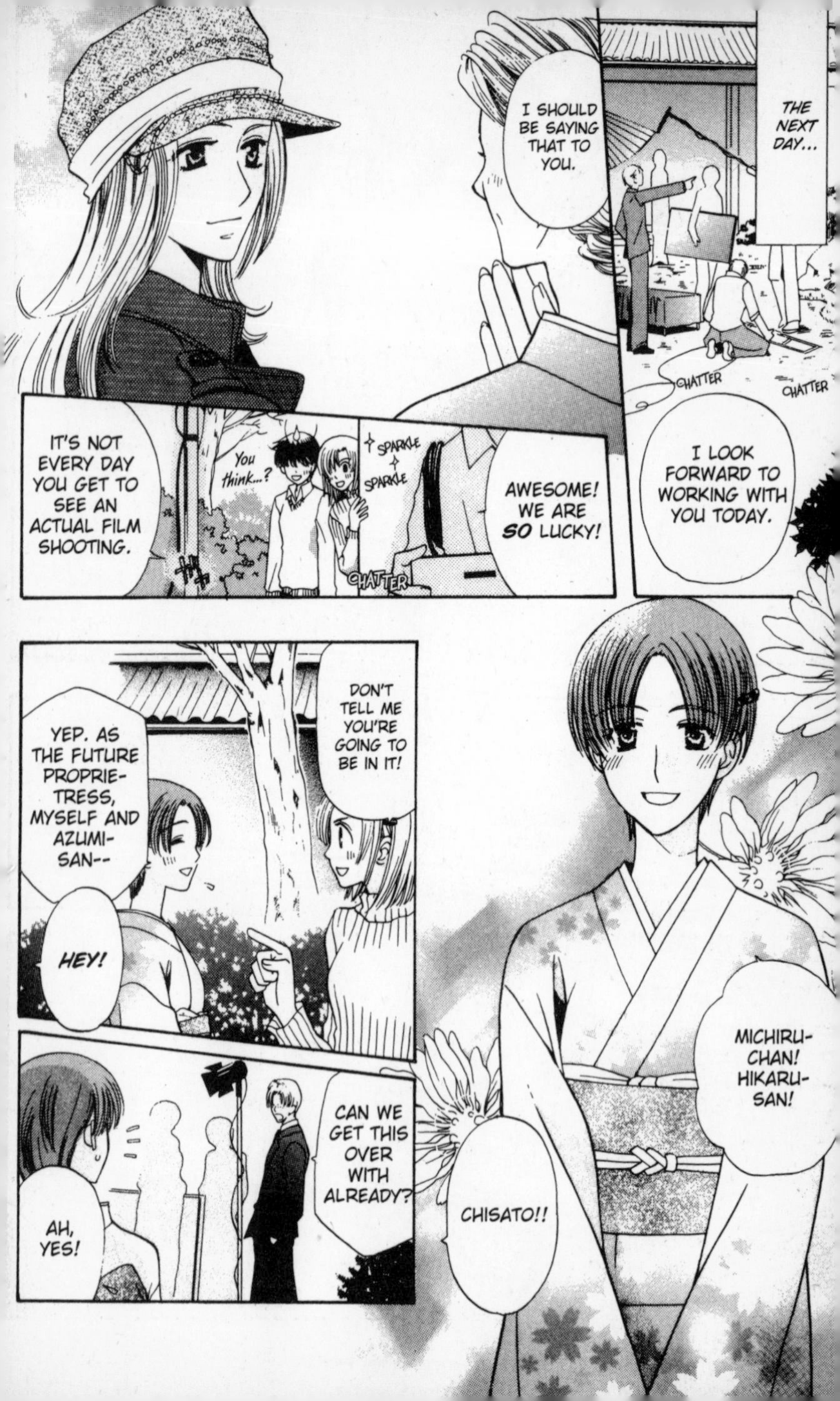
THE NEXT DAY...
CHATTER
CHATTER
I LOOK FORWARD TO WORKING WITH YOU TODAY.
I SHOULD BE SAYING THAT TO YOU.
SPARKLE
SPARKLE
AWESOME! WE ARE ***SO*** LUCKY!
CHATTER
IT'S NOT EVERY DAY YOU GET TO SEE AN ACTUAL FILM SHOOTING.
You think...?
MICHIRU-CHAN! HIKARU-SAN!
CHISATO!!
DON'T TELL ME YOU'RE GOING TO BE IN IT!
YEP. AS THE FUTURE PROPRIE-TRESS, MYSELF AND AZUMI-SAN--
HEY!
CAN WE GET THIS OVER WITH ALREADY?
AH, YES!

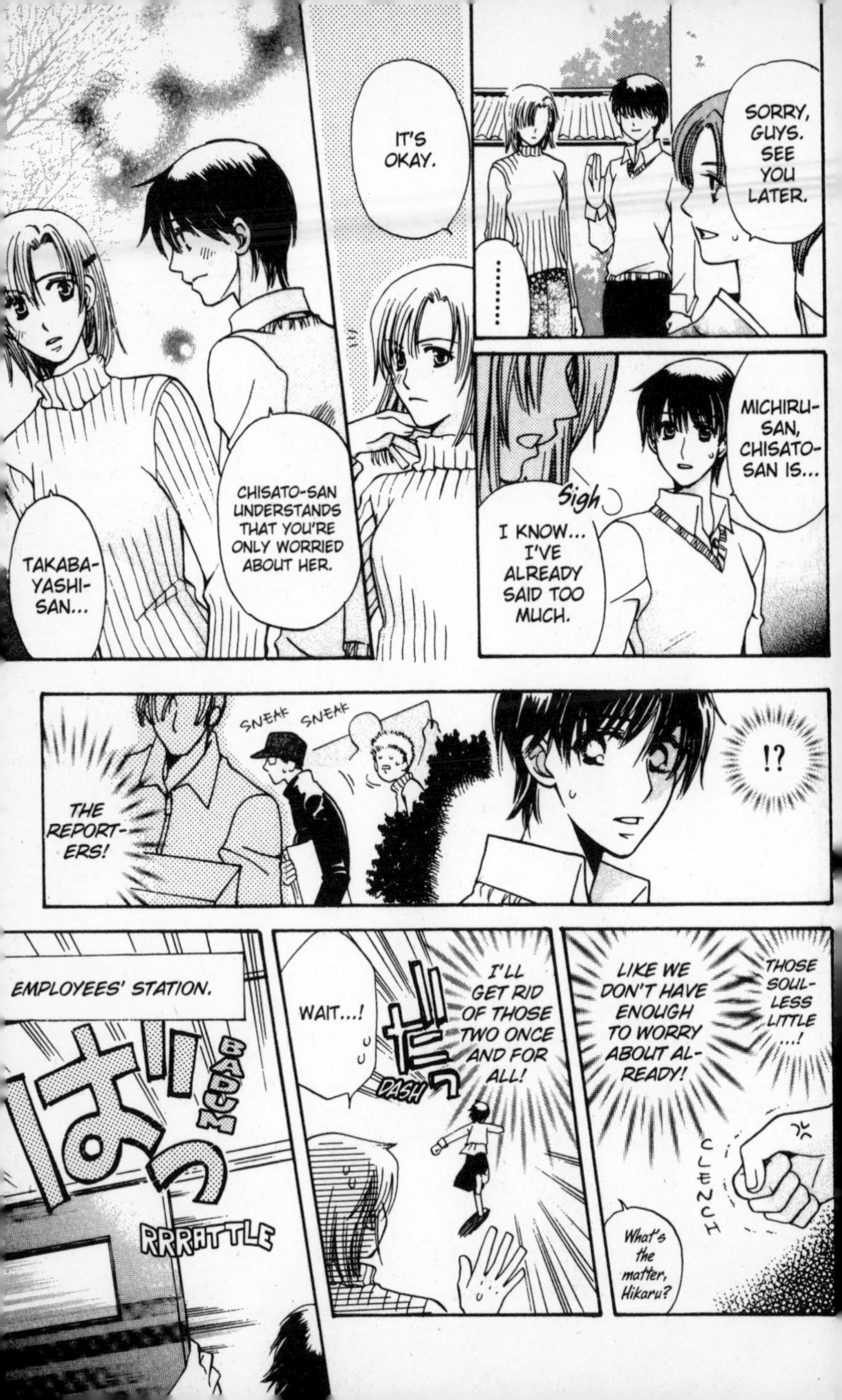
SORRY, GUYS. SEE YOU LATER.
......
MICHIRU-SAN, CHISATO-SAN IS...
Sigh
I KNOW... I'VE ALREADY SAID TOO MUCH.
IT'S OKAY.
CHISATO-SAN UNDERSTANDS THAT YOU'RE ONLY WORRIED ABOUT HER.
TAKABAYASHI-SAN...
!?
SNEAK SNEAK
THE REPORTERS!
THOSE SOULLESS LITTLE ...!
LIKE WE DON'T HAVE ENOUGH TO WORRY ABOUT ALREADY!
CLENCH
What's the matter, Hikaru?
I'LL GET RID OF THOSE TWO ONCE AND FOR ALL!
DASH
WAIT...!
EMPLOYEES' STATION.
BADUM
RRRATTLE

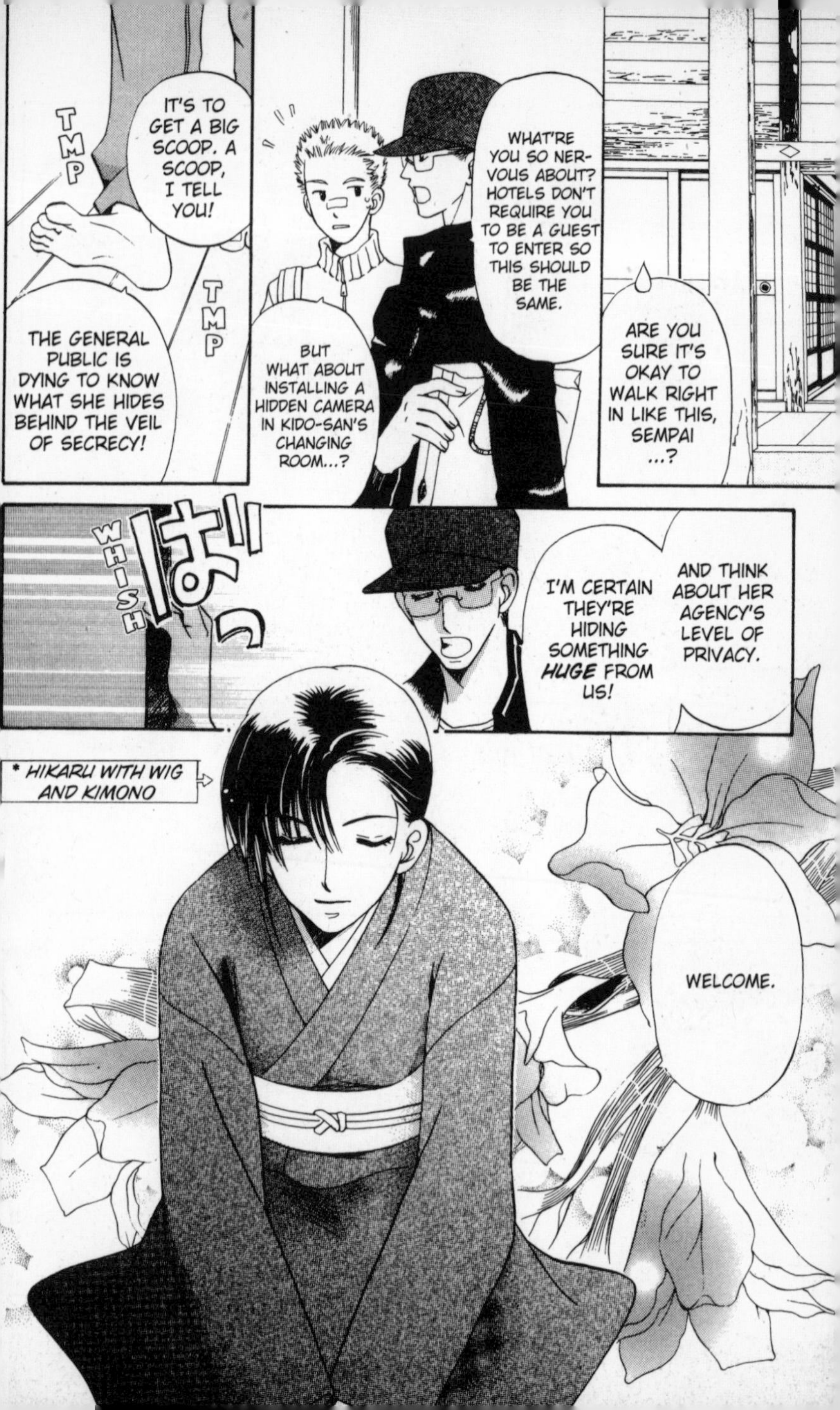

ARE YOU SURE IT'S OKAY TO WALK RIGHT IN LIKE THIS, SEMPAI ...?
WHAT'RE YOU SO NER-VOUS ABOUT? HOTELS DON'T REQUIRE YOU TO BE A GUEST TO ENTER SO THIS SHOULD BE THE SAME.
BUT WHAT ABOUT INSTALLING A HIDDEN CAMERA IN KIDO-SAN'S CHANGING ROOM...?
IT'S TO GET A BIG SCOOP. A SCOOP, I TELL YOU!
TMP
TMP
THE GENERAL PUBLIC IS DYING TO KNOW WHAT SHE HIDES BEHIND THE VEIL OF SECRECY!
AND THINK ABOUT HER AGENCY'S LEVEL OF PRIVACY.
I'M CERTAIN THEY'RE HIDING SOMETHING *HUGE* FROM US!
ばっ
WHISH
* HIKARU WITH WIG AND KIMONO
WELCOME.

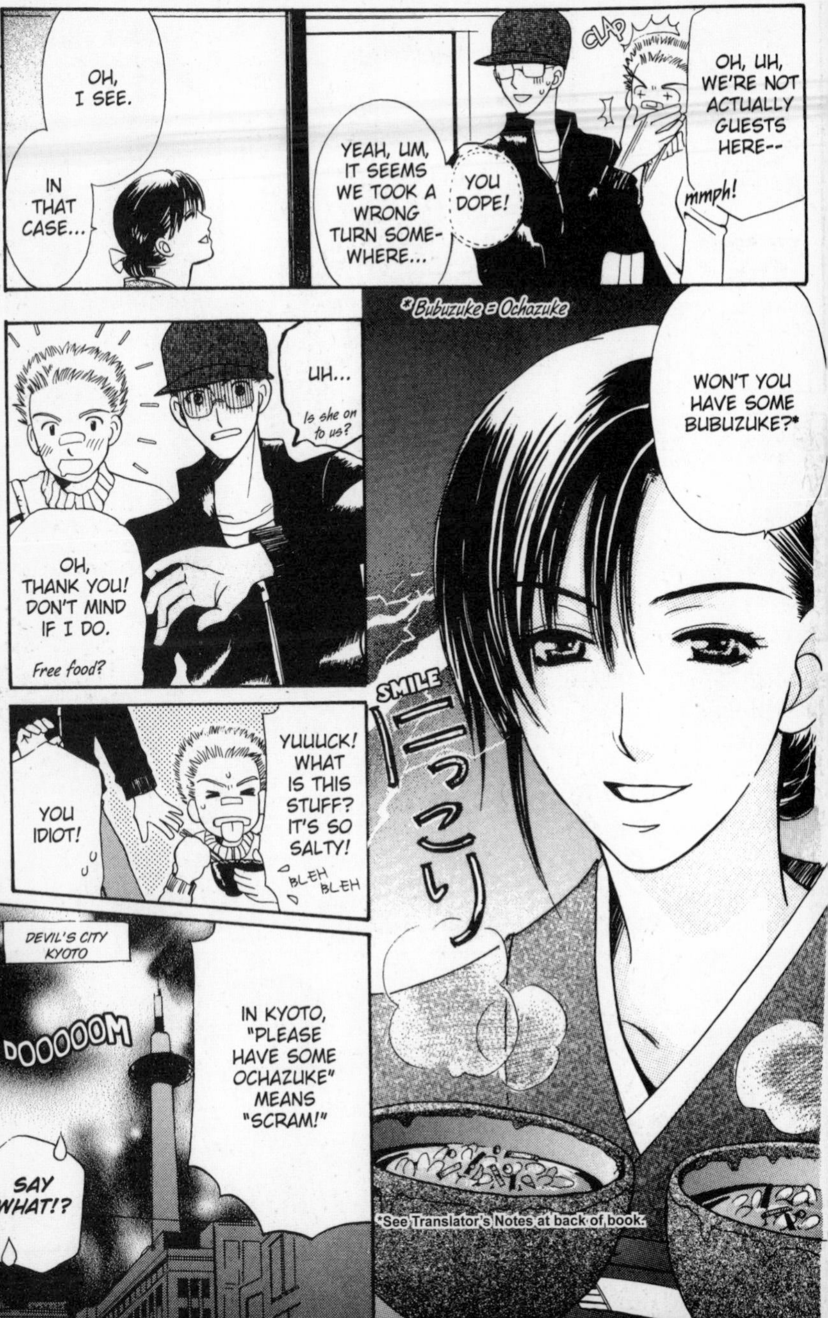
CLAP
OH, UH, WE'RE NOT ACTUALLY GUESTS HERE--
mmph!
YOU DOPE!
YEAH, UM, IT SEEMS WE TOOK A WRONG TURN SOMEWHERE...
OH, I SEE.
IN THAT CASE...
WON'T YOU HAVE SOME BUBUZUKE?*
*Bubuzuke = Ochazuke
SMILE
*See Translator's Notes at back of book.
UH...
Is she on to us?
OH, THANK YOU! DON'T MIND IF I DO.
Free food?
YUUUCK! WHAT IS THIS STUFF? IT'S SO SALTY!
BLEH BLEH
YOU IDIOT!
DEVIL'S CITY KYOTO
IN KYOTO, "PLEASE HAVE SOME OCHAZUKE" MEANS "SCRAM!"
DOOOOOM
SAY WHAT!?

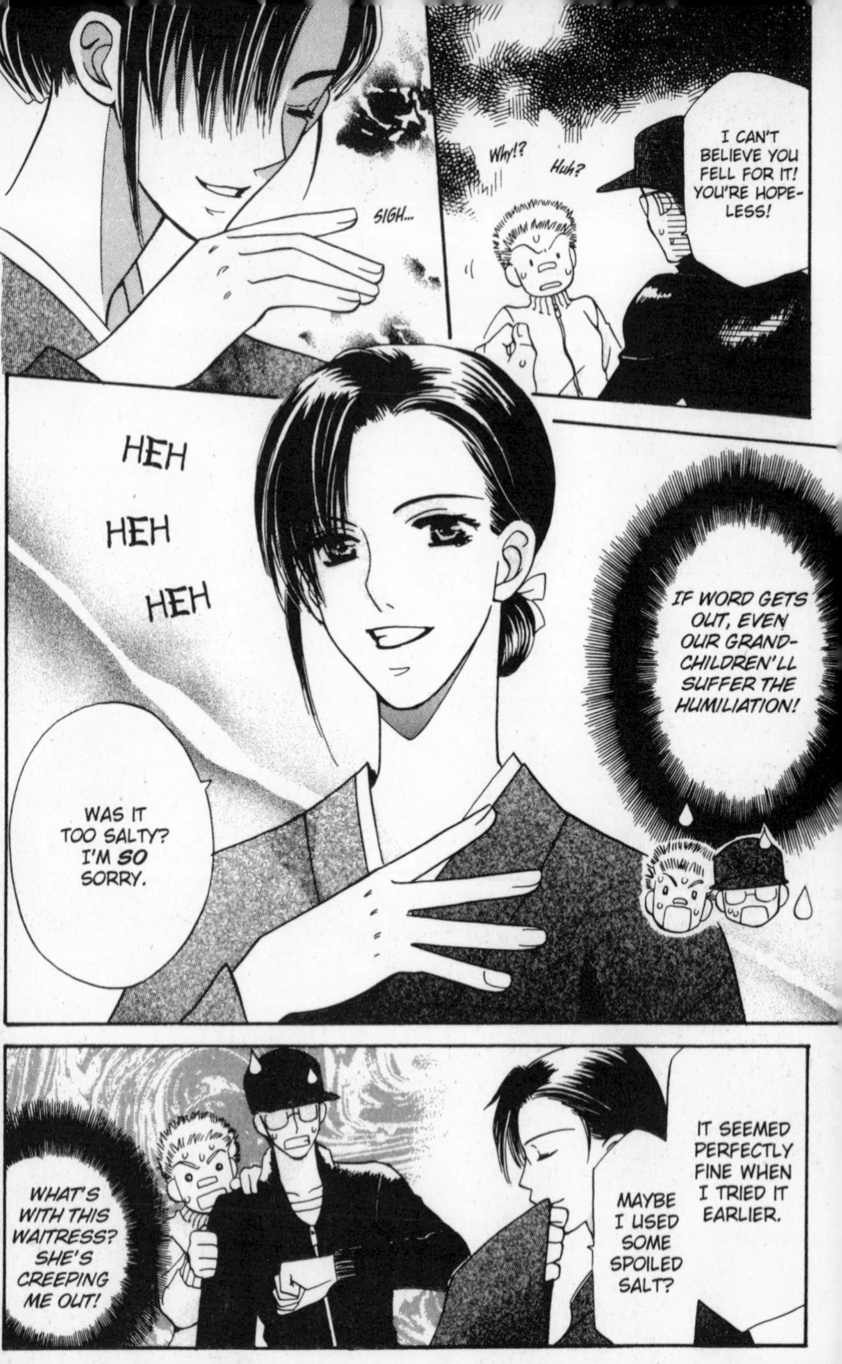
I CAN'T BELIEVE YOU FELL FOR IT! YOU'RE HOPE-LESS!
Huh?
Why!?
SIGH...
IF WORD GETS OUT, EVEN OUR GRAND-CHILDREN'LL SUFFER THE HUMILIATION!
HEH HEH HEH
WAS IT TOO SALTY? I'M SO SORRY.
IT SEEMED PERFECTLY FINE WHEN I TRIED IT EARLIER.
MAYBE I USED SOME SPOILED SALT?
WHAT'S WITH THIS WAITRESS? SHE'S CREEPING ME OUT!

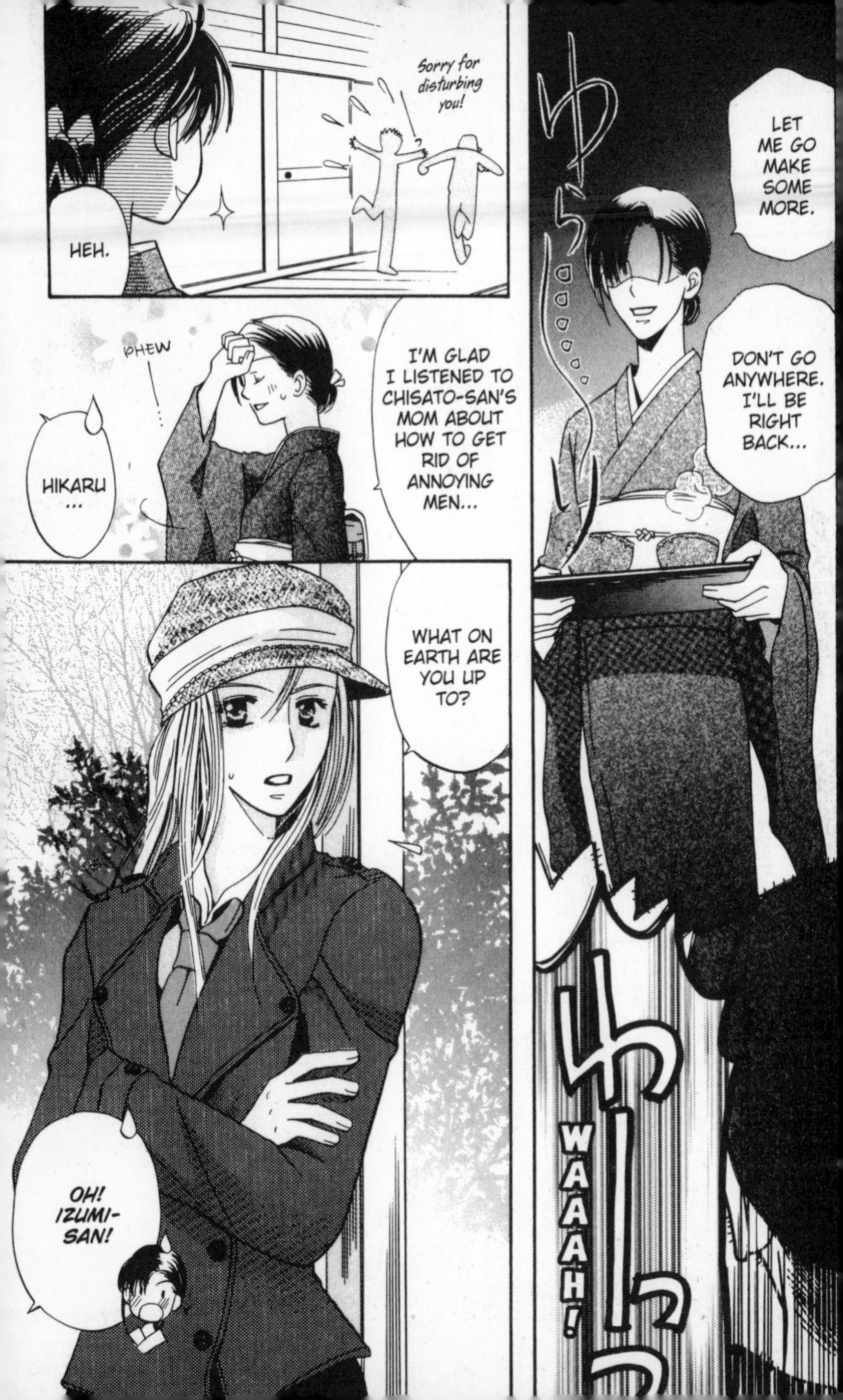
LET ME GO MAKE SOME MORE.
DON'T GO ANYWHERE. I'LL BE RIGHT BACK...
WAAAAH!
Sorry for disturbing you!
HEH.
I'M GLAD I LISTENED TO CHISATO-SAN'S MOM ABOUT HOW TO GET RID OF ANNOYING MEN...
PHEW
HIKARU ...
WHAT ON EARTH ARE YOU UP TO?
OH! IZUMI-SAN!

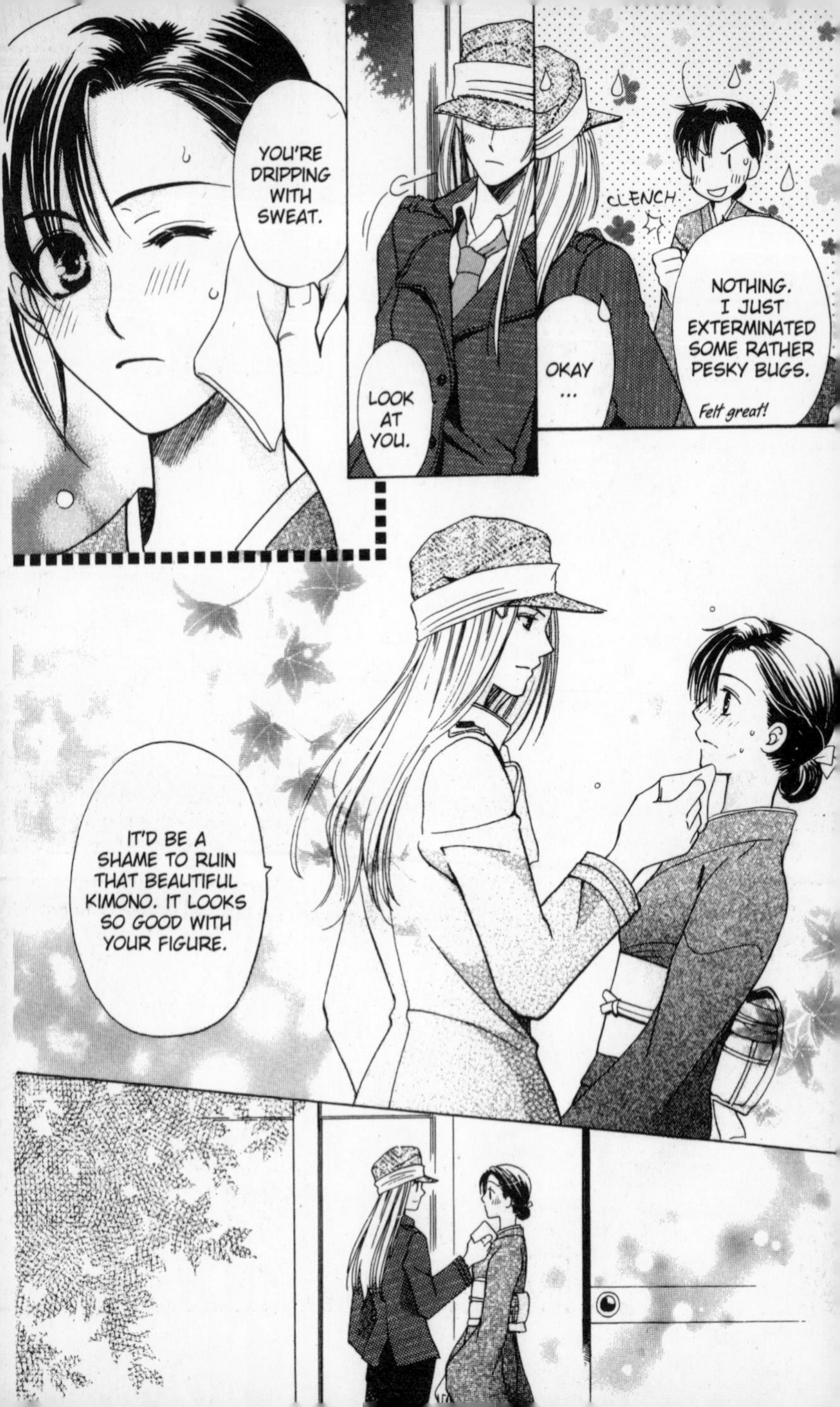
CLENCH
NOTHING. I JUST EXTERMINATED SOME RATHER PESKY BUGS.
Felt great!
OKAY ...
LOOK AT YOU.
YOU'RE DRIPPING WITH SWEAT.
IT'D BE A SHAME TO RUIN THAT BEAUTIFUL KIMONO. IT LOOKS SO GOOD WITH YOUR FIGURE.

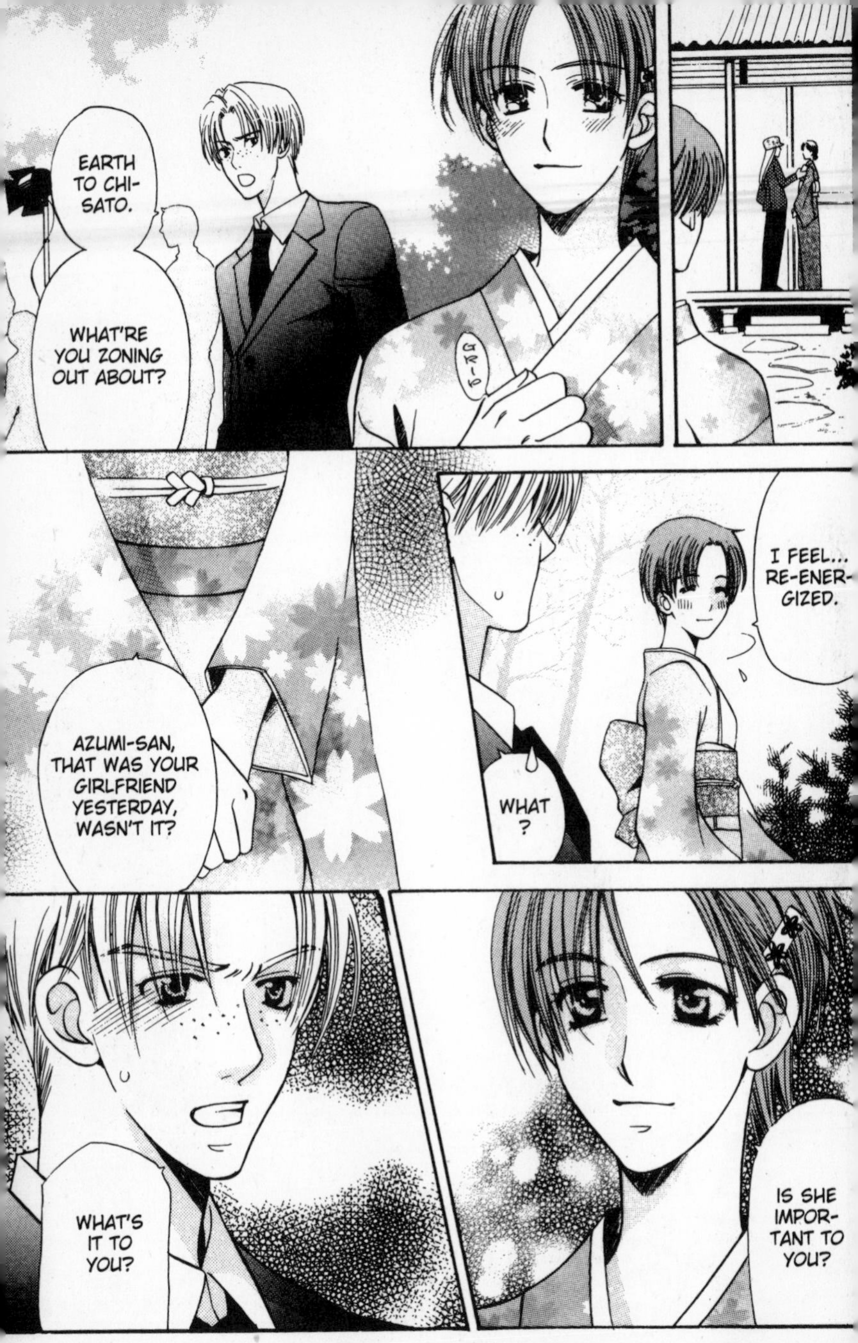
GRIP
EARTH TO CHI-SATO.
WHAT'RE YOU ZONING OUT ABOUT?
I FEEL... RE-ENERGIZED.
WHAT?
AZUMI-SAN, THAT WAS YOUR GIRLFRIEND YESTERDAY, WASN'T IT?
IS SHE IMPORTANT TO YOU?
WHAT'S IT TO YOU?

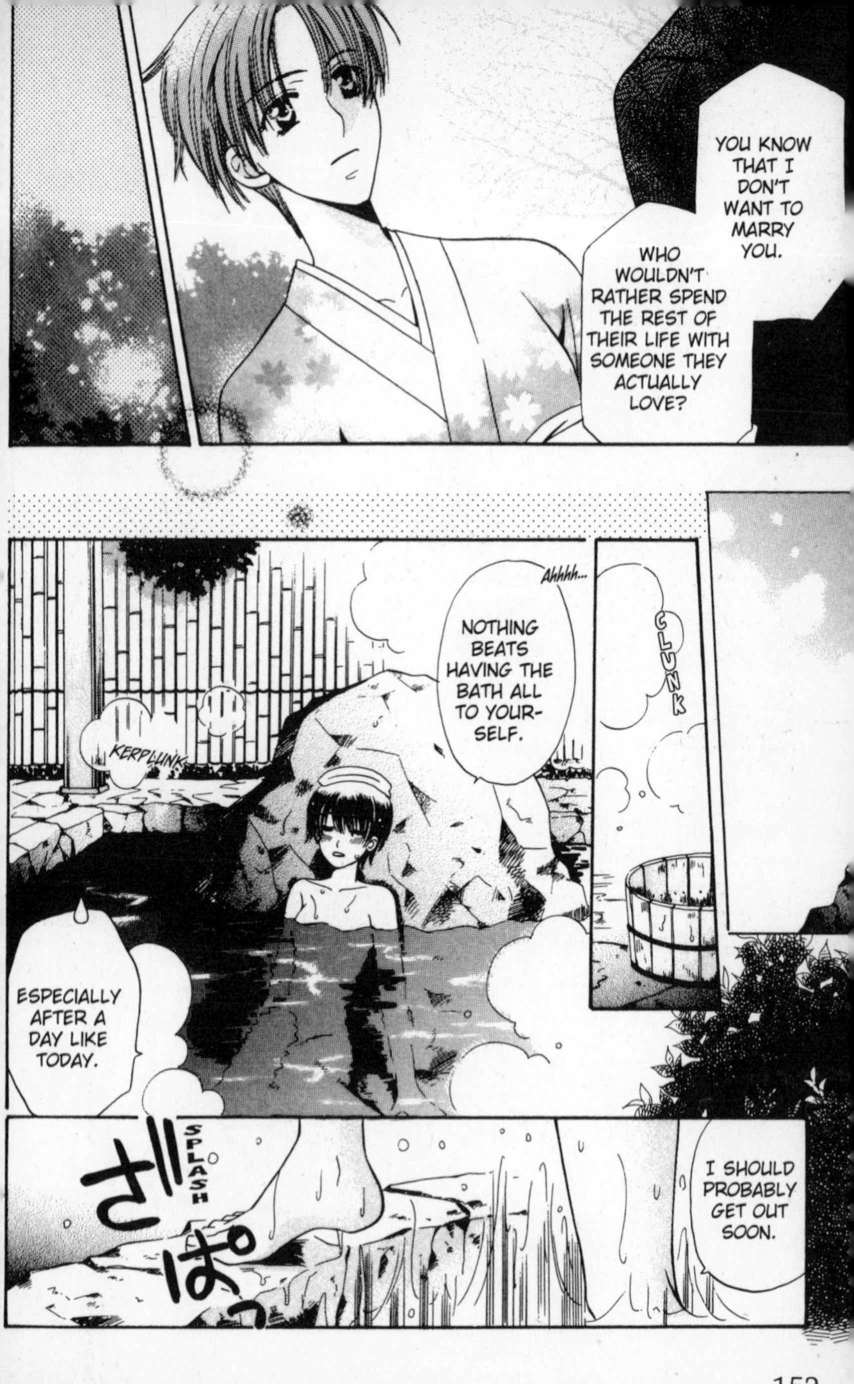
YOU KNOW THAT I DON'T WANT TO MARRY YOU.
WHO WOULDN'T RATHER SPEND THE REST OF THEIR LIFE WITH SOMEONE THEY ACTUALLY LOVE?
CLUNK
Ahhhh...
NOTHING BEATS HAVING THE BATH ALL TO YOUR-SELF.
KERPLUNK
ESPECIALLY AFTER A DAY LIKE TODAY.
I SHOULD PROBABLY GET OUT SOON.
ざぱっ
SPLASH

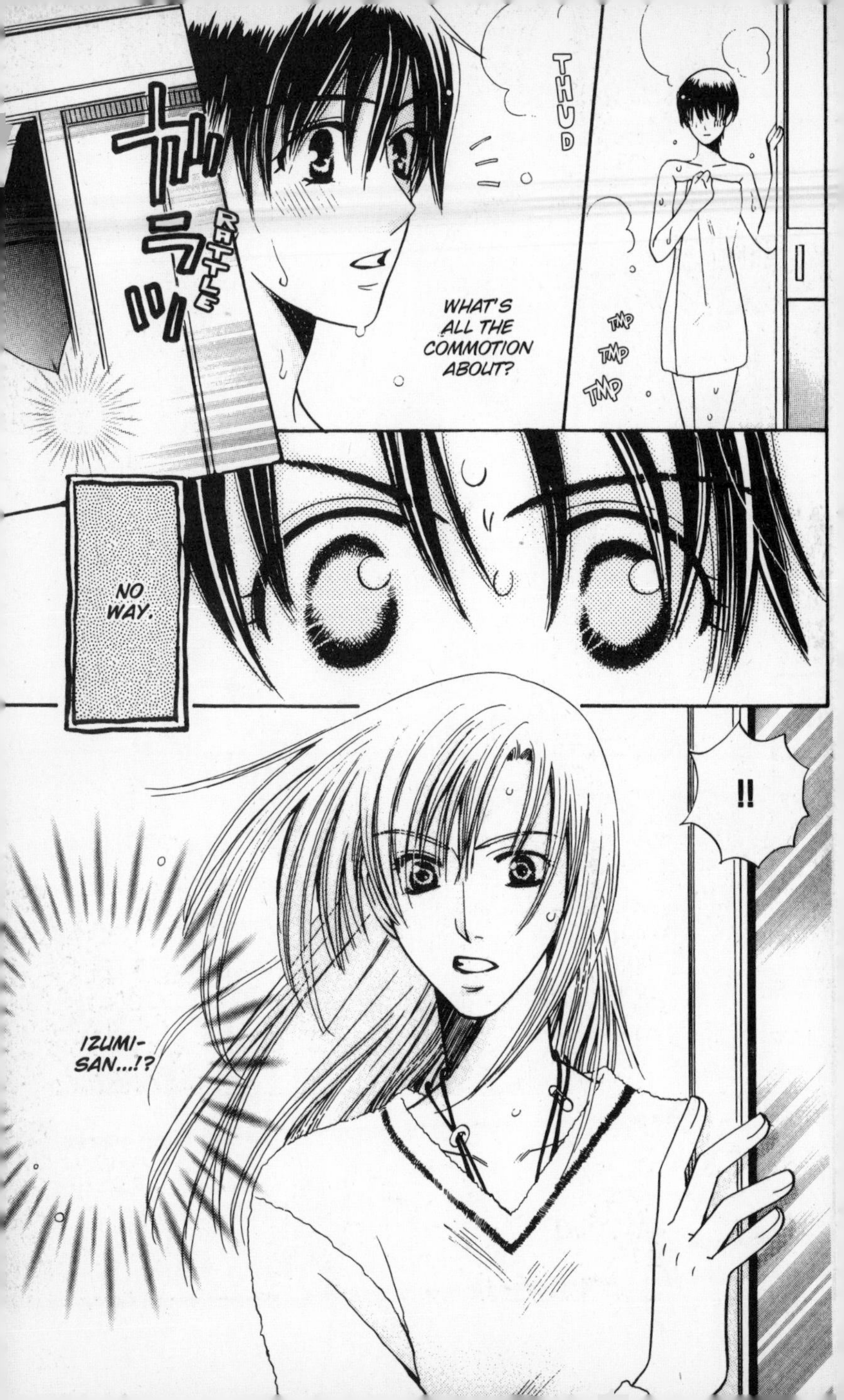
THUD
TMP
TMP
TMP
WHAT'S ALL THE COMMOTION ABOUT?
RATTLE
NO WAY.
!!
IZUMI-SAN...!?

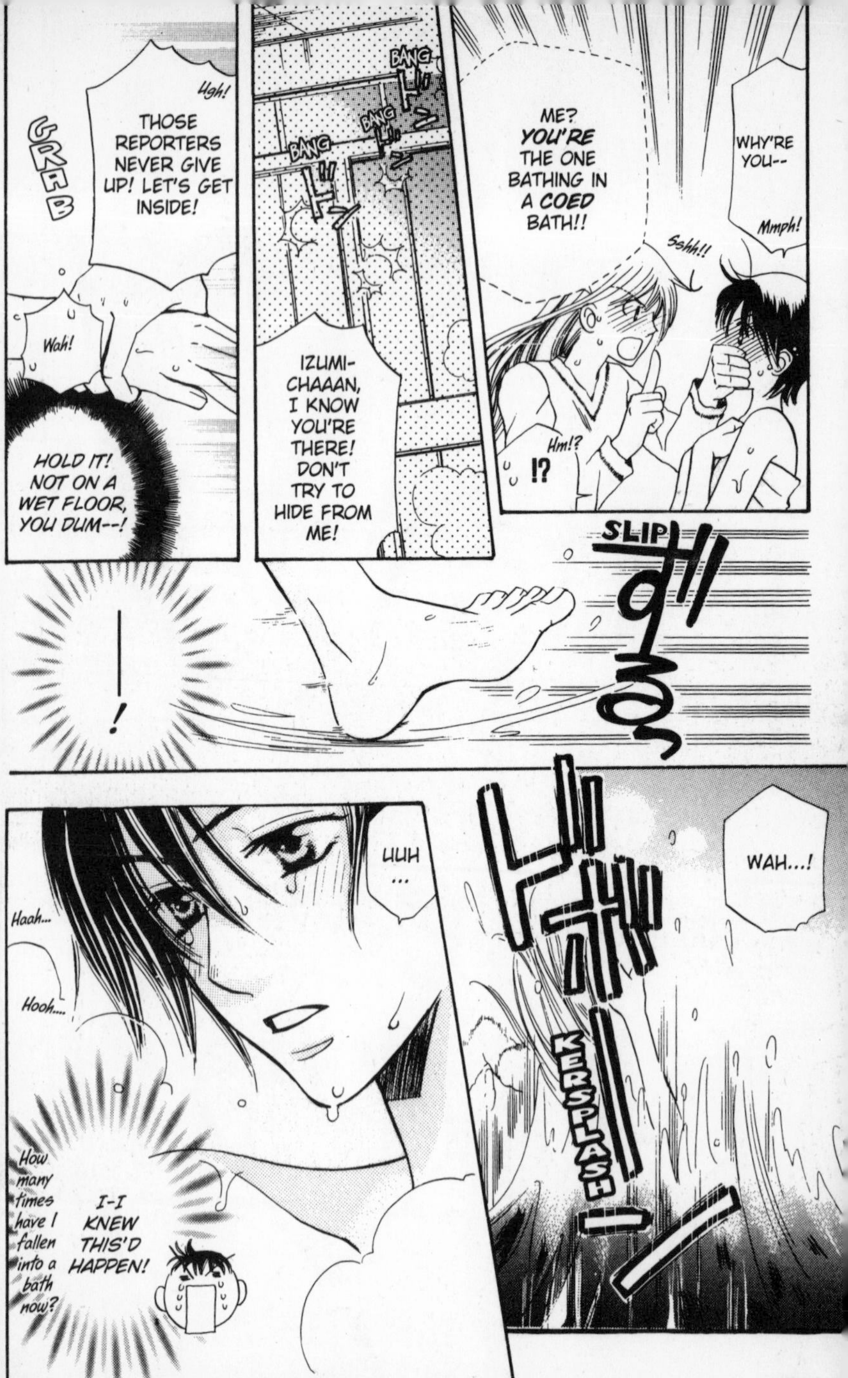
WHY'RE YOU--
Mmph!
ME? YOU'RE THE ONE BATHING IN A COED BATH!!
Sshh!!
Hm!?
!?
BANG
BANG
BANG
IZUMI-CHAAAN, I KNOW YOU'RE THERE! DON'T TRY TO HIDE FROM ME!
Ugh!
THOSE REPORTERS NEVER GIVE UP! LET'S GET INSIDE!
GRAB
Wah!
HOLD IT! NOT ON A WET FLOOR, YOU DUM--!
SLIP
!
WAH...!
KERSPLASH
UUH ...
Haah...
Hooh...
How many times have I fallen into a bath now?
I-I KNEW THIS'D HAPPEN!

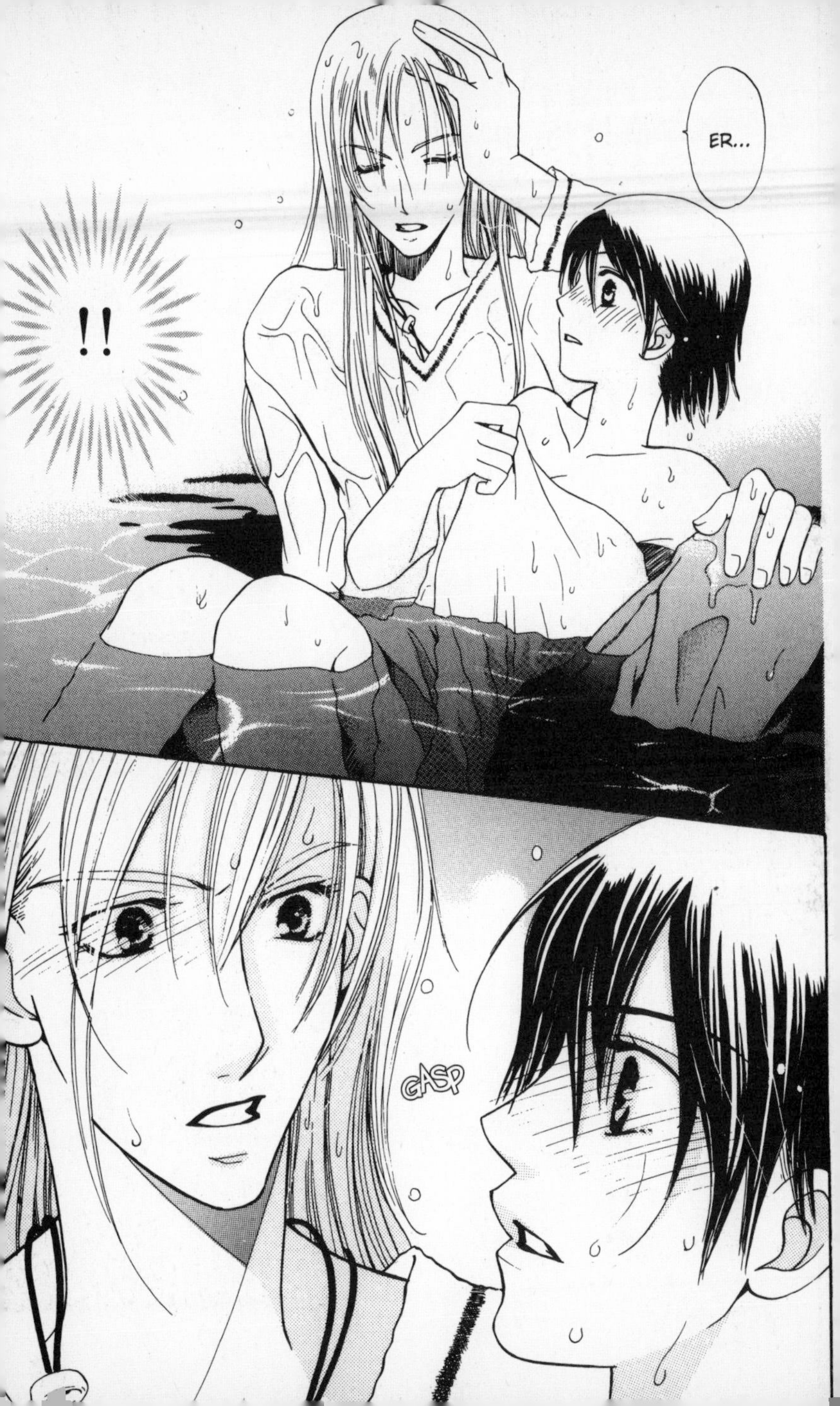
ER...
!!
GASP

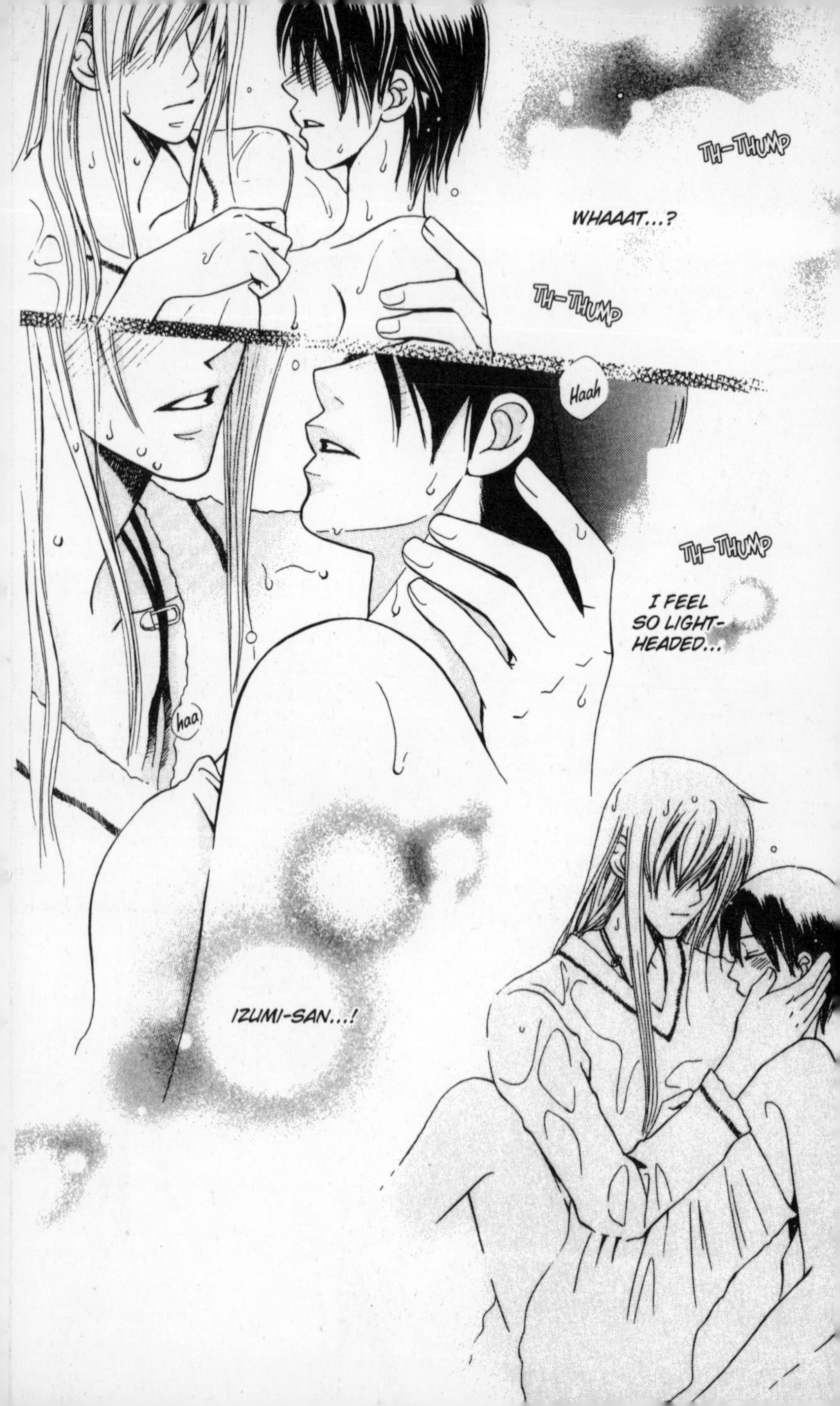

TH-THUMP
WHAAAT...?
TH-THUMP
Haah
TH-THUMP
I FEEL SO LIGHT-HEADED...
haa
IZUMI-SAN...!

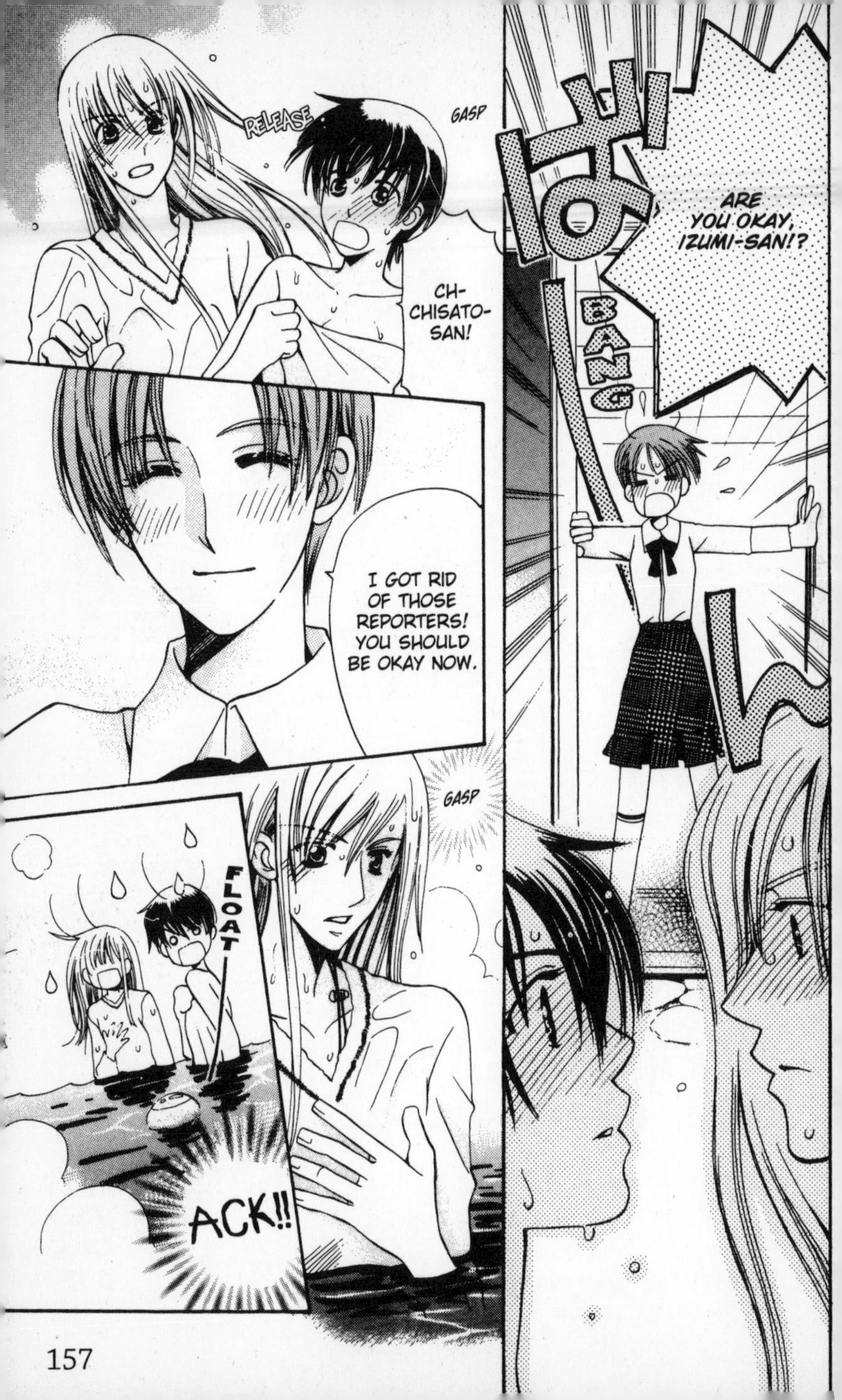
ARE YOU OKAY, IZUMI-SAN!?
BANG
RELEASE
GASP
CH-CHISATO-SAN!
I GOT RID OF THOSE REPORTERS! YOU SHOULD BE OKAY NOW.
GASP
FLOAT
ACK!!

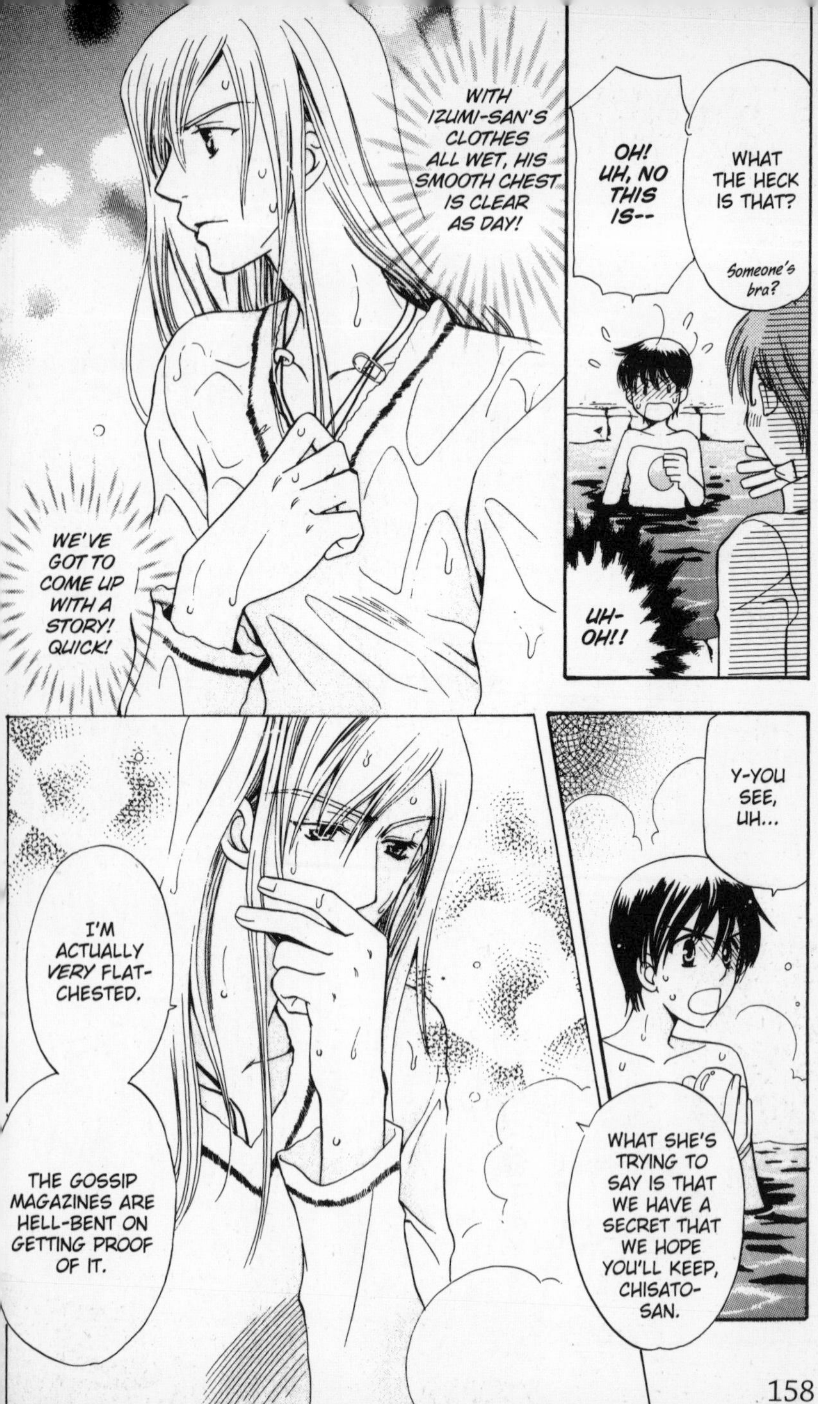
WHAT THE HECK IS THAT?
Someone's bra?
OH! UH, NO THIS IS--
UH-OH!!
WITH IZUMI-SAN'S CLOTHES ALL WET, HIS SMOOTH CHEST IS CLEAR AS DAY!
WE'VE GOT TO COME UP WITH A STORY! QUICK!
Y-YOU SEE, UH...
I'M ACTUALLY VERY FLAT-CHESTED.
THE GOSSIP MAGAZINES ARE HELL-BENT ON GETTING PROOF OF IT.
WHAT SHE'S TRYING TO SAY IS THAT WE HAVE A SECRET THAT WE HOPE YOU'LL KEEP, CHISATO-SAN.

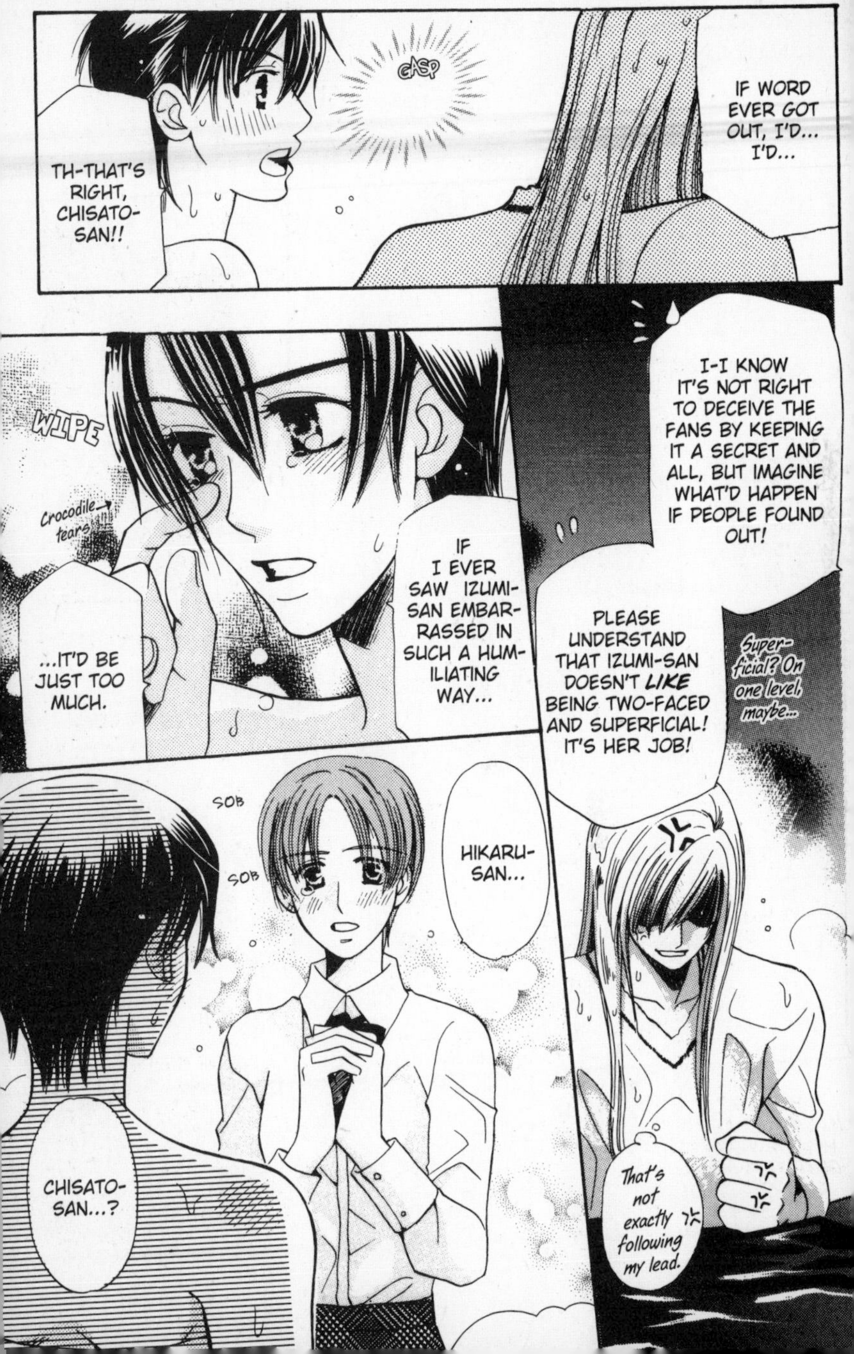
IF WORD EVER GOT OUT, I'D... I'D...
GASP
TH-THAT'S RIGHT, CHISATO-SAN!!
I-I KNOW IT'S NOT RIGHT TO DECEIVE THE FANS BY KEEPING IT A SECRET AND ALL, BUT IMAGINE WHAT'D HAPPEN IF PEOPLE FOUND OUT!
PLEASE UNDERSTAND THAT IZUMI-SAN DOESN'T LIKE BEING TWO-FACED AND SUPERFICIAL! IT'S HER JOB!
Superficial? On one level, maybe...
IF I EVER SAW IZUMI-SAN EMBARRASSED IN SUCH A HUMILIATING WAY...
...IT'D BE JUST TOO MUCH.
WIPE
Crocodile tears
That's not exactly following my lead.
HIKARU-SAN...
SOB
SOB
CHISATO-SAN...?

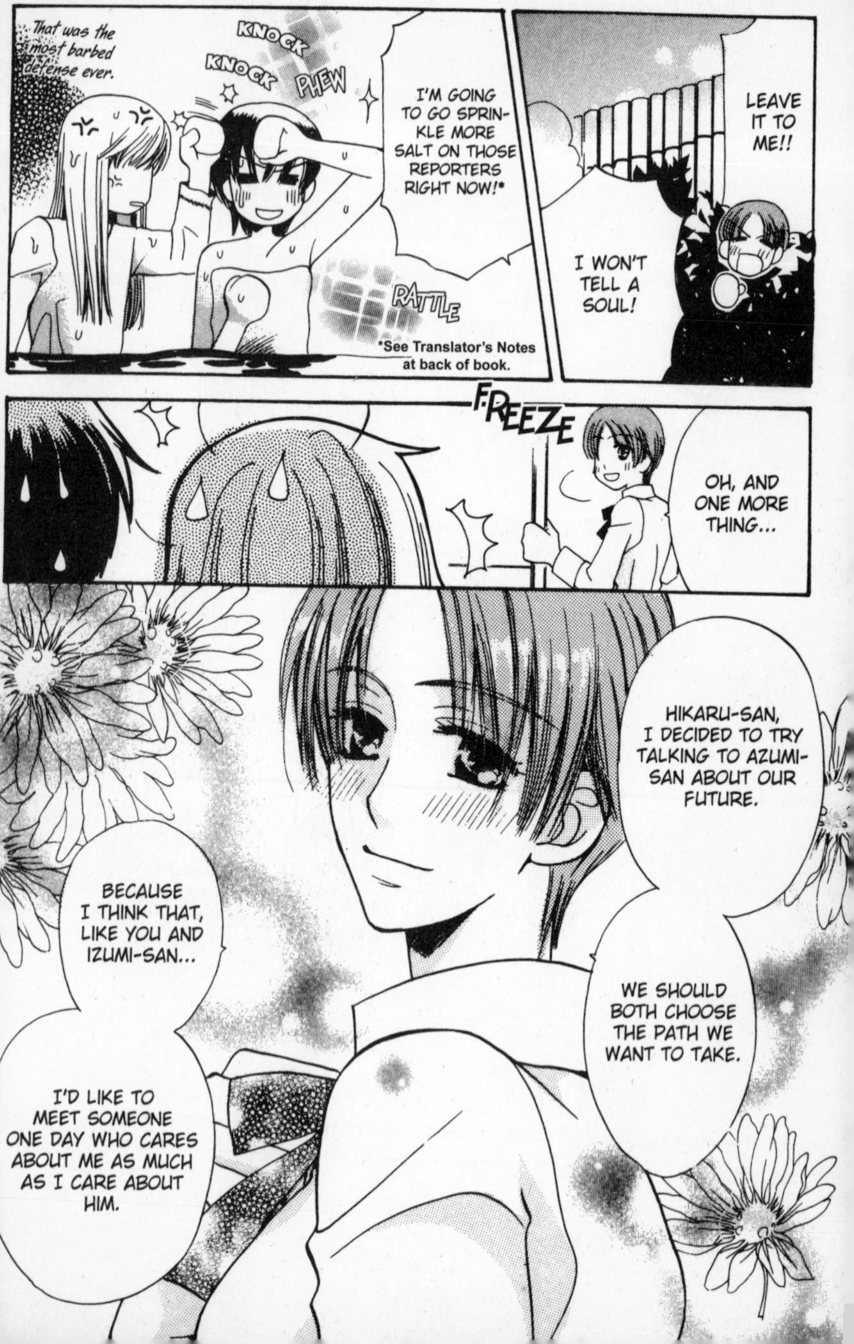
LEAVE IT TO ME!!
I WON'T TELL A SOUL!
I'M GOING TO GO SPRINKLE MORE SALT ON THOSE REPORTERS RIGHT NOW!*
KNOCK
KNOCK
PHEW
That was the most barbed defense ever.
RATTLE
*See Translator's Notes at back of book.
F-REEZE
OH, AND ONE MORE THING...
HIKARU-SAN, I DECIDED TO TRY TALKING TO AZUMI-SAN ABOUT OUR FUTURE.
WE SHOULD BOTH CHOOSE THE PATH WE WANT TO TAKE.
BECAUSE I THINK THAT, LIKE YOU AND IZUMI-SAN...
I'D LIKE TO MEET SOMEONE ONE DAY WHO CARES ABOUT ME AS MUCH AS I CARE ABOUT HIM.

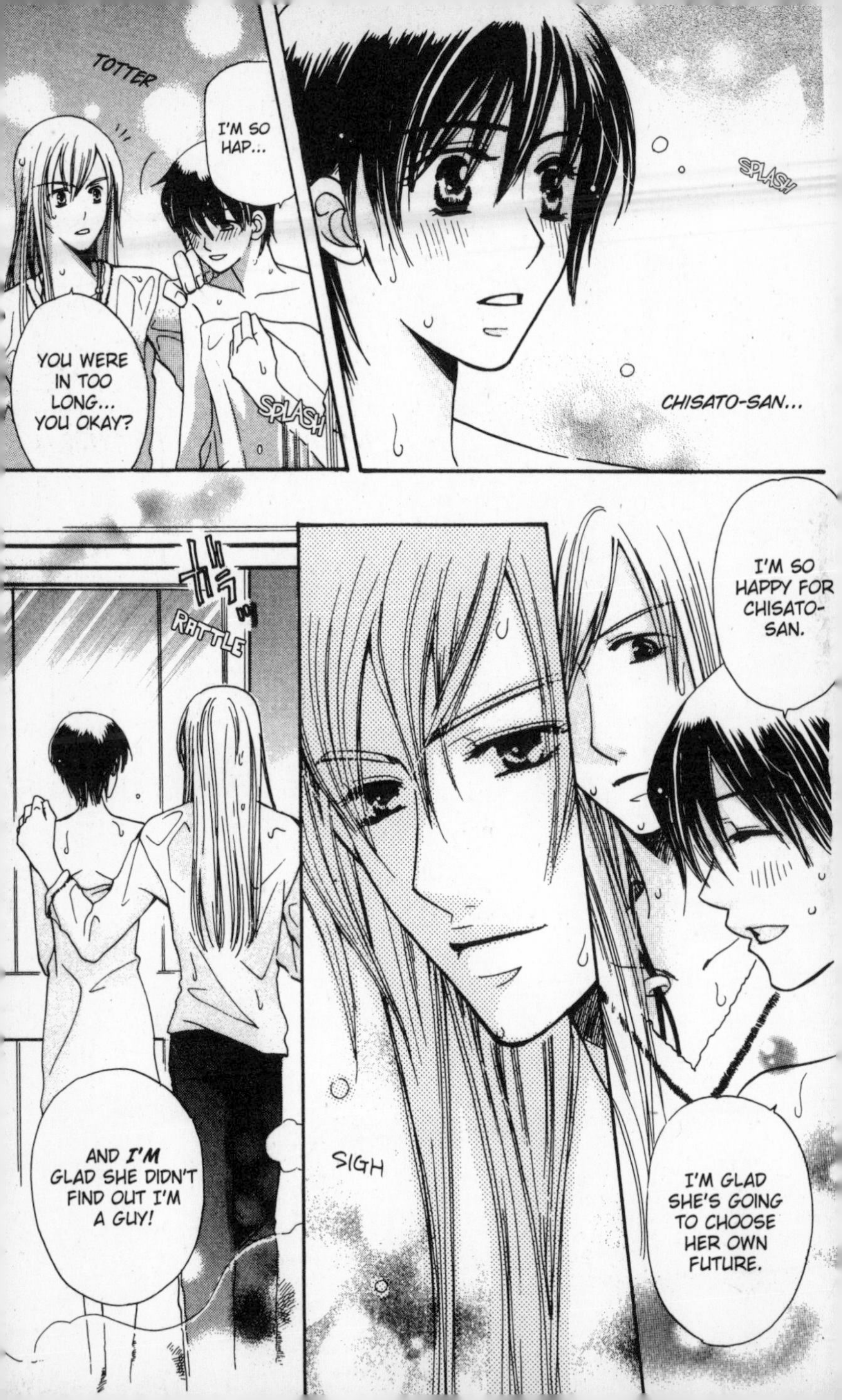
SPLASH
CHISATO-SAN...
TOTTER
I'M SO HAP...
YOU WERE IN TOO LONG... YOU OKAY?
SPLASH
I'M SO HAPPY FOR CHISATO-SAN.
I'M GLAD SHE'S GOING TO CHOOSE HER OWN FUTURE.
SIGH
RATTLE
AND *I'M* GLAD SHE DIDN'T FIND OUT I'M A GUY!

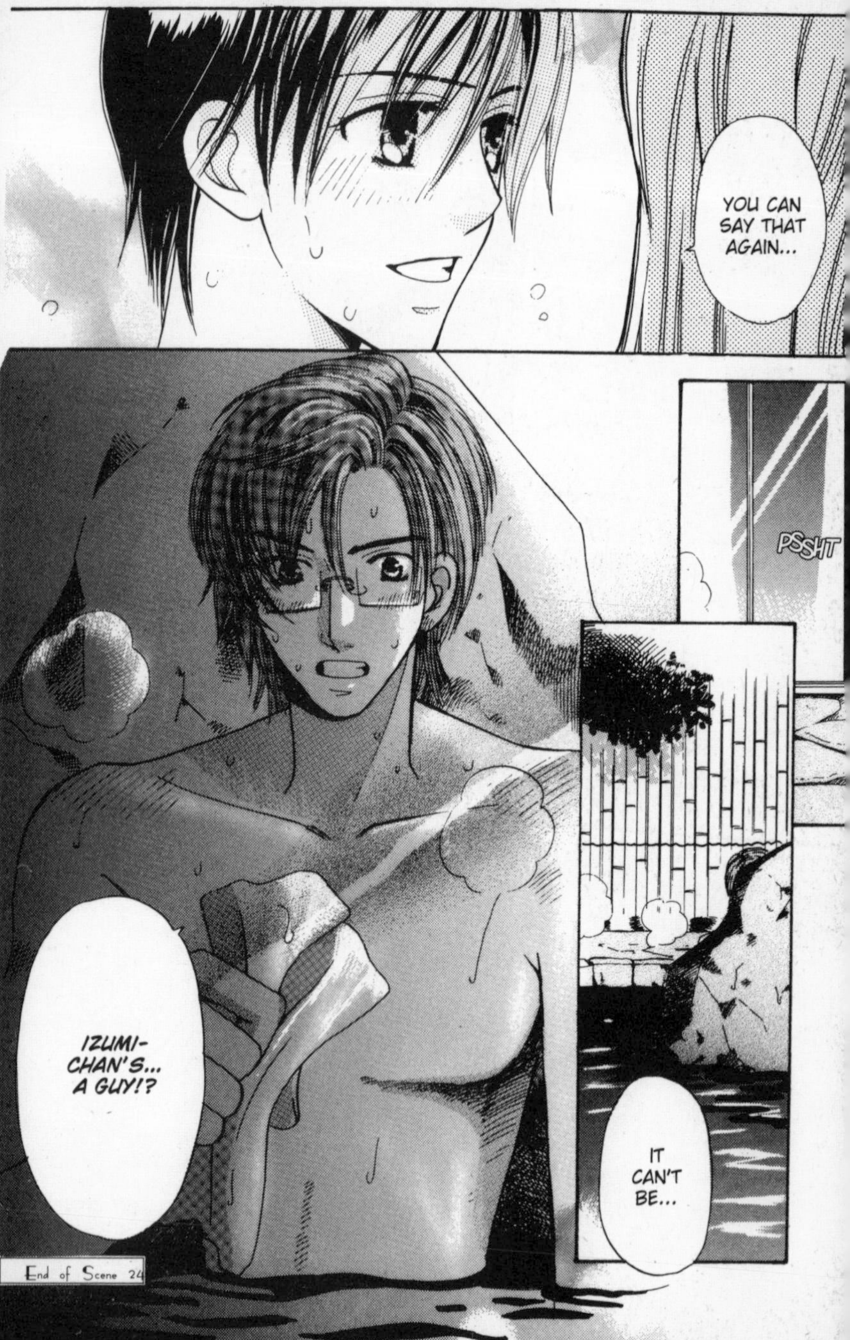
YOU CAN SAY THAT AGAIN...
PSSHT
IT CAN'T BE...
IZUMI-CHAN'S... A GUY!?
End of Scene 24

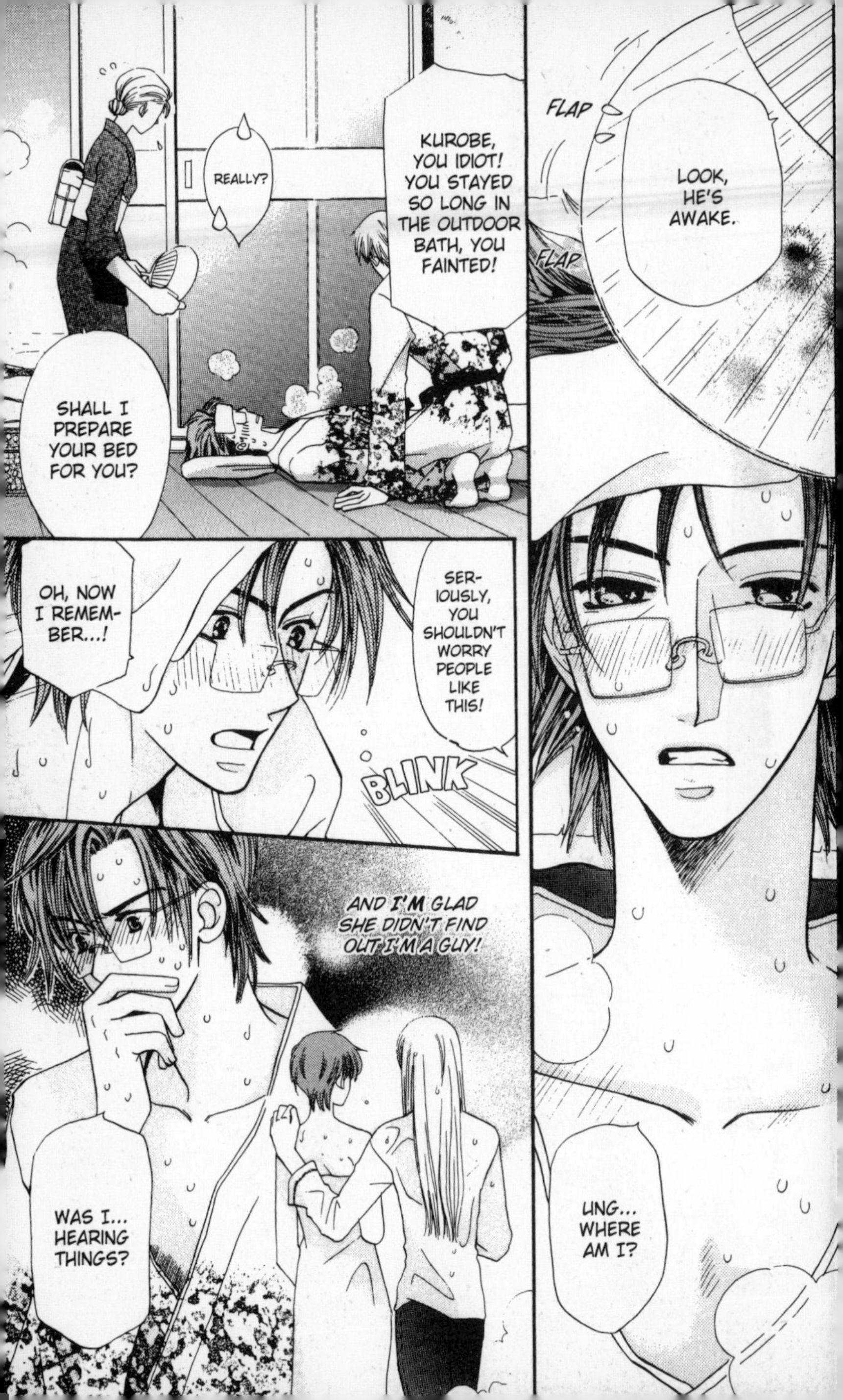
LOOK, HE'S AWAKE.
FLAP
FLAP
UNG... WHERE AM I?
KUROBE, YOU IDIOT! YOU STAYED SO LONG IN THE OUTDOOR BATH, YOU FAINTED!
REALLY?
SHALL I PREPARE YOUR BED FOR YOU?
SER-IOUSLY, YOU SHOULDN'T WORRY PEOPLE LIKE THIS!
BLINK
OH, NOW I REMEM-BER...!
AND I'M GLAD SHE DIDN'T FIND OUT I'M A GUY!
WAS I... HEARING THINGS?

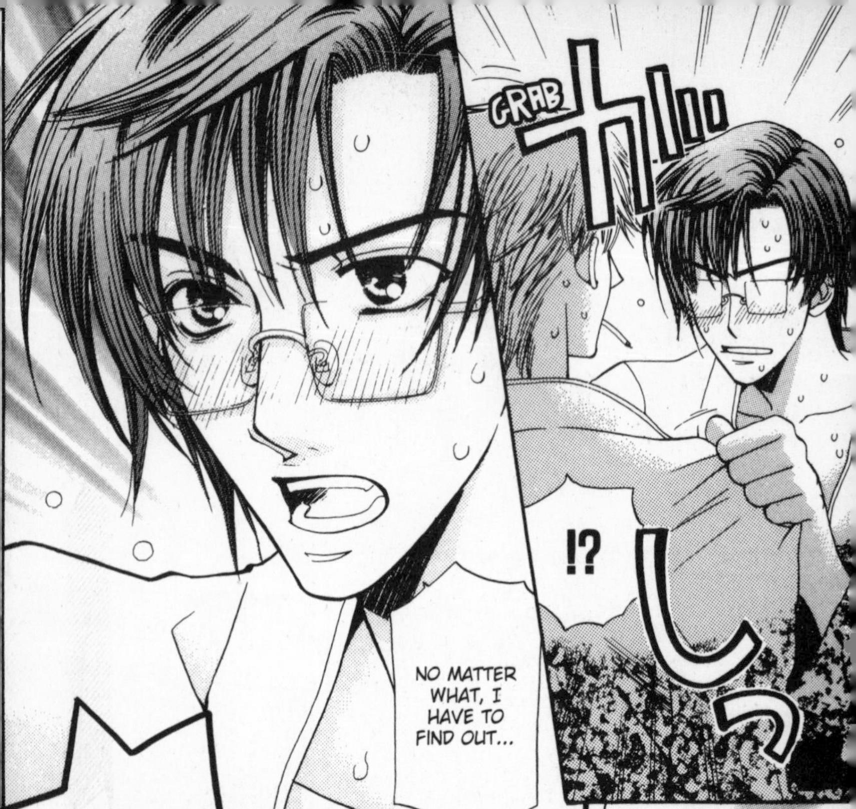
GRAB
!?
しっ
NO MATTER WHAT, I HAVE TO FIND OUT...
CAN I COUNT ON YOU TO HAVE MY BACK, PARTNER!?

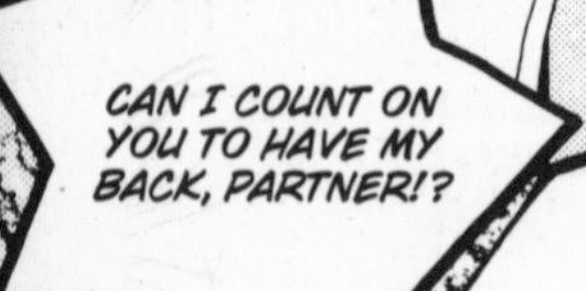
Comedy is easy money.
At least that's what I thought...
SHEESH

Kaoru Habashi (20 years old)
Born: November 10
Blood Type: AB
Wannabe-Host Type.
When I designed Kaoru, some of my assistants told me that he looks a lot like the stand-up comedian Hiroshi, which wasn't really a compliment at all. In reality, Kaoru's a very lazy guy. He's tied to his partner, Kurobe, who wants to do more than just comedy, and so he gets dragged around by Kurobe a lot.

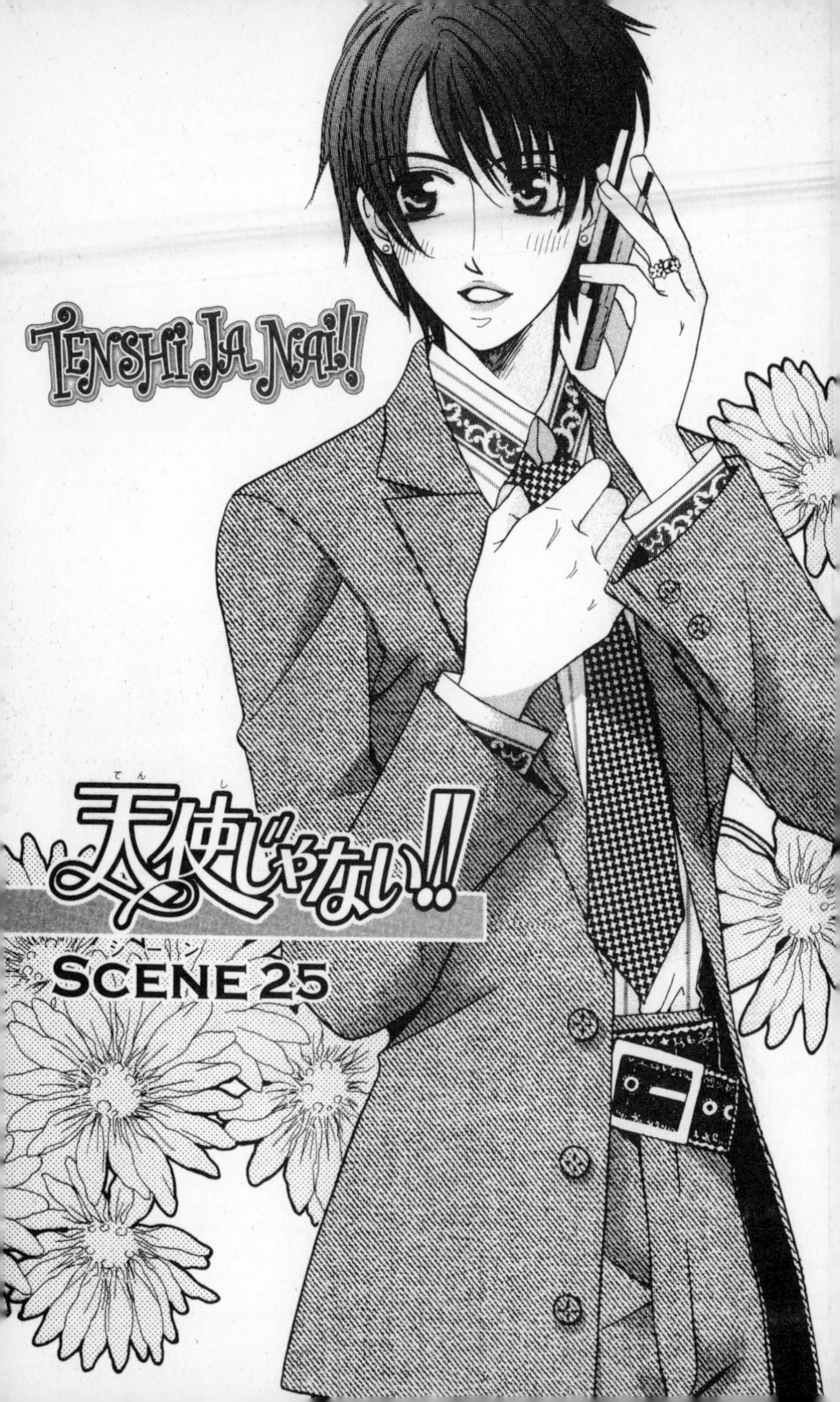
TENSHI JA NAI!!
天使じゃない!!
SCENE 25

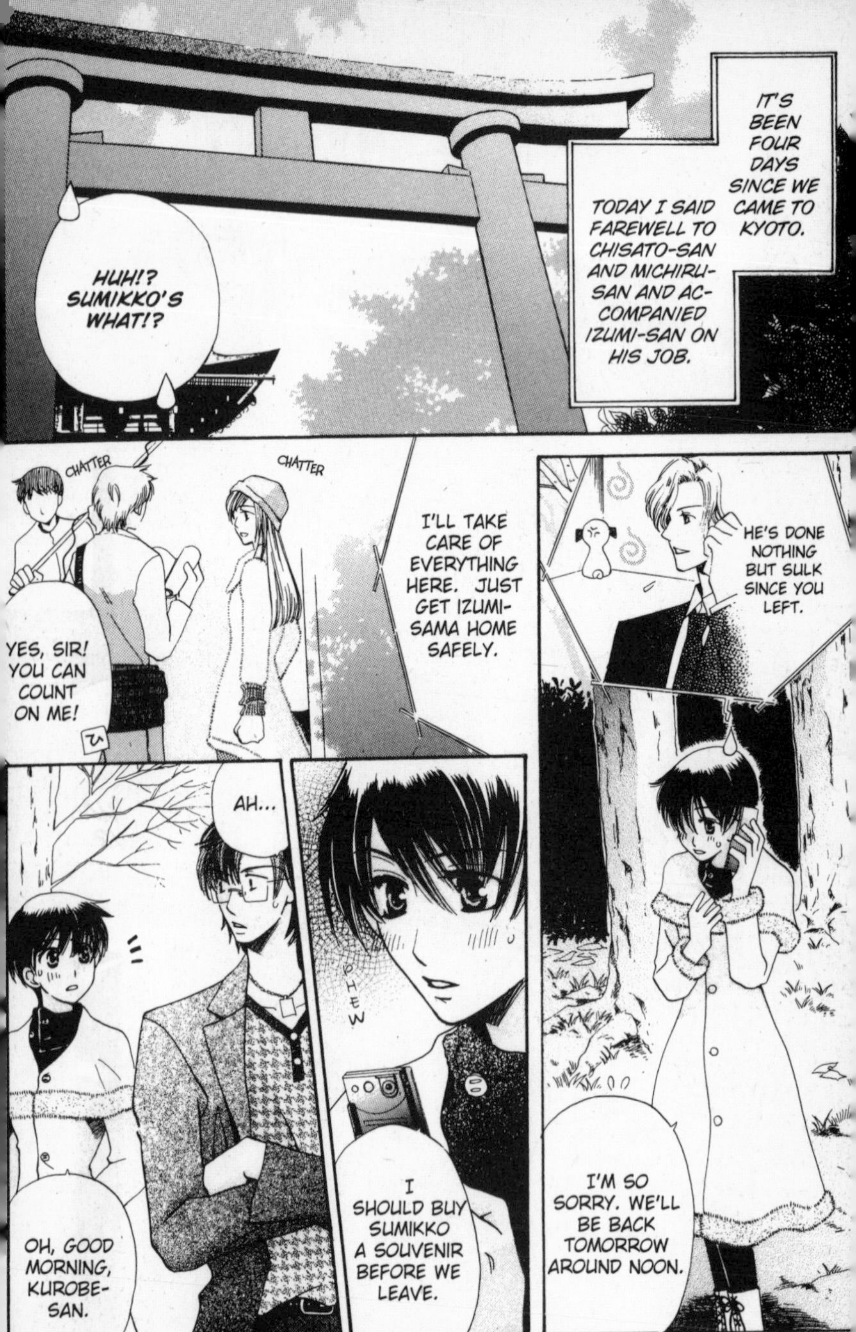
IT'S BEEN FOUR DAYS SINCE WE CAME TO KYOTO.
TODAY I SAID FAREWELL TO CHISATO-SAN AND MICHIRU-SAN AND AC-COMPANIED IZUMI-SAN ON HIS JOB.
HUH!? SUMIKKO'S WHAT!?
HE'S DONE NOTHING BUT SULK SINCE YOU LEFT.
I'M SO SORRY. WE'LL BE BACK TOMORROW AROUND NOON.
CHATTER
I'LL TAKE CARE OF EVERYTHING HERE. JUST GET IZUMI-SAMA HOME SAFELY.
CHATTER
YES, SIR! YOU CAN COUNT ON ME!
PHEW
I SHOULD BUY SUMIKKO A SOUVENIR BEFORE WE LEAVE.
AH...
OH, GOOD MORNING, KUROBE-SAN.

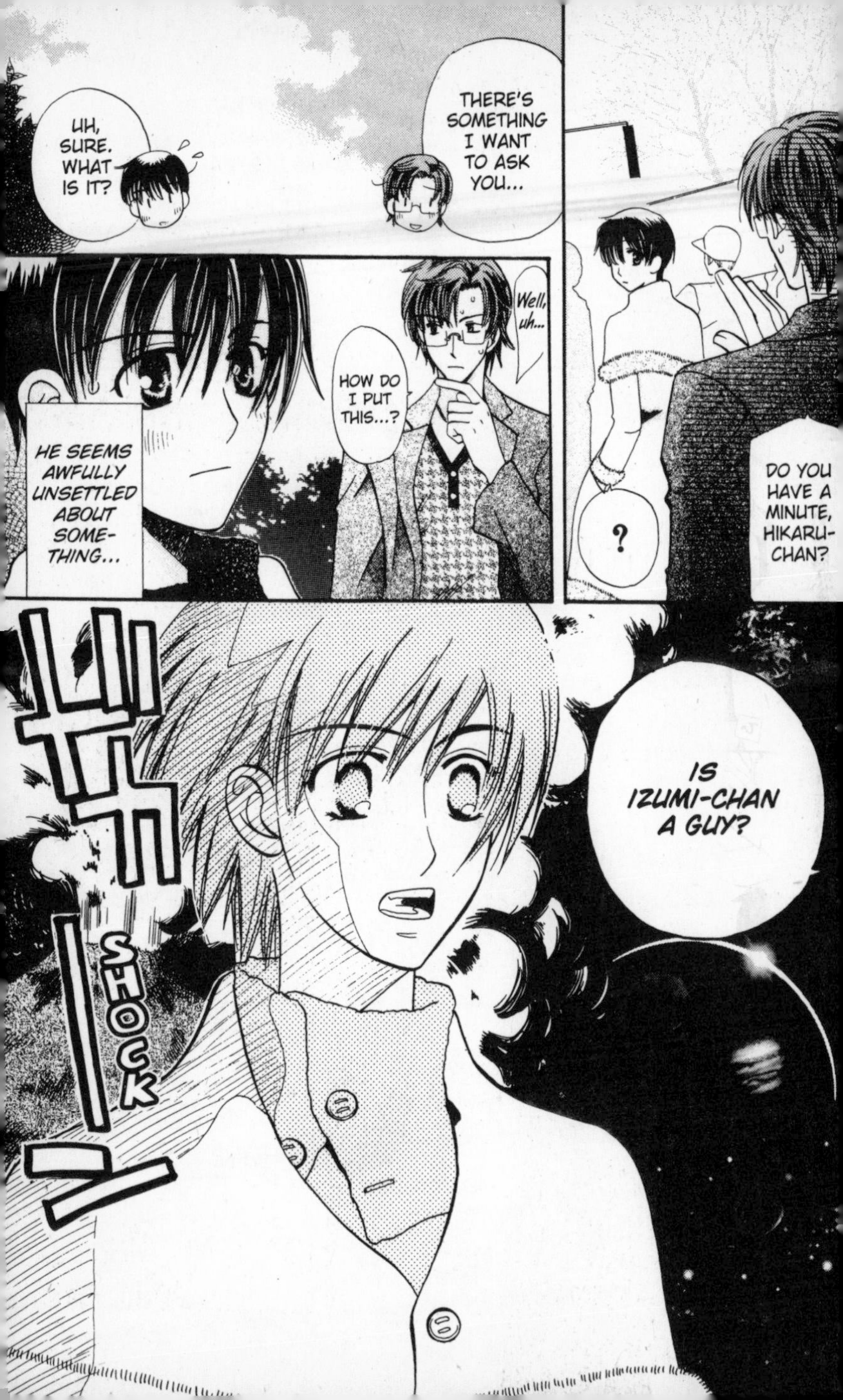
DO YOU HAVE A MINUTE, HIKARU-CHAN?
?
THERE'S SOMETHING I WANT TO ASK YOU...
UH, SURE. WHAT IS IT?
Well, uh...
HOW DO I PUT THIS...?
HE SEEMS AWFULLY UNSETTLED ABOUT SOME-THING...
IS IZUMI-CHAN A GUY?
SHOCK

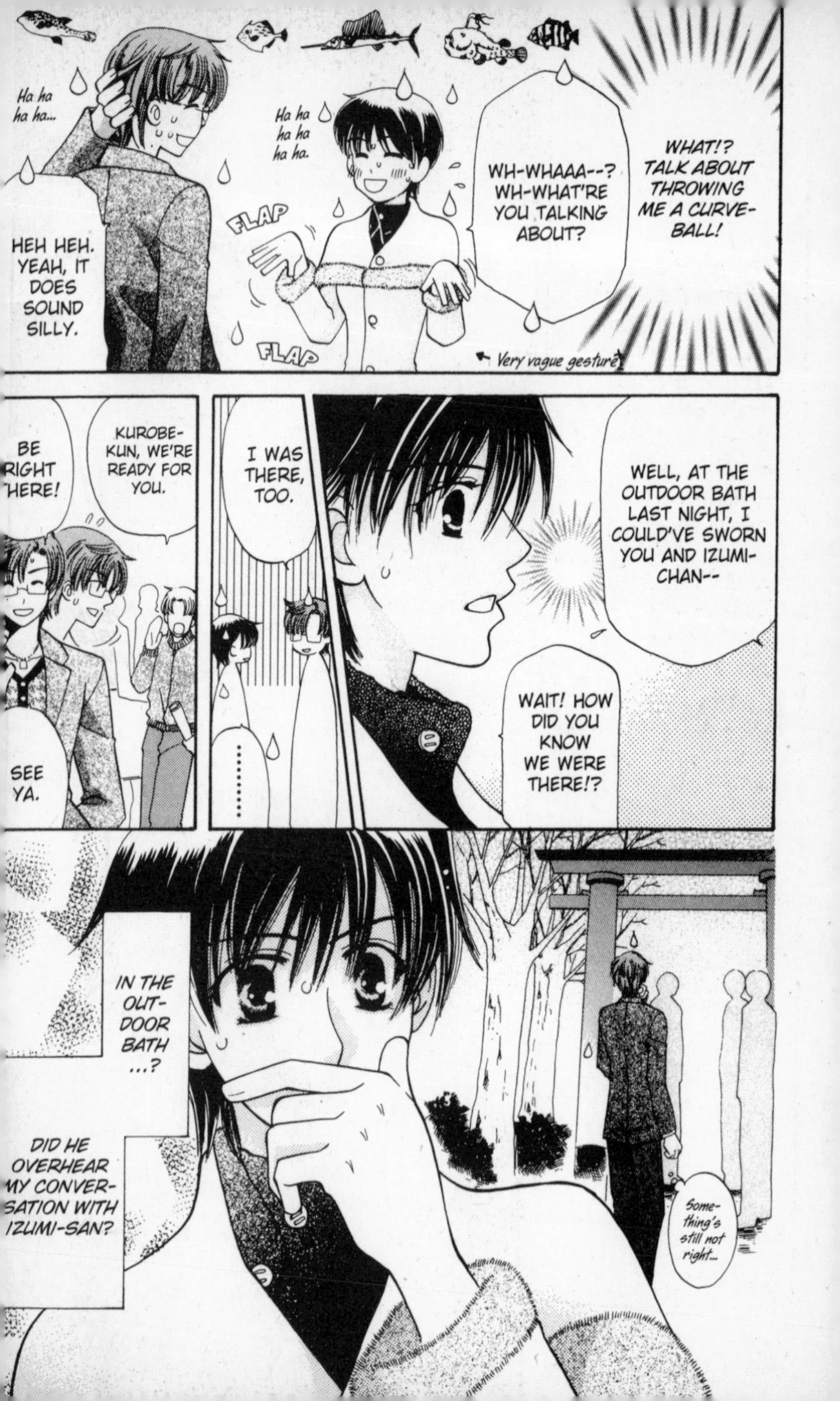
WHAT!? TALK ABOUT THROWING ME A CURVE-BALL!
WH-WHAAA--? WH-WHAT'RE YOU TALKING ABOUT?
Ha ha ha ha ha ha.
FLAP
FLAP
Very vague gesture
Ha ha ha ha...
HEH HEH. YEAH, IT DOES SOUND SILLY.
WELL, AT THE OUTDOOR BATH LAST NIGHT, I COULD'VE SWORN YOU AND IZUMI-CHAN--
WAIT! HOW DID YOU KNOW WE WERE THERE!?
I WAS THERE, TOO.
......
KUROBE-KUN, WE'RE READY FOR YOU.
BE RIGHT HERE!
SEE YA.
IN THE OUT-DOOR BATH ...?
Some-thing's still not right...
DID HE OVERHEAR MY CONVER-SATION WITH IZUMI-SAN?

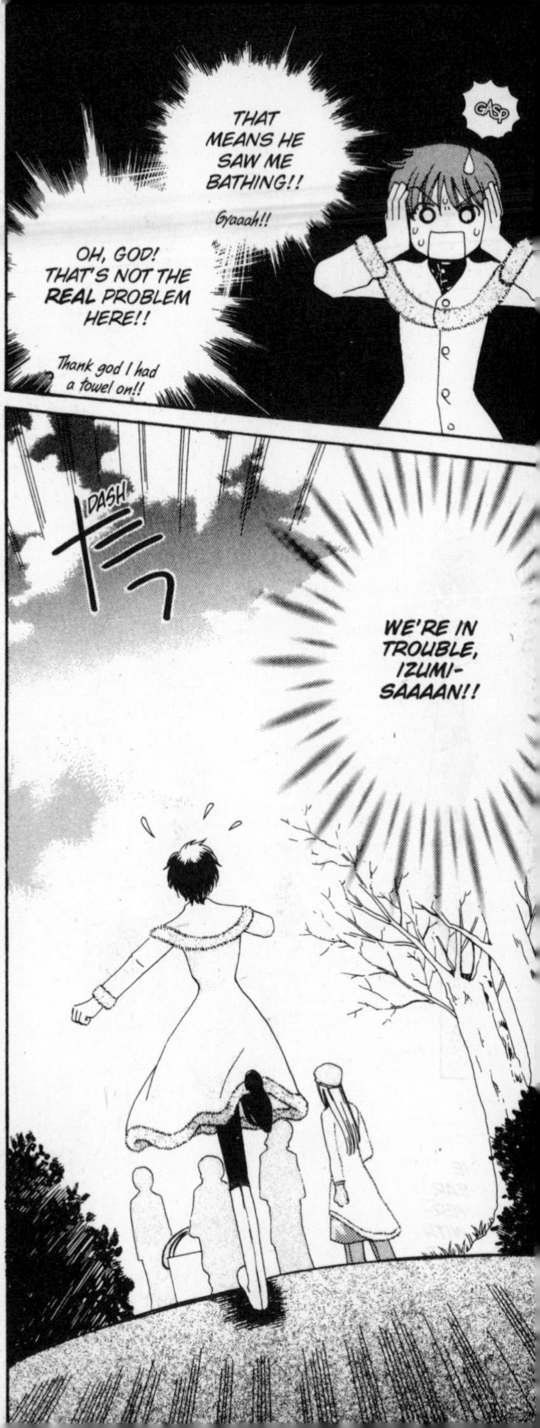
GASP
THAT MEANS HE SAW ME BATHING!!
Gyaaah!!
OH, GOD! THAT'S NOT THE **REAL** PROBLEM HERE!!
Thank god I had a towel on!!
WE'RE IN TROUBLE, IZUMI-SAAAAN!!
DASH

Confused By TV

✵ ✵ ✵

Er, maybe I shouldn't say that. I've been getting caught up in the QVC channel and watching documentaries, and it's got me thinking that I might be a shut-in. I even burst out crying whenever I watch anime. Then again, maybe that last one's not so abnormal...
I said I was into QVC, but these days I've calmed down about it. And the only reason I'm a shut-in is because work forces me to be. Yeah, that's it! My room's become my workplace!

✧

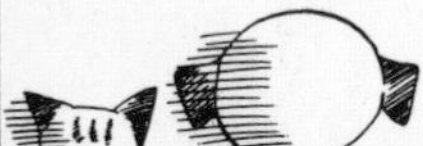

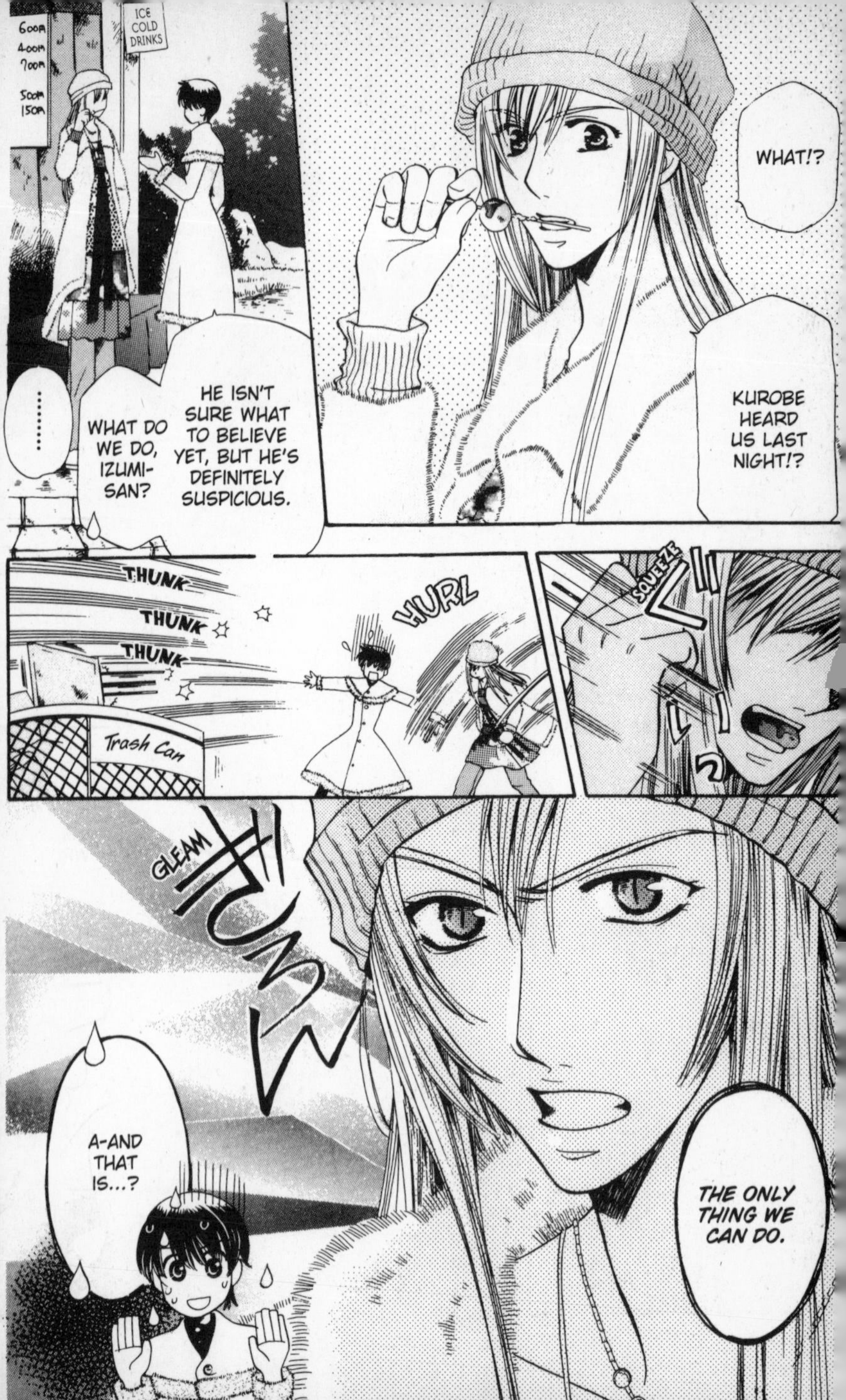
WHAT!?
KUROBE HEARD US LAST NIGHT!?
ICE COLD DRINKS
HE ISN'T SURE WHAT TO BELIEVE YET, BUT HE'S DEFINITELY SUSPICIOUS.
WHAT DO WE DO, IZUMI-SAN?
......
SQUEEZE
HURL
THUNK
THUNK
THUNK
Trash Can
GLEAM
THE ONLY THING WE CAN DO.
A-AND THAT IS...?

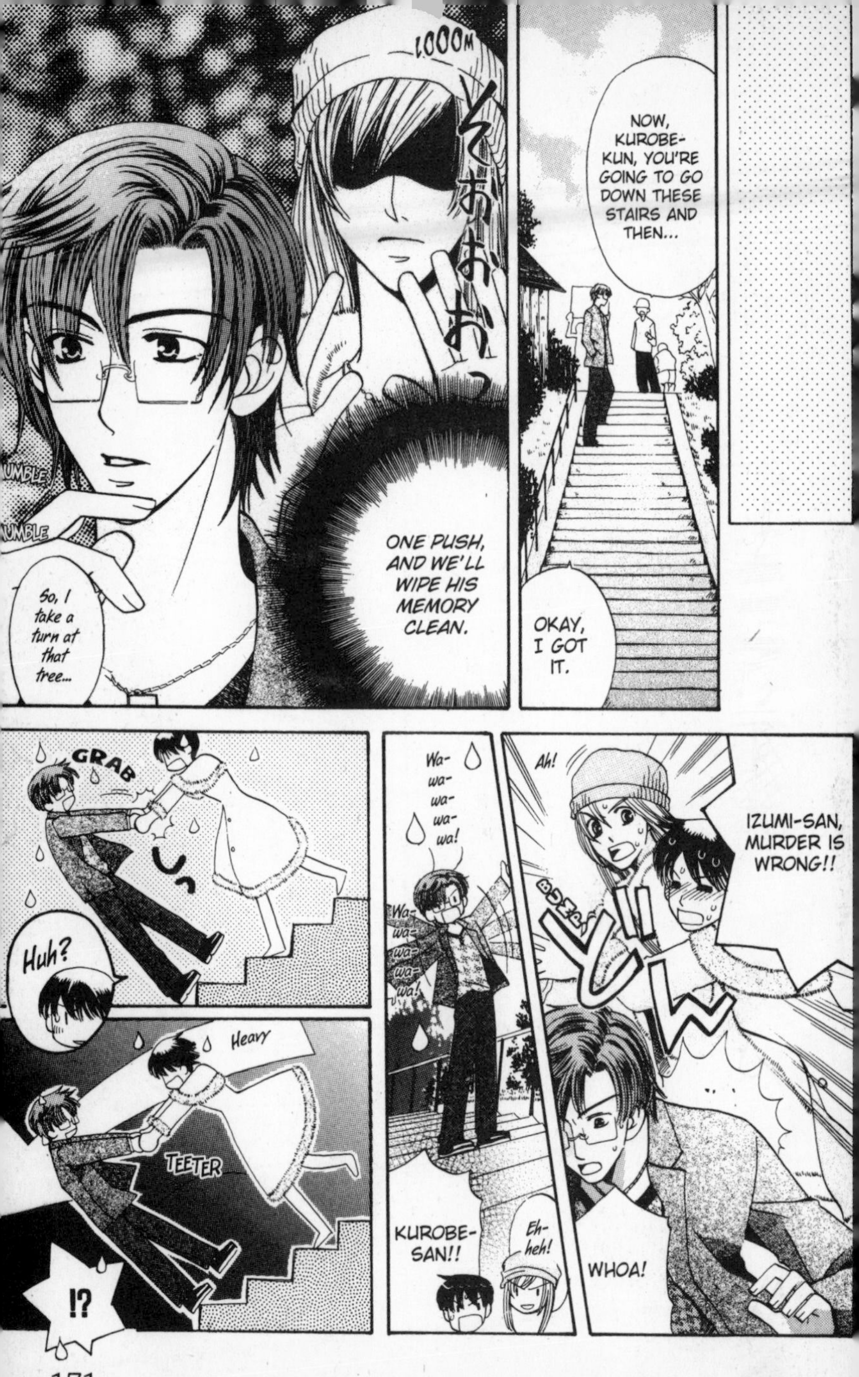
NOW, KUROBE-KUN, YOU'RE GOING TO GO DOWN THESE STAIRS AND THEN...
OKAY, I GOT IT.
LOOOM
ONE PUSH, AND WE'LL WIPE HIS MEMORY CLEAN.
So, I take a turn at that tree...
Ah!
IZUMI-SAN, MURDER IS WRONG!!
WHOA!
Wa-wa-wa-wa-wa!
Wa-wa-wa-wa-wa!
KUROBE-SAN!!
Eh-heh!
GRAB
Huh?
Heavy
TEETER
!?

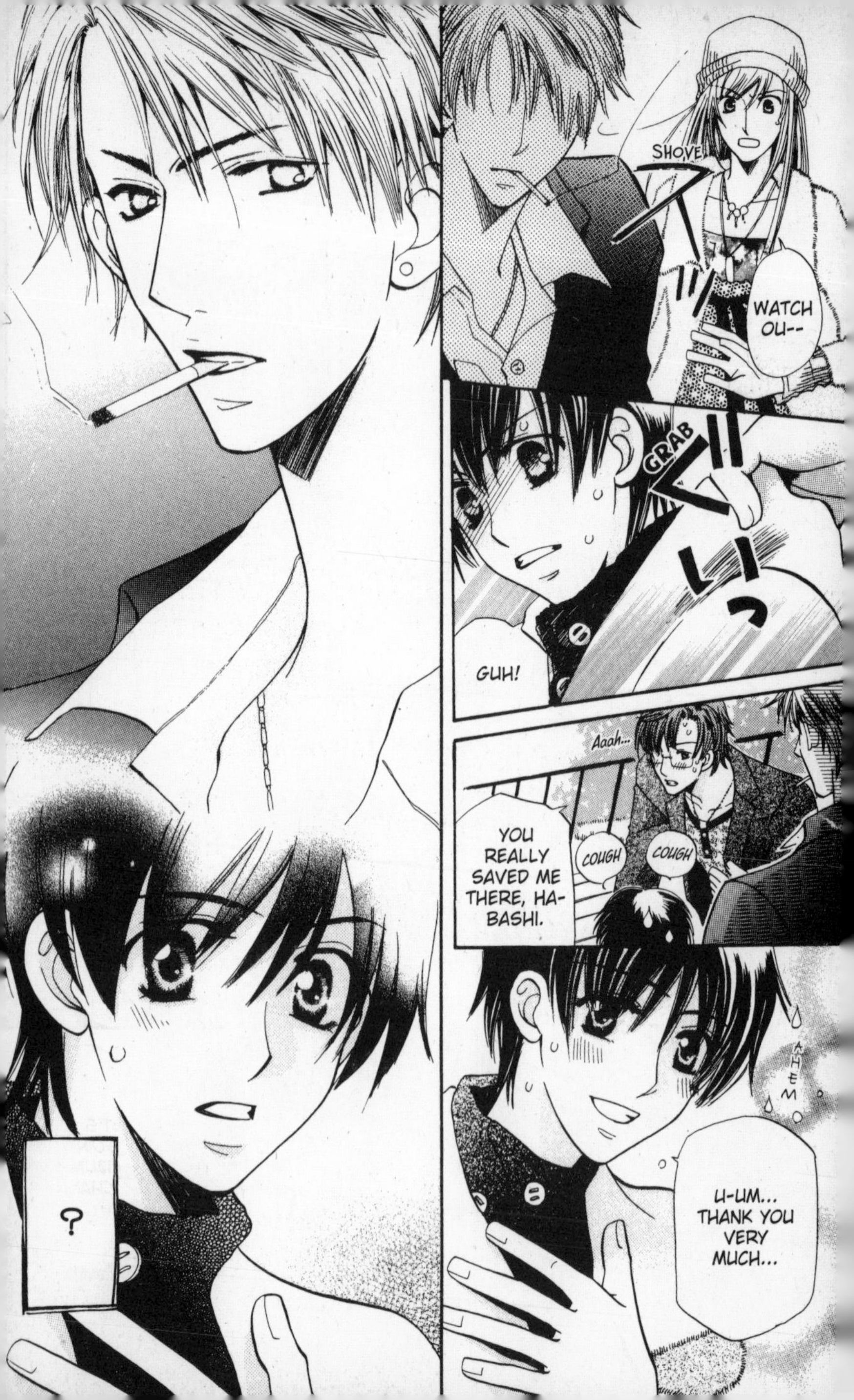
SHOVE
WATCH OU--
GRAB
GUH!
Aaah...
COUGH
COUGH
YOU REALLY SAVED ME THERE, HA-BASHI.
AHEM
U-UM... THANK YOU VERY MUCH...
?

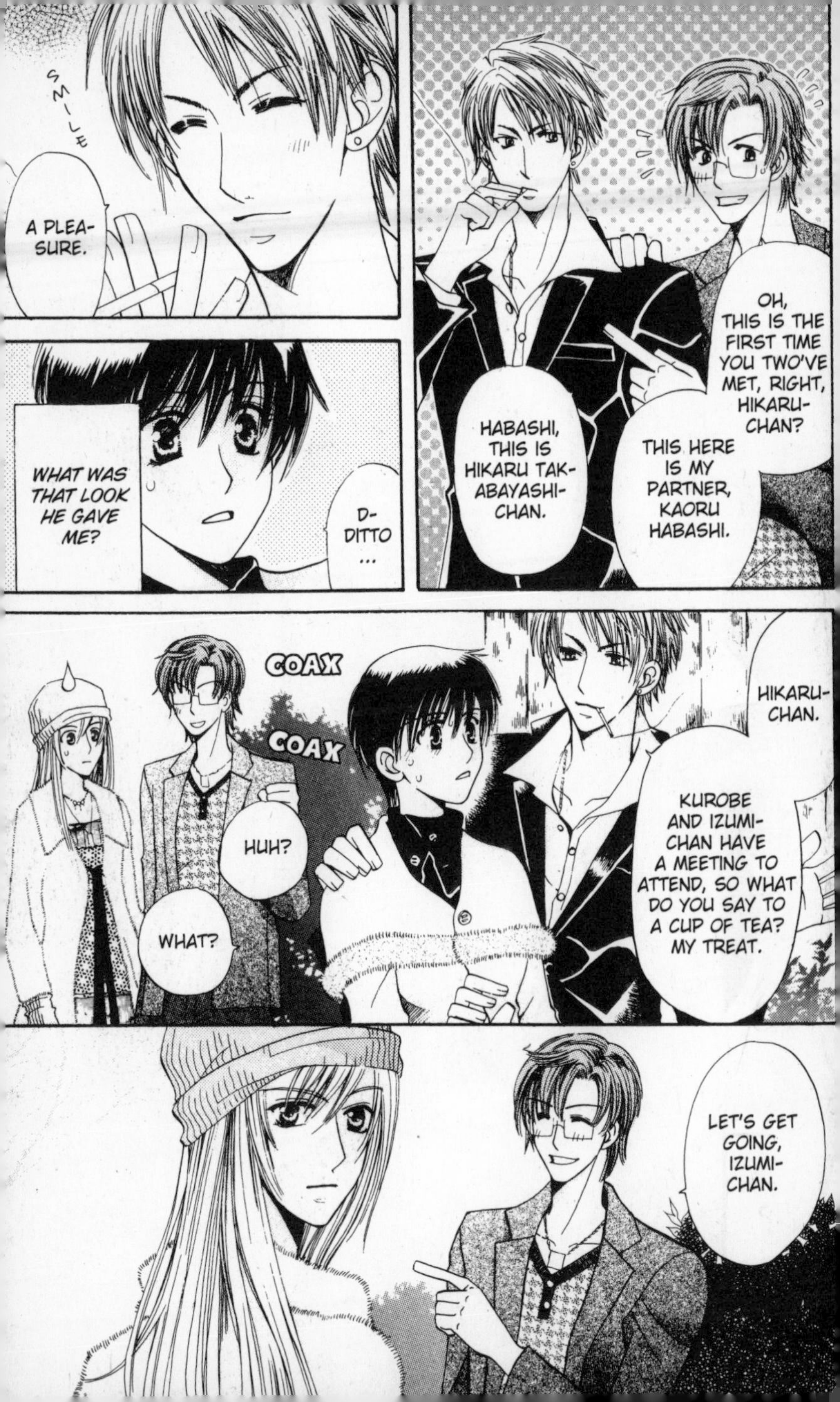
OH, THIS IS THE FIRST TIME YOU TWO'VE MET, RIGHT, HIKARU-CHAN?
THIS HERE IS MY PARTNER, KAORU HABASHI.
HABASHI, THIS IS HIKARU TAK-ABAYASHI-CHAN.
SMILE
A PLEA-SURE.
D-DITTO ...
WHAT WAS THAT LOOK HE GAVE ME?
HIKARU-CHAN.
KUROBE AND IZUMI-CHAN HAVE A MEETING TO ATTEND, SO WHAT DO YOU SAY TO A CUP OF TEA? MY TREAT.
COAX
COAX
HUH?
WHAT?
LET'S GET GOING, IZUMI-CHAN.

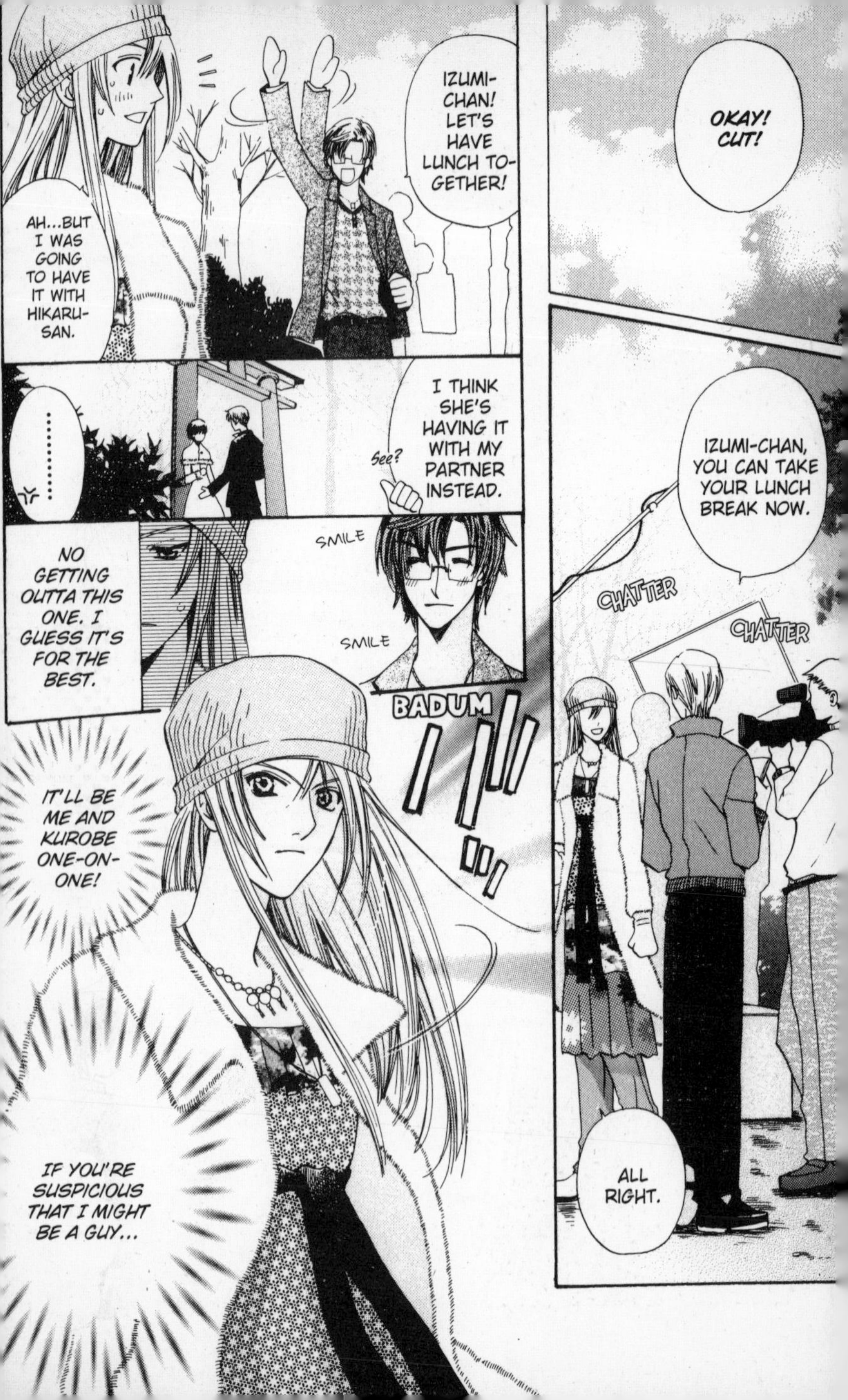
OKAY! CUT!
IZUMI-CHAN, YOU CAN TAKE YOUR LUNCH BREAK NOW.
CHATTER
CHATTER
ALL RIGHT.
IZUMI-CHAN! LET'S HAVE LUNCH TO-GETHER!
AH...BUT I WAS GOING TO HAVE IT WITH HIKARU-SAN.
I THINK SHE'S HAVING IT WITH MY PARTNER INSTEAD.
See?
....
SMILE
SMILE
NO GETTING OUTTA THIS ONE. I GUESS IT'S FOR THE BEST.
BADUM
IT'LL BE ME AND KUROBE ONE-ON-ONE!
IF YOU'RE SUSPICIOUS THAT I MIGHT BE A GUY...

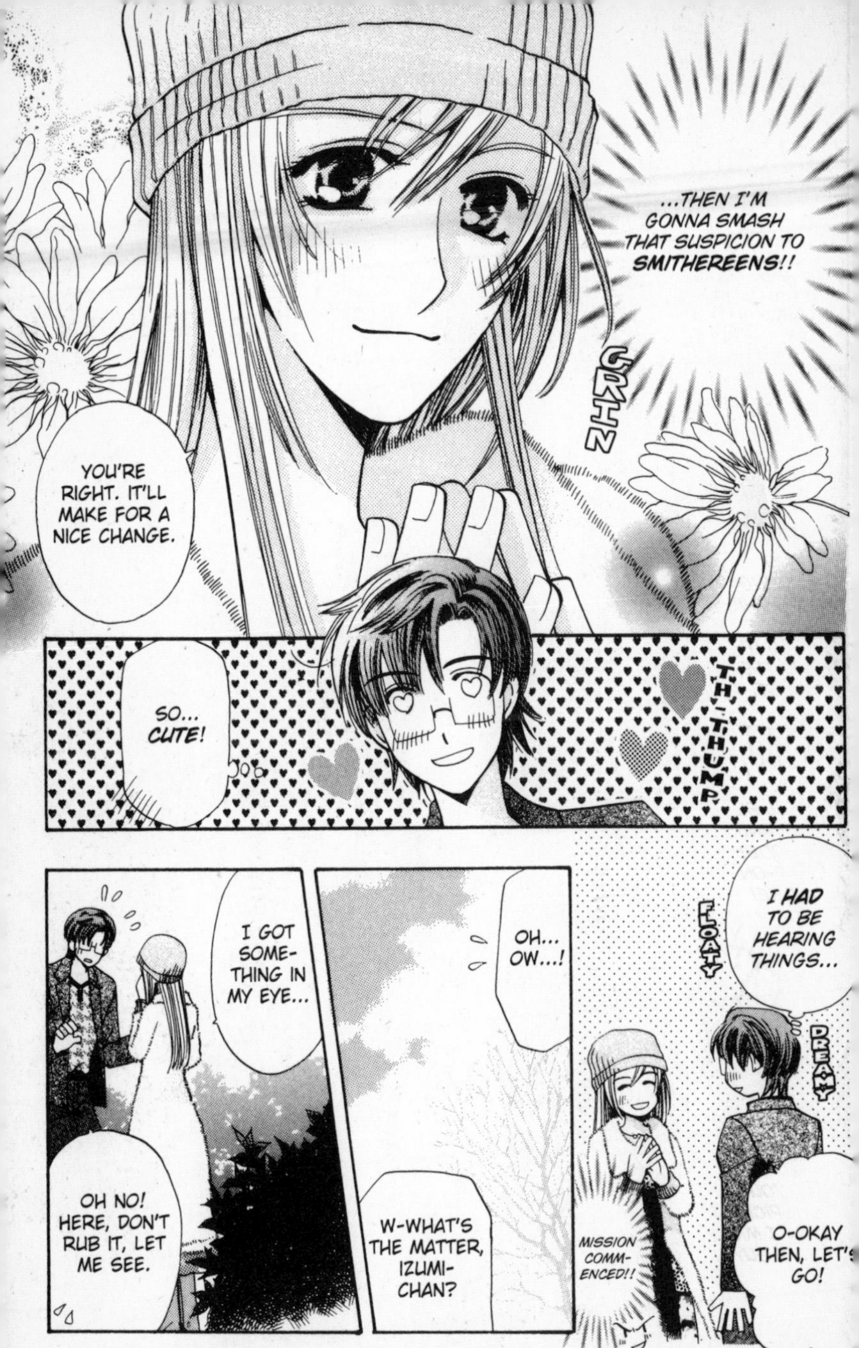
...THEN I'M GONNA SMASH THAT SUSPICION TO SMITHEREENS!!
GRIN
YOU'RE RIGHT. IT'LL MAKE FOR A NICE CHANGE.
TH-THUMP
SO... CUTE!
I HAD TO BE HEARING THINGS...
FLOATY
DREAMY
O-OKAY THEN, LET'S GO!
MISSION COMMENCED!!
OH... OW...!
W-WHAT'S THE MATTER, IZUMI-CHAN?
I GOT SOME-THING IN MY EYE...
OH NO! HERE, DON'T RUB IT, LET ME SEE.

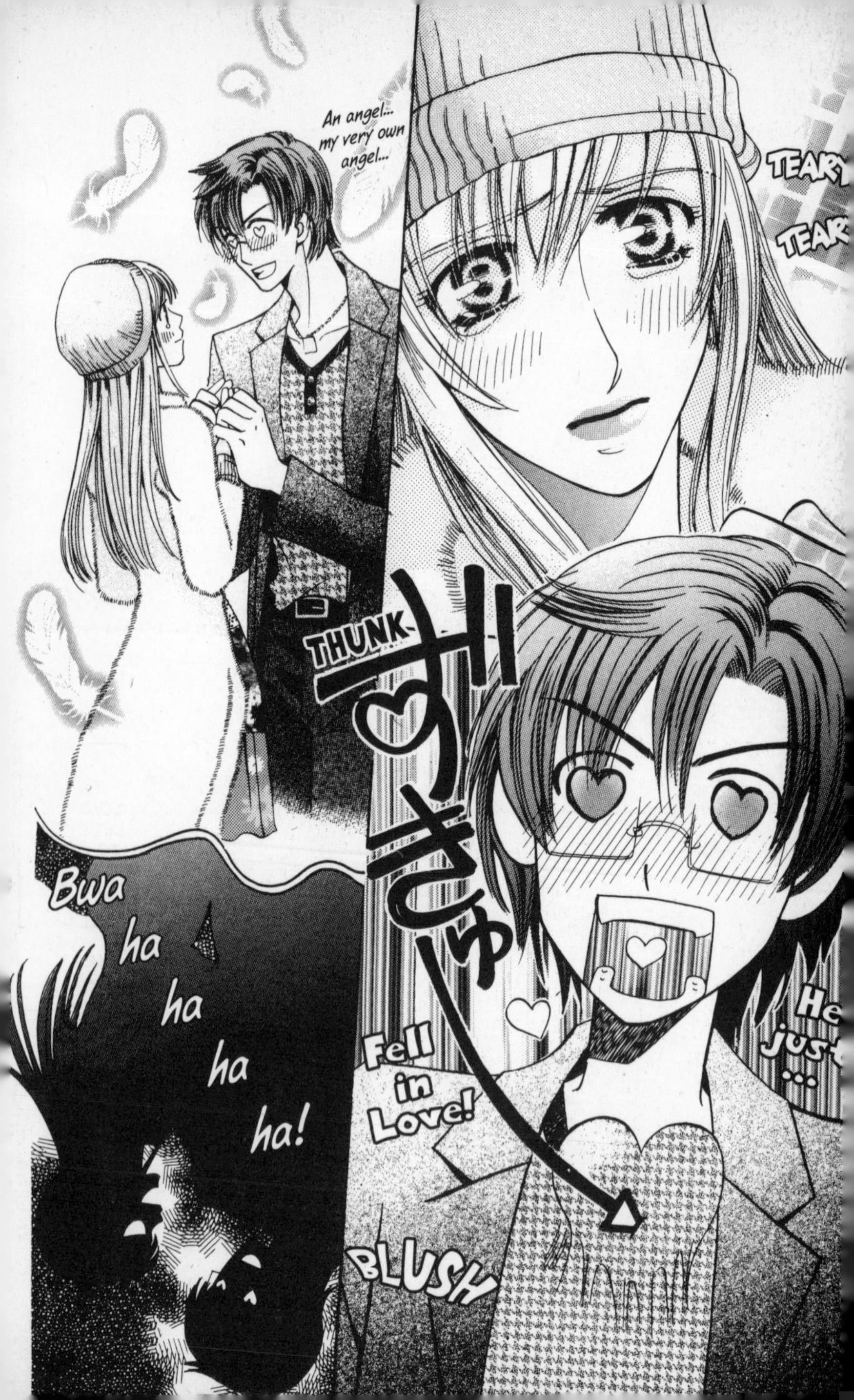
TEARY
TEAR
THUNK
He just...
Fell in Love!
BLUSH
An angel... my very own angel...
Bwa ha ha ha ha!

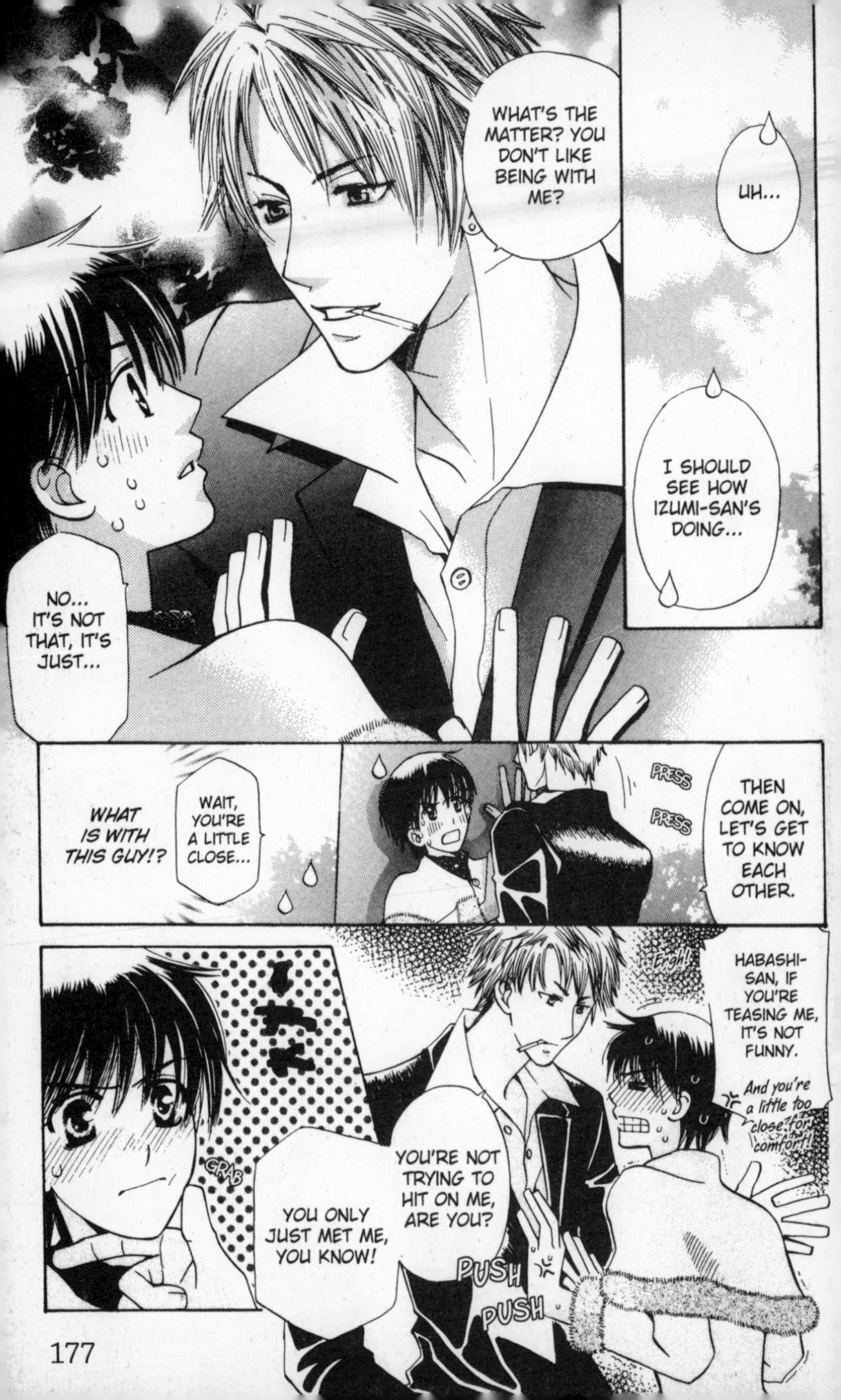

UH...
I SHOULD SEE HOW IZUMI-SAN'S DOING...
WHAT'S THE MATTER? YOU DON'T LIKE BEING WITH ME?
NO... IT'S NOT THAT, IT'S JUST...
PRESS
PRESS
THEN COME ON, LET'S GET TO KNOW EACH OTHER.
WAIT, YOU'RE A LITTLE CLOSE...
WHAT IS WITH THIS GUY!?
Ergh!
HABASHI-SAN, IF YOU'RE TEASING ME, IT'S NOT FUNNY.
And you're a little too close for comfort!
PUSH
PUSH
YOU'RE NOT TRYING TO HIT ON ME, ARE YOU?
YOU ONLY JUST MET ME, YOU KNOW!
GRAB

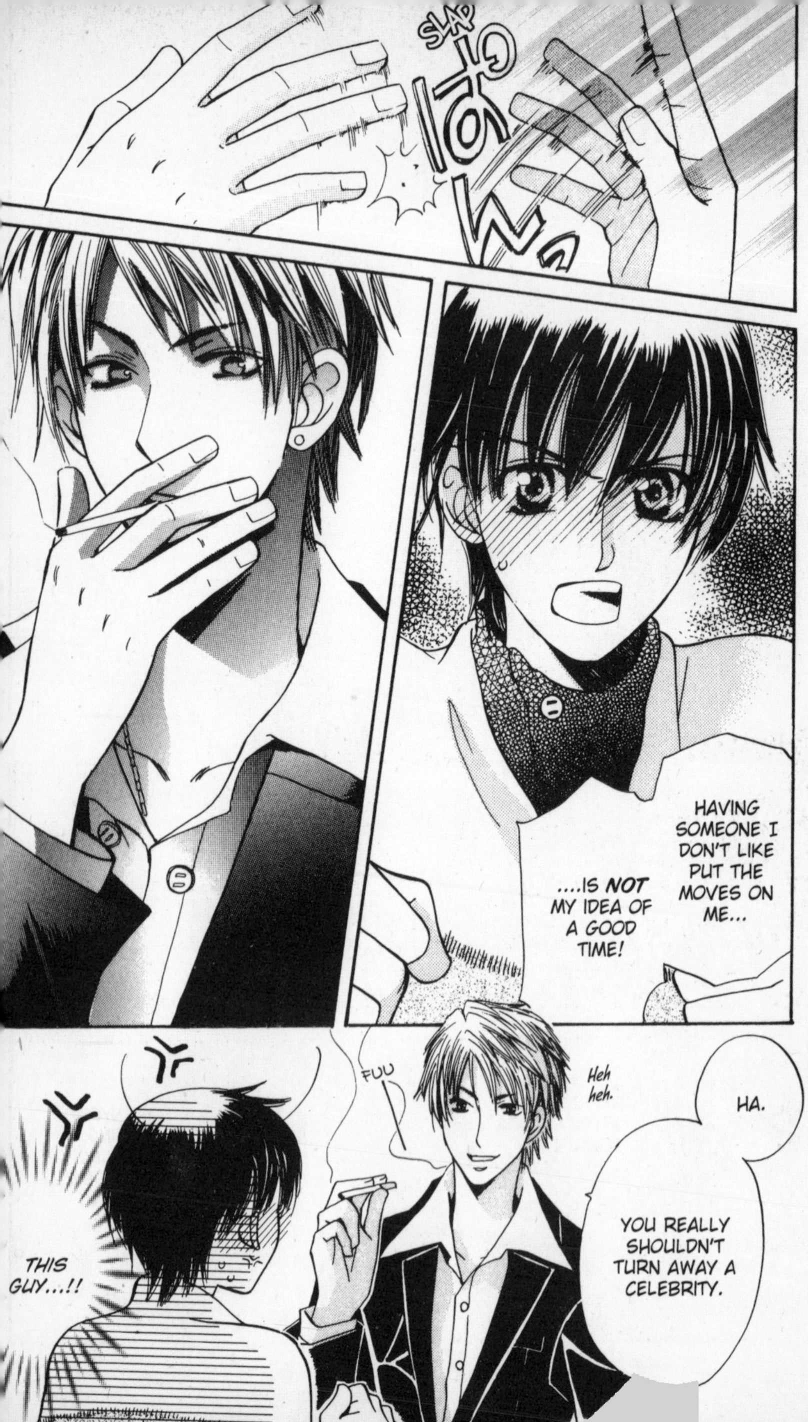
SLAP
HAVING SOMEONE I DON'T LIKE PUT THE MOVES ON ME...
....IS **NOT** MY IDEA OF A GOOD TIME!
HA.
YOU REALLY SHOULDN'T TURN AWAY A CELEBRITY.
Heh heh.
FUU
THIS GUY...!!

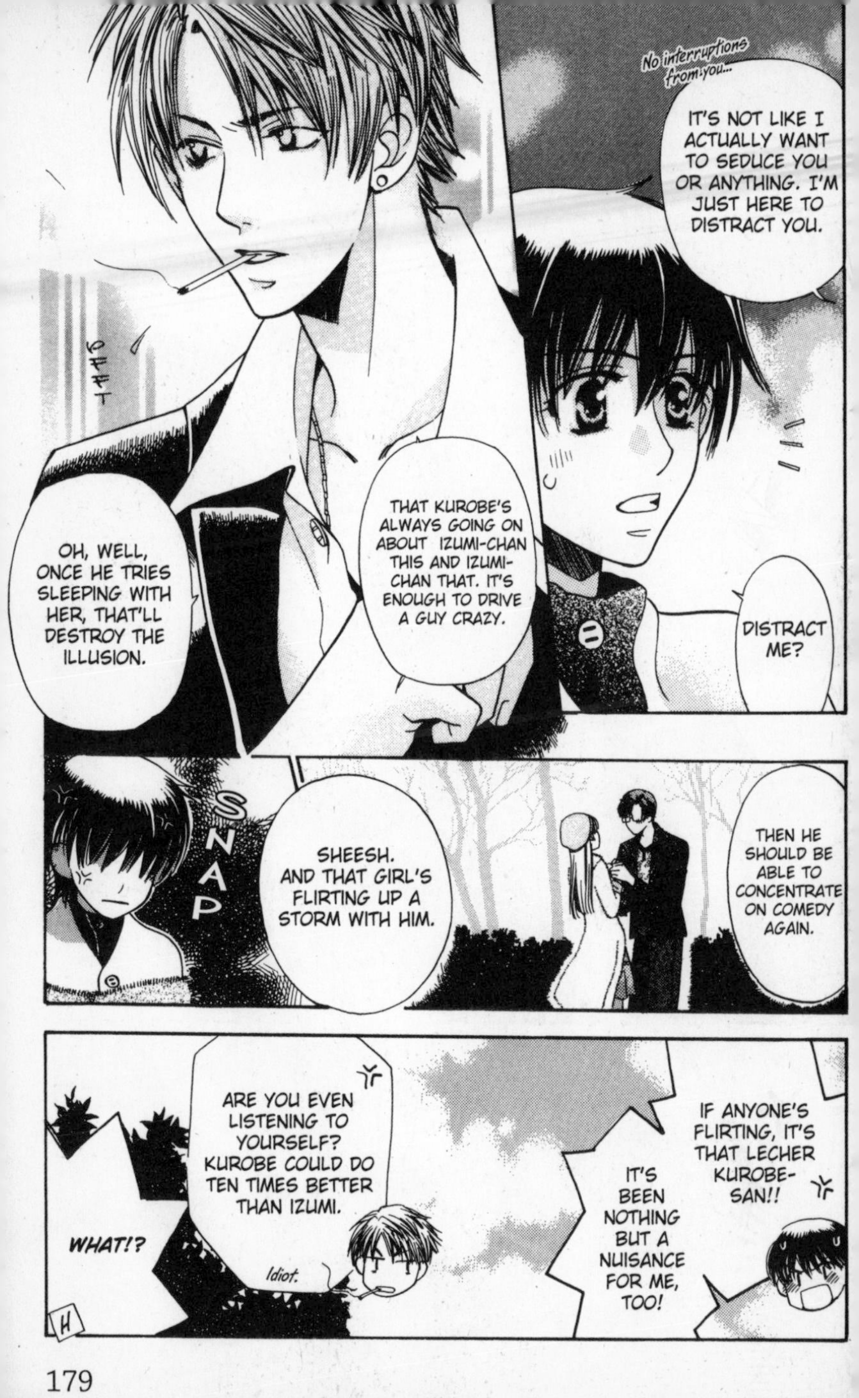
No interruptions from you...
IT'S NOT LIKE I ACTUALLY WANT TO SEDUCE YOU OR ANYTHING. I'M JUST HERE TO DISTRACT YOU.
DISTRACT ME?
SFFT
THAT KUROBE'S ALWAYS GOING ON ABOUT IZUMI-CHAN THIS AND IZUMI-CHAN THAT. IT'S ENOUGH TO DRIVE A GUY CRAZY.
OH, WELL, ONCE HE TRIES SLEEPING WITH HER, THAT'LL DESTROY THE ILLUSION.
THEN HE SHOULD BE ABLE TO CONCENTRATE ON COMEDY AGAIN.
SHEESH. AND THAT GIRL'S FLIRTING UP A STORM WITH HIM.
SNAP
IF ANYONE'S FLIRTING, IT'S THAT LECHER KUROBE-SAN!!
IT'S BEEN NOTHING BUT A NUISANCE FOR ME, TOO!
ARE YOU EVEN LISTENING TO YOURSELF? KUROBE COULD DO TEN TIMES BETTER THAN IZUMI.
Idiot.
WHAT!?

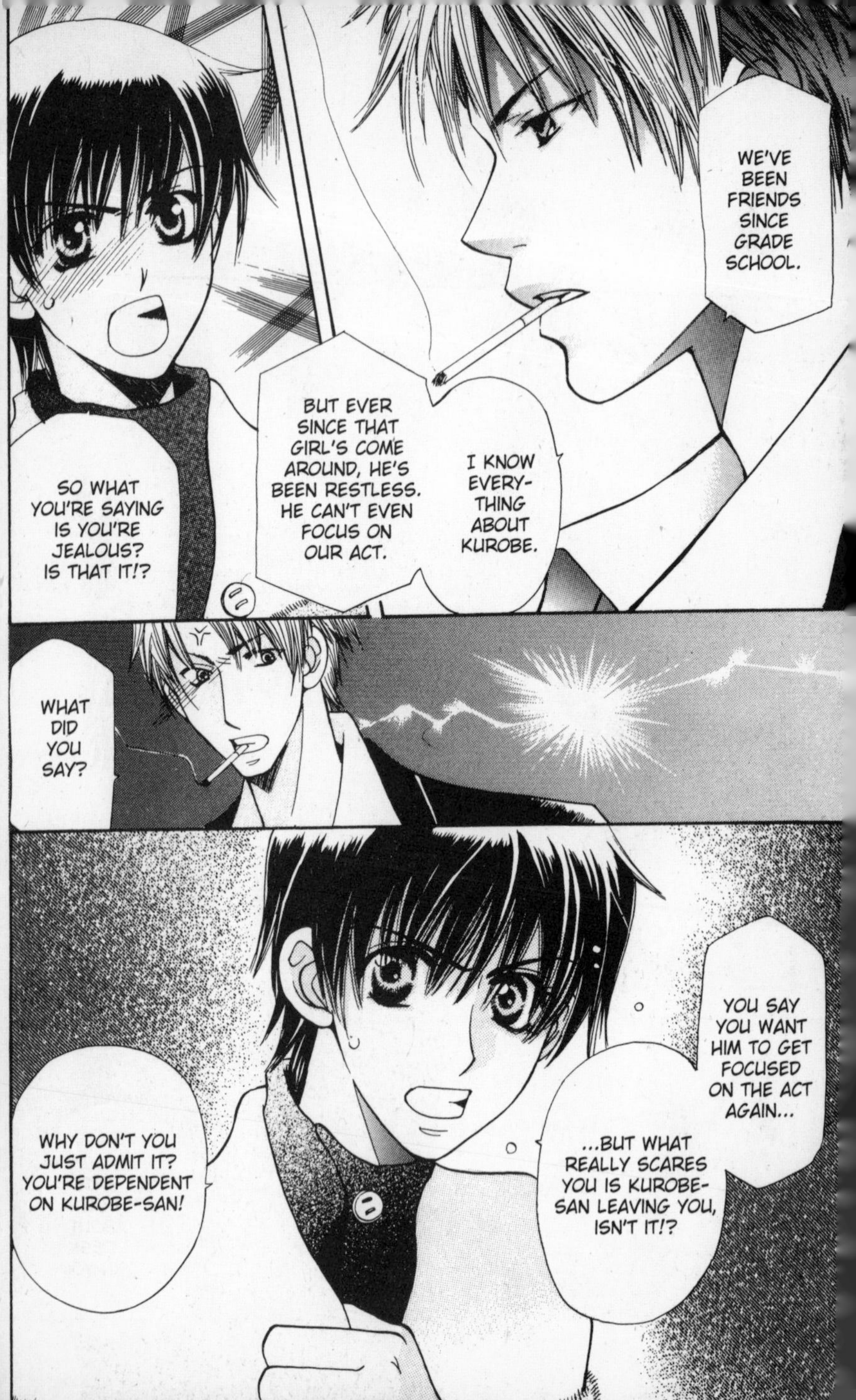
WE'VE BEEN FRIENDS SINCE GRADE SCHOOL.
I KNOW EVERY-THING ABOUT KUROBE.
BUT EVER SINCE THAT GIRL'S COME AROUND, HE'S BEEN RESTLESS. HE CAN'T EVEN FOCUS ON OUR ACT.
SO WHAT YOU'RE SAYING IS YOU'RE JEALOUS? IS THAT IT!?
WHAT DID YOU SAY?
YOU SAY YOU WANT HIM TO GET FOCUSED ON THE ACT AGAIN...
...BUT WHAT REALLY SCARES YOU IS KUROBE-SAN LEAVING YOU, ISN'T IT!?
WHY DON'T YOU JUST ADMIT IT? YOU'RE DEPENDENT ON KUROBE-SAN!

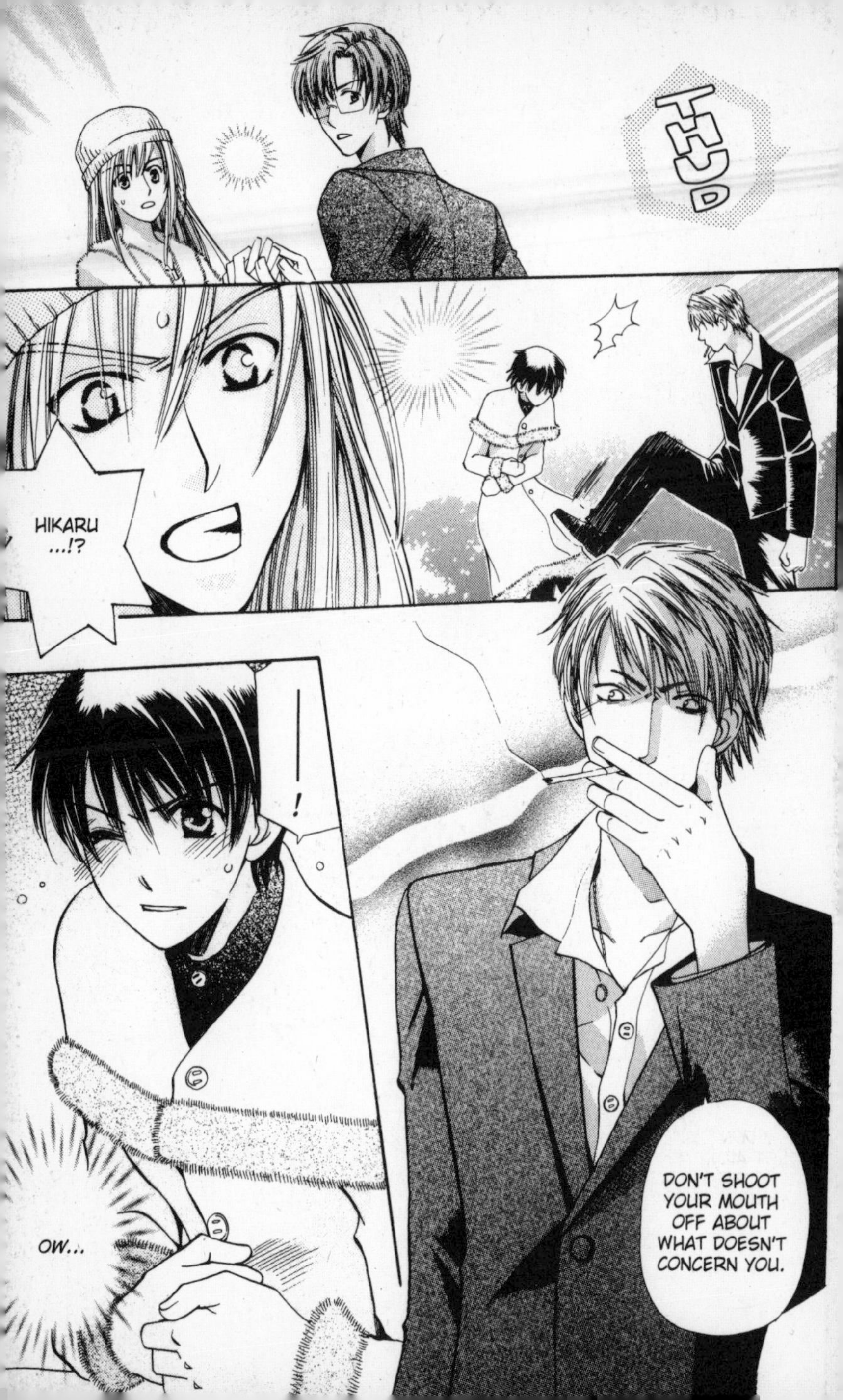
THUD
HIKARU ...!?
DON'T SHOOT YOUR MOUTH OFF ABOUT WHAT DOESN'T CONCERN YOU.
!
OW...

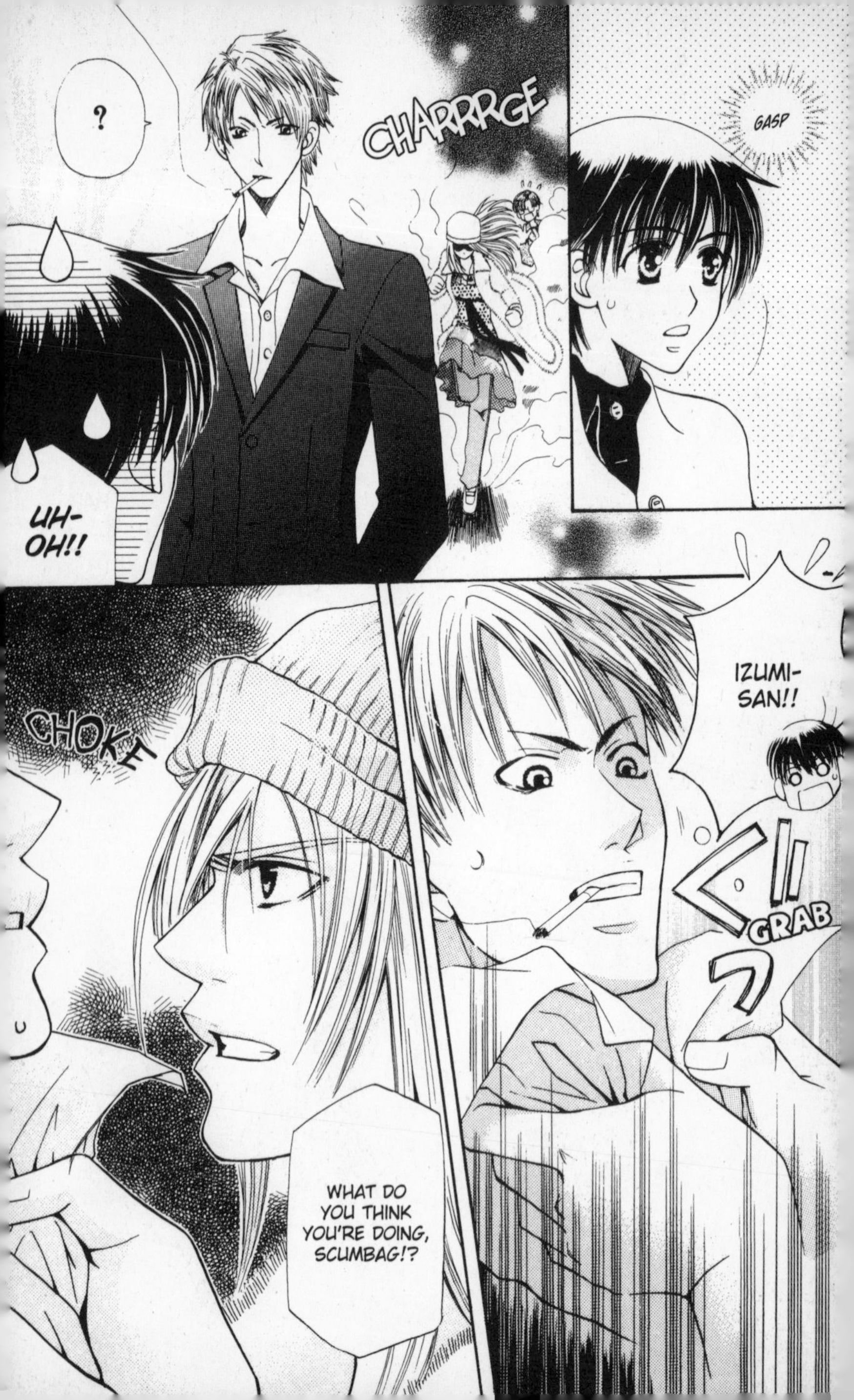
GASP
CHARRRGE
?
UH-OH!!
IZUMI-SAN!!
GRAB
CHOKE
WHAT DO YOU THINK YOU'RE DOING, SCUMBAG!?

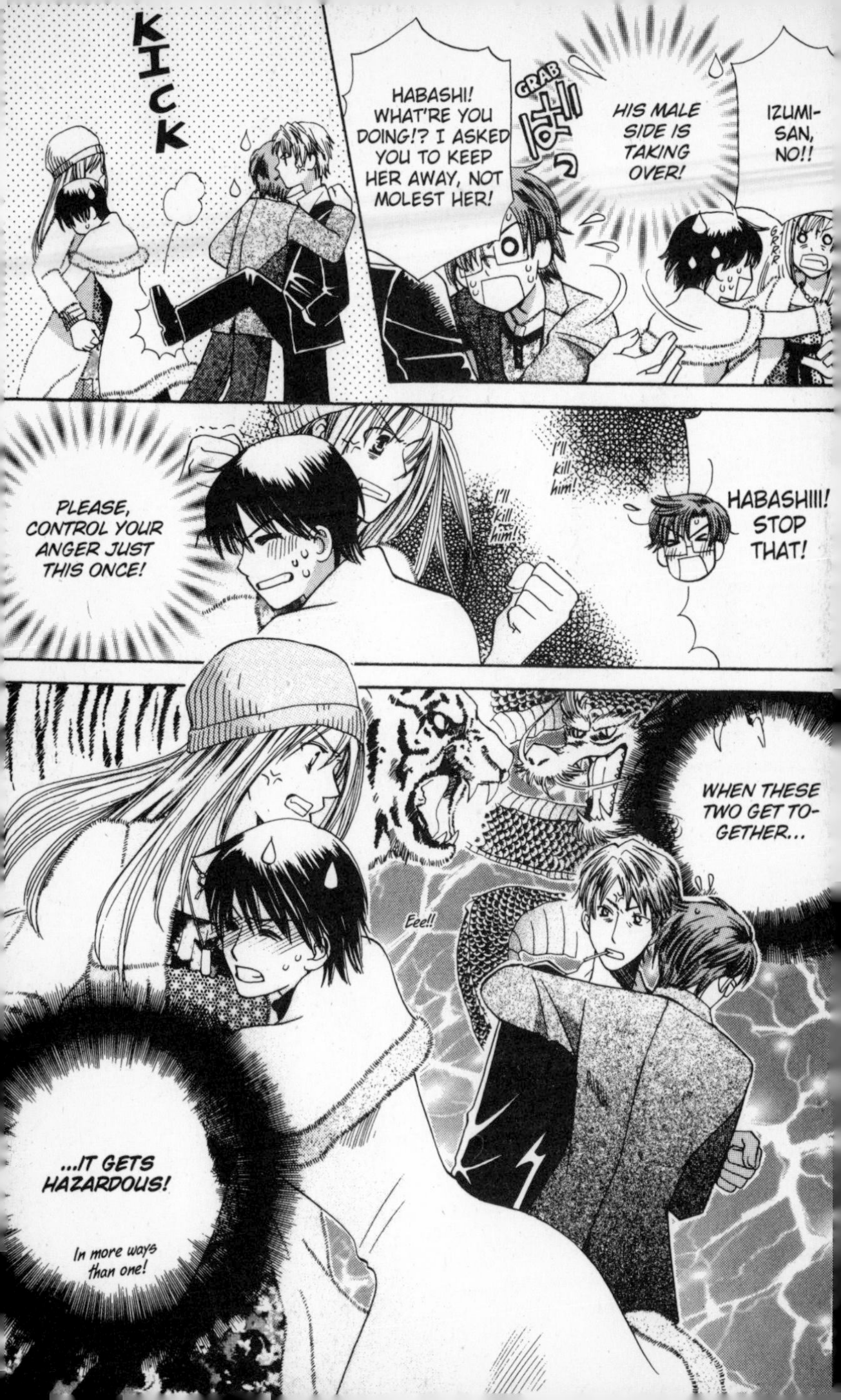
IZUMI-SAN, NO!!
HIS MALE SIDE IS TAKING OVER!
GRAB
ばっ
HABASHI! WHAT'RE YOU DOING!? I ASKED YOU TO KEEP HER AWAY, NOT MOLEST HER!
KICK
HABASHIII! STOP THAT!
I'll kill him!
I'll kill him!
PLEASE, CONTROL YOUR ANGER JUST THIS ONCE!
WHEN THESE TWO GET TO-GETHER...
Eee!!
...IT GETS HAZARDOUS!
In more ways than one!

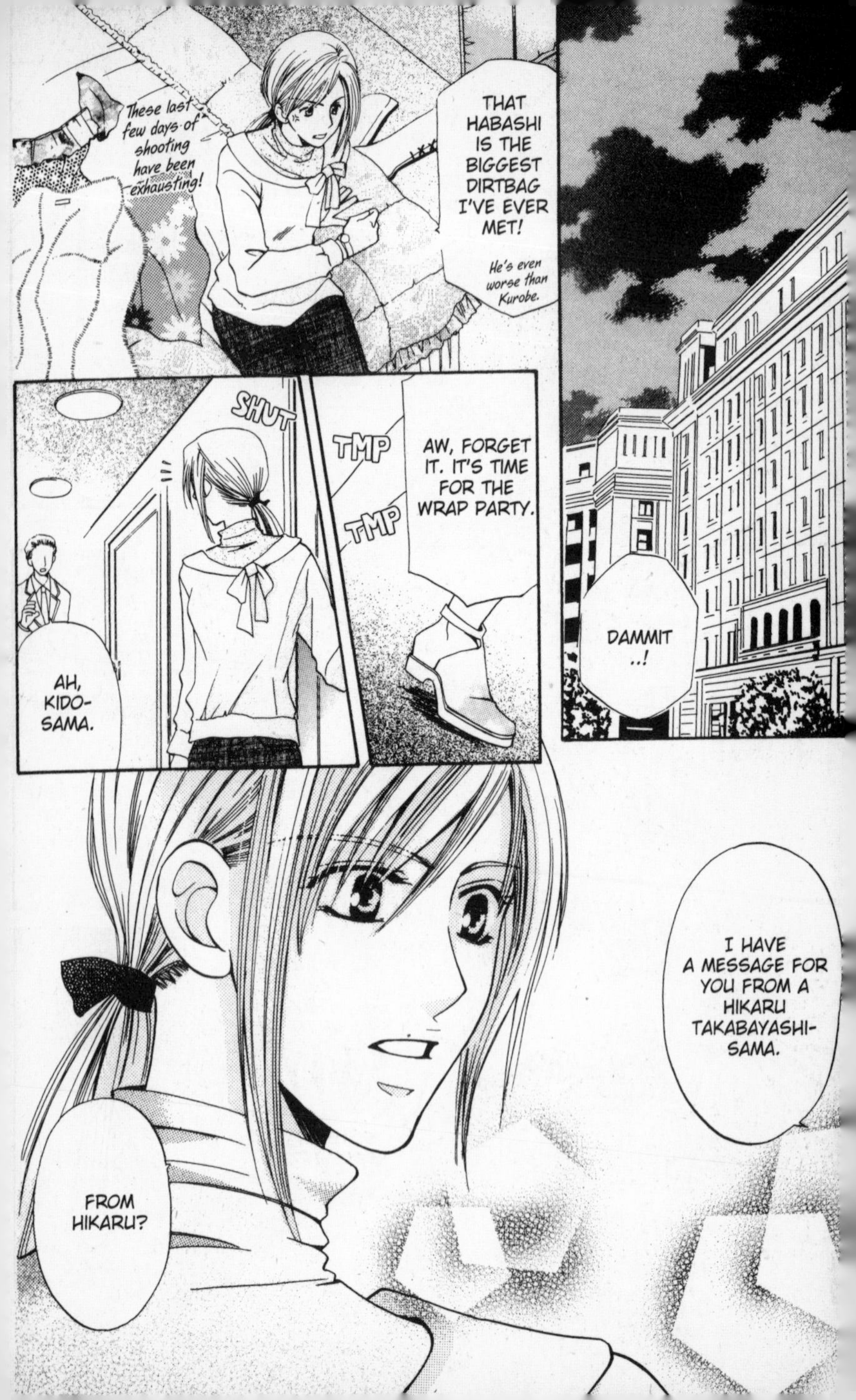
DAMMIT ..!
THAT HABASHI IS THE BIGGEST DIRTBAG I'VE EVER MET!
He's even worse than Kurobe.
These last few days of shooting have been exhausting!
TMP
TMP
AW, FORGET IT. IT'S TIME FOR THE WRAP PARTY.
SHUT
AH, KIDO-SAMA.
I HAVE A MESSAGE FOR YOU FROM A HIKARU TAKABAYASHI-SAMA.
FROM HIKARU?

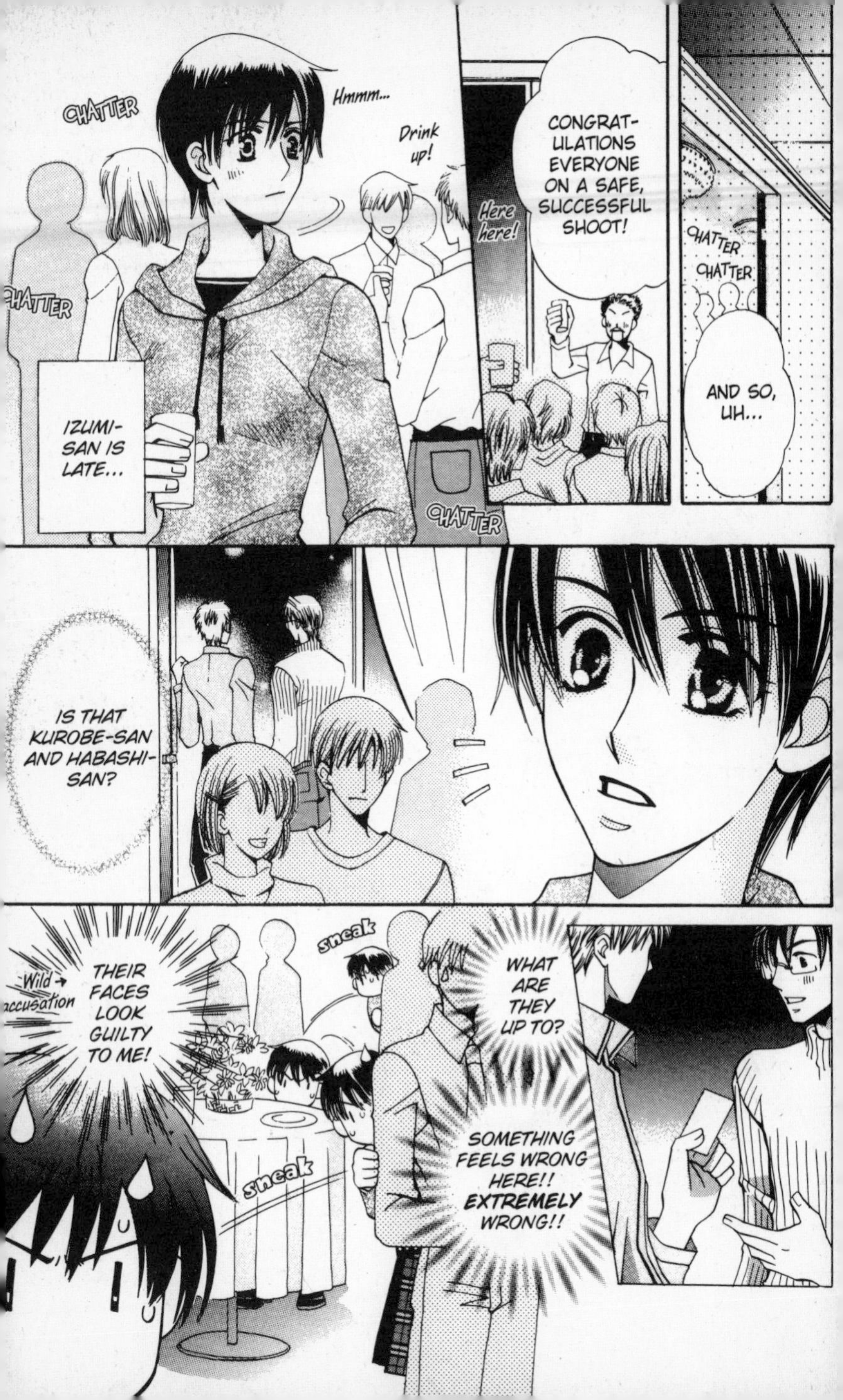
CHATTER
CHATTER
AND SO, UH...
CONGRAT-ULATIONS EVERYONE ON A SAFE, SUCCESSFUL SHOOT!
Here here!
Hmmm...
Drink up!
CHATTER
CHATTER
IZUMI-SAN IS LATE...
CHATTER
IS THAT KUROBE-SAN AND HABASHI-SAN?
WHAT ARE THEY UP TO?
SOMETHING FEELS WRONG HERE!! EXTREMELY WRONG!!
sneak
THEIR FACES LOOK GUILTY TO ME!
Wild accusation
sneak

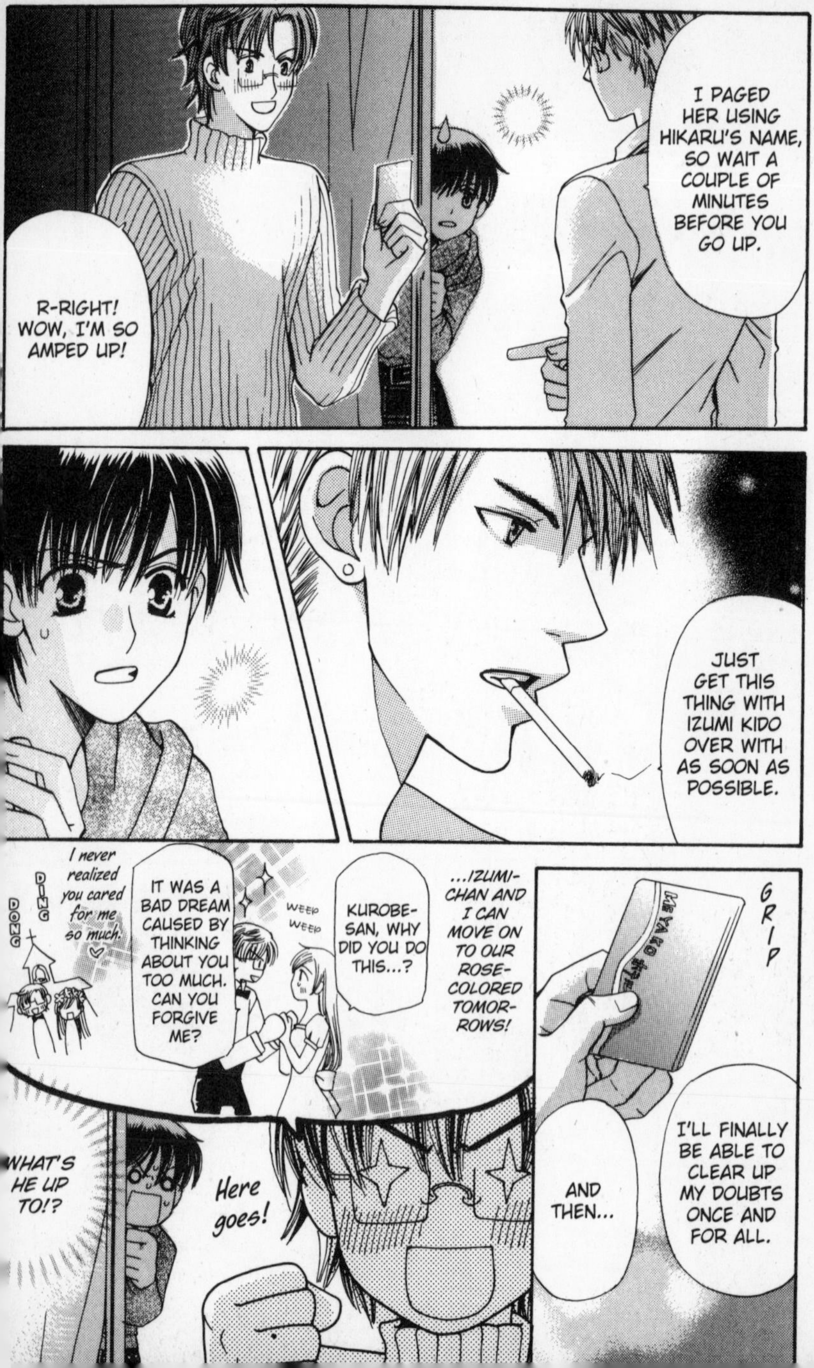
I PAGED HER USING HIKARU'S NAME, SO WAIT A COUPLE OF MINUTES BEFORE YOU GO UP.
R-RIGHT! WOW, I'M SO AMPED UP!
JUST GET THIS THING WITH IZUMI KIDO OVER WITH AS SOON AS POSSIBLE.
GRIP
I'LL FINALLY BE ABLE TO CLEAR UP MY DOUBTS ONCE AND FOR ALL.
AND THEN...
...IZUMI-CHAN AND I CAN MOVE ON TO OUR ROSE-COLORED TOMORROWS!
KUROBE-SAN, WHY DID YOU DO THIS...?
WEEP WEEP
IT WAS A BAD DREAM CAUSED BY THINKING ABOUT YOU TOO MUCH. CAN YOU FORGIVE ME?
I never realized you cared for me so much. ♡
DING DONG
Here goes!
WHAT'S HE UP TO!?

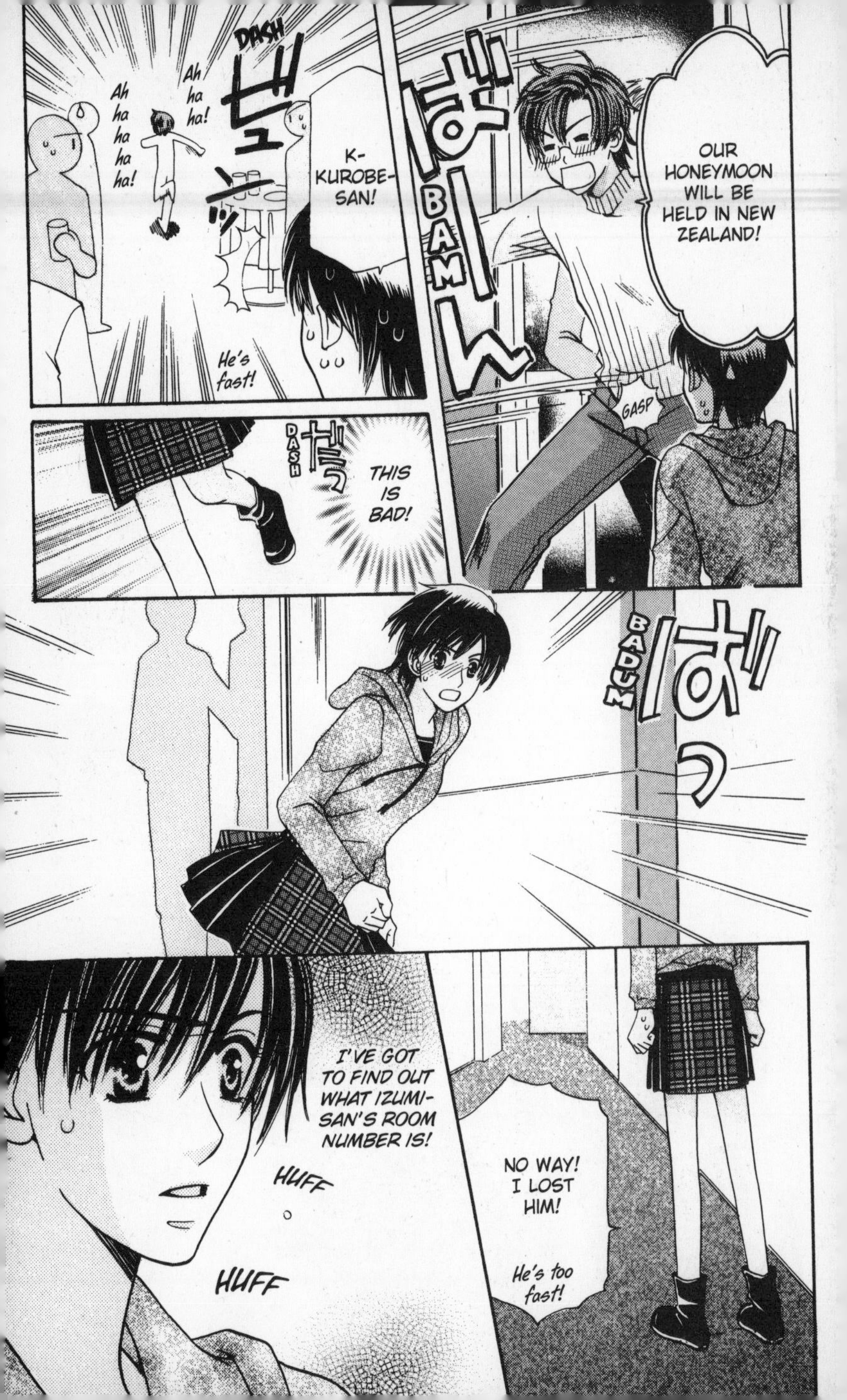
OUR HONEYMOON WILL BE HELD IN NEW ZEALAND!
BAM
GASP
K-KUROBE-SAN!
DASH
Ah ha ha!
Ah ha ha ha ha!
He's fast!
DASH
THIS IS BAD!
BADUM
NO WAY! I LOST HIM!
He's too fast!
I'VE GOT TO FIND OUT WHAT IZUMI-SAN'S ROOM NUMBER IS!
HUFF
HUFF

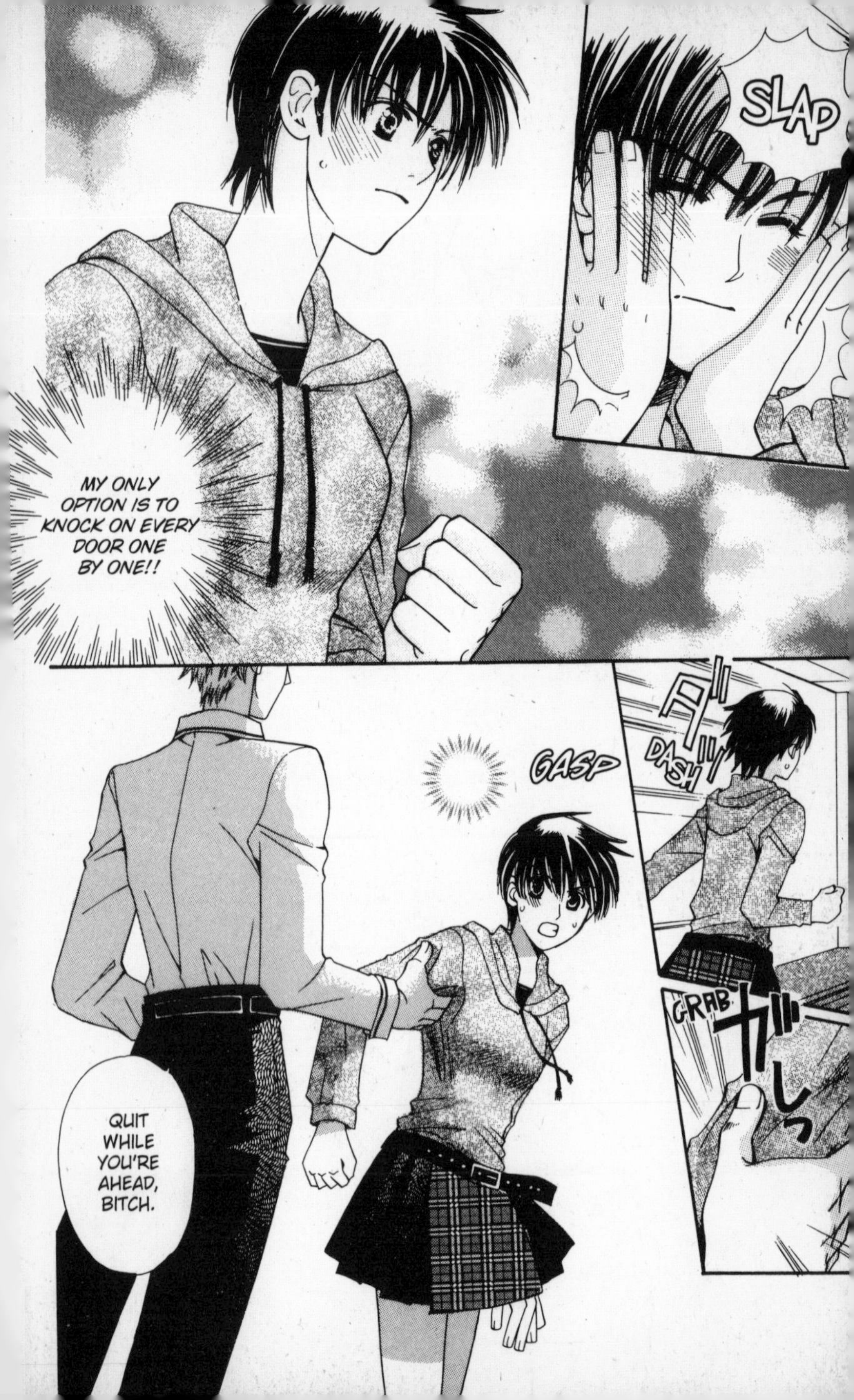
SLAP
MY ONLY OPTION IS TO KNOCK ON EVERY DOOR ONE BY ONE!!
DASH
GRAB
GASP
QUIT WHILE YOU'RE AHEAD, BITCH.

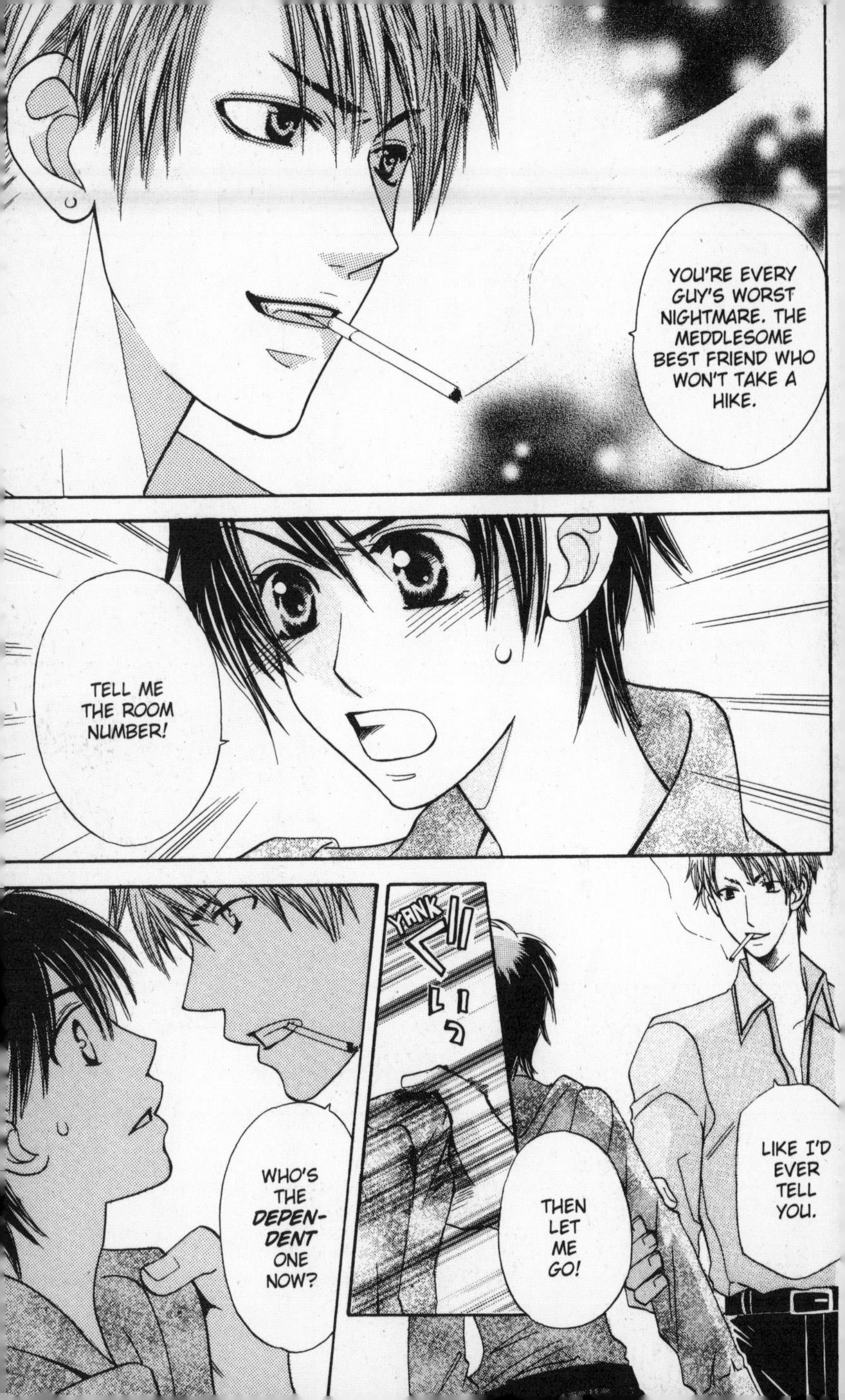
YOU'RE EVERY GUY'S WORST NIGHTMARE. THE MEDDLESOME BEST FRIEND WHO WON'T TAKE A HIKE.
TELL ME THE ROOM NUMBER!
LIKE I'D EVER TELL YOU.
THEN LET ME GO!
YANK
WHO'S THE *DEPENDENT* ONE NOW?

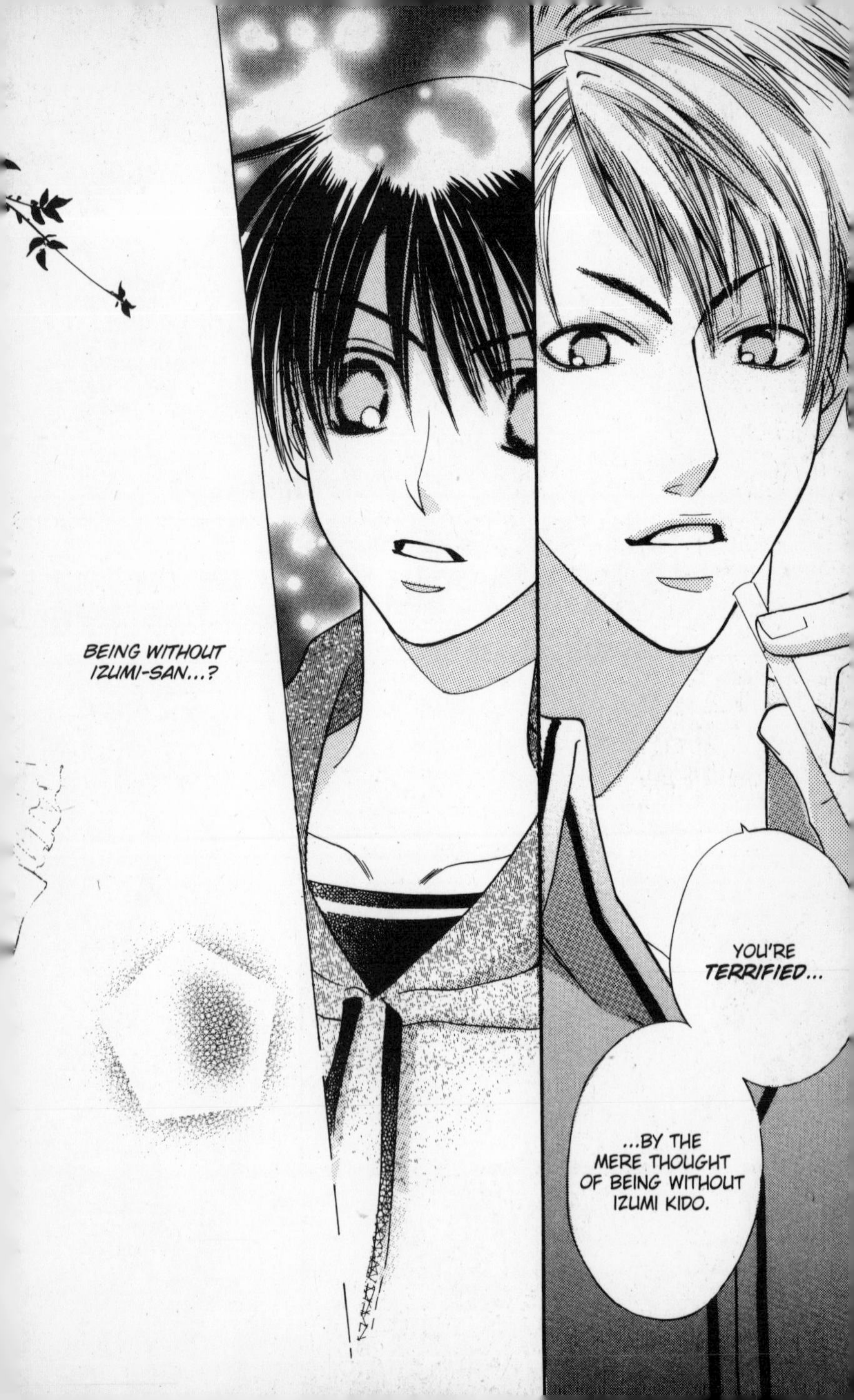
YOU'RE TERRIFIED...
...BY THE MERE THOUGHT OF BEING WITHOUT IZUMI KIDO.
BEING WITHOUT IZUMI-SAN...?

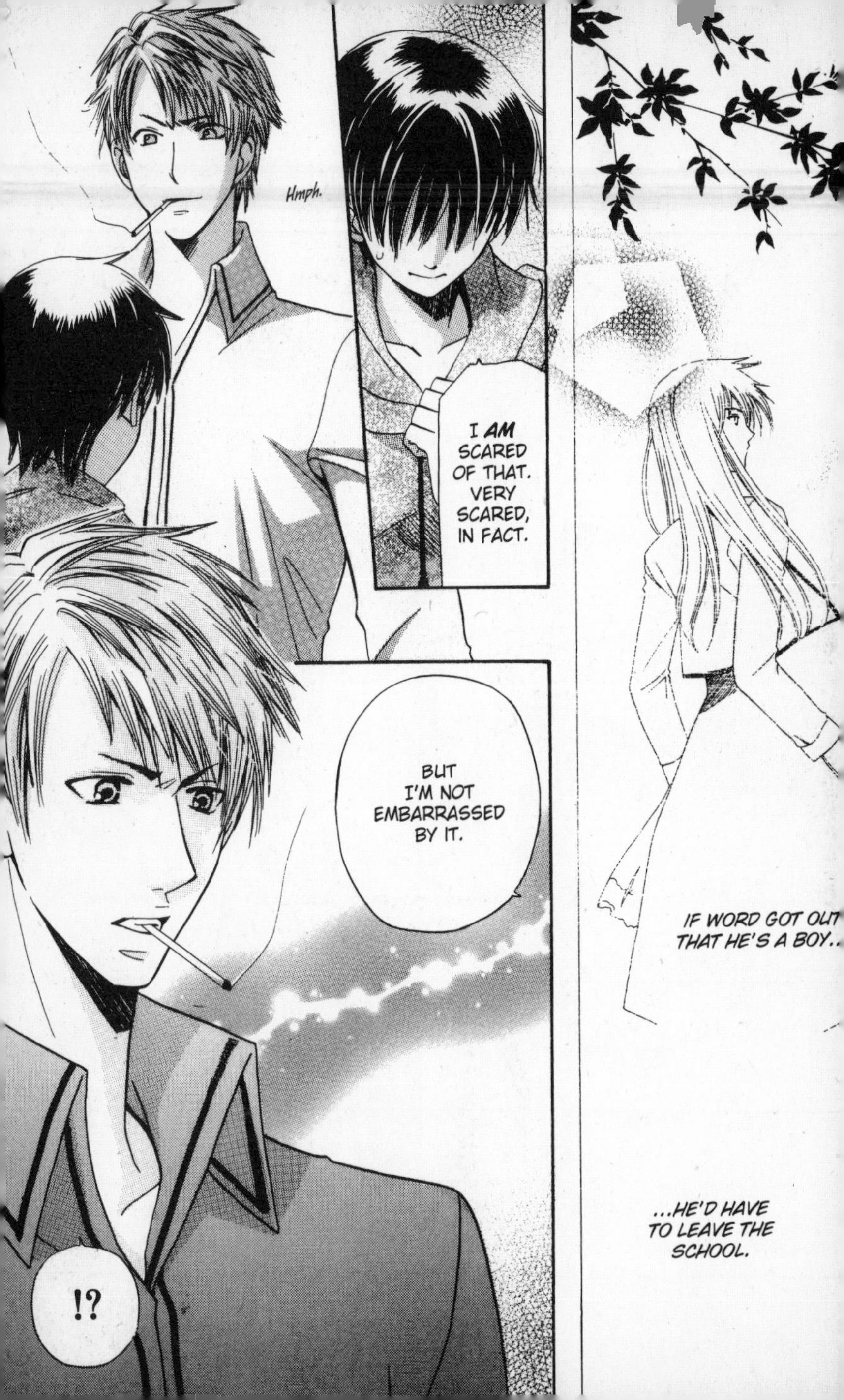
IF WORD GOT OUT THAT HE'S A BOY...
...HE'D HAVE TO LEAVE THE SCHOOL.
I *AM* SCARED OF THAT. VERY SCARED, IN FACT.
Hmph.
BUT I'M NOT EMBARRASSED BY IT.
!?

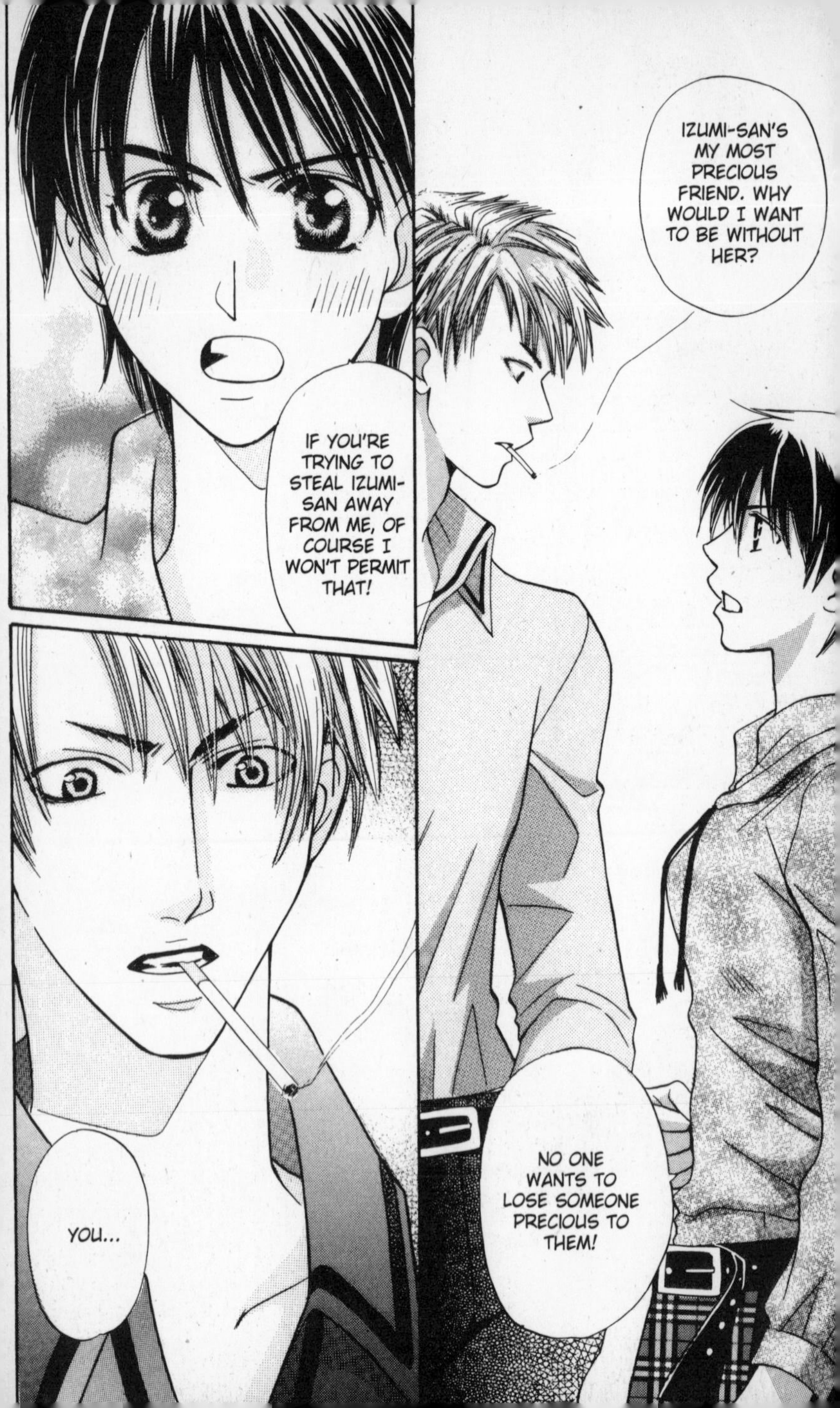
IZUMI-SAN'S MY MOST PRECIOUS FRIEND. WHY WOULD I WANT TO BE WITHOUT HER?
NO ONE WANTS TO LOSE SOMEONE PRECIOUS TO THEM!
IF YOU'RE TRYING TO STEAL IZUMI-SAN AWAY FROM ME, OF COURSE I WON'T PERMIT THAT!
YOU...

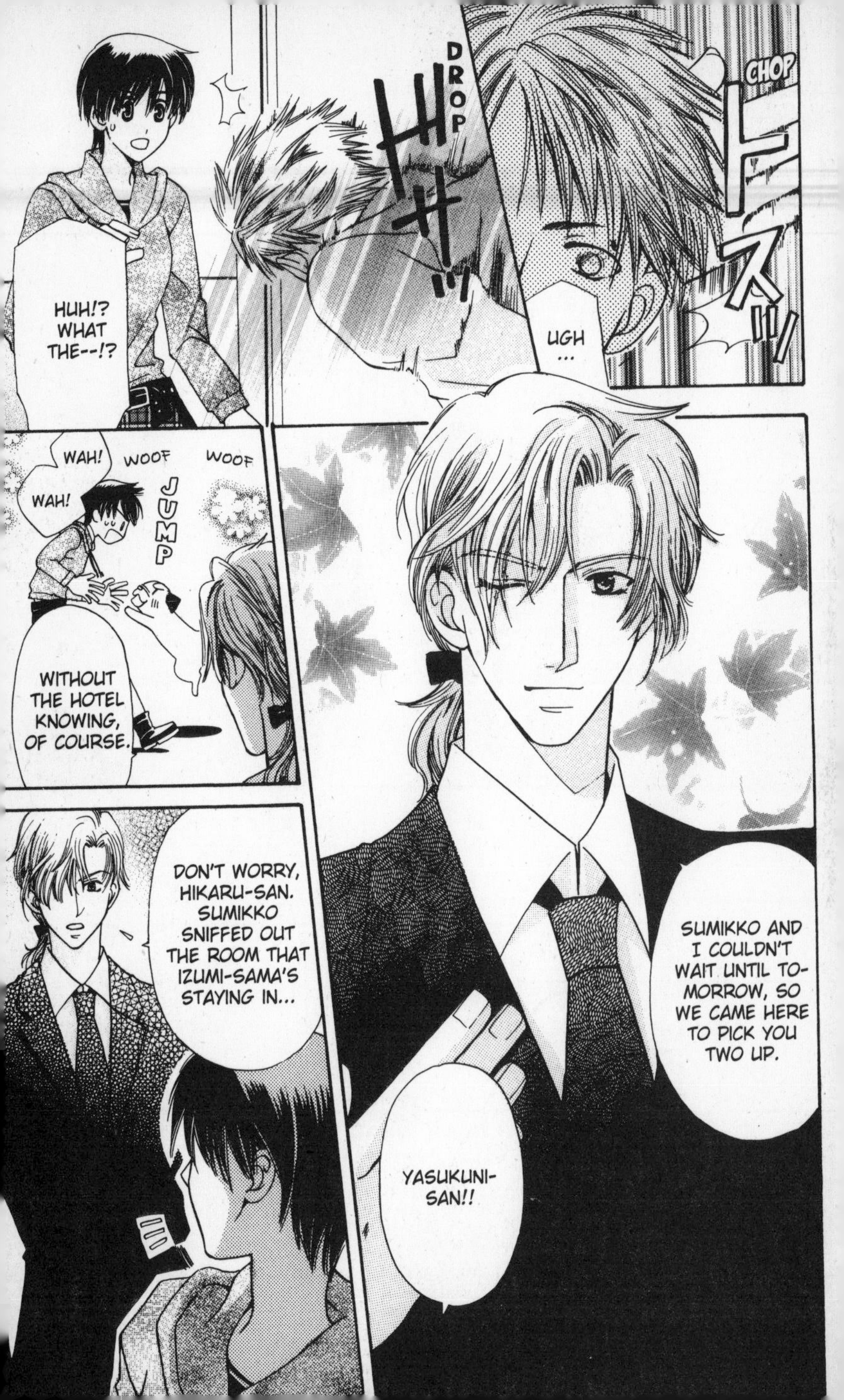

CHOP
UGH ...
DROP
HUH!? WHAT THE--!?
SUMIKKO AND I COULDN'T WAIT UNTIL TO-MORROW, SO WE CAME HERE TO PICK YOU TWO UP.
YASUKUNI-SAN!!
WAH!
WOOF
WOOF
JUMP
WAH!
WITHOUT THE HOTEL KNOWING, OF COURSE.
DON'T WORRY, HIKARU-SAN. SUMIKKO SNIFFED OUT THE ROOM THAT IZUMI-SAMA'S STAYING IN...

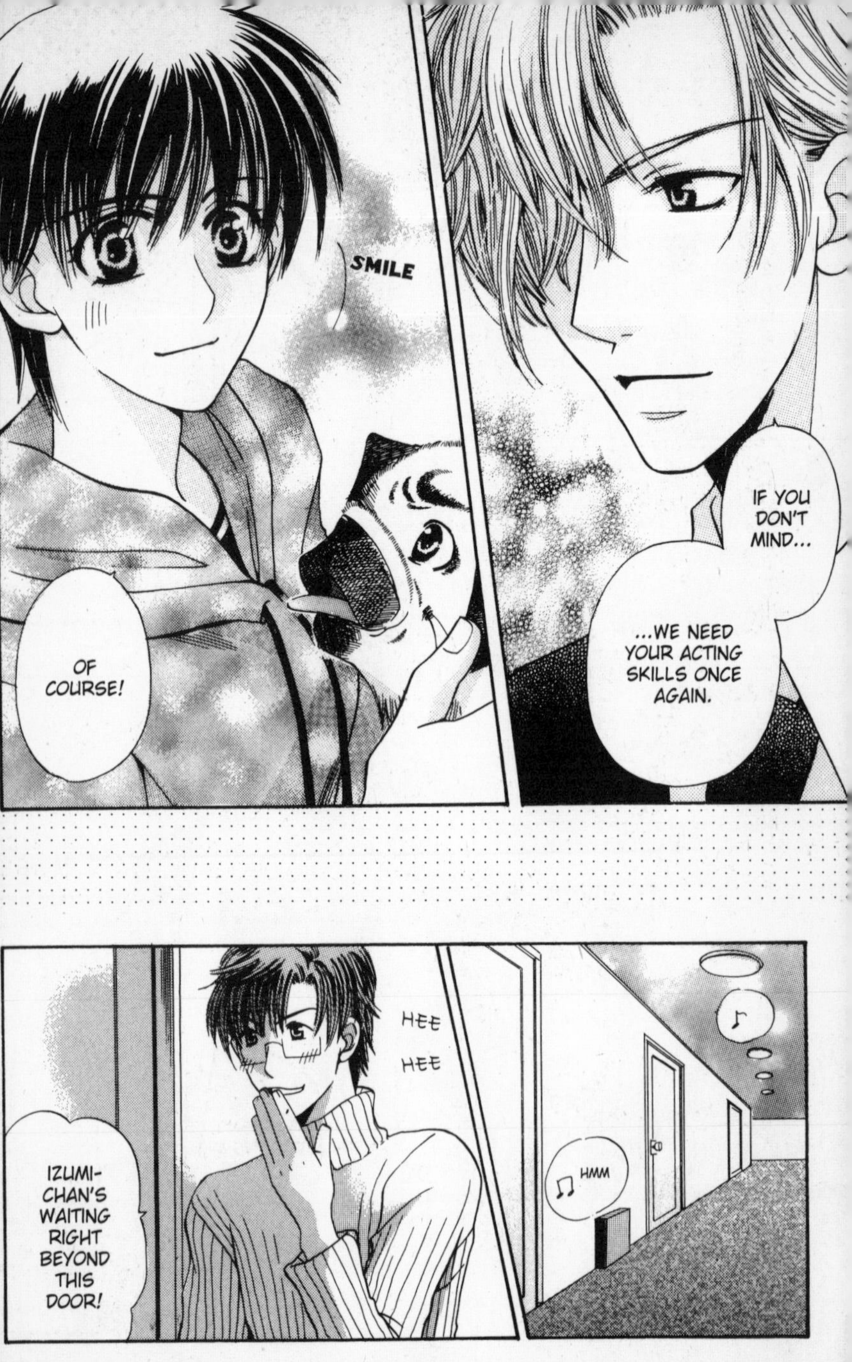
IF YOU DON'T MIND...
...WE NEED YOUR ACTING SKILLS ONCE AGAIN.
SMILE
OF COURSE!
♪ HMM
HEE HEE
IZUMI-CHAN'S WAITING RIGHT BEYOND THIS DOOR!

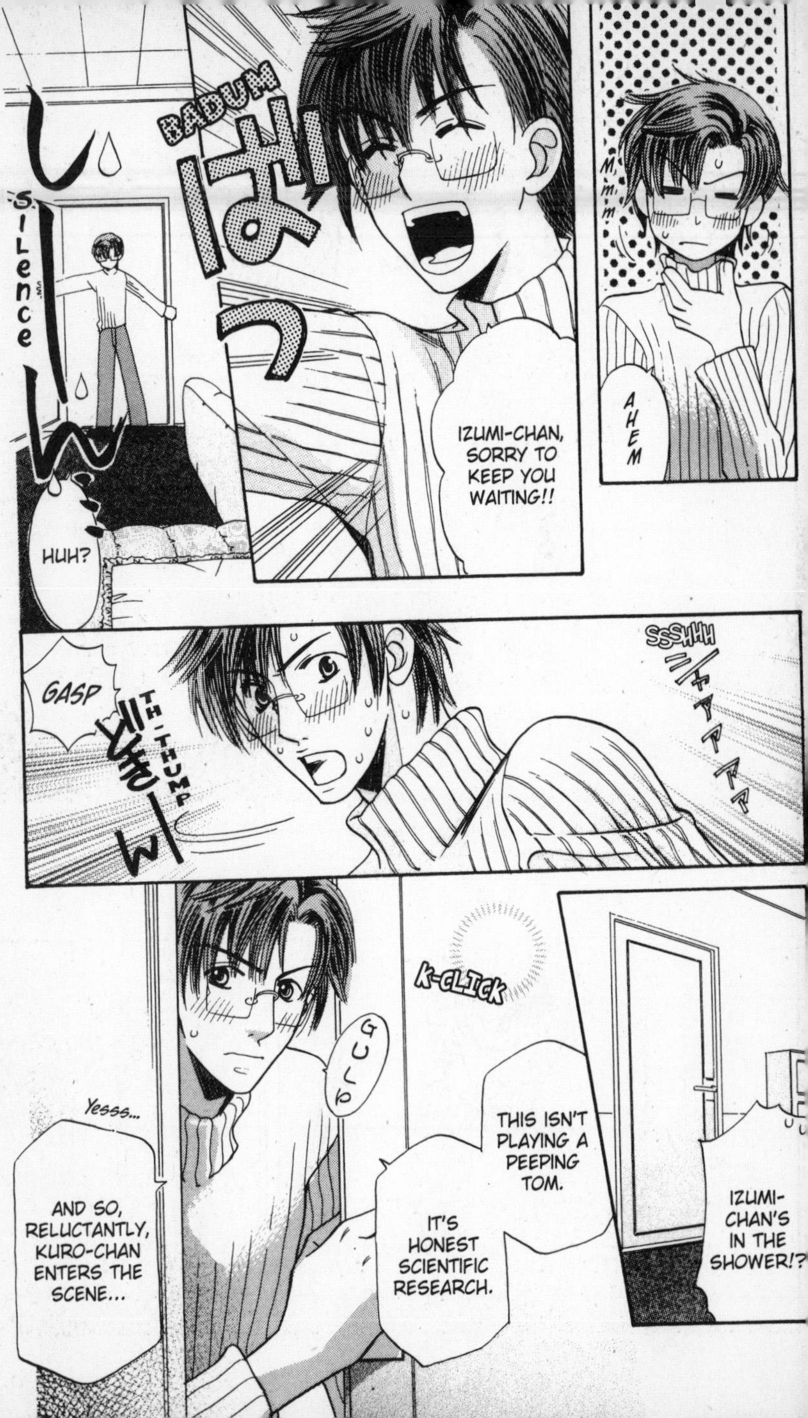
Mmm...
AHEM
BADUM
ばっ
IZUMI-CHAN, SORRY TO KEEP YOU WAITING!!
しーん
SILENCE
HUH?
SSSHHH
GASP
TH-THUMP
K-CLICK
IZUMI-CHAN'S IN THE SHOWER!?
THIS ISN'T PLAYING A PEEPING TOM.
IT'S HONEST SCIENTIFIC RESEARCH.
GULP
Yesss...
AND SO, RELUCTANTLY, KURO-CHAN ENTERS THE SCENE...

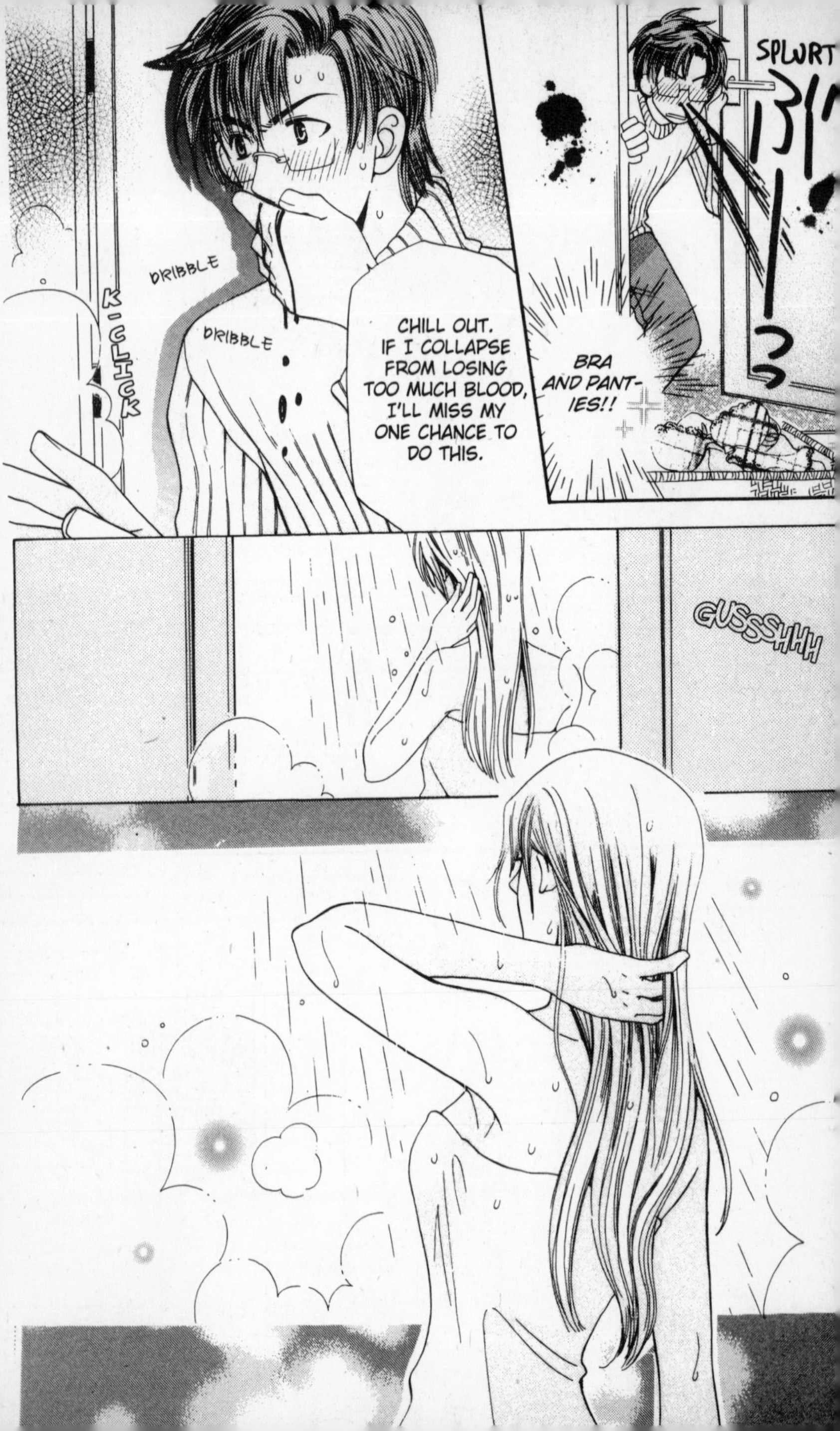
SPLURT
BRA AND PANTIES!!
DRIBBLE
DRIBBLE
K-CLICK
CHILL OUT. IF I COLLAPSE FROM LOSING TOO MUCH BLOOD, I'LL MISS MY ONE CHANCE TO DO THIS.
GUSSSHHH

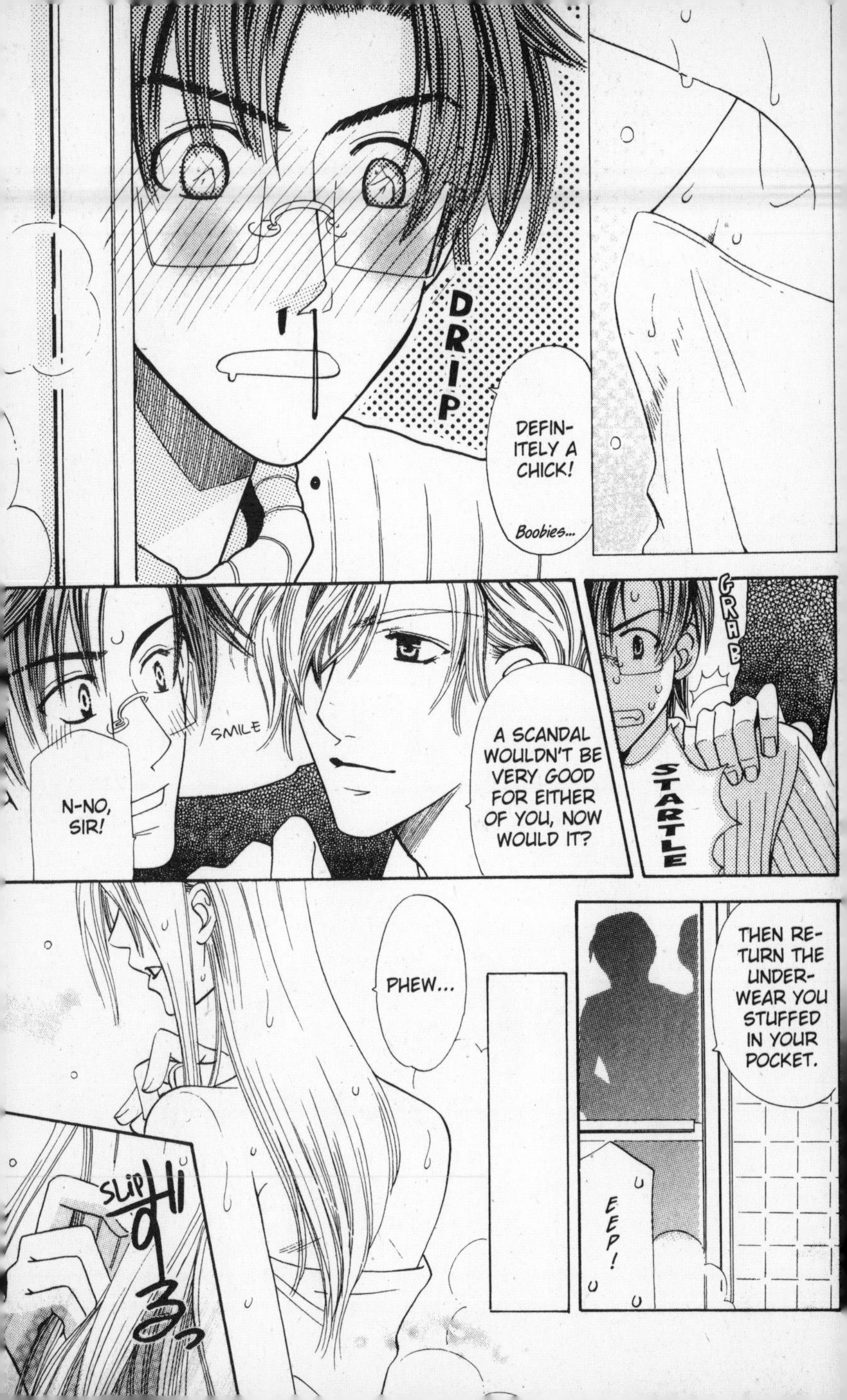
DRIP
DEFIN-ITELY A CHICK!
Boobies...
GRAB
STARTLE
A SCANDAL WOULDN'T BE VERY GOOD FOR EITHER OF YOU, NOW WOULD IT?
SMILE
N-NO, SIR!
THEN RE-TURN THE UNDER-WEAR YOU STUFFED IN YOUR POCKET.
EEP!
PHEW...
SLIP

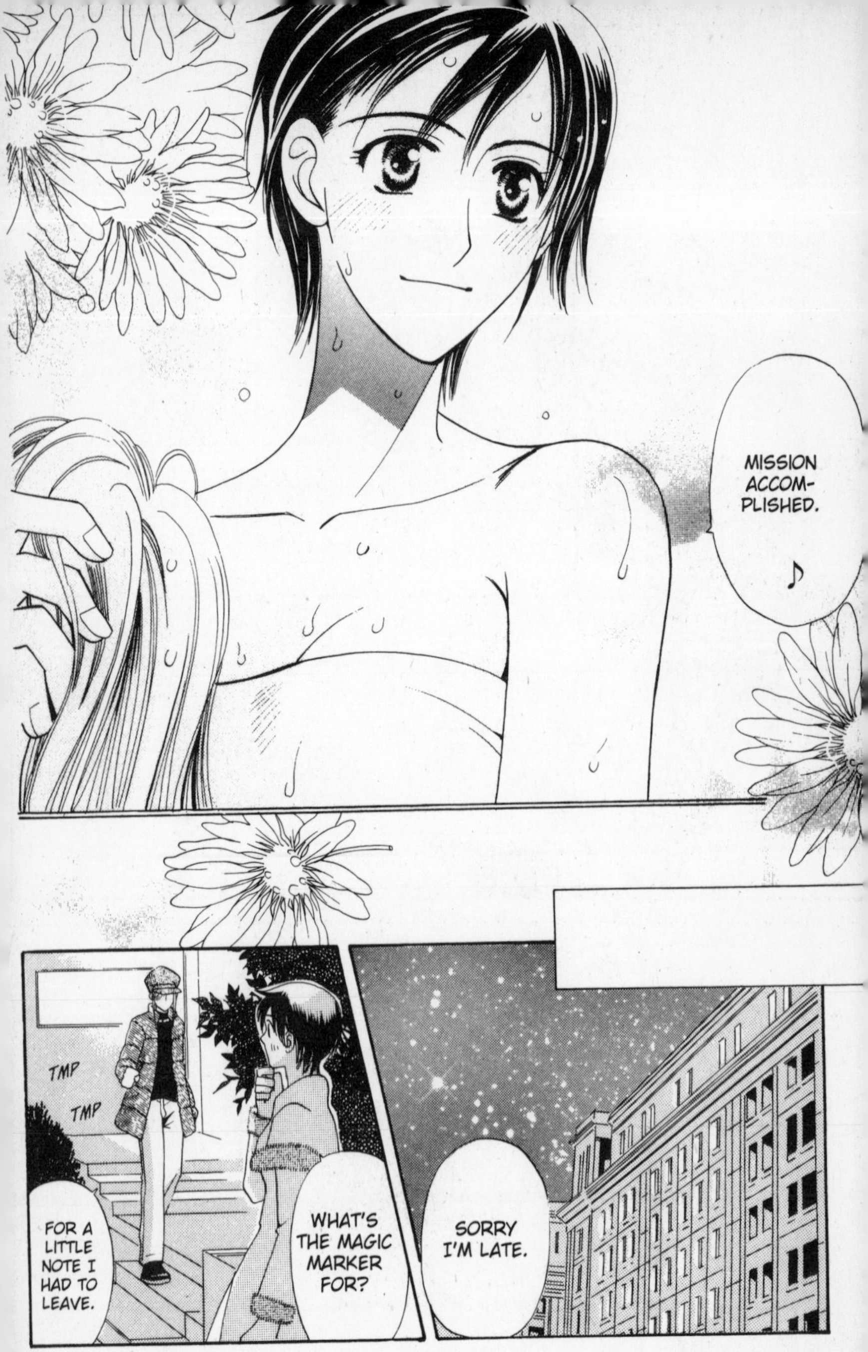
MISSION ACCOM-PLISHED. ♪
SORRY I'M LATE.
WHAT'S THE MAGIC MARKER FOR?
TMP
TMP
FOR A LITTLE NOTE I HAD TO LEAVE.

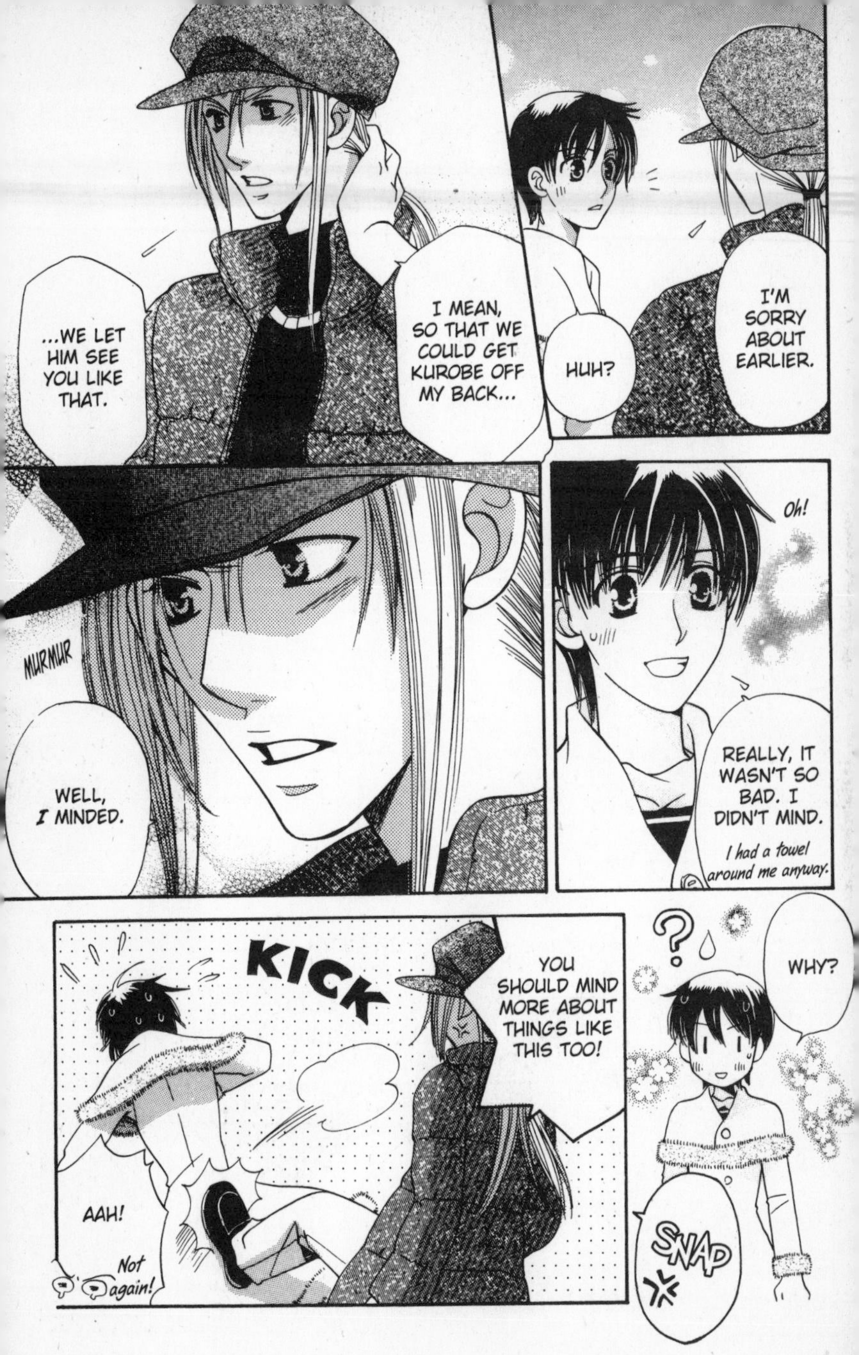
I'M SORRY ABOUT EARLIER.
HUH?
I MEAN, SO THAT WE COULD GET KUROBE OFF MY BACK...
...WE LET HIM SEE YOU LIKE THAT.
Oh!
REALLY, IT WASN'T SO BAD. I DIDN'T MIND.
I had a towel around me anyway.
MURMUR
WELL, I MINDED.
WHY?
SNAP
YOU SHOULD MIND MORE ABOUT THINGS LIKE THIS TOO!
KICK
AAH!
Not again!

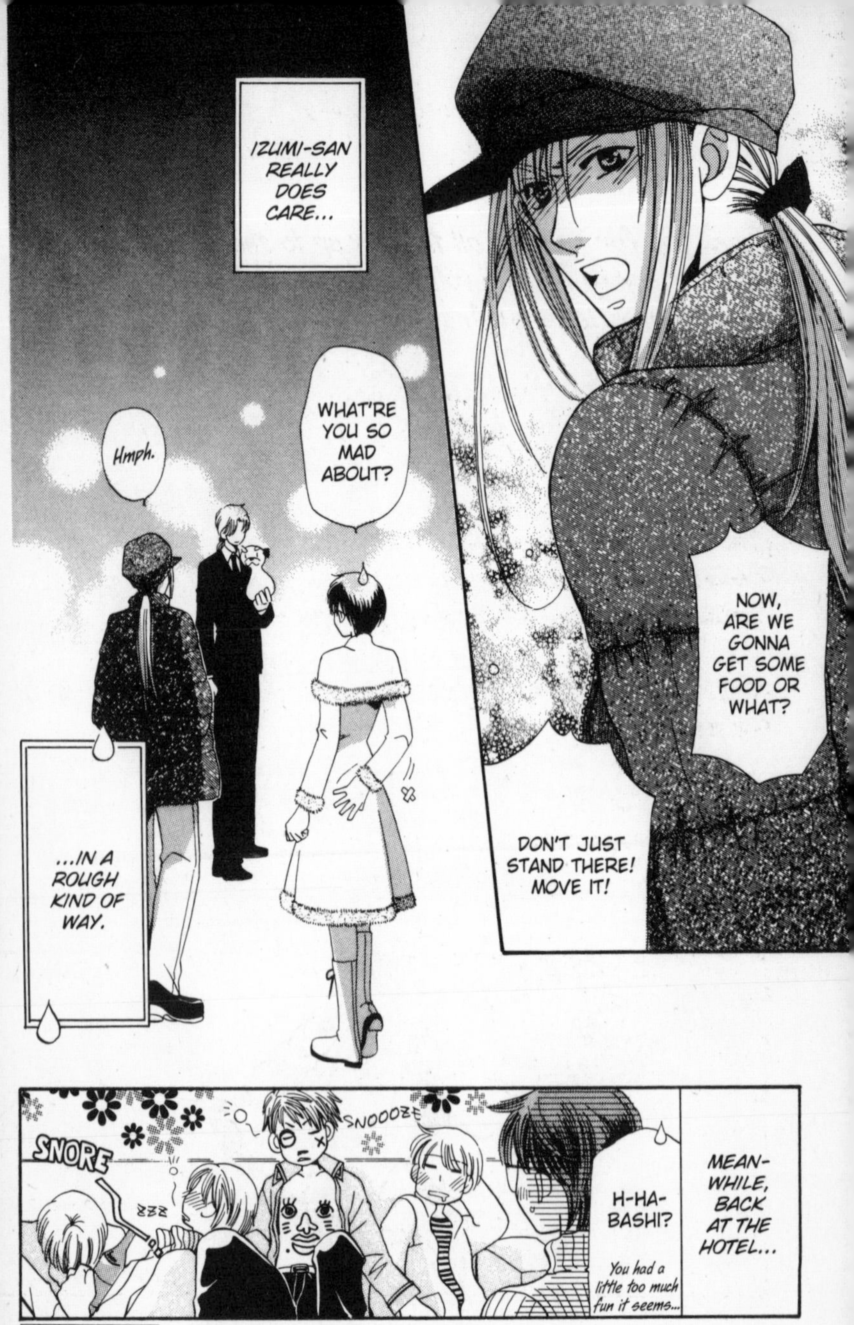
NOW, ARE WE GONNA GET SOME FOOD OR WHAT?
DON'T JUST STAND THERE! MOVE IT!
IZUMI-SAN REALLY DOES CARE...
WHAT'RE YOU SO MAD ABOUT?
Hmph.
...IN A ROUGH KIND OF WAY.
MEAN-WHILE, BACK AT THE HOTEL...
H-HA-BASHI?
You had a little too much fun it seems...
SNOOOZE
SNORE
zzz

End of Scene 25

Afterword and Special Thanks!

Thank you for reading all the way up to the afterword. And for buying the 5th volume of Tenshi Ja Nai!! And for all your lovely letters! And for visiting my website!

I am thrilled with the whole experience. My heart is quaking like the legs of a newborn baby deer... (tears of gratitude)

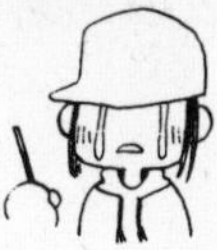

Also, to those who assisted in the production of this book: Hariguchi-san, Aihara-san, Hatayama-san, and my manager, Suguwara-san... Thank you all so very much!

Well, I'm keeping my fingers crossed that we all meet up in the next volume soon.

March 6, 2005
Takako Shigematsu

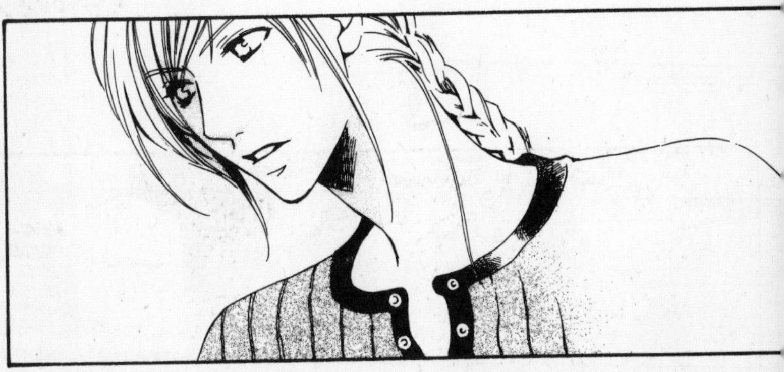

"Tenshi Ja Nai!! I'm No Angel!" Volume 5 - THE END

I'm eagerly awaiting your letters.

Homepage URL is:
http://www5b.biglobe.ne.jpg/~taka_s/index.html

I broke into tears and pleaded, "There are too many pages, please help me!!" As a result, this was drawn by my chief assistant, Hari-san.

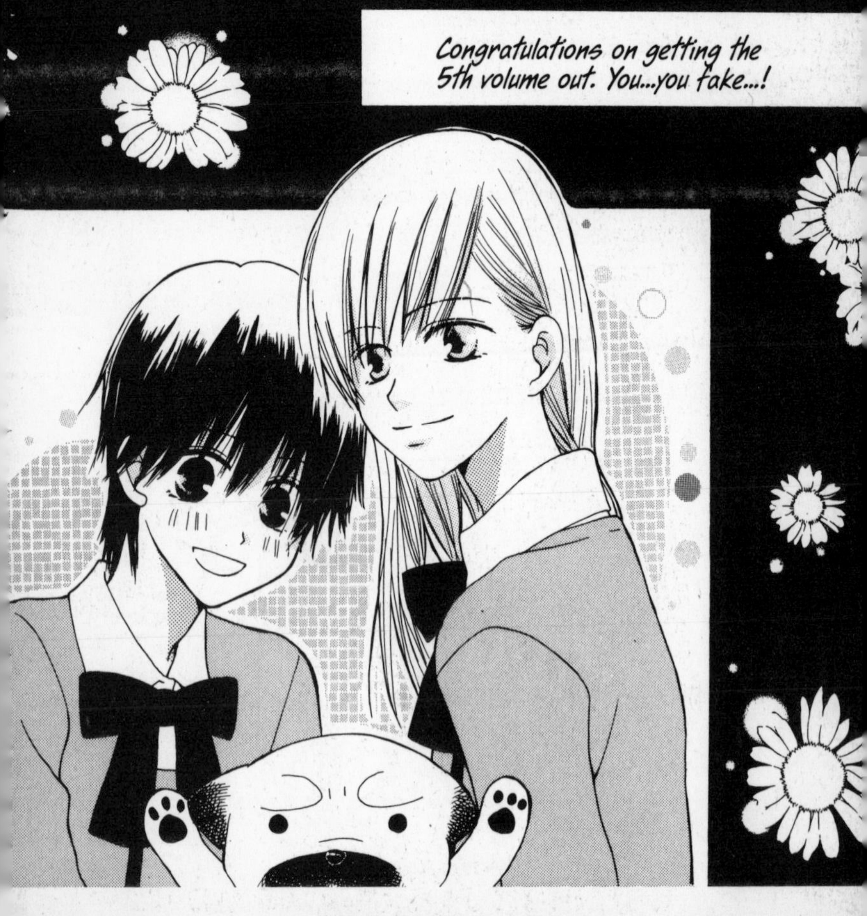
Congratulations on getting the 5th volume out. You...you fake...!

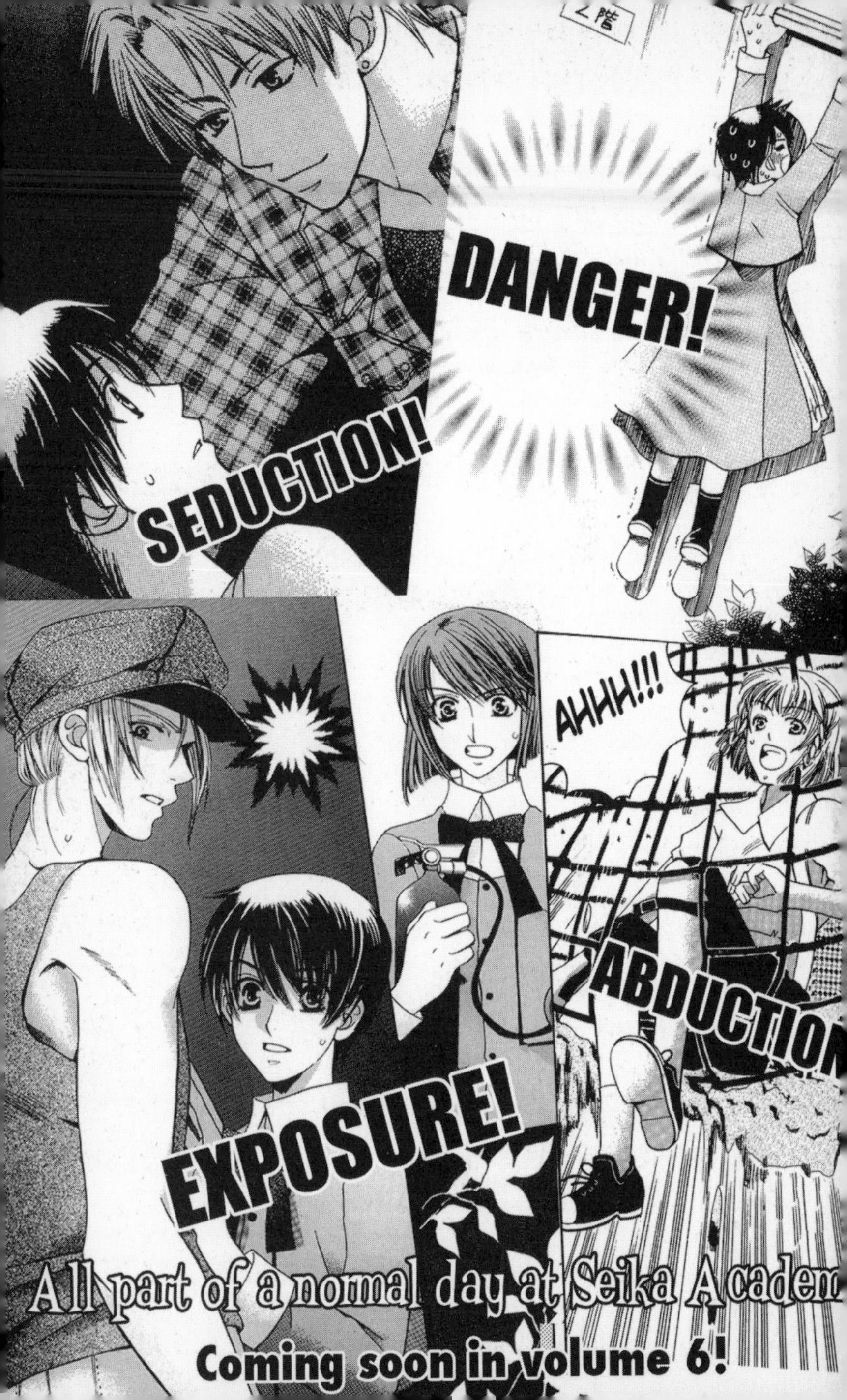
2階
DANGER!
SEDUCTION!
AHHH!!!
ABDUCTION
EXPOSURE!
All part of a normal day at Seika Academ
Coming soon in volume 6!

Translator's Notes

Pg. 31 – Serinentius and Melos

These are the names of two characters from the anime movie "Hashire Merosu" dating from the early 90's. Izumi and Hikaru's demonstration of friendship and trust is so moving, it reminds the girls of the friendship between the two male characters.

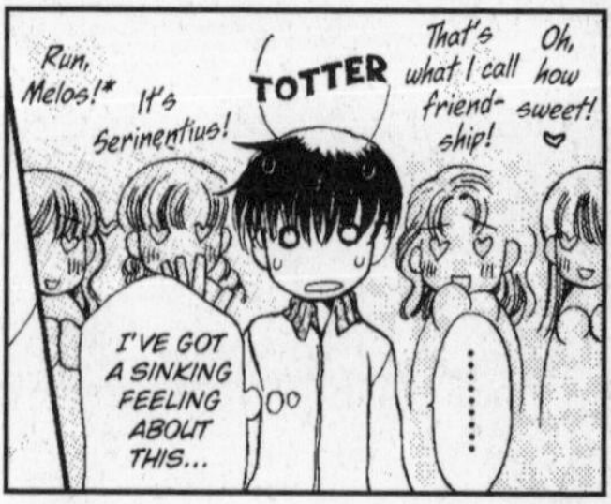
Oh, how sweet!
That's what I call friend-ship!
TOTTER
It's Serinentius!
Run, Melos!*
....
I'VE GOT A SINKING FEELING ABOUT THIS...

Pg. 116 – *Hanetsuki*

Japanese badminton, traditionally played on New Year's.

Pg. 134 – *Anko, Mitarashi, Ohagi*

Anko is a sweet red bean jam that the Kyoto region in particular is famous for. *Mitarashi* is a dumpling-style sweet that originally comes from Kyoto; its distinctive shape is said to mimic the foam and bubbles of the purifying waters at a traditional shrine. *Ohagi* are rice balls covered with sweet beans or sesame.

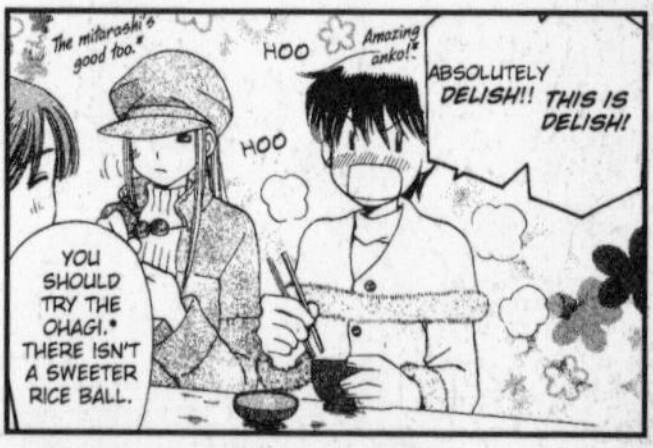
THIS IS DELISH!
ABSOLUTELY DELISH!!
Amazing anko!*
HOO
The mitarashi's good too.*
HOO
YOU SHOULD TRY THE OHAGI.* THERE ISN'T A SWEETER RICE BALL.

Pg. 147 – *Bubuzuke*

Rice with tea poured onto it, this obviously unappetizing "meal" is in fact a code of sorts in the Kansai region of Japan that a hostess will offer to guests as way to hint to them that they are not wanted.

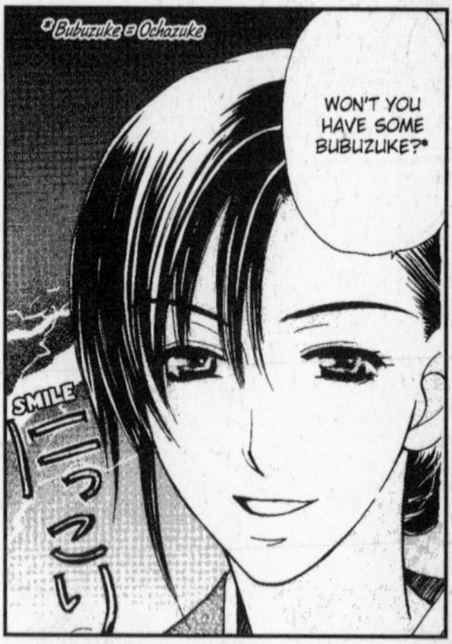
*Bubuzuke = Ochazuke
WON'T YOU HAVE SOME BUBUZUKE?*
SMILE

Pg. 160 – Sprinkling salt

This is referring to the Japanese superstition that sprinkling salt will ward off and vanquish evil spirits.

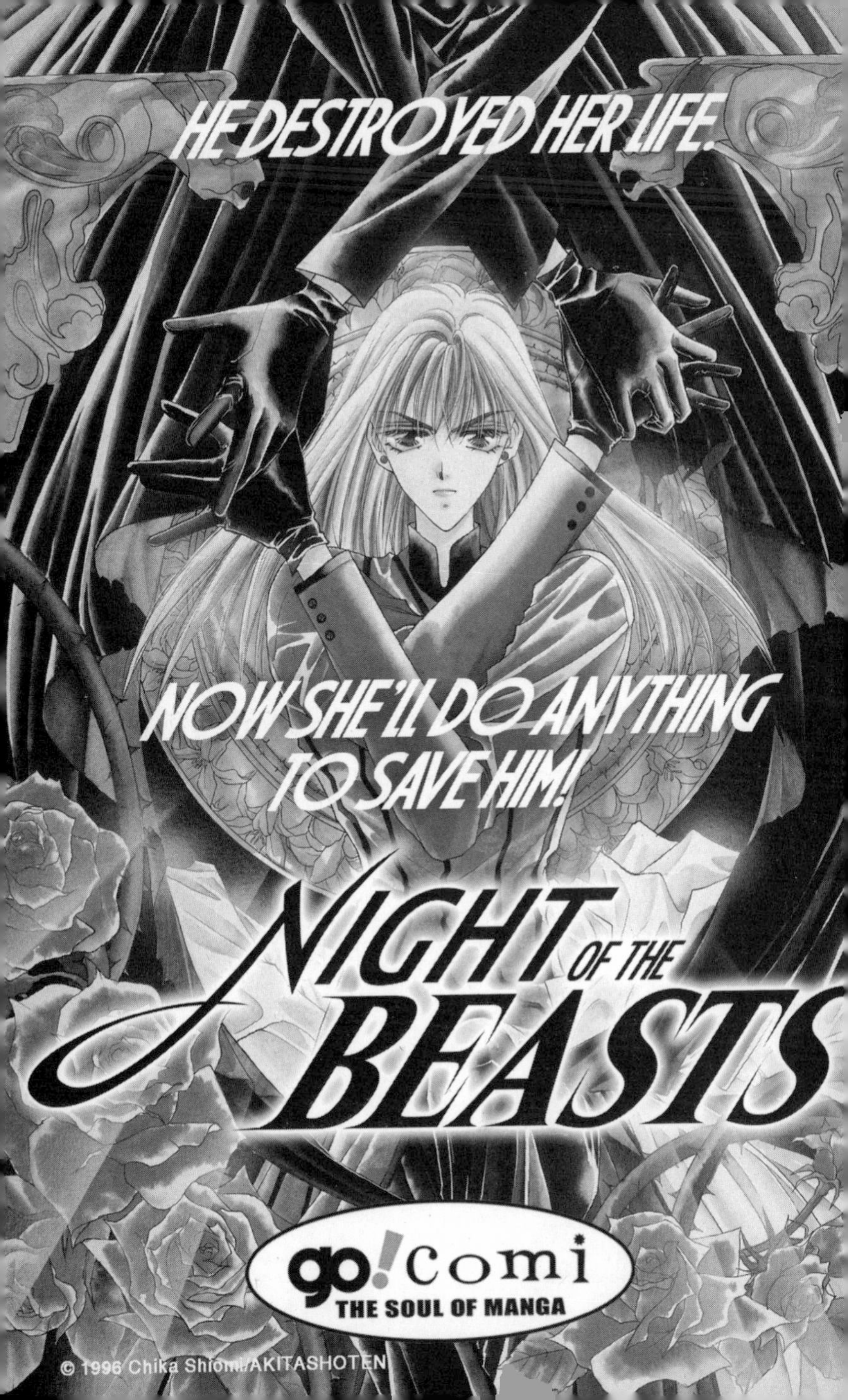
HE DESTROYED HER LIFE.
NOW SHE'LL DO ANYTHING TO SAVE HIM!
NIGHT OF THE BEASTS
go!comi
THE SOUL OF MANGA
© 1996 Chika Shiomi/AKITASHOTEN

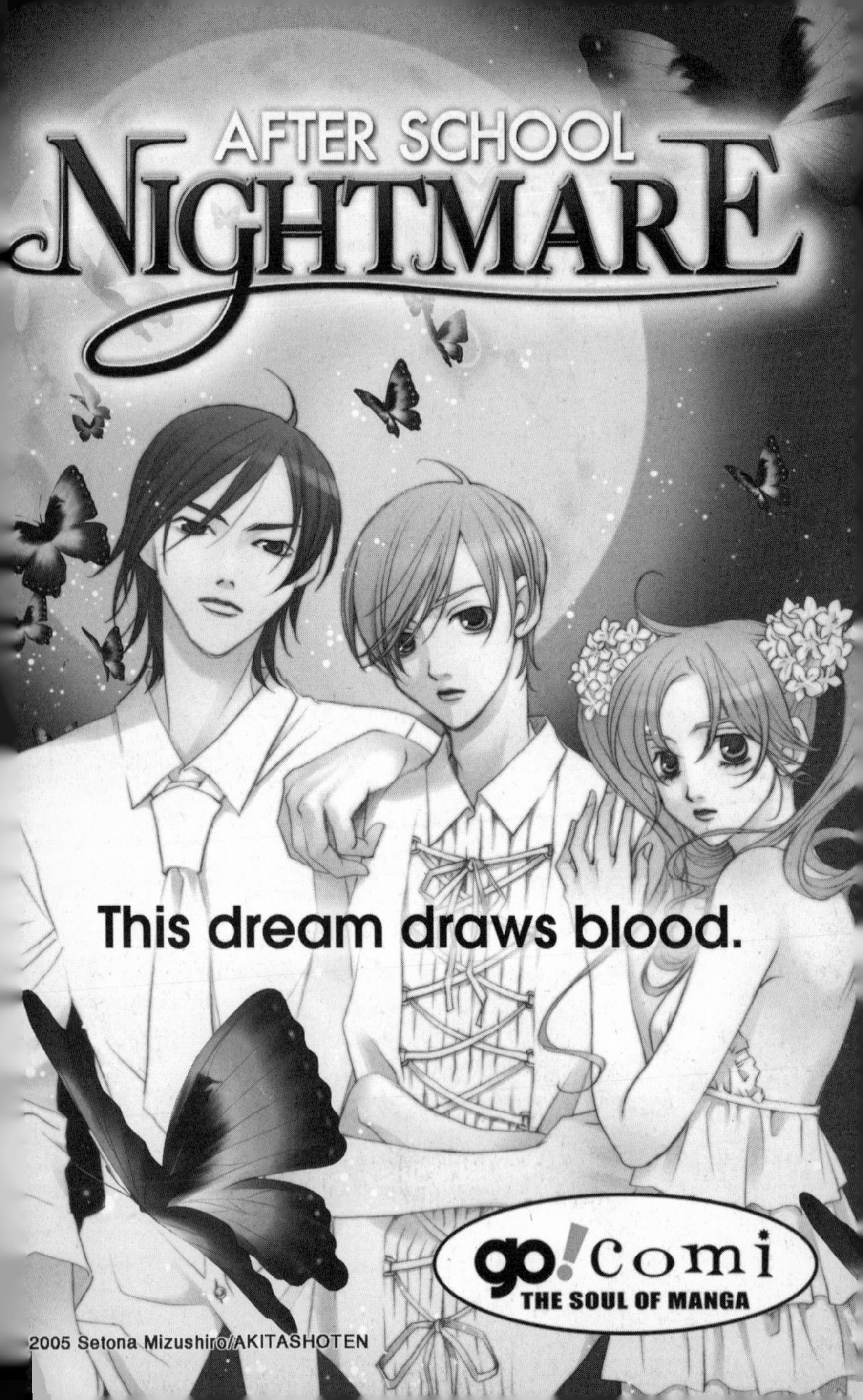
AFTER SCHOOL
NIGHTMARE
This dream draws blood.
go!comi
THE SOUL OF MANGA
2005 Setona Mizushiro/AKITASHOTEN

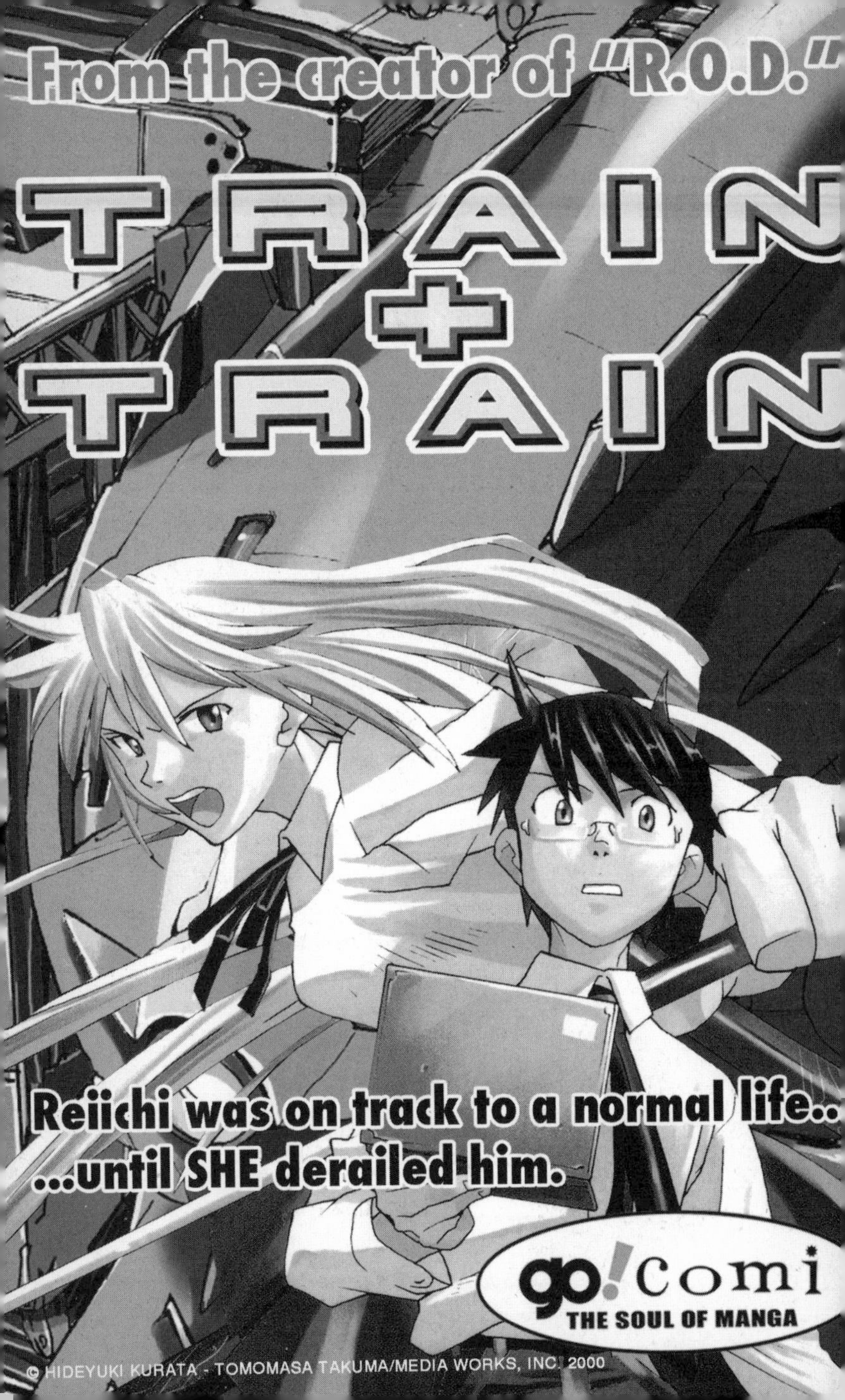
From the creator of "R.O.D."
TRAIN + TRAIN
Reiichi was on track to a normal life..
...until SHE derailed him.
go!comi
THE SOUL OF MANGA
© HIDEYUKI KURATA - TOMOMASA TAKUMA/MEDIA WORKS, INC. 2000

Author's Note

Here's a message from Molly, my pooch with the irresistible eyes: "Please buy our comics..." That's really what she's saying (J/K).

WITHDRAWN

CONTRA COSTA COUNTY LIBRARY

3 1901 05866 7124

Visit Shigematsu-sensi online at
http://www5b.biglobe.ne.jp/~taka_s/